Access My eLab

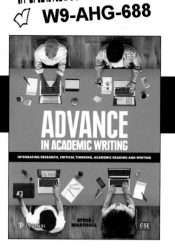

ADVANCE
IN ACADEMIC WRITING

TO REGISTER

❶ Go to **mybookshelf.pearsonerpi.com**

❷ Follow the instructions. When asked for your access code, please type the code provided underneath the blue sticker.

❸ To access **My eLab** at any time, go to mybookshelf.pearsonerpi.com. **Bookmark this page for quicker access.**

Access to My eLab is valid for 12 months from the date of registration.

WARNING! This book CANNOT BE RETURNED if the access code has been uncovered.

Note: Once you have registered, you will need to join your online class. Ask your teacher to provide you with the class ID.

TEACHER Access Code

To obtain an access code for My eLab, please contact your Pearson ELT consultant.

❓ I 800 263-3678, ext. 2
pearsonerpi.com/help

3076

W134150 (A38266)

W9-AHG-688

ADVANCE
IN ACADEMIC WRITING

INTEGRATING RESEARCH, CRITICAL THINKING, ACADEMIC READING AND WRITING

**STEVE
MARSHALL**

 Pearson

Product Owner
Stephan Leduc

Editor
Patricia Hynes

Proofreader
Mairi MacKinnon

Rights and Permissions Coordinator
Aude Maggiori

Text Rights and Permissions
Rachel Irwin

Art Director
Hélène Cousineau

Graphic Design Coordinator
Estelle Cuillerier

Book and Cover Design
Benoit Pitre

Book Layout
Pige communication

Cover Photo
SHUTTERSTOCK © Rawpixel.com

Dedication
I would like to dedicate this book to Jamie, Joey, and Miki.

The publisher wishes to thank the following people for their helpful comments and suggestions:

Jerry Block, Fraser International College

Jennifer Carioto, Algonquin College

Kristibeth Kelly Delgado, Fanshawe College

Michelle Duhaney, Seneca College

Glenda Fish, Trent University

Eldon Friesen, Brock University

Izabella Kojic-Sabo, University of Windsor Centre for English Language Development

Dagmar Kulikova, Seneca College

Jennifer Walsh Marr, University of British Columbia Vantage College

Darlene Murphy, University of Würzburg

Bobbi Reimann, Catholic University of Eichstätt-Ingolstadt

Cyndy Reimer, Douglas College

Daniel Riccardi, University of British Columbia Vantage College

Skye Skagfeld, Vancouver Island University

© ÉDITIONS DU RENOUVEAU PÉDAGOGIQUE INC. (ERPI), 2017
ERPI publishes and distributes PEARSON ELT products in Canada.

1611 Crémazie Boulevard East, 10th Floor
Montréal, Québec H2M 2P2
Canada
Telephone: 1 800 263-3678
Fax: 1 514 334-4720
information@pearsonerpi.com
pearsonerpi.com

Registration of copyright – Bibliothèque et Archives nationales du Québec, 2017
Registration of copyright – Library and Archives Canada, 2017

Printed in Canada   23456789   II   21 20 19 18
ISBN 978-2-7613-4150-9   134150 ABCD   OF10

INTRODUCTION

Success in Academic Writing

Effective academic writing is key to success in higher education, and *Advance in Academic Writing* has been written with success in mind. Success in academic writing depends on many factors. Of course, academic writers need to be able to use accurate sentence structure and vocabulary, as well as appropriate style; however, effective academic writing is not possible without effective academic reading and critical thinking. Writers have to be able to understand and engage critically with academic texts written by experts, and this engagement needs to be evident in their writing.

Integrating Research, Critical Thinking, Academic Reading and Writing

Advance in Academic Writing is an integrated textbook that interweaves writing and key skills for academic success, including a chapter dedicated to understanding the basics of academic research. Each chapter is based on a theme of scientific or social interest, includes authentic academic texts, and contains carefully constructed tasks that relate directly to the texts: active and critical reading, critical thinking, academic vocabulary, academic style, and effective sentence structure (writing-related grammar). Each chapter ends with a writing task that includes opportunities for editing and peer review.

Learning, Reviewing, Consolidating, and Applying Knowledge

Students need to apply what they learn on general academic writing courses in many contexts across the disciplines. Sometimes this application of knowledge to context takes place concurrently, during an academic writing course. More often, application to context takes place months later. In this sense, it is essential that academic writing courses build in ways for students to review and consolidate new knowledge so as to increase the likelihood of its successful application later on. Put simply, it is not enough for students to read a text, follow instructions, do a task, then move on. For learners to internalize and retain knowledge, continuous review and consolidation are required.

Multi-Stage Review and Consolidation

Advance in Academic Writing is structured to include multi-stage review and consolidation. The writing tasks at the end of each chapter encourage self- and peer review with task-specific checklists and structured evaluation sheets. To encourage long-term internalization of knowledge, students consolidate key aspects of the content between chapters, in two dedicated review chapters, in the Handbook at the end of the book, and in the customized My eLab.

Acknowledgements

I would like to acknowledge the students I have taught over the years at University College London and Simon Fraser University, from whom I have learned so much. I am especially grateful to the students who provided samples of their academic writing and to the reviewers, whose comments were invaluable. I would also like to acknowledge the support of the following people at Pearson ELT: Stephan Leduc, Aude Maggiori, and Benoit Pitre. Finally, I offer my gratitude to editor Patricia Hynes, whose expertise, knowledge, and attention to detail I greatly appreciated.

HIGHLIGHTS

Opening Page

Each chapter opens with a quotation for reflection, an introduction of the chapter topic and theme, and a list of contents. Students engage with the chapter theme by doing an exploratory task.

Active and Critical Reading

Authentic texts on the chapter theme introduce language and text features for analysis. The texts—primarily excerpts of academic journal articles—are the starting point for the critical-thinking, vocabulary, grammar, style, and writing tasks that follow.

Critical Thinking

Critical-thinking tasks are linked to in-depth engagement with academic texts, with a focus on how to create effective arguments and how expert authors avoid logical fallacies in their writing.

Vocabulary

Students build vocabulary that is particularly useful in academic writing, such as reporting verbs and language for describing data. A short list of words and expressions from the chapter texts is selected for vocabulary development in My eLab.

Effective Writing Style

Students practise essential aspects of effective style in academic writing, including objective and subjective styles, appropriate formality, and correct in-text citations and references.

Effective Sentence Structure

Examples from the chapter texts are used to show accurate structures in context. The chapter focus is linked to a Handbook unit, which develops the topic further.

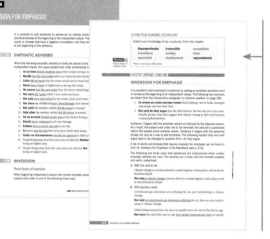

HANDBOOK: Writing Effective Sentences

Fourteen units expand on the grammar, sentence structure, and punctuation topics introduced in the chapters. Each unit is linked to additional practice in My eLab.

Write, Revise, and Edit

A final writing task gives students the opportunity to integrate their learning from the chapter. A checklist or review sheet is also provided for self- and peer reviews.

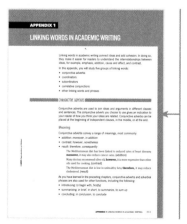

Appendices

Four appendices provide detailed explanations of linking words, cover the main aspects of APA and MLA citation styles, and highlight common mistakes to avoid in academic writing.

SCOPE AND SEQUENCE

Chapter	Active and Critical Reading	Critical Thinking	Vocabulary	Effective Sentence Structure
1 **Seven Stages of the Writing Process**	• Journal article on multi-lingual students' academic writing	• What is critical thinking?	• Strategies for learning vocabulary • Formality: phrasal verbs and Latinate verbs	• Tense and aspect → Handbook Unit 1
2 **Understanding Research**	• Expository text on the research process • Journal article on a historic double-blind control trial	• Evaluate types of research	• Research-related vocabulary	• Articles, nouns, and noun phrases • Passive voice → Handbook Unit 2
3 **Bringing in Others' Ideas: Reading**	• Reading around a text • Skimming • Journal and newspaper articles on self-driving cars • Scanning • Annotating	• Genre and style in writing	• Anaphoric and cataphoric reference words • Language of attribution	• Independent and dependent clauses • Simple, compound, and complex sentences → Handbook Unit 3
4 **Bringing in Others' Ideas: Writing**	• Journal article on writing from sources • Inferring meaning • Online article on plagiarism in the music industry • Assessing the reliability of sources	• Academic integrity versus plagiarism • "Standing on the shoulders of giants"	• Guessing meaning from context • Reporting verbs	• Relative clauses (defining and non-defining) → Handbook Unit 4
5 **Presenting Coherent Arguments**	• Newspaper article on prisons in Sweden • Note taking	• Role of prisons: rehabilitate or punish? • Logical fallacies: cause and effect	• Language of opinion	• Punctuation: commas → Handbook Unit 5
6 **Paragraphs**	• Selection of paragraphs on fair trade and slow food (various sources) • Model paragraphs	• Logical fallacies: generalization	• Conjunctive adverbs	• Participle phrases • Punctuation: semicolons → Handbook Units 5 and 6
7 **Introductions in Academic Writing**	• Model introduction • Selection of introductions from academic journal articles on business leadership in Asia and Africa	• Logical fallacies based on others' actions and ideas	• Linking words that perform different functions	• Passive voice → Handbook Unit 7
8 **Conclusions in Academic Writing**	• Model conclusion • Selection of conclusions from academic journal articles on business leadership in Asia and Africa	• Logical fallacies based on weak reasoning	• Synonyms	• Punctuation: colons and apostrophes • Review of relative clauses and participle phrases → Handbook Unit 8

The Writing Process	Effective Writing Style	Write, Revise, and Edit	My eLab
• Seven stages of the writing process	• Using or avoiding personal language	• Paragraph about personal background • Revise verb forms in paragraph	*Grammar diagnostic • Supplementary reading and writing activities • Vocabulary exercises • Exercises on tense and aspect
• 10 stages of the research process	• Writing in an objective, scientific style (passive voice)	• 100-word summary of the chapter article	• Supplementary reading and writing activities • Vocabulary exercises • Exercises on articles, nouns, and noun phrases
• Summary-writing process	• Adapting semi-formal style for academic writing • Paraphrasing	• 200-word academic summary • Self- and peer review (with review sheet)	• Supplementary reading and writing activities • Vocabulary exercises • Exercises on clauses and sentences
• Response paper writing process	• Shifting style from conversational to formal • Writing reference list entries in APA and MLA styles	• 200-word response paper • Self- and peer review (with review sheet)	• Supplementary reading and writing activities • Vocabulary exercises • Exercises on relative clauses
• Developing arguments	• Review shifting style from informal to formal	• Two opinion paragraphs • Peer review (with checklist)	• Supplementary reading and writing activities • Vocabulary exercises • Exercises on commas
• Writing paragraphs	• Writing in-text citations in APA and MLA styles • Shifting style, using linking words	• Improve paragraphs from Chapter 5 • Peer review (with checklist)	• Supplementary reading and writing activities • Vocabulary exercises • Exercises on participle phrases and semicolons
• Writing introductions	• Review of avoiding personal language	• Add an introduction to the paragraphs from Chapter 6 • Peer review (with checklist)	• Supplementary reading and writing activities • Vocabulary exercises • Exercises on the passive voice
• Writing conclusions	• Avoiding gender-exclusive language	• Add a conclusion to the paragraphs from Chapter 6 • Peer review (with checklist)	• Supplementary reading and writing activities • Vocabulary exercises • Exercises on colons and apostrophes

Chapter	Active and Critical Reading	Critical Thinking	Vocabulary	Effective Sentence Structure
9 **Review and Consolidation**	• Content overview: Chapters 1 to 8	• Consolidation tasks on logical fallacies, inferring meaning, and assessing the reliability of sources	• Consolidation tasks on language of attribution, reporting verbs, and reference words	→ Handbook Unit 9
10 **Describing Processes and Analyzing Data**	• Encyclopedia entry on 3D printing • Online article about air pollution statistics • Tabloid article	• Engaging critically with statistical data and media statistics	• Describing data	• Subject-verb agreement • Review of sentence fragments and punctuation → Handbook Unit 10
11 **Writing Arguments in Essays**	• Pre-reading research skills • Locating stance, opinion, and relevance in abstracts • Abstracts from academic journal articles and an academic blog on cellphone use in class	• Bringing life experience into one's writing	• Review of guessing meaning from context • Exemplification	• Conditional sentences → Handbook Unit 11
12 **Making Comparisons**	• Academic articles and an expert blog on nuclear versus solar and wind power • Inferring meaning and identifying stance • Model comparative paragraphs	• What is comparative analysis?	• Language of comparison	• Parallel structure → Handbook Unit 12
13 **Writing about Problems and Solutions**	• Academic journal articles and an online article on language endangerment and revitalization • Identifying problems, solutions, and background context in abstracts and articles	• Should special measures be taken to protect endangered languages?	• Describing problems, solutions, and evaluation	• Modal auxiliary verbs to express likelihood and obligation → Handbook Unit 13
14 **Writing about Causes and Effects**	• Academic journal article, with diagram, on the effects of climate change on children's health • Encyclopedia entry on El Niño	• Correlation versus causality	• Describing cause and effect	• Inversion for emphasis → Handbook Unit 14
15 **Review and Consolidation**	• Content overview: Chapters 10 to 14	• Consolidation tasks on analyzing causality, engaging critically with statistical data, and doing comparative analysis	• Consolidation tasks on guessing meaning from context; exemplification; making comparisons; and describing statistics, problems and solutions, and cause and effect	

The Writing Process	Effective Writing Style	Write, Revise, and Edit	My eLab
	• Consolidation tasks on APA and MLA citation styles, shifting style, using or avoiding personal language, and paraphrasing	• 700 to 1,000-word research essay, applying knowledge gained to this point • Self- and peer review (with review sheet)	• Exercises on sentence fragments, comma splices, and run-on sentences
• Expository writing	• Review of effective style	• Process paragraph based on a diagram • Paragraph describing data from two bar charts • Self- and peer review (with checklist)	• Supplementary reading and writing activities • Vocabulary exercises • Exercises on subject-verb agreement
• Forming outlines for argumentative essays	• Describing the genre features of an academic blog • Review of describing statistical data	• Four-page argumentative essay • Self- and peer review (with review sheet)	• Supplementary reading and writing activities • Vocabulary exercises • Exercises on conditional sentences
• Forming outlines for comparative essays	• Review of shifting style	• Comparative research essay OR • Two comparative paragraphs • Self- and peer review (with review sheet)	• Supplementary reading and writing activities • Vocabulary exercises • Exercises on parallel structure
• Writing about problems and solutions, and evaluating the solutions	• Techniques for defining and classifying	• Two-page problem-solution essay • Self- and peer review (with checklist)	• Supplementary reading and writing activities • Vocabulary exercises • Exercises on modal auxiliary verbs to express likelihood and obligation
• Writing about causes and effects	• Review of defining • Review of improving style	• Four paragraphs on the causes, effects, and solutions described in a diagram • Self- and peer review (with checklist)	• Supplementary reading and writing activities • Vocabulary exercises • Exercises on inversion for emphasis
	• Consolidation tasks on improving style, defining and classifying, and shifting style		

TABLE OF CONTENTS

PART 3 WRITING FOR DIFFERENT ACADEMIC PURPOSES

WRITING AND RESEARCH: GETTING STARTED

CHAPTER 1

SEVEN STAGES OF THE WRITING PROCESS

The two most engaging powers of an author: new things are made familiar, and familiar things are made new.

Samuel Johnson

Academic writing is a process. It is a sequence of stages. You go through these stages cognitively as you take each step in the process of creating the finished product: the essay, the lab report, the summary, or another type of text. At each step, you engage critically with new ideas to address a problem or answer your question. Following the words of the great English writer Samuel Johnson, to be successful in writing, you need to find new ideas and make them understandable to your reader while adding new perspectives to your reader's existing knowledge.

In this chapter, you will:

- read a journal article about multilingual students' experiences of academic writing
- learn four strategies for dealing with academic vocabulary
- practise using formal and informal vocabulary
- study tense and aspect in English
- study seven key stages of the writing process
- analyze the use of personal language in academic writing
- write about your background and writing style

TASK 1 EXPLORE THROUGH WRITING

What kind of writer are you?

When you do exploratory writing, the main purpose is to generate ideas about the topic. The style of the writing is less important; just try to write down as many ideas as possible. Take five minutes. After you have finished, share your notes with peers.

MULTILINGUAL STUDENTS AND ACADEMIC WRITING

In the following article, the authors analyze how students in an English for Academic Purposes (EAP) program deal with their writing assignments. The authors focus on three multilingual students and examine how their understanding changed as they did research and writing during their first year of university. The following are excerpts from the writing samples and interviews with two of the participants in the study: Fei and Laura.

What Our Students Tell Us: Perceptions of Three Multilingual Students on Their Academic Writing in First Year

by Janne Morton, Neomy Storch, and Celia Thompson

Fei is a Chinese student who at the time of the study was 20 years old and had been living in Australia for more than two years. After finishing her secondary education in China, Fei had "repeated" the last two years of education at an Australian high school. Fei lived with her family in Australia
5 and only spoke Cantonese at home. At university, she was enrolled in an Economics and Business degree, majoring in Marketing and Management, and taking subjects such as Introductory Macroeconomics, Finance, Marketing, Organisational Behaviour, and Academic English: Economics and Business. . . . Fei . . . went on to successfully complete all subjects in the
10 second semester, and by taking extra subjects in the summer semester, was able to graduate with a degree within three years. . . .

At the start of this study, Fei's description of what academic writing meant to her focused on technical vocabulary and simple overall structure of an assignment:

15 *good academic writing is meant to present high-level knowledge by efficient use of academic vocabulary . . . a group of non-popular words that are specially used in academic reports and professional speeches . . . academic assignments need to have an introduction body conclusion.* (First Writing Task)

She added that when writing an academic assignment:

20 *I spend most of my time on looking up in the dictionary and forming academic-style sentences.* (Interview 1)

Over the duration of her first year, Fei's understanding shifted to one that saw writing in the academy as more complex and as much about process as product. In her mid-year interview, she spoke of the importance of:

25 *picking up key words in instructions . . . guessing words in a paragraph by looking at the topic sentence . . . "parawriting" because teachers tell us it's not good to use many quotes because someone has done much effort for original writing and you need to give more detail to show you understand.* (Interview 3)

By the end of the year, her focus was on the choice of sources and their effect on potential readers:

I need to find suitable research sources and to incorporate these to fit cohesively with my own words and . . . to be traced by the reader. (Interview 5)

as well as on her developing meta-awareness of how rhetorical differences in the subjects she was studying influenced the selection of appropriate sources:

Assignments in Management are relevant to a lot of theories that might be hard to find online but described in academic books frequently. Accordingly, to organise a good research-based Management assignment, students should reference more from academic books. Finance 1 assignments might rely on online material because you need to talk about real life and environment outside the university. (Final Writing Task) . . .

The third student is Laura, who was born in Brazil and at the time of this study, was aged 25 having already lived in Australia for five years. She was thus a little older than Fei and Kevin and had spent more time in an English-speaking country than either of them. Laura described herself as a speaker of Portuguese ("first" language), Spanish ("second" language) and English ("third" language), but a writer of Portuguese and English only. She had been educated in Portuguese and Spanish in primary and secondary school, with some of her secondary education delivered in English. In Australia, Laura lived with her Brazilian husband and spoke Portuguese at home. At university, Laura was enrolled in a Bachelor of Arts degree, and in her first year she successfully completed subjects in a broad range of Arts disciplines including: Medieval History, Philosophy, Politics and Economics, Academic English 2 (first semester), and Ecological History of Humanity, Second Language Teaching and Learning, and International Relations (second semester). . . .

For Laura, the main challenge of academic writing was how to construct an effective academic identity for herself in her writing. . . . Throughout the year, Laura spoke of struggling to find a way to articulate her opinions, her experience, and her knowledge. . . . In linguistic terms, she noted that the first person singular ("I") could be used in academic writing to express opinions if one was also careful to use formal language:

We can use the first person if someone is asking our response and interpretation of a expecific discussion and be academic at the same time using very respectful formal language. (First Writing Task)

But Laura also understood that the relationship between the personal and the academic was as much about knowledge and meaning-making as about academic conventions . . .:

Sometimes we start writing in a very confusing and personal manner because we don't know what to write about, and once we discover the path to follow and which way we should write, it makes it easier to write in a formal academic manner. (First Writing Task)

Disciplinary knowledge was viewed by Laura as central to the process of becoming a clear and authoritative writer. She described how in first semester she felt uncertain sometimes as to exactly what her thoughts were about the topics she was studying (Interview 2). By the end of the year, the process of engaging with content from a range of sources had enabled her to develop her own opinions. She was learning to be, as she put it, "more myself":

I feel that I have much stronger views than before that relate to the subjects I am studying . . . I have my own opinion now. That has changed . . . I would like to impose myself more. (Interview 5) . . .

She also revealed that if she wanted to obtain high grades, she would sometimes have to change her views and opinions when they conflicted with those of her tutors or lecturers—a recognition that academic success required her to negotiate heterogeneous disciplinary contexts with often highly asymmetrical power relations (cf. Canagarajah, 2002; Prior & Bilbro, 2012).

In her final interview, Laura was still struggling with the concept of authorship in academic writing:

I used to use more quotes than I use now . . . I use a lot more of my own words . . . I paraphrase more . . . sometimes you're more of an author . . . sometimes I see my text going exactly the way that I want with that idea [from a source text] . . . [but] I don't think I'm an author yet—I think it's a process. (Interview 5) . . .

Fei's understanding of academic writing gradually moved from one of acquisition of "non-popular" vocabulary, grammar, and the mechanics of citation towards a more sophisticated view of writing as situated in the rhetoric of particular disciplines, with this shaping, for example, the relevance and appropriacy of types and locations of source materials. This shift, according to Fei, was the result of increased discipline knowledge and her growing awareness of the wide range of people and resources (both formal and informal) that she could draw upon when needed. . . . For Laura, university writing was a very different sort of struggle. From the start of the year, Laura saw this primarily in terms of the search for an authentic and authoritative academic identity in the disciplines she was engaged with. Her development in academic writing over the year was for her related to the interaction between increasing disciplinary knowledge, language, and identity.

References

Canagarajah, A. S. (2002). Multilingual writers and the academic community: Towards a critical relationship. *Journal of English for Academic Purposes, 1*, 29–44. doi:10.1016S1475-1585(02)7-3

Casanave, C. P. (2002). *Writing games: Multicultural case studies of academic literacy practices in higher education*. Mahwah, NJ: Lawrence Erlbaum Associates.

Green, S. (2013). Novice ESL writers: A longitudinal case-study of the situated academic writing processes of three undergraduates in a TESOL context. *Journal of English for Academic Purposes, 12*, 180–191. doi:10.1016/j.jeap.2013.04.001

Pennycook, A. (2012). *Language and mobility: Unexpected places*. Bristol, UK: Multilingual Matters.

Prior, P., & Bilbro, R. (2012). Academic enculturation: Developing literate practices and disciplinary identities. In M. Castelló & C. Donahue (Eds.), *University writing: Selves and texts in academic societies* (pp. 19–31). Bingley, UK: Emerald.

Excerpts from Morton, J., Storch, N., & Thompson, C. (2015). What our students tell us: Perceptions of three multilingual students on their academic writing in first year. *Journal of Second Language Writing*, *30*, 1–13.

TASK 2 DISCUSS

In groups of two or three, talk about the following question: What is good academic writing? In your discussion, refer to your own opinions, your experiences as a student, and the ideas in the article. Also, consider the quotation from Samuel Johnson at the beginning of the chapter, regarding the powers of an author.

VOCABULARY

FOUR STRATEGIES FOR VOCABULARY LEARNING

When you read academic articles, you will frequently come across words that you do not fully understand. The following are four strategies for dealing with such words; you will practise these strategies throughout this book.

Strategy 1: Pass over the Word or Phrase

If you feel that understanding the word is not necessary to understanding the general idea of the sentence, you may decide to pass over it and carry on reading.

Strategy 2: Look at the Structure of the Word

Sometimes you can guess meaning from the different parts that make up a word. For example, if you came across the phrase *deregulation of banking* and did not know what *deregulation* meant, you could find clues in the parts of the word:

- *de*—a prefix that can mean "to reverse or remove"
- *regulate*—a verb meaning "to set rules"
- *ation*—a suffix meaning "the process of doing something" and indicating that the word is a noun

From this analysis of the parts of the word, you can guess that the meaning might be "the process of removing rules or controls in banking."

Strategy 3: Guess the Meaning from the Context

You can try to guess the meaning from the context by looking at the surrounding text for clues. For example, you may find a sentence such as "The researchers attempted replication of a previous experiment" in an academic article about a medical experiment. If you did not know the meaning of *replication*, you could search for clues in the surrounding text. If, further on in the text, you were to find a phrase such as "after repeating the experiment with a different group to test the findings," you could guess the meaning of *replication* without having to look it up in a dictionary.

Strategy 4: Look Up the Word in a Dictionary

In many cases, you will need to look up the meaning in a reliable dictionary. When you look up a word or phrase in a dictionary, you will often find more than one possible meaning. You then need to return to the text you are reading and decide which of the definitions best fits the context.

It can be difficult to understand vocabulary in academic journal articles and books. This is because authors use vocabulary in specialized ways in different fields. Even if you know what a word or phrase means in a general sense, an author may have a different, specialized meaning in mind.

When you do not understand a word or phrase, or a specific use of a word or phrase, you need to choose and apply one of the four strategies above.

TASK 3 PRACTISE THE FOUR STRATEGIES

Find the word or phrase in the first column of the table by referring to the line indicated in the Morton, Storch, and Thompson article. Read the whole sentence. If you think that the word is not important to the overall meaning, you can pass over it (1). If you feel that the word is important, use one of the other three strategies to try to define it: look at the structure of the word (2), guess the meaning from the context (3), or look up the word in a dictionary (4). Write a definition in the Meaning column and indicate the strategy, or strategies, that you used. Remember: authors use vocabulary for specific meanings in academic texts, so even if you think you know the general meaning of the word or phrase, make sure that you understand its specific meaning in the article.

Word/Phrase	Line	Meaning	Strategies Used			
			1	2	3	4
shifted	22					
process	23					
product	24					
cohesively	31					
traced	32					
meta-awareness	33					
rhetorical differences	33					
articulate	57					
first person	58					
conventions	66					
disciplinary knowledge	71					
viewed	71					

Word/Phrase	Line	Meaning	Strategies Used			
			1	2	3	4
authoritative writer	72					
impose myself	79					
negotiate	83					
cf.	84					
paraphrase	89					
acquisition	95					
mechanics of	96					
sophisticated	97					
draw upon	102					
primarily	104					
interaction between	106					

*Words in bold type are Academic Word List (AWL) entries.

Practise Chapter 1 vocabulary online.

TASK 4 MAKE SENSE OF COMPLEX ACADEMIC VOCABULARY

The following are three examples of complex academic vocabulary from the Morton et al. article. As a reader, you need to understand the overall meaning of the sentence. Read each example, and choose which of the two explanations, written in less technical language, is correct.

1. . . . a recognition that academic success required her to negotiate hetero-geneous disciplinary contexts with often highly asymmetrical power relations. [LINES 82–84]

    Explanation 1: This means that she realized that if she wanted to do well at university, she would have to figure out how to write in different subject areas, from a position of much less power than the people teaching her.

    Explanation 2: This means that she realized that if she wanted to do well at university, she had to meet and agree with her teachers, who were strict and powerful.

2. . . . a more sophisticated view of writing as situated in the rhetoric of particular disciplines, with this shaping, for example, the relevance and appropriacy of types and locations of source materials. [LINES 97–99]

    Explanation 1: She is now a better writer and can persuade her readers in different subject areas. As a result, she can now also choose better evidence and information from books and articles.

    Explanation 2: She now has a more complex understanding of writing, accepting that it reflects how people persuade each other in different ways in different subject areas. These strategies affect how students find and use relevant and appropriate evidence and information in books and articles.

3. Laura saw this primarily in terms of the search for an authentic and authoritative academic identity in the disciplines she was engaged with. [LINES 103–105]

Explanation 1: Laura's main struggle was finding a real and confident sense of who she was as a writer in the different subjects she was studying.

Explanation 2: Laura had to look for examples of university writing that focused on reality, confidence, and identity in the different subjects she was studying.

VOCABULARY

FORMALITY: PHRASAL VERBS AND LATINATE VERBS

This book is written in Standard Modern English, a language that did not exist a thousand years ago. To understand formality in academic writing, it is useful to trace the origins of the English language. After the French Norman invasion of Britain in 1066, French was established as the high-status language of the elite in Britain, while Anglo-Saxon, a Germanic dialect, remained the lower-status, everyday language of many people. Over the next three hundred years, the two languages merged into Old English, which later became Modern English. The result of this history is that there are often two ways to say things in English, one with its origins in Anglo-Saxon and the other with its origins in Latin, which came to English via French.

Consider the following sentences:

1. I **looked into** the room to see if anyone had arrived early. (verb + preposition)

2. I **looked into** the possibility of moving closer to college. (phrasal verb)

3. I **investigated** the possibility of moving closer to college. (Latinate verb)

The words in bold in example 1 are a verb and a preposition. The preposition indicates the direction in which the speaker looked (i.e., into the room); it does not change the meaning of the verb.

Example 2 contains a phrasal verb, formed by combining a verb (*look*) with a particle (*into*). The particle in phrasal verbs changes the meaning of the verb—in this case, from "look + into" to "investigate."

In example 3, the verb *investigate* is a Latinate verb. Latinate verbs tend to be longer than the verb components of phrasal verbs.

In academic writing, Latinate verbs are usually seen to be more formal than phrasal verbs, and many writers prefer to use them. In everyday speech and in less formal writing genres, phrasal verbs are more commonly used. English is rich in phrasal verbs; many have an equivalent, more formal alternative, often with its origins in Latin.

If you use too many Latinate verbs in your academic writing, it may seem overly formal. Equally, if you use too many phrasal verbs, your writing may seem overly informal or conversational. You need to strike a balance that makes your writing readable yet authoritative.

TASK 5 FIND THE LESS FORMAL VERBS

In Fei's interview and writing excerpts quoted in the Morton et al. article, she uses some less formal phrasal verbs and verb–preposition combinations. Match the following formal words and phrases to the less formal ones used by Fei.

1. searching in a book [LINE 20]: _____

2. acquiring [LINE 25]: _____

3. analyzing [LINE 25]: _____

4. discuss [LINE 39]: _____

TASK 6 FIND THE MORE FORMAL VERBS

The Morton et al. article contains many examples of formal academic vocabulary in the authors' writing as well as in Fei's and Laura's interviews and writing excerpts. Match the following less formal phrasal verbs to the more formal verbs used in the article.

1. bring into (my writing) [LINE 31]: _____

2. put together [LINE 37]: _____

3. build up [LINE 55]: _____

4. get across [LINE 57]: _____

5. find out [LINE 68]: _____

6. put together [LINE 75]: _____

7. went against [LINE 81]: _____

TASK 7 REWRITE FORMAL AND LESS FORMAL SENTENCES

1. Increase the formality of the following sentences by replacing the phrasal verbs.

   a) I **tried out** the theory in my lab experiment.

   _____

   _____

   b) I had to **make sure** that all of the equipment was working.

   _____

   _____

   c) I **got over** failing and passed the second time around.

   _____

   _____

2. Reduce the formality of the following sentences by using phrasal verbs.

   a) The medical students **performed** the procedure under supervision.

   _____

   _____

   b) I wasn't sure what my instructor **was implying** in his feedback.

   _____

   _____

   c) I **admire** my sister, who graduated within three years.

   _____

   _____

EFFECTIVE SENTENCE STRUCTURE

TENSE AND ASPECT

Tense

We use different verb tenses to situate actions and states at certain times in the past, present, and future. In the following examples, the time idea is underlined and the verb, in bold.

The assessed essay **is** due <u>now</u>.	(present simple tense for present time)
<u>At the time of the study</u>, Fei **was** 20 years old and Laura, 25.	(past simple tense for past time)
Both students **will graduate** <u>next year</u>.	(future time)

Aspect

Aspect is slightly different. It refers to how an action or state relates to different time ideas rather than when it is situated in time. There are two kinds of aspect: perfect and continuous. Perfect aspect indicates a relationship between two time periods (for example, past and present, past and past, present and future, or future and future), while continuous aspect indicates that an action is, was, or will be in progress at a certain time.

Perfect Aspect

> I feel that I have much stronger views than before that relate to the subjects I am studying ... I have my own opinion now. That **has changed** ... I would like to impose myself more.

In the example above, the present perfect tense is used by Laura to explain a relationship between the past and the present. When Laura states "That has changed," the past-time idea is indefinite (in other words, we do not know when the change took place). In this use of the present perfect tense, it is not important when the change took place in the past; the present result (Laura's stronger views and desire to impose herself) is more important and is thus emphasized. This type of relationship between the past and present characterizes perfect aspect.

To form perfect aspect, use the auxiliary verb *to have*, followed by the past participle of the main verb:

> That **has changed**.

Continuous Aspect

> I feel that I have much stronger views than before that relate to the subjects I **am studying** . . . I have my own opinion now. That has changed . . . I would like to impose myself more.

In the same example, Laura uses the present continuous to explain that an action is in progress at the time of speaking. In this instance of the present continuous, Laura describes a temporary continuing action that is not necessarily taking place at the time of speaking. This illustrates the main feature of continuous aspect: an action in progress at a certain time.

To form continuous aspect, use the auxiliary verb *to be*, followed by the main verb + *ing*:

> . . . the subjects I **am studying**.

Perfect and Continuous Aspect Together

> Fei is a Chinese student who <u>at the time of the study</u> was 20 years old and **had been living** in Australia for more than two years.

In the example above, the authors use the past perfect continuous, which combines perfect and continuous aspect. The past perfect continuous is used to describe perfect aspect (a relationship between two past-time ideas: Fei began to live in Australia *before* the study took place) and continuous aspect (an unfinished past state in progress at a certain time: Fei *was still living* in Australia at the time of the study).

Do Unit 1: Tense and Aspect in the Handbook, pp. 321–326.

TASK 8 FIND APPROPRIATE PAST-TENSE FORMS

In the following paragraphs from the Morton et al. article, the verbs that refer to the past have been removed. Without looking at the article, fill in the blanks with appropriate past-time forms of the verbs in brackets. There may be more than one correct answer. If you know the names of the different tenses, make note of them in the margin. After you have finished, compare your verb forms with those in the article.

Fei is a Chinese student who at the time of the study _____ [be] 20 years old and _____ [live] in Australia for more than two years. After finishing her secondary education in China, Fei _____ [repeat] the last two years of education at an Australian high school. Fei _____ [live] with her family in Australia and only _____ [speak] Cantonese at home. At university, she _____ [be] enrolled in an Economics and Business degree . . . . Fei . . . _____ [go on] to successfully complete all subjects in the second semester, and by taking extra subjects in the summer semester, _____ [be able] to graduate with a degree within three years.

The third student is Laura, who _____ [be] born in Brazil and at the time of this study, _____ [be] aged 25, _____ [live] in Australia for five years. She _____ [be] thus a little older than Fei and Kevin and _____ [spend] more time in an English-speaking country than either of them. Laura _____ [describe] herself as a speaker of Portuguese ("first" language), Spanish ("second" language) and English ("third" language), but a writer of Portuguese and English only. She _____ [be educated] in Portuguese and Spanish in primary and secondary school, with some of her secondary education delivered in English. In Australia, Laura _____ [live] with her Brazilian husband and _____ [speak] Portuguese at home. At university, Laura _____ [be] enrolled in a Bachelor of Arts degree, and in her first year she successfully _____ [complete] subjects in a broad range of Arts disciplines.

TASK 9 IDENTIFY PERFECT AND CONTINUOUS ASPECT

Now look again at the Morton et al. article. Underline any examples you find of perfect aspect and highlight any examples of continuous aspect. You will need to underline *and* highlight some examples that represent both perfect and continuous aspect.

TASK 10 RESPOND TO PROMPTS

The prompts below provide context about tense and aspect. Read the prompts and write a corresponding sentence.

1. Your study period was interrupted by the fire alarm.

   _____

   _____

2. You came to Canada three years ago. You are living in Toronto.

   _____

   _____

3. You started university two years ago. You lived in Toronto for one year before that.

   _____

   _____

4. You have read your friend's essay. You predict success in her final exams.

   _____

   _____

5. You have arranged a visit to New York next week.

_____

_____

TASK 11 WRITE A PARAGRAPH

Write a paragraph about your own background as if you were a participant in the same study as Fei and Laura. Write in the first person, using _I_ rather than the third-person _he_ or _she_. Try to use a range of past tenses. Later in the chapter, you will review what you have written to add precision and variety to the ways you refer to past time.

THE WRITING PROCESS

SEVEN STAGES OF THE WRITING PROCESS

Academic writing can be understood as both _process_ and _product_.

The _product_ is the final piece of work, which you usually submit for a grade. This product will normally be assessed and graded by your instructors according to a list of criteria. The criteria are the things that you have to do well for grades, for example, organization and structure, content, and accuracy and style of language.

Process refers to the different stages of study and writing that you go through to create the final product, ranging from reading and note taking to writing and editing your work. Each stage requires specific skills in reading, thinking, and writing. People write in different ways, so writers may go through many stages to create the final written product. Below are seven important stages of the writing process to consider each time you face the challenge of a new writing assignment.

Stage 1: Understand Your Audience, Genre, and Purpose

Before you start writing, it is important to think about your audience, genre, and purpose. If you understand these three concepts, it will help you organize your ideas, decide on appropriate writing styles, and engage critically with your topic.

Audience

Your audience is your reader or readers. It is important to think about the expectations of your audience when you write and to consider the following questions:

- Who is my audience?
- Does my reader have expert knowledge of the subject?
- Does my reader expect me to write in a certain way?

Genre

Put simply, the term _genre_ refers to different types of text, for example, a lab report, a summary, or an online news article. You need to pay attention to genre conventions—the rules or common practices that are associated with each type of text. Some texts may be written more formally than others, some may require evidence to back up arguments, and some may be structured differently from others. Genre conventions are determined not only by individual writers but also by different academic communities, or fields. For example, the rules for using personal language in academic writing are different in a lab report written for a biology class than in a reflective essay written for an education course. It is important to think about genre when you do different forms of academic writing and to consider the following questions:

- What genre is this text?
- What genre conventions do I need to follow?

Purpose

Every time you write, you have a reason. This is your purpose. If you are writing notes, you do not need to worry about style. However, if you are writing an exam essay or an assignment to be graded, then you need to take considerable care to meet your reader's expectations and to follow the genre conventions associated with the text. Ask yourself the following questions regarding your purpose for writing:

- Why am I writing?
- What is at stake?
- Can I take risks and be creative, or should I play safe?

To sum up, always consider the relationship between you, the writer, and your audience, the reader(s). Also, remember that different types of text have different genre conventions. If the stakes are high, you need to take care to follow those conventions.

TASK 12 IDENTIFY AUDIENCE, GENRE, AND PURPOSE

Look back at the exploratory writing you did for Task 1 and compare it with the academic article you read. Analyze each in terms of audience, genre, and purpose, and then describe how the writing styles differ.

1. Your writing for Task 1

   Audience: _____

   Genre: _____

   Purpose: _____

   _____

2. Morton, Storch, and Thompson (2015)

   Audience: _____

   Genre: _____

   Purpose: _____

   _____

3. Describe how the writing styles differ.

_____

_____

_____

_____

Stage 2: Find Your Focus and Question

You will regularly encounter two kinds of writing assignment: closed assignments that require you to respond to a question set by an instructor, and more open assignments that require you to choose your own question.

Understanding Your Focus and Task

If you are given a specific question to answer for a writing assignment during a course, or in an examination, you need to break down the focus and task so that you keep your writing _in focus_ and _on task_. Consider the following example:

general topic ⟶ The <u>use of fossil fuels for transportation</u> is still dominant in the world today,

task ⟶ but this dominance is beginning to face challenges from <u>alternative energy sources</u>. <u>Discuss the potential of alternative energy sources to replace fossil fuels for transportation in the next 20 years.</u>

The specific focus in the question is the dominance of fossil fuels in transportation today and the extent to which this dominance is being challenged by emerging alternative energy sources.

The specific task of a question is often indicated by a verb or phrase such as _discuss_, _analyze_, _compare and contrast_, or _describe_. This is what you have to do. Most of what you write needs to be about the focus and the task.

TASK 13 IDENTIFY THE FOCUS AND TASK IN AN ESSAY QUESTION

Read the following essay question and write the focus and task below.

Fossil fuels have been blamed for causing climate change, yet there are also several natural causes of climate change to consider. Compare the effects of fossil fuels and at least two natural phenomena on climate change. Do your findings support the view that governments should financially support the development of alternative energy sources?

Focus: _____

_____

_____

Task: _____

_____

_____

Choosing a Question and Subquestion

Many writing assignments require you to choose your own focus and task. In such cases, you first need to choose a question, research problem, or issue. Then you should bring in a number of subquestions to narrow your focus. For example, if you were asked to write an assignment on the topic of fossil fuels and alternative energy, you could form questions and subquestions as follows:

Question: Which alternative energy sources can feasibly replace fossil fuels for transportation?

Subquestions:

- Which fossil fuels are most commonly used for transportation in the world today?

- Which alternative energy sources are beginning to make an impact?

- What factors will determine their success? Technology, cost, environmental awareness?

- Which alternative energy sources therefore have the greatest chance for success?

When you are searching for academic articles, you can often find the main question and subquestion(s) in the abstract of the article. The abstract is normally a short summary (100–150 words) that includes the following: the main question, problem, or issue being analyzed; main supporting theories; methodology; findings; and conclusion. When you read the abstract, you can get a general idea of whether the article will be useful and relevant for your assignment.

TASK 14 IDENTIFY THE QUESTION AND SUBQUESTION(S)

Read the abstract below from the article by Morton et al. (2015). (See p. 7 for the full source.) Identify the main question and subquestions.

Abstract

Over the last couple of decades, there has been a growing recognition of the complexity of academic writing, including an interest in how learners negotiate the contexts within which they learn to write. As teachers in an EAP program, we approached this study with an interest in how our multilingual students negotiate the demands of their written assignments within particular disciplinary communities. The focus of the paper is thus on students' perceptions of what it means to "do" academic writing in their first year at university. A case study approach revealed the diversity of student perceptions of academic writing (as an issue of "skills" development, interpersonal relations, or the negotiation of authorial identities), as well as the multiplicity of resources that the multilingual students had at their disposal. It also allowed for insights into unexpected practices contributing to the students' progress as academic writers. Our findings suggest that the social context relevant for student writing includes but extends beyond the formal and academic, and embraces spaces and practices outside the institution. The current study was conducted in an Australian university, and one of its purposes is to add an Australian perspective to the growing body of case study research in academic literacy.

Main question: _____

_____

_____

Subquestion(s): _____

_____

_____

_____

Stage 3: Gather Your Ideas

As a writer, you may do some research before you write down your ideas, write down your ideas first and then do the research, or do both concurrently. Whatever the order, you can use several strategies for gathering your ideas. In this chapter, you will practise three: free writing, concept mapping, and linear notes.

Free writing: This involves writing down as many ideas as you can in any style you choose. The main goal is to generate as many ideas as possible to get started with the writing process.

Concept mapping: Instead of writing ideas down freely, you may prefer to map out your ideas in interconnected circles or bubbles in a concept map. Then you can place and label arrows between the bubbles to represent the relationships between the ideas. As with free writing, the aim of concept mapping is to generate as many ideas as possible and to begin the process of understanding the inter-relationships of ideas.

Linear notes: You may prefer to write down your ideas in linear notes, listing as many ideas as possible in note form and organizing them under headings and subheadings.

TASK 15 GATHER IDEAS

Practise gathering ideas in the three ways to see which method works best for you. After you have finished, discuss the effectiveness of the methods in pairs.

The topic is "How to become an effective writer in higher education."

1. **Free writing:** Write as many ideas as possible on the topic. You do not need to worry about formal style and sentence structure—notes are fine. The most important thing is to generate as many good ideas as possible.

_____

_____

_____

_____

_____

_____

_____

_____

_____

_____

_____

_____

_____

_____

_____

_____

_____

_____

2. **Concept mapping:** Now try gathering your ideas on the same topic, using the concept map below. Fill in the bubbles with your ideas; then draw arrows between the bubbles and describe their interrelationships. Add bubbles as needed.

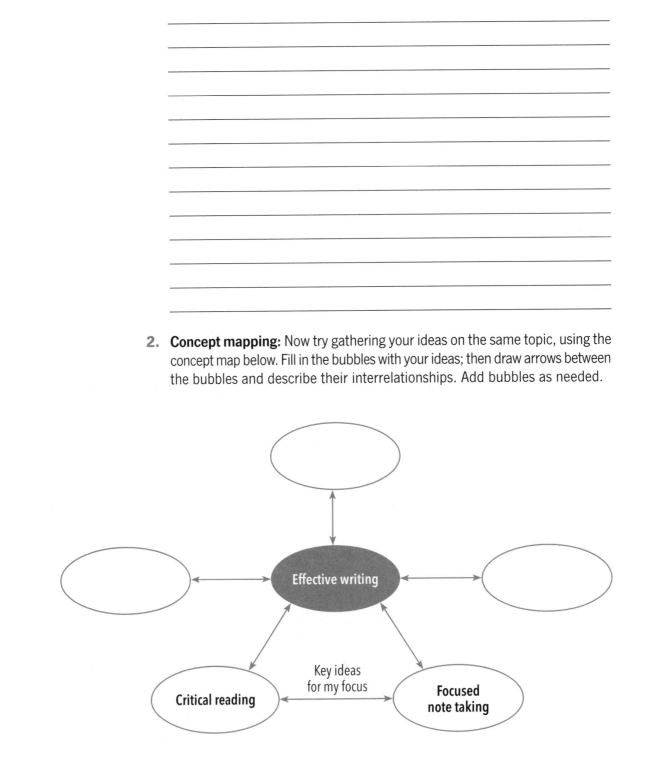

3. **Linear notes:** Write down any ideas you can think of and organize them under subheadings.

How to become an effective writer in higher education.

a) Critical reading: critically engage with ideas in the text — consider relevance + my opinion; keep in mind my focus and task

_____

b) Focused note taking: annotate text as I read — include key ideas, my opinions, questions I have

_____

c) _____

_____

_____

d) _____

_____

_____

e) _____

_____

_____

Stage 4: Form an Outline

Once you have analyzed your focus and task, identified questions and subquestions, and generated some ideas about the subject, you should form an outline for the essay. Different genres require different types of outline; for example, the outlines for a lab report and an argument essay would be very different. You need to be flexible as a writer and learn to arrange your ideas into different structures. In Part 3 of this book, you will study different strategies for forming outlines.

Stage 5: Add Research through Reading and Note Taking

Depending on the nature of the writing assignment and on your personal preferences as a learner, you may do research before, during, and/or after you form your outline. Two important skills you need to apply as you add research are assessing reliability and taking effective notes.

Make sure that the materials you use (e.g., articles, books, and other materials) come from reliable sources. You will study how to assess the reliability of sources in Chapter 4.

Second, make sure to take notes effectively. Your notes should include key ideas, questions that come to your mind as you read, and your personal opinions about the ideas. Taking effective notes also involves recording the information you will need for in-text citations and reference lists (e.g., author(s), date, place of publication, publisher, page numbers). You should use quotation marks for information that you copy directly. All of these aspects of note taking will help you write more clearly and will save you time.

The example on the next page is from the conclusion of the Morton et al. article. (See pp. 6–7 for the references and full source.) The text has been annotated for key information, the reader's personal opinion, questions that arise, and bibliographic information. Annotation involves taking notes as you read and may include highlighting key points in the text. You will practise annotating texts more in the coming chapters.

We conclude this paper with reflections on case study methodology. We approached this study with an interest in the experiences of our multilingual students. We found that longitudinal case studies were able to capture some of the complexity and diversity of the three students' trajectories as academic writers. In particular, we found that the five in-depth interviews over the duration of the study fostered student–researcher relationships that opened up space for insights into the unpredictable and unexpected practices contributing to the students' progress as academic writers (cf. Casanave, 2002; Pennycook, 2012). All three students told us they enjoyed the opportunities to talk at length with the researchers and especially to reflect upon their learning experiences—opportunities they said were not available to them elsewhere in the university. The in-depth interviews, in our experience, encouraged self-reflection and contributed to "the learning that happens as people listen to themselves put feelings and experiences into words" (Casanave, 2002, p. 33). The kind of reflexivity and the meta-knowledge about writing that was built up in these interviews have been linked in other research to success in academic writing (Green, 2013), and could thus be seen as an unexpected benefit of participating in this type of research.

TASK 16 ANNOTATE A PARAGRAPH

The following paragraph is from an article that looks at the sense of belonging (the extent to which people feel they belong to a community) among undergraduate students who are taking a first-year academic writing course called ALC at a university in Canada. The paragraph is from the Discussion section of the article, in which the authors bring together the analysis of their findings.

Read the paragraph and take notes, including the following:

- key ideas
- questions that come to your mind as you read
- your personal opinions about the ideas
- a direct quotation (something that stands out for you)

Sense of Belonging and First-Year Academic Literacy

A broad range of factors affected ALC students' sense of belonging both to the university and to the course. First, participants described their sense of belonging to the university as being affected by interacting with peers, making new friends, interacting with faculty and advisers, living in residence, and having a manageable course load. Those who described a lack of sense of belonging to the university linked it to two of these factors (interacting with peers and not making friends) as well as to the size of the campus and concerns about maintaining GPA. When participants described their sense of belonging in relation to ALC, they referred to improved academic literacy, small class size, new friendships, supportive learning environment, pedagogy, and instruction. Others perceived a lack of connection between their sense of belonging and ALC, stating that their sense of belonging was unrelated to the course. For those who referred to a lack of sense of belonging to ALC, the reasons they gave were a poor fit with curriculum and peers, lack of improvement in academic literacy, over-

demanding course load, class size, linguistic difference, and national identity. Finally, a number of participants described a sense of being between belonging and not belonging, and uncertainty about their sense of belonging, citing the following factors: it was too soon to say, they were still finding their way around the large campus, and they had concerns about their academic success and GPA.

Excerpt from Marshall, S., Zhou, M., Gervan, T., & Wiebe, S. (2012). Sense of belonging and first-year academic literacy. *Canadian Journal of Higher Education, 42*(3), 116–142.

Stage 6: Write the Essay Sections

Once you have completed stages 1 to 5, it is time to start writing the introduction, main body paragraphs, and conclusion, in whatever order suits your style of writing.

If you like to write in a linear fashion (i.e., you like to do things in order, one at a time, from *a* to *z*), you would typically start with the introduction, work through the main body sections, and then finish with the conclusion and reference list.

If you are not a linear writer, then you might write the sections in any order. For some writers, the introduction is the last section they turn to rather than the first.

As you write, keep in mind the three concepts introduced in this chapter: audience, genre, and purpose. Remember to keep *in focus* and *on task*.

Stage 7: Review and Edit Your Work

When you write, it is important to review and edit your work as you go along. You need to check the language for accuracy of grammar, vocabulary, and punctuation. You should also make sure you are writing in a style that is appropriate for the task. Equally important (many would say *more* important) is the content: make sure your ideas, arguments, and statements are clear, logical, well supported, and convincing.

WHAT IS CRITICAL THINKING?

Critical thinking is essential for successful academic writing. In the following chapters, you will study different aspects of critical thinking that will allow you to include arguments in your writing that are both coherent and convincing.

TASK 17 EXPLORE THROUGH WRITING

What is critical thinking?

Take five minutes to answer the question. You can write in any style you like. The main aim is to generate ideas. After you have finished, share your writing with peers.

TASK 18 DISCUSS

In the Morton et al. article, do the strategies described by Fei or Laura for becoming a successful academic writer convince you? Which aspects of critical thinking help you answer the question?

EFFECTIVE WRITING STYLE

USING OR AVOIDING PERSONAL LANGUAGE

In this chapter, you have studied excerpts from an academic journal article in which the authors did not use personal language such as *I* and *we* in their analysis of multilingual students' understanding of academic writing. In contrast, for Tasks 1 and 11, you most likely used personal language to describe your writing style and your background. The decision to use personal language or not depends on the genre and common practices in your field, the expectations of your reader(s), and your purpose for writing.

It is important to understand that using personal language in academic writing does not mean that your writing is informal. Rather, choosing to use personal language is a choice of style. In many subject areas, personal language is encouraged; for example, in the field of education studies, students are often encouraged to express their views subjectively with personal language. In other subjects, it is discouraged because it is seen to be unscientific and subjective.

When you write an assignment, be sure to find out if you should or should not use personal language. Regardless of the subject area you are studying, it is a useful skill to be able to use language effectively, switching from the personal to the impersonal as required.

Consider the following example sentences written in personal language and the four strategies for making them less personal.

> **I will discuss** the extent to which natural phenomena contribute to climate change.

> **My** analysis is based on the view that certain natural phenomena do cause climate change.

Four Strategies to Make Writing Less Personal

Learn more about the passive voice in Unit 7 of the Handbook, p. 364.

1. **Use the passive voice instead of the active voice.**

   I will discuss the extent to which natural phenomena contribute to climate change. (active voice)

   The extent to which natural phenomena contribute to climate change **will be discussed**. (passive voice)

2. **Use an impersonal subject instead of a personal subject pronoun.**

   I will discuss the extent to which natural phenomena contribute to climate change. (personal subject pronoun)

   This essay will discuss the extent to which natural phenomena contribute to climate change. (impersonal subject)

3. **Use an impersonal phrase instead of a personal subject pronoun.**

   I will discuss the extent to which natural phenomena contribute to climate change. (personal subject pronoun)

   The focus of this essay is the extent to which natural phenomena contribute to climate change. (impersonal phrase)

4. **Replace *my* with an impersonal determiner.**

   My analysis is based on the view that certain natural phenomena do cause climate change. (possessive determiner)

   The analysis is based on the view that certain natural phenomena do cause climate change. (impersonal determiner)

   Determiners are words such as *the*, *this*, *those*, and *my* that come before a noun to explain its context.

TASK 19 MAKE SENTENCES LESS OR MORE PERSONAL

Refer to the strategies above and make the following sentences less personal (1 and 2) and more personal (3 and 4).

1. In the previous sections, I discussed the significance of natural causes of climate change. I suggested that certain natural phenomena do cause climate change.

   _____

   _____

   _____

2. I strongly believe that human-produced CO_2 remains the most controllable factor in reducing climate change.

   _____

   _____

   _____

3. It has been argued that climate change will pose the greatest threat to economic stability in the 21st century.

_____

_____

_____

4. The above paragraphs focused on two natural causes of climate change: volcanic activity and solar activity. Several impacts were then analyzed.

Find supplementary reading, writing, and critical-thinking activities online.

_____

_____

_____

REVISE AND EDIT

REVISE VERB FORMS

Review the paragraph you wrote about your background in Task 11. Check your verb forms for appropriate tense and aspect, and try to improve them. Look again at Unit 1 in the Handbook for ideas on how to write about past time with more precision. After you have improved your text, complete the checklist below.

Checklist for Revising and Editing

☐ Have you checked your tenses and made changes to add more precision regarding the time ideas of actions and states?

Do the online grammar diagnostic. Draw up a checklist of areas for improvement.

☐ Have you considered perfect and continuous aspect and changed verb forms accordingly?

☐ Do you now have a broader range of tenses and verb forms?

☐ Does your paragraph flow better, and have you made it more readable?

CHAPTER 2

UNDERSTANDING RESEARCH

> If we knew what it is we were doing,
> it would not be called research, would it?
>
> Albert Einstein

As suggested by Albert Einstein, research is a pursuit of new knowledge, a process of questioning and searching for answers in new ways. Understanding research is key to success in academic writing. Whether you are doing your own research project or reviewing existing research for an assignment, you need to be aware of the research process and of different types of research.

In this chapter, you will:

- learn about the research process
- study research vocabulary
- read a journal article about scientific research
- study articles (*a* and *the*) and noun phrases in English
- analyze the use of the passive voice in objective, scientific writing style
- write a 100-word summary

TASK 1 EXPLORE THROUGH WRITING

What is research, and why do it?

Take five minutes to answer the questions. Try to write as many ideas as you can.

After you have finished, discuss what you have written with peers.

WHAT IS RESEARCH?

Research involves collecting and analyzing data in a systematic way to further your understanding of knowledge by looking at theories, asking questions, forming hypotheses, and reaching conclusions. Research can be carried out to test and prove existing theories and to form new ones.

Why Do Research?

If you are carrying out your own research project, you are looking for answers to a specific problem or question. If you are reviewing existing literature, you are learning about the current state of your research field: who is studying what, what the main issues of contention are, and how these may relate to your own studies.

Empirical versus Non-Empirical Research

Empirical research involves answering questions and furthering knowledge by observation and experimentation. Non-empirical research seeks answers to questions and tests theory by analyzing existing knowledge.

Quantitative versus Qualitative Research

There is an important division in academic research between quantitative and qualitative research.

A researcher's decision to employ one type of research or the other can depend on a number of factors:

- the research questions
- the phenomenon, group, or population under investigation
- personal philosophical beliefs about knowledge, behaviour, and society

Quantitative Research

In quantitative research, the researcher normally builds on existing theory by forming a hypothesis, that is, a prediction that will be tested to see whether a theory is valid. Quantitative researchers usually study large populations and use random sampling of study participants. Random sampling is the use of mathematical formulas to select participants in a way that makes them representative of a broader population, for example, by age, gender, race, class, and socio-economic status. Data are often gathered via surveys and experiments. In quantitative research, data are analyzed numerically and usually presented in tables and graphs.

> In English, *data* can act as a subject to both singular and plural verbs. It is possible to write "the data is" or "the data are."

In quantitative experimental research, it is common practice to divide participants randomly between study and control groups. In medical research, for example, the study group would receive a new treatment, while the control group would receive a placebo, which is a substance with no medical effect. Such experiments are described as "blind" if participants in each group do not know whether they are receiving medicine or a placebo, and "double-blind" if neither the researchers nor the participants know.

The following are three important concepts in quantitative research:

- **Correlation:** Quantitative researchers create statistical representations of the data and look for correlations. Drawing a correlation means finding a link. For example, in early investigations of the negative health effects of smoking, researchers were able to draw a correlation between smoking and cancer. When further study proved this correlation, cigarette manufacturers began to write warnings on their packaging, such as "Smoking can cause cancer."

- **Causality:** When quantitative researchers find a correlation between *a* and *b*, this does not mean that they can claim causality. In other words, they cannot state that *a* causes *b*. In order to claim causality, they need to eliminate variable factors. In the early research into smoking-related diseases, the variables were any factors, other than smoking tobacco, that may have caused cancer in the smokers being studied, for example, age, gender, diet, lifestyle, and socio-economic status. Only through further investigation and analysis were researchers able to establish causality and claim that smoking *caused* cancer in the people they studied.

- **Generalizability:** Generalizability means that the research findings can be applied to the broader general population. For researchers to claim that their findings are generalizable, they need to replicate their studies. Replication involves repeating the same research procedure with different groups. If the results are the same, then the findings become generalizable. After the early research into smoking-related illnesses was replicated and the same findings emerged, cigarette manufacturers around the world began to change the warning on their packaging to "Smoking causes cancer."

Qualitative Research

In qualitative studies, researchers do not always build on existing theory by testing a hypothesis; the tendency to focus on smaller populations makes hypothesis testing less relevant and less feasible. Accordingly, qualitative researchers are unlikely to use random sampling to get a representative group of participants. Data are commonly gathered via interviews and observation. While qualitative researchers

may sometimes suggest correlations in their findings, they do not aim for causality (by eliminating variable factors) or generalizability (by replicating the study).

In qualitative research, data are coded (organized into groups and categories) and analyzed through detailed written description rather than numerically.

Mixed-Method Research

It is common for researchers to combine quantitative and qualitative research. For example, a researcher may carry out observations and interviews with a small group of participants in the exploratory phase of a research project and then follow up this stage with surveys or experiments with larger groups. Mixed-method researchers may also work in the opposite direction, for example, by carrying out surveys or experiments with a large group of participants and then doing follow-up interviews with a smaller group to expand on initial findings in more detail.

TASK 2 UNDERSTAND STATEMENTS ABOUT QUANTITATIVE AND QUALITATIVE RESEARCH

Read the statements below about quantitative and qualitative research and answer the questions that follow.

1. The researchers suggested that the use of hand-held devices while driving may have been linked to the increase in fatal road accidents.

   Which did the researchers establish in their findings: causality or a possible correlation?

   _____

   _____

   _____

2. Swiss psychologist Jean Piaget's studies of brothers and sisters in the 1920s were successfully replicated several times. It is now accepted that young children conceptualize brother-and-sister relations in three important stages (Elkind, 1962).

   Does this statement illustrate generalizability? Why or why not?

   _____

   _____

   _____

3. After eliminating 10 key variable factors ranging from age to social class, the researchers concluded that a diet high in sugar caused chronic illness in 72% of the participants.

   Does the statement illustrate causality or generalizability? Why or why not?

   _____

   _____

   _____

4. After eliminating 10 key variable factors ranging from age to social class, and replicating the procedure with different groups over a 15-year period, the researchers concluded that a diet high in sugar causes chronic illness.

How does the statement show that the researchers moved from causality to generalizability?

_____

_____

_____

_____

_____

10 STAGES OF THE RESEARCH PROCESS

When you read about research while reviewing literature, or if you write about your own research, it is important to understand and evaluate the research process. Carrying out effective research usually involves some or all of the following 10 stages, although not always in this order.

Stage 1: Find a Research Problem or Question

In the planning stages, researchers focus on a question or find a problem. They often justify their choice of question or problem, explaining why it is interesting, relevant, and important.

Stage 2: State the Purpose and/or Goals

Researchers should also state why they are doing the research, explaining what they want to find out and what they want to achieve.

Stage 3: Review Relevant Literature

The purpose of the literature review is to analyze theories that are relevant to the upcoming research data. In order to show a clear understanding of a specific field, researchers need to critically engage with relevant literature by assessing the strengths and weaknesses of the studies reviewed. To do this, they evaluate the methodology, analysis, and findings of the studies. If possible, they highlight a gap in the literature and attempt to address that gap with their own research.

Stage 4: Adopt a Theoretical Position

After critically engaging with relevant literature and finalizing the research problem or question, researchers develop and adopt a theoretical position. This position usually involves accepting or applying a specific theory or framework, or a combination of theories and frameworks.

Stage 5: State a Hypothesis

Researchers often state a hypothesis, which is a prediction that will be tested in the study. As mentioned above, stating a hypothesis is less common in qualitative research.

Stage 6: Discuss Methodology and Select Methods

The term *methodology* refers to a discussion of possible research methods. Research methods are the different tools that are used to collect data, such as surveys, experiments, interviews, and observation. Researchers choose specific methods to address the problem or answer the research question. Before selecting the methods, it is necessary to review those used in other related studies, assessing their strengths, weaknesses, relevance, and applicability.

Stage 7: Collect Data

Next, researchers follow through with the data-gathering methods chosen during the methodology stage. They try to stick as closely as possible to these methods and take note of any deviations from the original plan.

Stage 8: Code and Analyze the Data

The ways that researchers code and analyze their data will depend on whether the research is quantitative or qualitative. Nonetheless, in both cases, they are looking for answers to questions, and solutions to problems. Quantitative and qualitative researchers typically code data—that is, they organize the data into groups and categories—and look for emerging themes. Quantitative researchers often form themes and categories by using statistical analysis software such as SPSS (Statistical Package for the Social Sciences) and represent their findings in tables, graphs, figures, illustrations, and written description. Qualitative researchers may use coding software such as NVivo to find categories and emerging themes in their data; they usually present their findings in detailed written form, with fewer tables and figures.

Stage 9: Present and Evaluate Results and Conclusions

After analyzing data, researchers present and evaluate their results. This involves clearly addressing the original research problem and answering any research questions. Researchers should also assess whether their findings are valid (put simply, whether they are scientifically solid and convincing), recognize the limitations of their study, and consider future research directions.

Stage 10: Disseminate the Research

The final stage of the research process is to disseminate the results by submitting an essay or a report, presenting it to peers in class or at a conference, and publishing it if possible.

TASK 3 IDENTIFY THE RESEARCH PROCESS IN AN ABSTRACT

In the following abstract from an article on homeopathic medicine, the paragraph headings have been removed and replaced with lines.

1. Match each of the following paragraph headings to the correct part of the abstract. Write the heading on the appropriate line.

   Background — Conclusion — Keywords — Research Methods — Results

Abstract

a) _____

Homeopathic medicine is a branch of integrative medicine that has been gaining increasing popularity. However, its clinical application remains controversial.

To improve the understanding of homeopathy, observational studies—which monitor the effects of homeopathy in real-life clinical settings—are a helpful **adjunct** to **randomized controlled trials**.

The goal of this controlled observational study was to investigate the role of the homeopathic medicine in preventing **respiratory tract infections** (RTIs).

b) _____

This **retrospective** analysis of patients' medical records focused on a single centre from 2002 to 2011, and examined 459 patients, out of whom 248 were treated with homeopathic medicine (specific extract of duck liver and heart) and 211 were not treated. All patients were followed-up for at least 1 year, and up to a maximum of 10 years.

c) _____

A significant reduction in the frequency of **onset** of RTIs was found in both the homeopathic medicine and untreated groups. The reduction in the **mean number** of RTI episodes during the period of observation vs. the year before inclusion in the study was significantly greater in the homeopathic-treated group than in untreated patients (-4.76 ± 1.45 vs. -3.36 ± 1.30; $p = 0.001$). The beneficial effect of the homeopathic medicine was not significantly related to gender, age, smoking habits or **concomitant** respiratory diseases when compared to the effect observed in untreated patients.

d) _____

These results suggest that homeopathic medicine may have a positive effect in preventing RTIs. However, randomized studies are needed before any firm conclusion can be reached.

e) _____

Comparative study, Integrative therapies, Homeopathy, Observational study, Oscillococcinum, Respiratory tract infections

Beghi, G. M., & Morselli-Labate, A. M. (2016). Does homeopathic medicine have a preventive effect on respiratory tract infections? A real life observational study. *Multidisciplinary Respiratory Medicine*, *11*(12), 1. doi:10.1186/s40248-016-0049-0

adjunct: addition

randomized controlled trials: experiments in which one group receives treatment and the other does not

respiratory tract infections: infections occurring between the lungs and the nose

retrospective: historical

onset: beginning

mean number: average

concomitant: happening at the same time

2. <u>Underline</u> the words or phrases that bring the reader's focus to the following information in the Background section:

   a) Why the topic is interesting

   b) The research problem

   c) The aims of the study

3. In paragraph d), the authors state the following: "These results suggest that homeopathic medicine may have a positive effect in preventing RTIs."

   Are the authors suggesting causality or a possible correlation?

   _____

   _____

VOCABULARY

RESEARCH-RELATED VOCABULARY

The language of research includes many terms that have their origins in Latin and Greek.

TASK 4 DEFINE TERMS RELATED TO RESEARCH

Review the following key terms from the sections titled "What Is Research?" and "10 Stages of the Research Process." Refer back to the texts and write a definition of each term. Compare your answers with a partner.

1. empirical research: _____

   _____

2. non-empirical research: _____

   _____

3. quantitative research: _____

   _____

   _____

   _____

4. qualitative research: _____

   _____

   _____

   _____

5. phenomenon: _____

   _____

6. hypothesis: _____

   _____

7. random sampling: _____

   _____

8. study group: _____

   _____

9. control group: _____

   _____

10. placebo: _____

    _____

11. blind: _____

    _____

12. double-blind: _____

    _____

13. correlation: _____

    _____

14. eliminate variable factors: _____

    _____

15. generalizability: _____

    _____

16. replication: _____

    _____

CRITICAL THINKING

EVALUATE TYPES OF RESEARCH

TASK 5 DISCUSS

In pairs or small groups, discuss the following questions:

1. What kind of research is most common in your field of study?

2. What do you see as the strengths and weaknesses of quantitative and qualitative research?

THE DOUBLE-BLIND CONTROL TRIAL AND HOMEOPATHY

In homeopathic medicine, people are treated with minute doses of the substances that would lead to illness in healthy people if they were given a larger dose. For example, a homeopathic treatment for people with a pollen allergy (hay fever, or

allergic rhinitis) is to find out which pollen they are allergic to and then administer minute doses of that pollen over a period of months to prevent an allergic reaction when the people breathe in pollen.

Many homeopathic medicines are sold in pharmacies on a separate counter for alternative or complementary treatments. In many cases, they are not sold as approved medicine because their effectiveness in treating illness has not been conclusively proven in a double-blind control trial.

TASK 6 READ AND TAKE NOTES

Read the text below. In the article, author Michael Stolberg refers to the famous Nuremberg salt test of 1835, in which homeopathic medicine was put to the test in a double-blind control trial. As you read, take notes on the main ideas. You will use your notes later to write a 100-word summary of the article.

Inventing the Randomized Double-Blind Trial: The Nuremberg Salt Test of 1835

by Michael Stolberg

Control groups, randomization, blinding, placebos and related methods designed to eliminate bias have become widely recognized as key features of efforts to identify more effective and safer treatments. . . . A very early example of randomization and double blinding was an evaluation of
5 homeopathy conducted in Nuremberg in 1835 by a 'society of truth-loving men' (Stolberg, 1996, 1999; Löhner, 1835).

At the time, homeopathy had **garnered** considerable support among the upper classes in the then Kingdom of Bavaria. In Nuremberg, one of Bavaria's largest and most **affluent** cities, Karl Preu and Johann Jacob Reuter had
10 treated some of the most **prominent** families with homeopathy, including members of the **high aristocracy**. In 1834, annoyed by homeopathy's rising popularity, Friedrich Wilhelm von Hoven, the city's highest ranking public health official and head of the local hospitals, . . . accused homeopathy of lacking any scientific foundation. He suggested that homeopathic drugs were
15 not real medicines at all and alleged homeopathic cures were either due to **dietetic regimens** and the healing powers of nature, or showed the power of belief. He called for an objective, comparative assessment by **impartial**

garnered: gathered

affluent: wealthy, rich

prominent: leading

high aristocracy: highest social class, often with inherited land and titles

dietetic regimens: planned diets

impartial experts: experts who are not biased

drastic measures: strong or extreme actions

deceived patients: patients who have been given the wrong impression

physician: doctor

lunatics: people with mental illness (pejorative in modern usage)

C30 dilution of salt: measured mixture of a tiny amount of salt and distilled water

The odds were ten to one: There was a 10% chance.

took up: accepted

vials: small glass containers

distilled snow water: snow heated to gas then collected after evaporating

allopathic drugs: non-homeopathic drugs

protocol: design of the experiment

experts. If, as he expected, homeopathic treatment proved ineffective, the government would need to take **drastic measures** to protect the lives of
20 **deceived patients**.

In 1835, . . . Johann Jacob Reuter was the sole remaining **physician** homeopath in the city. He reacted . . . with an ardent defence of homeopathy (Reuter, 1835) and pointed out that even children, **lunatics** and animals had been successfully cured. . . . He challenged von Hoven to try the effects of a **C30**
25 **dilution of salt** on himself. **The odds were ten to one**, he claimed, that his opponent would experience some extraordinary sensations as a result—and these were nothing compared to the much stronger effects on the sick. Perhaps surprisingly, Reuter's opponents **took up** his challenge. . . .

Following a widely publicized invitation to anyone who was interested, more
30 than 120 citizens met in a local tavern. The minimum number needed to proceed had been fixed at 50. The design of the proposed trial was explained in detail. In front of everyone, 100 **vials** were numbered, thoroughly shuffled and then split up at random into two lots of 50. One lot was filled with **distilled snow water**, the other with ordinary salt in a homeopathic C30-dilution of
35 distilled snow water, prepared just as Reuter had demanded: a grain of salt was dissolved in 100 drops of distilled snow water and the resulting solution was diluted 29 times at a ratio of 1 to 100. Great care was taken to avoid any contamination with **allopathic drugs**. . . .

A list indicating the numbers of the vials with and without the salt dilution,
40 respectively, was made and sealed. The vials were then passed on to a 'commission' which distributed 47 of the vials to those among the audience who had declared their willingness to participate . . . . The participants' names and the number of the vial that each had received were written in a second list. . . .

45 Three weeks later, at a second meeting, the participants were asked to report whether they had experienced anything unusual after ingesting the vial's content. Those who did not come to the meeting were asked to send this information in. Responses were thus obtained from 50 of the 54 participants. Those participants who had perceived something unusual described their
50 symptoms, as required by the **protocol**.

Finally, the sealed lists were opened to see who had received water and who the homeopathic dilution, and a list of results was compiled. . . . The vast majority of those who had received the homeopathic salt dilution had thus not experienced any 'effect'. The investigators concluded that Reuter was
55 wrong.

From a modern point of view, the major features of the trial can be summarized as follows:

(1) The trial design (protocol) was carefully set out and the details of the study were made public in advance.

60 (2) The number of participants was relatively large and the differences between the two groups would have been significant if Reuter had been right.

(3) Assignment to one group or the other was apparently perfectly randomized.

(4) A control group receiving only placebo was used.

65 (5) The trial was double blind: neither the participants nor those who organized the trial, distributed the vials and documented the effects had any idea whether a vial contained the homeopathic high dilution or **merely** water.

(6) A rough comparative statistics of the results was compiled.

(7) Irregularities were carefully recorded, such as the failure of four partici-
70 pants to report back, and the fact that several vials were distributed only after the first tavern meeting.

The organizers concluded that the symptoms or changes which the homeo-paths claimed to observe as an effect of their medicines were the **fruit of imagination**, **self-deception** and **preconceived opinion**—if not **fraud**.
75 In spite of their efforts to achieve perfect blinding and randomization, they seem to have been aware, however, that the homeopaths could come up with solid methodological reasons for not accepting this interpretation: in this specific setting, even randomization and double blinding could not eliminate bias. Most participants seem to have opposed homeopathy, and if they wanted
80 to discredit it, they could do so simply by reporting that they had not experienced anything unusual. . . .

Historically, the value of the trial report thus lies above all in the principles it set out. The organizers called on others and, in particular, on the homeopaths themselves, to perform and repeat similar trials, with different dilutions, and
85 to make the results public. They stressed once more the *punctum saliens*, the crucial element of their design: one must avoid anything that might enable the participants and those responsible for the trial to guess whether the actual medicine was given or not.

References

Löhner, G., on behalf of a society of truth-loving men. (1835). Die homöopathischen Kochsalzversuche zu Nürnberg [The homeopathic salt trials in Nuremberg]. Nuremberg.

Reuter, J. J. (1835). Sendschreiben an Dr E Fr Wahrhold als Erwiederung auf dessen Schrift "Auch etwas über die Homöopathie" [Letter to Dr. E. F. Wahrhold in response to his paper on homeopathy]. Nuremberg.

Stolberg, M. (1996). Die Homöopathie auf dem Prüfstein: Der erste Doppelblindversuch der Medizingeschichte im Jahr 1835 [Homeopathy put to the test: The first double-blind experiment in medical history, in 1835]. *Münchener medizinische Wochenschrift*, *138*, 364–366.

Stolberg, M. (1999). *Die Homöopathie im Königreich Bayern (1800–1914)* [Homeopathy in the kingdom of Bavaria, 1800–1914]. Heidelberg: Haug.

Excerpts from Stolberg, M. (2006). Inventing the randomized double-blind trial: The Nuremberg salt test of 1835. *Journal of the Royal Society of Medicine*, *99*, 642–643. Retrieved from http://www.jameslindlibrary.org/articles/inventing-the-randomized-double-blind-trial-the-nurnberg-salt-test-of-1835/

merely: only

fruit of imagination: not real, imagined

self-deception: making yourself believe something that is not true

preconceived opinion: opinion formed before evidence is available

fraud: cheating, dishonesty

EXTEND YOUR ACADEMIC VOCABULARY

Extend your knowledge of key vocabulary from this chapter.

bias	**foundation**	**significant**
compile	**proceed**	**stress**
conduct	respective(ly)	thorough(ly)

*Words in bold type are Academic Word List (AWL) entries.

Practise Chapter 2 vocabulary online.

TASK 7 ENGAGE CRITICALLY WITH RESEARCH

When you read about research, you need to engage critically with the text. This kind of critical engagement through reading involves identifying strengths and weaknesses, arguments that do or do not convince you, information that is missing, and the author's opinions. After developing an in-depth understanding of the text, you then need to represent that understanding clearly in your writing.

Show your in-depth understanding of the text by answering the following questions.

1. According to the author, Johann Jacob Reuter provided a strong defence of homeopathy, and to support his argument, he pointed out "that even children, lunatics and animals had been successfully cured." [LINES 23–24]

   Are you convinced by Reuter's support for his argument? Why or why not?

   _____

   _____

   _____

   _____

   _____

2. The following numbers appear in the article between lines 29 and 50. Write what each number refers to.

   a) 120 [LINE 30]: _____

   b) 50 [LINE 31]: _____

   c) 100 [LINE 32]: _____

   d) 50 [LINE 33]: _____

   e) 47 [LINE 41]: _____

   f) 50 [LINE 48]: _____

   g) 54 [LINE 48]: _____

3. What information is missing for these numbers to make sense, and what assumptions do you have to make as a reader about the missing information?

_____

_____

_____

_____

_____

_____

4. Despite the trial results, the homeopaths could have argued that randomization (randomly allocating the treatment to the participants) did not eliminate bias: "even randomization and double blinding could not eliminate bias." [LINES 78–79]

Opponents of homeopathy could sign up for the experiment and discredit it by providing biased responses: "if they wanted to discredit it, they could do so simply by reporting that they had not experienced anything unusual." [LINES 79–81]

Could random sampling have reduced or eliminated bias? Why or why not?

_____

_____

_____

_____

_____

5. In lines 82 to 83, the author states that "the value of the trial report thus lies above all in the principles it set out."

What does this imply about the author's opinion of the experiment and its findings?

_____

_____

_____

EFFECTIVE SENTENCE STRUCTURE

ARTICLES, NOUNS, AND NOUN PHRASES

What Are Nouns and Noun Phrases?

Nouns are words that are used to name things, and noun phrases are phrases that include a noun as the main word.

dictionary	(noun)
the dictionary on my shelf	(noun phrase)

Countable and Uncountable Nouns

There are two types of nouns: countable and uncountable. Countable nouns can have a plural form; uncountable nouns have no plural form.

I'm looking for a **dictionary**. (singular countable noun)

You can use two **dictionaries**. (plural countable noun)

I did some **research** last week. (uncountable noun)

Rules for Describing Things in English

You can use articles such as *a* and *the*, or no articles, with nouns and noun phrases. You should use different forms depending on whether the noun you are describing is countable or uncountable and whether you are referring to the thing in a general or specific way. The following statements about the Stolberg article illustrate different types of noun phrases, highlighted in bold.

General Noun Phrases (G)

G1. Friedrich Wilhelm von Hoven was looking for **a local tavern** where he could carry out the experiment.

(*a* + singular countable noun ⟶ general meaning: "any tavern")

G2. He thought **homeopathic drugs** were not real medicine.

(plural countable noun with no article ⟶ general meaning: "all homeopathic drugs")

G3. Homeopathy had become popular among the upper middle classes.

(uncountable noun with no article ⟶ general meaning: "all forms of homeopathy")

G4. The double-blind control trial has become the standard for testing medicine.

(*the* + singular countable noun ⟶ general meaning: "all double-blind control trials")

Note that the G4 form is the only way to use *the* in general noun phrases and is reserved for inventions, species, and academic analysis of the impact and relevance of things.

Specific Noun Phrases (S)

S1. The experiment led by von Hoven showed that homeopathy was not effective.

(*the* + singular countable noun ⟶ specific meaning: "the specific experiment carried out by von Hoven")

S2. The participants in von Hoven's experiment each received a vial of liquid.

(*the* + plural countable noun ⟶ specific meaning: "the specific participants in the experiment")

S3. The randomization of the vial distribution was insufficient to eliminate bias.

(*the* + uncountable noun ⟶ specific meaning: "the specific randomization in distributing the vials")

S4. Van Hoven set up **an experiment** to test the effectiveness of homeopathy.

(*an* + singular countable noun ⟶ specific meaning: "a specific experiment")

Note that the S4 form is the only way to use *a/an* in specific noun phrases and is reserved for information being mentioned for the first time. Thereafter, *the* is used as in sentence S1.

TASK 8 IDENTIFY TYPES OF NOUNS AND NOUN PHRASES

1. The sentences below come from the Stolberg article. Indicate whether the nouns or noun phrases in bold are countable or uncountable, and whether the author is referring to things in general (any or all members of a group) or specifically (specific member[s] of a group). If a phrase is underlined, focus only on that phrase.

    a) **Control groups**, randomization, blinding, **placebos** and **related methods designed to eliminate bias** have become widely recognized as key features of efforts to identify more effective and safer treatments. [LINES 1–3]

        ☐ countable ☐ uncountable   ☐ general ☐ specific

    b) Control groups, **randomization**, **blinding**, placebos and related methods designed to eliminate **bias** have become widely recognized as key features of efforts to identify more effective and safer treatments. [LINES 1–3]

        ☐ countable ☐ uncountable   ☐ general ☐ specific

    c) **A very early example of randomization and double blinding** was **an evaluation of homeopathy conducted in Nuremberg in 1835**. [LINES 3–5]

        ☐ countable ☐ uncountable   ☐ general ☐ specific

    d) At the time, **homeopathy** had garnered considerable support among the upper classes. [LINES 7–8]

        ☐ countable ☐ uncountable   ☐ general ☐ specific

    e) He suggested that **homeopathic drugs** were not real medicines at all. [LINES 14–15]

        ☐ countable ☐ uncountable   ☐ general ☐ specific

    f) **The design** of the proposed trial was explained in detail. [LINES 31–32]

        ☐ countable ☐ uncountable   ☐ general ☐ specific

    g) **A list indicating the numbers of the vials with and without the salt dilution**, respectively, was made and sealed. [LINES 39–40]

        ☐ countable ☐ uncountable   ☐ general ☐ specific

    h) **The vials** were then passed on to a 'commission' which distributed 47 of the vials to those among the audience who had declared their willingness to participate. [LINES 40–42]

        ☐ countable ☐ uncountable   ☐ general ☐ specific

i) The vast majority of those who had received **the homeopathic salt dilution** had thus not experienced any 'effect'. [LINES 52–54]

☐ countable ☐ uncountable ☐ general ☐ specific

j) Historically, **the value** of the trial report thus lies above all in the principles it set out. [LINES 82–83]

☐ countable ☐ uncountable ☐ general ☐ specific

2. The four sentences below are related to the Stolberg article. Look at the phrases in bold in each sentence and categorize them as in Task 1 above.

a) **A randomized blind control trial** can assess the effectiveness of homeopathy.

☐ countable ☐ uncountable ☐ general ☐ specific

b) **A randomized blind control trial** was carried out to assess the effectiveness of homeopathy.

☐ countable ☐ uncountable ☐ general ☐ specific

c) **The double-blind control trial** has been highly effective in the last hundred years.

☐ countable ☐ uncountable ☐ general ☐ specific

d) **The double-blind control trial** carried out by von Hoven has great historical significance.

☐ countable ☐ uncountable ☐ general ☐ specific

Shared Knowledge in Specific Noun Phrases

In specific noun phrases, the speaker and listener, or writer and reader, can share knowledge about the specific thing(s) being described in two ways: explicitly or implicitly. Consider the two examples below.

Explicitly Shared Knowledge

> The participants **in von Hoven's experiment** each received a vial of liquid.

In this sentence, the specific noun phrase is in bold: *the participants in von Hoven's experiment*. It includes specifying information, which is underlined: *in von Hoven's experiment*.

The writer includes the specifying information so that the reader knows exactly which participants are being described. Without the specifying information, the reader might be confused and ask, "Which participants?"

When you include specifying information in this way, knowledge is being shared *explicitly*, which means it is stated clearly in the noun phrase.

Implicitly Understood Knowledge

> **The salt dilution** was made from a grain of salt and snow water.

In this sentence, the specific noun phrase is in bold: *the salt dilution*. The writer does not include specifying information because it is not necessary. The reader

understands which salt solution is being described from the context, provided by previous sentences about the dilution.

When you do not include specifying information in a specific noun phrase, knowledge is being shared *implicitly*, which means it is *not* stated. The reader can understand the specific sense from the context.

TASK 9 IDENTIFY EXPLICITLY AND IMPLICITLY SHARED KNOWLEDGE

Look at the specific noun phrases in bold in the following three sentences from the Stolberg article. Indicate whether shared knowledge is stated explicitly, with specifying information, or understood implicitly. <u>Underline</u> any specifying information.

		Explicitly Shared Knowledge	Implicitly Shared Knowledge
1	**The design of the proposed trial** was explained in detail.		
2	**The vials** were then passed on to a 'commission' which distributed 47 of the vials to those among the audience who had declared their willingness to participate.		
3	Historically, **the value of the trial report** thus lies above all in the principles it set out.		
4	Historically, the value of **the trial report** thus lies above all in the principles it set out.		
5	Historically, the value of the trial report thus lies above all in **the principles it set out**.		

Do Unit 2: Articles, Nouns, and Noun Phrases in the Handbook, pp. 327–334.

EFFECTIVE WRITING STYLE

WRITING IN AN OBJECTIVE, SCIENTIFIC STYLE: THE PASSIVE VOICE

A common feature of academic writing—most notably, scientific writing—is the use of the passive voice instead of the active voice.

Active Voice

Active-voice sentences are formed with a subject followed by a corresponding verb, and sometimes an object.

<u>Preu and Reuter</u> **treated** <u>the patients</u>.

| subject | verb | object |

Look at the following three examples of active-voice sentences from the Stolberg article. The subjects are underlined and the corresponding verbs, in bold.

> <u>Karl Preu and Johann Jacob Reuter</u> **had treated** some of the most prominent families with homeopathy.

> <u>He</u> **suggested** that homeopathic drugs were not real medicines at all.

> <u>He</u> **reacted** with an ardent defence of homeopathy.

In these three sentences, the author places the subject at the beginning of the sentence, possibly to give the subject greater emphasis.

Passive Voice

Passive-voice sentences are formed with transitive verbs (verbs that are followed by an object).

To form a passive-voice sentence from one in the active voice, take the object of the active-voice sentence and place it in the subject position, use a form of the verb *to be*, and add the past participle of the transitive verb:

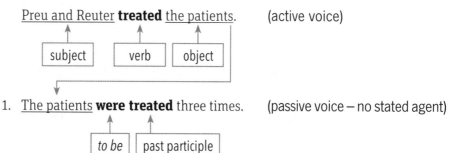

<u>Preu and Reuter</u> **treated** <u>the patients</u>.   (active voice)

1. <u>The patients</u> **were treated** three times.   (passive voice – no stated agent)

2. <u>The patients</u> **were treated** three times by Preu and Reuter.   (passive voice – stated agent)

In sentence 1, there is no stated agent; in other words, the writer does not mention who applied the treatment. This type of agentless passive-voice sentence is used when the agent is unknown or unimportant; the process of treating is more important.

In sentence 2, the agent is stated: "by Preu and Reuter." This type of passive-voice sentence emphasizes the agent(s).

TASK 10 LOCATE THE PASSIVE VOICE

1. Read the paragraphs below (lines 29–44 from the Stolberg article) and <u>underline</u> the examples of the passive voice.

Following a widely publicized invitation to anyone who was interested, more than 120 citizens met in a local tavern. The minimum number needed to proceed had been fixed at 50. The design of the proposed trial was explained in detail. In front of everyone, 100 vials were numbered, thoroughly shuffled and then split up at random into two lots of 50. One lot was filled with distilled snow water, the other with ordinary salt in a homeopathic C30-dilution of distilled snow water, prepared just as Reuter had demanded: a grain of salt was dissolved in 100 drops of distilled snow water and the resulting solution was diluted 29 times at a ratio of 1 to 100. Great care was taken to avoid any contamination with allopathic drugs . . . .

A list indicating the numbers of the vials with and without the salt dilution respectively was made, and sealed. The vials were then passed on to a 'commission' which distributed 47 of the vials to those among the audience who had declared their willingness to participate. The participants' names and the number of the vial that each had received were written in a second list.

2. Why do you think the author does not state the agent in any of the passive-voice sentences?

_____

_____

_____

_____

TASK 11 EXPLAIN TYPICAL USE OF THE PASSIVE VOICE

Look at three more examples of passive-voice sentences from the Stolberg article. Each sentence illustrates a typical use of the passive voice to create an objective, scientific style. Answer the questions that follow.

A grain of salt was dissolved in 100 drops of distilled snow water.

Finally, the sealed lists were opened.

Irregularities were carefully recorded.

1. Can the sentences be rewritten using the active voice?

_____

_____

_____

_____

_____

_____

_____

2. Why do you think the author used the passive voice in these sentences instead of the active voice?

_____

_____

_____

Learn more about the passive voice in Unit 7 of the Handbook, p. 364.

TASK 12 REWRITE ACTIVE-VOICE SENTENCES

Now look at four examples of active-voice sentences.

1. Rewrite the following sentence in the passive voice:

   <u>Karl Preu and Johann Jacob Reuter</u> **had treated** some of the most prominent families with homeopathy.

   _____

   _____

2. Rewrite the following sentence in the passive voice:

   (Note: You will need to begin the sentence with _It_.)

   <u>He</u> **suggested** that homeopathic drugs were not real medicines at all.

   _____

   _____

3. It is not possible to rewrite the following sentence in the passive voice. Why not?

   <u>He</u> **reacted** with an ardent defence of homeopathy.

   _____

   _____

Find supplementary reading, writing, and critical-thinking activities online.

4. Rewrite the following sentence in the passive voice:

   Perhaps surprisingly, <u>Reuter's opponents</u> **took up** his challenge.

   _____

   _____

A SUMMARY

TASK 13 WRITE A SUMMARY

Write a 100-word summary of the article "Inventing the Randomized Double-Blind Trial: The Nuremberg Salt Test of 1835." Refer to the notes you took for Task 6.

In pairs, read each other's first draft of the summary. Assess the use of articles in general and specific noun phrases and the use of the passive voice. Then improve your summary by rewriting sentences as required.

Checklist for Revising and Editing

☐ Have you included the main ideas of the article?

☐ Have you revised noun phrases according to the rules presented in the Effective Sentence Structure section?

☐ Have you used passive-voice sentences for an objective, scientific style?

☐ Does your paragraph flow better, and have you made it more readable?

CHAPTER 3

BRINGING IN OTHERS' IDEAS: READING

Books are like mirrors: if a fool looks in,
you cannot expect a genius to look out.

J. K. Rowling

Effective academic writing requires effective reading. The ways you read play a major role in your success as a writer. Or, as suggested by novelist J. K. Rowling, the way you write mirrors what you read.

Academic reading is different from other types of reading. To be an effective academic reader, you should not read passively, but actively and critically. You then need to transmit to your writing what you have learned through your reading. Remember: your reader will apply the same active and critical reading skills to your work!

In this chapter, you will:

- read two articles about self-driving cars
- practise active and critical reading skills
- study reference words and language of attribution
- practise shifting style from semi-formal to academic
- learn how to paraphrase a text effectively
- study clauses and sentences
- learn how to write a summary
- write an academic summary

TASK 1 EXPLORE THROUGH WRITING

What do you read, and how do you read?

Take three minutes to answer the questions. In pairs, compare what you have written.

SKIMMING FOR GENERAL MEANING

What Is the Difference between Active and Critical Reading?

Active reading is the opposite of passive reading. When you read passively, you wait for the ideas to come to you while you read, for example, when you are reading a book for pleasure, not for a specific academic task such as writing an essay. When you read actively, you seek out the information you need for your task. Active reading includes the following:

- skimming a text for general meaning
- scanning a text for specific information
- highlighting key information
- taking notes as you read

Critical reading involves engaging with the ideas in a text, looking at the text from different angles, and gaining an in-depth understanding of it. The process requires several skills:

- assessing whether a source is reliable
- distinguishing between facts and opinions
- recognizing multiple opinions in a text
- inferring meaning when it is not stated clearly
- agreeing and disagreeing with what you read
- considering the relevance of a text to your task
- considering what is missing from a text

Reading around a Text

When you are researching a topic and looking for relevant material to support your writing, you will not have time to read every text you find. Therefore, it is helpful to *read around a text* to see quickly whether it will be useful or not. When you read around a text, focus on finding the following information:

- What is the title? (The title indicates the general topic.)
- What is the subtitle? (The subtitle indicates the specific focus.)
- Who is the author? (Is the author well known in the field?)
- Is there relevant information in the abstract? (In journal articles, the abstract summarizes the article.)
- When was the text published? (Is it up to date?)
- Who published it? (Is the publisher recognized in the field?)
- Are there any images? (Images give clues about the focus and seriousness of an article.)

TASK 2 READ AROUND A TEXT

Take four minutes to read around the two articles on the topic of self-driving cars on pages 52 and 59. Find and write the following:

1. **Article 1** (page 52)

    Title: _____

    _____

    _____

    Subtitle: _____

    Author(s): _____

    Publication date: _____

    Who published it? _____

    Image(s): _____

2. **Article 2** (page 59)

    Title: _____

    _____

    Subtitle: _____

    Author(s): _____

    Publication date: _____

    Who published it? _____

    Image(s): _____

Skimming a Text

After you read around a text and decide that it may be useful for your assignment, instead of reading the text from start to finish, a more efficient next step is to skim the text. When you skim a text, you read it at surface level for *gist*, to find out the general idea. You do not read in depth. Skimming a text is helpful when you are searching for and reviewing literature and need to see whether an article or book will be useful for your writing task.

One way to skim a text is to locate the main idea of each paragraph in the article. When you find the main idea, rather than continuing to read the whole paragraph, you should move on to the next paragraph and do the same. As you read, take notes on the main ideas so you can locate information more quickly when you return to the article later.

TASK 3 SKIM A TEXT

Take five minutes to skim the following article. As you read, write the topic of each paragraph in the margin.

To Delegate or Not to Delegate: A Review of Control Frameworks for Autonomous Cars

by Dale Richards and Alex Stedmon

1. Introduction

[1] With increasingly congested road networks the existing road infrastructure is unsufficient at meeting the growing and future demands that will be placed on it. Alongside this is a strong desire to improve efficiency and safety. At the centre of accident causality, human error remains a primary concern and advances in autonomous systems are **hailed** as the **harbinger** of a technology that can potentially reduce road fatalities in the future. In the scope of this paper, the term *autonomous system* will be defined as the quality of a technology that is able to perceive information from the environment and its ability to act upon it without human intervention. With the advent of autonomous systems, what better way to reduce human error than by removing the human driver? The **impetus** behind an initiative such as this is directly related to the advances in technology that can assist in the management of the traffic **infrastructure** such as intelligent transport systems (ITS) or in-vehicle driver assistance systems such as advanced driver assistance systems (ADAS).

[2] Several states in the United States (i.e. Nevada, Florida, Michigan and California) have reflected this growing appetite by passing legislation that allows the introduction of autonomous vehicles onto public highways. If we look across the current range of autonomous cars (Google, Toyota, Nissan, BMW, to name but a few) we can see they are all actively researching the integration of autonomous decision-making technologies. Although there are differences across these manufacturers in terms of their approach to integrating autonomous systems, they all have one thing in common: the driver who is **ultimately** responsible for the vehicle.

[3] With the onset of smaller and cheaper sensors we have seen a migration of such technology transfer from other domains into the automotive community. For example, the development of Light Radar (LiDAR) was initially designed for uses in analysing **meteorological** conditions (specifically cloud density). Modern LiDAR systems have been used in unmanned ground vehicles for detecting obstacles whilst navigating. Perhaps the best-known use of this within the automotive domain is the Google 'Chauffeur' car with its recognisable spinning LiDAR sensor mounted on the roof. At the moment this technology is expensive but there are already initiatives to produce a more affordable and mainstream version of this technology that could be integrated into other cars. LiDAR is **but one of** the many different sensor technologies available that could be integrated within an intelligent automotive system. Within current ADAS functions, **ultrasound** technology is predominantly used for parking and proximity/separation such as adaptive cruise control (ACC), collision warning systems (CWS) and driver awareness functions such as blindspot and intersection warning. . . .

hailed: welcomed or acclaimed with enthusiasm

harbinger: forerunner, signal of what is to come

impetus: force or motivation behind something

infrastructure: public facilities such as roads, bridges, communications

ultimately: basically, in the end

meteorological: related to weather

but one of: only one of

ultrasound: producing images with sound that humans cannot hear

[4] With these technologies employed to assist the driver, if we assume that ADAS functions such as intelligent collision warning/avoidance are integrated into the wider traffic network, how might these forms of automation actually
45 support drivers? There would appear to be two key ways in which the autonomous system could interact with the user. For example, an autonomous car will be able to respond to an event or situation that is perceived by the system as a potential threat (using on-board sensors) and either advise the driver on the appropriate action to take and place authority on the driver to respond;
50 or the car will be authorised to take action on behalf of the driver in order to avoid an accident. Both cases highlight the need for a framework of **delegating** authority between the user and the system so that future solutions are developed with a common user-centred perspective.

delegating: giving responsibility or a task to someone/something else

2. Automation and Human Performance

55 **[5]** The implication of incorporating an element of autonomy within a system **predicates** the delegation of authority, by the user, to the system. That is, the user who traditionally is seen as being in control of the system and '**in-the-loop**' (Wiener and Curry, 1980) accepts that the system is performing certain functions either without their full knowledge (e.g. a 'blackbox' scenario) or
60 whilst they adopt a supervisory role. However, this can lead to 'out-of-loop' situations where the operator is not fully engaged in the task and may have diverted their attention to other activities but then be faced with taking back control at short notice and without fully understanding the current situation.

predicates: is based on

in-the-loop: connected, informed

[6] A certain degree of transparency must exist, which Norman (1990)
65 argues, is the operator's ability to understand the automated systems and 'see through' the system's processes. Thus, the lower the transparency, the more removed the human is from the information processing which might have serious implications for situation awareness (SA). . . .

3. Frameworks for Delegating Control Authority

70 **[7]** Autonomous cars are sometimes, rather **misleadingly**, referred to as 'driverless' vehicles. It is not about taking control from the driver, but allowing them to delegate authority to the system in a manner that they understand and feel comfortable with. To **facilitate** the interaction between the user and the system a framework is required that defines the delegation of authority
75 under a variety of different circumstances.

misleadingly: giving the wrong impression or idea

facilitate: make easier

[8] The traditional model for defining the levels of automation was put forward by Sheridan and Verplank (1978), and later revised by Parasuraman et al. (2000). This framework . . . provides ten levels of automation distributed between the user and the system. These range from the system making all
80 decisions on behalf of the user (Level 10) to the human making all decisions (Level 1). . . .

4. Control Delegation in Autonomous Vehicles

[9] . . . It can be argued that with increasing levels of automation or decision

cognitively: mentally

vigilance: careful attention

pertaining to: relating to

detrimental: damaging

susceptibility: tendency

perceptual thresholds: levels at which people become aware of things

degrade: break down

failure track: gradual process of breakdown

future proofed: developed to minimize future problems

graceful degradation: continued but limited function when a system fails

vulnerable to: exposed to, at risk of

mature: developed

complacency: lack of awareness

support available to the user, it is equally important to provide the user with
85 a better understanding of what the system is doing (Bainbridge, 1983;
Norman, 1990). The active monitoring of a highly automated system is
cognitively demanding (Tsang and Johnson, 1989) and requires a high degree
of **vigilance** on behalf of the user (Molloy and Parasuraman, 1996). In order
to reduce the likelihood of human error it is important that the individual
90 attains a sufficient level of SA **pertaining to** their situation and the context
in which the system they are interacting with operates (Endsley, 1995;
Endsley and Jones, 2012). Mental workload has also been cited as having a
detrimental effect on human performance and safety (Tsang and Vidulich,
2006). The potential for a lack of vigilance has been linked to a number of
95 accidents (Warm et al., 2008). Humans are poor at monitoring systems due
to **susceptibility** of cognitive processing to switch off and miss stimuli where
perceptual thresholds are low (Kantowitz and Sorkin, 1987). . . .

[10] A further aspect of a reliance on automation is that the reliability of
such systems will **degrade** over time just as current mechanical ones do.
100 The design of the **failure track** is presumably part of the process for the
systems engineers and it is important to consider the autonomy lifecycles so
that systems are **future proofed** and potentially incorporate principles of
graceful degradation so that the entire system is not **vulnerable to** complete
failure.

5. Discussion

[11] . . . The technology that will facilitate the introduction of the autonomous
car has entered a phase of demonstration, with the Technology Readiness
Levels (TRL) getting closer to market introduction. What is less **mature** is
the associated understanding of how drivers will adapt to this new style of
110 driving. . . . On the occasion that the human is happy to delegate control to
the system, thought is needed as to how to keep the user 'in the loop' in terms
of maintaining SA. Good SA is essential not just for monitoring the system
in terms of ensuring it is safe, but more so for predicate events that suddenly
occur when there is a system failure or the system recommends or hands
115 control back to the user. In such instances human trust in the system may
very well lead to a dangerous degree of **complacency** (Bainbridge, 1983).
As illustrated in other domains this is all too common and can lead to tragic
consequences. This is why, for the foreseeable future, a driver of an autonomous car will be legally required to be paying attention to the road at all
120 times (as is legally required in some of the US States that have already passed
legislation). . . .

6. Conclusion

[12] The use of an autonomous car is not about taking control away from the
driver, but allowing the driver to delegate authority to the system. This
125 changes the nature of the driving role with the driver adopting a more supervisory approach to monitoring an intelligent system. In order for this interaction to be effective it is important to design the system that allows the user

determine: make
something happen

to understand not only what the system is currently doing (and plans to do) but also what the system is not able to do. This builds a partnership of trust

130 between the user and the system that recognises not just human limitations but combines these with systemic limitations in order to **determine** a user-centred socio-technical system for autonomous driving.

References

Bainbridge, L. (1983). Ironies of automation. *Automatica*, *19*(6), 775–779.

Endsley, M. R. (1995). Toward a theory of situation awareness in dynamic systems. *Human Factors*, *37*(1), 32–64.

Endsley, M. R., & Jones, D. G. (2012). *Designing for situation awareness: An approach to human-centered design* (2nd ed.). London: Taylor & Francis.

Kantowitz, B. H., & Sorkin, R. D. (1987). Allocation of functions. In G. Salvendy (Ed.), *Handbook of human factors and ergonomics* (pp. 355–370). New York: Wiley.

Molloy, R., & Parasuraman, R. (1996). Monitoring an automated system for a single failure: Vigilance and task complexity effects. *Human Factors*, *38*(2), 311–322.

Parasuraman, R., Sheridan, T. B., & Wickens, C. D. (2000). A model for types and levels of human interaction with automation. In *IEEE Transactions on Systems, Man, and Cybernetics – Part A: Systems and Humans*, *30*, 286–297.

Sheridan, T. B., & Verplank, W. (1978). *Human and computer control of undersea tele-operators*. Cambridge, MA: Man-Machine Systems Laboratory, Department of Mechanical Engineering, MIT.

Tsang, P. S., & Johnson, W. W. (1989). Cognitive demands in automation. *Aviation, Space, and Environmental Medicine*, *60*, 130–135.

Tsang, P., & Vidulich, M. A. (2006). Mental workload and situation awareness. In G. Salvendy (Ed.), *Handbook of human factors and ergonomics* (pp. 243–268). New York: Wiley.

Warm, J. S., Parasuraman, R., & Matthews, G. (2008). Vigilance requires hard mental work and is stressful. *Human Factors*, *50*, 433–441.

Wiener, E. L., & Curry, R. E. (1980). Flight-deck automation: Promises and problems. *Ergonomics*, *23*, 995–1011.

Excerpts from Richards, D., & Stedmon, A. (2016). To delegate or not to delegate: A review of control frameworks for autonomous cars. *Applied Ergonomics*, *53*(2016), 383–388. doi:10.1016/j.apergo.2015.10.011

TASK 4 MATCH YOUR NOTES

Look again at the 12 paragraph topics you wrote for Task 3. Match them to the topics listed below. Write the paragraph number on the line beside the matching topic. After you have finished, read the complete text.

_____ **a)** Users delegating authority to systems: problems

_____ **b)** Reliability and degradation

_____ **c)** Technology to reduce human error and improve safety

_____ **d)** How best to delegate authority

_____ **e)** Integrating autonomous decision-making technologies

_____ **f)** Transparency and situation awareness

_____ **g)** How autonomous systems can support drivers

_____ **h)** 10 levels of automation

_____ **i)** Understanding and monitoring a system

_____ **j)** Building a partnership between user and system

_____ **k)** Human adaptation: trust and complacency

_____ **l)** Sensor technologies borrowed from other fields

VOCABULARY

ANAPHORIC AND CATAPHORIC REFERENCE WORDS

A common feature of academic texts is the use of reference words such as *it* and *this* to refer to information and ideas in the text. Anaphoric reference words refer back to information and ideas already mentioned. Cataphoric reference words refer forward to ideas that are coming in the text.

Look at the reference words (in bold) in the examples below from the Richards and Stedmon article.

> In the scope of this paper, the term *autonomous system* will be defined as the quality of a technology that is able to perceive information from the environment and its ability to act upon **it** without human intervention. [LINES 7–10]

It is an anaphoric reference word referring back to "information from the environment." In this case, the use of *it* is effective and economical because the authors do not have to repeat the words "information from the environment," which would be wordy and repetitive.

> …**it** is important that the individual attains a sufficient level of SA pertaining to their situation and the context in which the system they are interacting with operates. [LINES 89–91]

It refers forward to the idea that the individual should attain "a sufficient level of SA pertaining to their situation and the context in which the system they are interacting with operates." The use of *it* in a sentence with cataphoric reference adds a scientific tone to the writing.

TASK 5 IDENTIFY AND UNDERSTAND REFERENCE WORDS

In the following sentences, indicate whether the reference words *it*, *this*, and *these* are anaphoric or cataphoric. Then look at the surrounding text and write the information or idea the word refers to.

1. Alongside **this** is a strong desire to improve efficiency and safety. [LINES 4–5]

   ☐ anaphoric   ☐ cataphoric

   Reference: _____

   _____

2. **These** range from the system making all decisions on behalf of the user (Level 10) to the human making all decisions (Level 1). [LINES 79–81]

   ☐ anaphoric   ☐ cataphoric

   Reference: _____

   _____

3. **It** can be argued that with increasing levels of automation or decision support available to the user, it is equally important to provide the user with a better understanding of what the system is doing. [LINES 83–85]

   ☐ anaphoric   ☐ cataphoric

   Reference: _____

   _____

4. The design of the failure track is presumably part of the process for the systems engineers and **it** is important to consider the autonomy lifecycles so that systems are future proofed. [LINES 100–102]

   ☐ anaphoric   ☐ cataphoric

   Reference: _____

   _____

5. As illustrated in other domains **this** is all too common and can lead to tragic consequences. [LINES 117–118]

   ☐ anaphoric   ☐ cataphoric

   Reference: _____

   _____

ACTIVE AND CRITICAL READING

SCANNING FOR SPECIFIC INFORMATION

When you scan a text, you do not read the whole text; you look only for specific information, usually for a related writing task. An effective technique for scanning a text is to look for keywords, synonyms (words with similar or the same meaning), and associated words (words that are related to the specific information you are looking for).

For example, if you were scanning the Richards and Stedmon article for information on how ADAS technology might assist drivers, you could look for the following:

- keywords: ADAS, technology, assist, drivers
- synonyms: advanced, technical development, aid, help, road users
- associated words: driverless, integration, support, transportation

With these words in mind, you could find the specific information on lines 42 to 45: "if we assume that ADAS functions such as intelligent collision warning/avoidance are integrated into the wider traffic network, how might these forms of automation actually support drivers?"

This sentence acts as an introduction to the information that you require: the ways ADAS can help drivers.

TASK 6 SCAN A TEXT FOR INFORMATION

Now take five minutes to scan the article on the next pages from the *Washington Post*. Do not read the complete article; look only for the following information. Make note of the answers as you read.

1. What will the real weather challenge be for autonomous vehicles? [para. 2]

_____

_____

2. What special skill does the forward radar have? [para. 4]

_____

_____

3. What two risk factors are mentioned as possibly preventing the sensitive systems of an autonomous vehicle from working? [para. 7]

_____

_____

4. When might people realize that it is safer to disobey the rules of the road? [para. 12]

_____

_____

5. When will the first all-weather driverless vehicles be built? [para. 16]

_____

_____

Driverless Cars Work Great in Sunny California. But How About in a Blizzard?

by Brian Fung

[1] As cities along the east coast finally finish digging their way out of last weekend's historic snowstorm, drivers braving the streets have to contend with icy conditions, snowbanks along the curb and other hazards they would probably rather avoid if they could help it.

5 [2] Enter the self-driving car, which someday may alleviate that anxiety. But although the technology appears to work well in dry, sunny weather, those are just the best-case scenarios. The real test for autonomous vehicles will be when the roads are wet or even icy and invisible to the computerized eye. What then?

10 [3] Researchers who work on driverless cars say we're still five to 10 years away from developing an all-weather self-driving capability. That's because there are a host of challenges when it comes to driving in bad weather that humans 15 have learned to overcome—but computers have not. This issue has taken on even greater urgency given that an initial wave of high-tech cars, such as Tesla's sedans that can go on auto-pilot, are already on the road.

20 [4] "The forward radar is very good at detecting fast moving large objects and can actually see through fog, rain, snow, and dust," said Tesla chief executive Elon Musk in November. "So, the forward radar is the car's super human feature. It can see through things a person cannot."

[5] For the most part, self-driving cars being tested by Google and other 25 carmakers are running their experiments in relatively safe environments in California and Texas, where the weather is generally fine. But last month, a company spokesman said, Google sent its self-driving cars to snowy Lake Tahoe to collect important test data. Google's car is equipped with special wiper blades that help keep the car's camera lenses clear in bad weather. 30 And if it's in the middle of a particularly nasty storm, the vehicle can automatically pull over and wait it out, according to a recent company report.

[6] "Our cars can determine the severity of the rain," the report reads, "and just like human drivers they drive more cautiously in wet conditions when roads are slippery and visibility is poor."

35 [7] Like real people, being unable to see can be a huge problem for a machine that relies on cameras, radar and laser-based sensing systems. In addition to the risk of snow or ice building up on external sensors, even an inch of snow cover on the ground could disrupt an autonomous vehicle's sensitive systems. . . . That's because the sensing systems designed to bounce signals 40 off of distant objects are reflecting off of the snow instead, resulting in what looks like a cloud of angry bees surrounding the car.

[8] "If we can't see the world around us really well, our ability to estimate where we are falls apart," said Edwin Olson, an associate professor of computer science at the University of Michigan who's working with Ford. "The standard approach to figuring out where you are very accurately is to look at the ground—and the ground is the first thing to go when it's snowing or raining."

[9] The solution, Olson said, is to train the car's cameras on its surroundings—to rely on passing buildings, street poles and even trees to determine its location. From there, the car can match those reference points to the map that's stored in its brain.

[10] But low visibility is just one aspect of the problem.

[11] "In a snowy climate, people aren't driving in their lanes anymore. They're driving in the tire tracks of the guy in front of them," said Ryan Eustice, who directs the University of Michigan's Perceptual Robotics Lab and has also been working with Ford.

[12] In other words, humans know that it's sometimes safer to break the rules of the road when it's snowing than it is to obey them. But how do you teach a machine to defy its own programming?

[13] That's not all. On top of knowing the difference between bad weather and a sensor malfunction—and how to behave "improperly"—autonomous vehicles may also have to communicate with, or even fight, other safety systems in the car in order to drive the way a human would.

[14] For example, anti-lock brakes and electronic stability control have helped human drivers avoid crashes for years. But software makers for driverless cars don't necessarily have control over those features because they are sometimes made by third-party suppliers, said Olson. The result could be that these features kick in when the computer least expects it.

[15] "Stability control systems, those are really going on at very low levels in the vehicle, almost like a reflex," said Olson. "The autonomous vehicle is almost cognitive, at a much higher level. There's a real concern that these safety systems—which are great for human drivers—will it just confuse the autonomous control? Getting that interaction right is pretty tricky."

[16] The fact that we're still so far from building an all-weather driverless car will probably mean that manufacturers will release their earliest autonomous vehicles only to certain cities at first, or allow drivers to turn on the robotic features under a specific set of conditions. So while driverless cars are definitely coming, don't expect them to be able to get you through a whiteout anytime soon.

Fung, B. (2016, January 28). Driverless cars work great in sunny California. But how about in a blizzard? *The Washington Post*. Retrieved from https://www.washingtonpost.com/news/the-switch/wp/2016/01/28/driverless-cars-work-great-in-sunny-california-but-how-about-in-a-blizzard/

TASK 7 READ CRITICALLY

Now read the full text. When you have finished, answer the questions below. First, write your answers in the spaces provided; then discuss your answers in pairs.

1. Reread paragraphs 3 and 4 of the article. What issue is the author referring to when he writes, "This issue has taken on even greater urgency given that an initial wave of high-tech cars, such as Tesla's sedans that can go on auto-pilot, are already on the road"?

    _____

    _____

2. The author goes on to quote Tesla chief executive Elon Musk as follows: "The forward radar is very good at detecting fast moving large objects and can actually see through fog, rain, snow, and dust. . . . So, the forward radar is the car's super human feature. It can see through things a person cannot."

    Is there a contradiction between the quotation and the statement preceding it?

    _____

    _____

    _____

3. In line 73, Edwin Olson states, "Getting that interaction right is pretty tricky." Which interaction is he describing?

    _____

    _____

    _____

4. In lines 74 to 76, the author writes, "The fact that we're still so far from building an all-weather driverless car will probably mean that manufacturers will release their earliest autonomous vehicles only to certain cities at first." Which cities does he mean when he writes "certain cities"?

    _____

    _____

EXTEND YOUR ACADEMIC VOCABULARY

Extend your knowledge of key vocabulary from this chapter.

contend with	**facilitate**	necessarily
definitely	impetus	**ultimately**
determine	in addition to	
detrimental	increasingly	

*Words in bold type are AWL entries.

Practise Chapter 3 vocabulary online.

ADAPTING SEMI-FORMAL STYLE FOR ACADEMIC WRITING

In the second article, journalist Brian Fung writes in a semi-formal style that is designed to catch readers' attention and engage them. The style is appropriate for the genre. When you summarize ideas and information from this article in Task 17 (p. 74), you will need to write in a more objective, academic style that matches the genre features of an academic summary.

The following are four stylistic features of Fung's text that would seem informal and/or inappropriate in many forms of academic writing:

1. contractions: using abbreviated forms such as *isn't* instead of *is not*

2. addressing the reader as *you*: using phrases such as *you can see* instead of *people can see* or *it can be seen*

3. starting sentences with *and, but,* or *so*: using these simple coordinating linking words instead of conjunctive adverbs (for example, *moreover, however,* and *therefore*) or different sentence structures

4. rhetorical questions: asking questions for rhetorical effect (to persuade your reader) but not answering them

> Learn more about conjunctive adverbs as linking words in Appendix 1, p. 423.

TASK 8 LOCATE EXAMPLES OF NON-ACADEMIC STYLE

Go back through the Fung article and note any examples you can find of the four stylistic features of non-academic style (ignore non-academic style in direct quotations). Write the examples and line numbers.

1. Contractions:

   _____

   _____

2. Addressing the reader as *you*:

   _____

   _____

3. Starting sentences with *and, but,* or *so*:

   _____

   _____

4. Rhetorical questions:

   _____

   _____

TASK 9 REWRITE SENTENCES IN ACADEMIC STYLE

Rewrite the sentences below from the Fung article to make them more academic and formal. Less formal language is in bold type.

1. The real test for autonomous vehicles will be when the roads are wet or even icy and invisible to the computerized eye. **What then**?

   _____

   _____

   _____

   _____

2. From there, the car can match those reference points to the map **that's** stored in its brain. **But** low visibility is just one aspect of the problem.

   _____

   _____

   _____

   _____

3. In other words, humans know that **it's** sometimes safer to break the rules of the road when **it's** snowing than it is to obey them. **But how do you teach a machine to defy its own programming?**

   _____

   _____

   _____

   _____

4. **So** while driverless cars are definitely coming, **don't** expect them to be able to get **you** through a whiteout anytime soon.

   _____

   _____

   _____

   _____

CRITICAL THINKING

GENRE AND STYLE

TASK 10 DISCUSS

1. What do you notice about the genres and writing styles of the two articles?

2. What style characterizes writing in your subject area?

LANGUAGE OF ATTRIBUTION

It is common for academic and journalistic texts to present a range of ideas and opinions from different people, groups, or organizations. When you summarize a text with multiple views, it is important to attribute ideas and opinions to the appropriate sources. You do this by using words and phrases, known as *language of attribution*, to make it clear to your reader who thinks what. If you do not include adequate language of attribution, your reader may confuse your sources, and worse, you could be accused of plagiarism for appropriating others' ideas and presenting them as your own.

TASK 11 ANALYZE A TEXT FOR LANGUAGE OF ATTRIBUTION

1. Read the example paragraph below, which summarizes some of the ideas from the Fung article without any language of attribution. Is it clear to you as a reader who thinks what?

   Autonomous vehicles will face their biggest test when they operate in icy and wet winter conditions. In fact, it will take up to 10 years before driverless cars have the ability to drive in all weather conditions. However, the forward radar in Tesla autonomous cars is already able to function properly in fog and snow. At the moment, if the weather is bad during test drives, autonomous cars have the capacity to pull over and wait for a change in weather.

2. Now read the same text with language of attribution. <u>Underline</u> the language of attribution that makes it clear to you who thinks what.

   According to *Washington Post* journalist Brian Fung, autonomous vehicles will face their biggest test when they operate in icy and wet winter conditions. Researchers in the field believe that it will take up to 10 years before driverless cars have the ability to drive in all weather conditions. However, Tesla chief executive Elon Musk claims that the forward radar in Tesla autonomous cars is already able to function properly in fog and snow. A recent Google report found that at the moment, if the weather is bad during test drives, its autonomous car has the capacity to pull over and wait for a change in weather.

TASK 12 LOCATE LANGUAGE OF ATTRIBUTION

1. Reread the Fung article and <u>underline</u> any examples of language of attribution.

2. Look at the following two examples of ideas Fung presents without any language of attribution. Who do you attribute these ideas to, and why?

a) The result could be that these features kick in when the computer least expects it. [LINES 67–68]

_____

_____

_____

_____

b) The fact that we're still so far from building an all-weather driverless car will probably mean that manufacturers will release their earliest autonomous vehicles only to certain cities at first, or allow drivers to turn on the robotic features under a specific set of conditions. [LINES 74–77]

_____

_____

_____

_____

EFFECTIVE WRITING STYLE

PARAPHRASING

When you paraphrase a text effectively, you use your own words to rewrite information you have read, changing vocabulary, grammar, and sentence structure to make the writing your own. When the ideas are not your own, you need to indicate clearly who they belong to, using language of attribution. In writing assignments that require APA or MLA citation style, make sure to include accurate, correctly formatted in-text citations every time you present someone else's ideas in your writing.

> Find detailed rules and formats for APA and MLA citation styles in Appendices 2 and 3.

Patchwriting

Patchwriting is different from paraphrasing. Patchwriting occurs when a writer copies text from a source and changes only some of the words and grammar. Patchwriting is unacceptable paraphrasing, a type of plagiarism.

TASK 13 IDENTIFY PARAPHRASING AND PATCHWRITING

In the two paragraphs you are about to read, a writer has attempted to paraphrase an excerpt from the Fung article. One example represents effective paraphrasing: the writer has made sufficient changes to the vocabulary and grammar of the original. The other example represents unacceptable paraphrasing, or patchwriting: the writer has changed only a few words and structures here and there.

Read examples 1 and 2 and decide which is acceptable paraphrasing and which is patchwriting. Underline words and phrases that are copied exactly from the original text to support your answers. Compare your answers with a partner.

Excerpt from the Original Text

> Researchers who work on driverless cars say we're still five to 10 years away from developing an all-weather self-driving capability. That's because there are a host of challenges when it comes to driving in bad weather that humans have learned to overcome—but computers have not. This issue has taken on even greater urgency given that an initial wave of high-tech cars, such as Tesla's sedans that can go on autopilot, are already on the road. "The forward radar is very good at detecting fast moving large objects and can actually see through fog, rain, snow, and dust," said Tesla chief executive Elon Musk in November. "So, the forward radar is the car's super human feature. It can see through things a person cannot."

1. According to researchers working on driverless cars, we are still 5 to 10 years away from developing an all-weather self-driving capability because of many challenges when it comes to driving in bad weather that humans have learned to overcome—but computers have not. This issue has become more urgent given that an initial wave of high-tech cars, such as Tesla's sedans that can go on autopilot, are already being driven on roads. Tesla chief executive Elon Musk stated in November that the forward radar is excellent at detecting fast moving large objects and can actually see through fog, rain, snow, and dust, saying it is the car's superhuman feature.

   Example 1: Acceptable paraphrasing or patchwriting? Why or why not?

   _____

   _____

   _____

2. According to researchers of autonomous car technology, it will take perhaps a decade before all-weather self-driving capability is developed as computers have yet to learn to deal with the many challenges that are associated with driving in poor weather conditions. Since the first phase of high-tech vehicles are already being driven on roads—for example, Tesla's sedans that have an autopilot function—this challenge requires urgent attention. According to Elon Musk, however, the Tesla forward radar can detect large fast-moving objects very effectively even in inclement weather; the Tesla chief executive sees the forward radar as "the car's superhuman feature."

   Example 2: Acceptable paraphrasing or patchwriting? Why or why not?

   _____

   _____

   _____

Effective Paraphrasing

In Task 13, you highlighted the words and phrases copied directly from the original text in an effective paraphrase. Now study the following paragraphs to learn how the vocabulary, grammar, and sentence structure of the original text were changed.

Vocabulary Changes

According to researchers of **autonomous car technology, it will take perhaps a decade** before all-weather self-driving capability is developed **as** computers have yet to learn to deal with the **many** challenges **that are associated with** driving in **poor** weather conditions. **Since** the first phase of high-tech vehicles are already being driven on roads—for example, Tesla's sedans that **have an** autopilot **function**—this challenge **requires urgent attention.** According to Elon Musk, however, the Tesla forward radar can detect large fast-moving objects very effectively even in **inclement weather**; the Tesla chief executive sees the forward radar **as** "the car's superhuman feature."

Grammar Changes

According to researchers of autonomous car technology, **it will take** perhaps a decade before all-weather self-driving capability is developed as computers **have yet to learn** to deal with the many challenges that are associated with driving in poor weather conditions. Since the first phase of high-tech vehicles **are already being driven on roads**—for example, Tesla's sedans that have an autopilot function—this challenge requires urgent attention. According to Elon Musk, however, the Tesla forward radar **can detect** large fast-moving objects very effectively even in inclement weather; the Tesla chief executive sees the forward radar as "the car's superhuman feature."

Sentence Structure Changes

According to researchers of autonomous car technology, it will take perhaps a decade before all-weather self-driving capability is developed **as computers have yet to learn** to deal with the many challenges that are associated with driving in poor weather conditions. **Since the first phase of high-tech vehicles are already being driven on roads**—for example, Tesla's sedans that have an autopilot function—this challenge requires urgent attention. **According to Elon Musk, however,** the Tesla forward radar can detect large fast-moving objects very effectively even in inclement weather; **the Tesla chief executive sees the forward radar as** "the car's superhuman feature."

TASK 14 PARAPHRASE SENTENCES

Consider the techniques you have just studied to avoid patchwriting, and paraphrase the following sentences from the Richards and Stedmon article. Remember to keep the meaning as close as possible to the original.

1. There would appear to be two key ways in which the autonomous system could interact with the user.

   _____

   _____

2. Autonomous cars are sometimes, rather misleadingly, referred to as 'driverless' vehicles.

   _____

   _____

3. A further aspect of a reliance on automation is that the reliability of such systems will degrade over time just as current mechanical ones do.

_____

_____

4. The use of an autonomous car is not about taking control away from the driver, but allowing the driver to delegate authority to the system.

_____

_____

▐ EFFECTIVE SENTENCE STRUCTURE ▐

TWO TYPES OF CLAUSE AND THREE TYPES OF SENTENCE

What Is a Clause?

A clause is a group of words that forms a whole sentence, or part of a sentence. Clauses have a subject and a verb, unlike phrases, which do not. Understanding the difference between independent and dependent clauses is the first step to improving your sentence structure.

Independent Clauses

Independent clauses, sometimes called _main clauses_, have a subject and a corresponding verb. They can stand alone as a sentence and as a complete thought or idea. Below are two examples from the Richards and Stedmon article:

1. In such instances human trust in the system may very well lead to a dangerous degree of complacency.

2. . . . human error remains a primary concern . . . .

Example 1 is an independent clause that makes up a complete simple sentence. Example 2 does not make up a complete sentence; it is part of a larger sentence.

Dependent Clauses

Dependent clauses, also called _subordinate clauses_, cannot stand alone as a sentence or as a complete thought or idea. Below are two examples from the Richards and Stedmon article:

1. Although there are differences across these manufacturers in terms of their approach to integrating autonomous systems . . .

2. . . . that could be integrated within an intelligent automotive system.

Learn more about subordinators as linking words in Appendix 1, p. 427.

Example 1 is a dependent clause because the clause begins with the subordinator _although_. Other subordinators that make clauses dependent are linking words such as _while_, _because_, and _unless_.

Example 2 is a dependent clause because it begins with the relative pronoun *that*. Other relative pronouns that make clauses dependent in this way are *which*, *who*, *when*, *where*, *why*, and *what*. You will study different kinds of relative clauses in Chapter 4.

Learn more about sentence fragments in Unit 9 of the Handbook, p. 379.

To make either of the two dependent clauses above into a complete sentence, join the dependent clause with an independent clause to form a complex sentence (see below). If the two clauses are left as they are, they are considered sentence fragments, which are incomplete sentences.

Simple Sentences

A simple sentence is an independent clause that forms a complete sentence. Below is an example from the Richards and Stedmon article. The simple sentence contains one complete idea.

> In such instances human trust in the system may very well lead to a dangerous degree of complacency.

Compound Sentences

A compound sentence is made up of two (or more) independent clauses joined by one of the "FANBOYS" coordinators (*for*, *and*, *nor*, *but*, *or*, *yet*, *so*). Below is an example adapted from the Richards and Stedmon article. The independent clauses are underlined, and the coordinator is in bold. The information or ideas in the clauses of a compound sentence usually have equal emphasis.

> Human error remains a primary concern, **and** advances in autonomous systems may reduce road fatalities in the future.

Complex Sentences

A complex sentence can be formed by combining one or more dependent and independent clauses. Below are two examples adapted from the Richards and Stedmon article. The dependent clauses are in italics, and the independent clauses are underlined. When the independent clause comes second in a complex sentence (as in sentence 1 below), it usually carries more emphasis than the preceding dependent clause.

1. *Although there are differences across these manufacturers in terms of their approach to integrating autonomous systems*, they all have one thing in common.
2. LiDAR is one of the many different available sensor technologies *that could be integrated within an intelligent automotive system*.

TASK 15 PRACTISE FORMING SIMPLE, COMPOUND, AND COMPLEX SENTENCES

Use what you have learned from the two articles in this chapter to complete the simple, compound, and complex sentences below.

1. Simple sentence: Autonomous cars _____

_____.

2. Compound sentence: Car manufacturers are working to develop autonomous technology, but self-driving cars _____ _____.

3. Compound sentence: Self-driving cars have no steering wheel, and _____ _____.

4. Complex sentence: If autonomous cars are used in snowy conditions, _____ _____.

Do Unit 3: Clauses and Sentences in the Handbook, pp. 335–342.

5. Complex sentence: Self-driving cars, which _____ _____, are still not ready to deal with certain weather conditions.

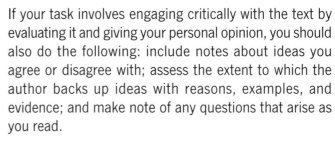

ACTIVE AND CRITICAL READING

ANNOTATION

When you annotate a text, you take notes as you read, for example, in the margins of the text. The type of notes you take will depend on your task. If you are making annotations for a summary in which you are not required to give your opinion, you should focus on the ideas that you think are most important in the text.

If your task involves engaging critically with the text by evaluating it and giving your personal opinion, you should also do the following: include notes about ideas you agree or disagree with; assess the extent to which the author backs up ideas with reasons, examples, and evidence; and make note of any questions that arise as you read.

Annotation is a more active and effective note-taking strategy than just highlighting or underlining the main information in a text. First, when you annotate, you can also add your own opinions and questions if necessary. Second, highlighting and underlining alone are passive forms of note taking that do not allow you to internalize the information as effectively as when you write it down. Third, annotating saves time in the long term because it makes it quicker and easier to find information when you come back to a text later.

TASK 16 ANNOTATE AN ARTICLE

Reread the Fung article and make annotations while you read. You will use your annotations later to write a 200-word summary of the article in which you are not required to give your personal opinion.

WRITING SUMMARIES

Summarizing is an important academic writing skill to master. Not only is it necessary to summarize information for most types of writing assignments, it is also common to write summaries as stand-alone assignments.

When you write a summary, remember the following key points about representation and style:

Representation

- Select the main ideas: avoid including minor information.
- Represent ideas accurately: do not change the original meaning or add new ideas.
- Represent ideas in your own words: make sure to paraphrase; avoid too many quotations.
- Represent the whole text: give your reader a sense of the complete original text.
- Attribute: use language of attribution to make it clear who thinks what (e.g., X states that . . .).

Style

- Be concise: get the main information across in as few words as possible; keep to the word limit.
- Write in an objective style: represent ideas rather than give your opinion.
- Use formal language: adopt an academic style even if the article you are summarizing is less formal.

The Summary-Writing Process

The following are five common stages in the process of writing an academic summary.

Stage 1: Skim the Text

Read the text for gist, highlight or underline the main ideas, and write notes in the margin.

Stage 2: Read the Complete Text

Follow up the skimming with a detailed reading of the text. Add to your notes as you read if you find other important information to include in the summary.

Stage 3: Decide on Your Structure

There are different ways to structure the summary. The most common way is to follow the original structure of the text you are summarizing. Alternatively, you may use a thematic structure and organize the summary according to main themes you identify as you read.

Stage 4: **Start Writing**

Once you have gone through stages 1 to 3, it is time to start writing.

4.1 Write the opening sentences. Include the following information in the first sentence of the summary (if the information is available):

- the title of the article
- the author's name
- the name and date of the publication
- the main topic

For example, if you were summarizing the Richards and Stedmon article, you could introduce the summary in one of the following three ways:

1. **In the article** "To Delegate or Not to Delegate: A Review of Control Frameworks for Autonomous Cars," published in *Applied Ergonomics* in 2016, **Dale Richards and Alex Stedmon analyze** the relationship between autonomous systems and human drivers in cars.

2. **The article** "To Delegate or Not to Delegate: A Review of Control Frameworks for Autonomous Cars," written by Dale Richards and Alex Stedmon and published in *Applied Ergonomics* in 2016, **analyzes** the relationship between autonomous systems and human drivers in cars.

3. **In the article** "To Delegate or Not to Delegate: A Review of Control Frameworks for Autonomous Cars," written by Dale Richards and Alex Stedmon and published in *Applied Ergonomics* in 2016, the relationship between autonomous systems and human drivers in cars **is analyzed**.

Example 1 begins with the preposition phrase *in the article*. Avoid making the mistake of using the preposition phrase as the subject of the verb *analyze*:

"**In the article** 'To Delegate or Not to Delegate: A Review of Control Frameworks for Autonomous Cars,' written by Dale Richards and Alex Stedmon and published in *Applied Ergonomics* in 2016, **analyzes** the relationship between autonomous systems and human drivers in cars" is *incorrect*.

Example 2 begins with the noun phrase *the article*, which acts as a subject to the verb *analyzes*. Example 3 is in the passive voice: *the relationship between autonomous systems and human drivers in cars is analyzed*.

You can choose any of these three approaches; there is no difference in meaning or formality. Make sure to avoid making the mistake shown above for example 1.

After writing the introductory sentence, write a sentence that sums up the general focus and main argument or idea of the article. You can do this by paraphrasing or by using a direct quotation. You can usually locate this information in the notes you have taken in the margin of the first paragraph of the article, as illustrated below:

congestion

improve safety

human error = main concern

With increasingly <u>congested road networks</u> the existing road infrastructure is unsufficient at meeting the growing and future demands that will be placed on it. Alongside this is a strong desire to <u>improve efficiency and safety</u>. At the centre of accident causality, <u>human error</u> remains a primary concern and advances in autonomous systems are hailed as the harbinger of a technology that can

autonomous tech. may
reduce deaths

replace the driver?

with ITS & ADAS

potentially <u>reduce road fatalities</u> in the future. In the scope of this paper, the term *autonomous system* will be defined as the quality of a technology that is able to perceive information from the environment and its ability to act upon it without human intervention. With the advent of autonomous systems, what better way to reduce human error than by <u>removing the human driver?</u> The impetus behind an initiative such as this is directly related to the advances in technology that can assist in the management of the traffic infrastructure such as <u>intelligent transport systems (ITS)</u> or in-vehicle driver assistance systems such as <u>advanced driver assistance systems (ADAS)</u>.

Example of a paraphrase:

> Richards and Stedmon begin by highlighting the existence of increased traffic congestion and the need to make roads safer and more efficient. The authors suggest that, as human error plays a major part in many road deaths, replacing the driver with intelligent transport systems (ITS) and advanced driver assistance systems (ADAS) may be the way forward. They use the term *autonomous system* with reference to technology that can perceive environmental information and respond to it without human action.

Example with a direct quotation:

> Richards and Stedmon begin by highlighting the existence of increased traffic congestion and the need to make roads safer and more efficient. The authors suggest that, as human error plays a major part in many road deaths, replacing the driver with intelligent transport systems (ITS) and advanced driver assistance systems (ADAS) may be the way forward. They use the term *autonomous system* with reference to "technology that is able to perceive information from the environment and its ability to act upon it without human intervention" (para. 1).

In each of the examples above, the general focus and main idea of the article are stated. If you are using direct quotations in your summary, remember not to use too many.

4.2 Write the rest of the summary. After writing the introductory sentences of the summary, write the remaining sections or paragraphs according to the structure you chose in stage 3. Your decision on the number of paragraphs to write will depend primarily on the required length of the summary but may also depend on the structure you have chosen and the number of main themes you have identified. Make sure to finish the summary with an appropriate concluding sentence so that it does not end too abruptly.

Stage 5: Edit Your Work

After you have finished writing your first draft, edit your work for accuracy and variety of language and for accurate representation of ideas and information. After self-editing, ask a peer to review your work.

My eLab

Find supplementary reading, writing, and critical-thinking activities online.

AN ACADEMIC SUMMARY

TASK 17 WRITE A SUMMARY

Write a 200-word summary of the Fung article. Follow the five stages you just studied. Do not give your opinion in this summary.

Peer Review

The purpose of peer review is to learn from reading others' writing, and to benefit from peers' positive comments about your writing and from their constructive criticism. When you read a text that is well written, make sure to give positive feedback. However, giving and responding to constructive criticism is also central to the success of peer review. As you read others' writing, look for aspects that could be improved and make your recommendations in a friendly way. When you receive constructive criticism about your writing, decide which recommendations you should follow and which you should set aside.

When you have finished the first draft of your summary in Task 17, use the Summary Review Sheet to first do a review of your own work. Then ask two peers to review your work, also using the Review Sheet. Compare your self-evaluation with the peer review and look for similarities, differences, and areas to improve.

Find the Summary Review Sheet in the online Documents.

Identify useful criticism and recommendations in the reviews; revise and edit your summary accordingly.

CHAPTER 4

BRINGING IN OTHERS' IDEAS: WRITING

> . . . standing on the shoulders of giants.
>
> Sir Isaac Newton

To be a successful academic writer, you need to search for useful sources, select relevant and important ideas, and incorporate these ideas into your own writing. When you use the ideas of experts to make your writing more effective and convincing, you are metaphorically standing on their shoulders to improve your vision and understanding in your subject area. However, those ideas do not belong to you. The rules of academic integrity require that you acknowledge your sources.

In this chapter, you will:

- learn about plagiarism and how to avoid it
- read two articles about plagiarism
- guess meaning from context
- study inference
- practise shifting style and writing reference list entries
- study reporting verbs
- study relative clauses
- learn how to write a response paper
- write a 200-word response paper

TASK 1 EXPLORE THROUGH WRITING

What is academic integrity, and what is plagiarism?

Take five minutes to answer the questions. Try to write as many ideas as possible. After you have finished, in groups of three, read each other's notes and discuss what you have written.

ACADEMIC INTEGRITY

Exercising academic integrity means behaving honestly and ethically as a student, following the rules of an institution, and respecting and acknowledging the intellectual property of others in your work. Accordingly, it means avoiding cheating and plagiarizing.

Plagiarism and Intention

Plagiarism can be defined as using others' ideas, statistics, or creative works in your writing as if they were your own, without acknowledging your source.

When a writer commits plagiarism, it is not always clear whether he or she intended to. Sometimes, plagiarism may be unintentional, for example, when a writer forgets to add an in-text citation for an idea paraphrased from someone else's work. However, if a student pays for an essay from an Internet essay mill and passes it off as his or her own work, the intention is clear.

Remember: your instructors cannot read your intentions, only your writing. Many will assume intention.

Common Knowledge

When writing, if you use an idea or a piece of information that is considered common knowledge, it is not necessary to acknowledge your source. The following two examples illustrate what common knowledge is and is not:

> The North American Free Trade Agreement (NAFTA) came into effect on January 1, 1994.

This is common knowledge because it is a historical fact.

> The North American Free Trade Agreement (NAFTA), which came into effect in 1994, has mainly benefited large corporations in the United States, Canada, and Mexico.

This is not common knowledge because it is not a historical fact. It is a writer's opinion about the results of the historical fact. If you copy this idea without acknowledging your source, you are committing plagiarism by passing off another writer's idea as your own.

TASK 2 IDENTIFY ACTS OF PLAGIARISM

Read the following eight examples of students incorporating others' ideas into their writing. Circle the number from 1 to 3 that fits your understanding of the situation, and then explain your answer.

1. A student included a direct quotation and did not include quotation marks and an in-text citation with a page number.

1	2	3
plagiarism	not sure	not plagiarism

_____

_____

_____

2. A student paraphrased original ideas from another source and did not include an in-text citation.

1	2	3
plagiarism	not sure	not plagiarism

_____

_____

_____

3. A student paraphrased several sentences from another source, making only a few changes to the vocabulary and grammar, and included a citation.

1	2	3
plagiarism	not sure	not plagiarism

_____

_____

_____

4. A student asked for help from a private tutor, who rewrote some sections of an essay so the student could get a better grade.

1	2	3
plagiarism	not sure	not plagiarism

_____

_____

_____

5. A student asked for help from a private tutor, who corrected only grammar and vocabulary errors so the student could get a better grade.

1	2	3
plagiarism	not sure	not plagiarism

_____

_____

_____

6. A student submitted an essay in an academic writing course that he or she had previously submitted in another course.

1	2	3
plagiarism	not sure	not plagiarism

_____

_____

_____

7. A student downloaded an essay from the Internet and submitted it without changing anything.

1	2	3
plagiarism	not sure	not plagiarism

_____

_____

_____

8. A student included in-text citations for all paraphrases and direct quotations in an essay but did not include a corresponding reference for each of them in the reference list at the end of the essay.

1	2	3
plagiarism	not sure	not plagiarism

_____

_____

_____

ACTIVE AND CRITICAL READING

WRITING FROM SOURCES AND PLAGIARISM

The following excerpt is from an academic journal article on the challenges students face when writing from sources.

Student Perceptions of the Value of Turnitin Text-Matching Software as a Learning Tool

by Carol Bailey and Rachel Challen

Introduction

Academic writing is a challenging venture, especially when writing from sources. It involves reading widely yet selectively, understanding and questioning what we read, and **weaving together** multiple authors' voices with
5 our own, indicating both their relationships to each other and how they have influenced our own thinking on the topic. When writing for scholarly

weaving together: combining, joining together

publication, we engage in conversation with our academic peers; thus it is of crucial importance that we correctly represent and attribute each other's views.

10 Student writing follows a similar process but has a rather different purpose. When teachers set written coursework, they hope that by reading and writing students will develop not only their knowledge but also their thinking and communication skills. However, a key function of student writing is assessment 15 of said knowledge and skills. The student writer has a limited readership …, and conversation is restricted to **tutor feedback**, often with little scope for student response. **Baffled** by sometimes inexplicable and apparently contradictory **exhortations** to read more widely yet be selective, to 'use your own words and 20 ideas' yet provide a citation for every statement, novice writers may find themselves engaging in a 'hollow simulacrum of research' (Jamieson and Howard, 2011b:n.p.). This can include behaviours such as falsification of references, copy-pasting citations to sources the student has not read, and what Howard et al. call 'quote-mining' 25 (2010:186), all in the belief that more references will placate the lecturer and lead to higher grades (Harwood and Petric, 2012; Ellery, 2008).

This article will explore student perceptions of the text-matching software Turnitin. Because Turnitin is commonly employed to detect inappropriate textual borrowing (Badge and Scott, 2009), studies on its use often commence 30 with a discussion of plagiarism: its incidence, causes and solutions. Since we will be focussing on the use of Turnitin in developing academic writing skills, we begin by examining some of the challenges students face when writing from sources.

Although most students now arrive at university with some **grounding** in 35 information technology, recent studies suggest that young Internet users, while confident with the technology, are less competent when it comes to **sourcing** and critically evaluating online information (Bartlett and Miller, 2011). In Higher Education, this reveals itself as a tendency to depend on sources which educators may consider insufficiently reliable or 'academic'. …
40 While students are likely to access increasingly authoritative sources as they progress through their studies, Judd and Kennedy found that even in their final year students were relying on Google and Wikipedia 41% of the time, and only 40% of the sources they accessed via Google were classified by the authors as highly reliable (2011:355–57). Similarly, iParadigms relate that of 45 112 million content matches in 28 million student papers submitted to Turnitin between July 2011 and June 2012, 43% were to 'sites that are academically suspect, including … user-generated content' (2012:3). The most popular source, representing 11% of all matched text, was Wikipedia.

A further finding of the Citation Project is that a high proportion of citations 50 were to the first page of a source (46%) or to the first three pages (77%). … Most of the citations were quotations, sentence-level paraphrase or patchwriting. …

tutor feedback: comments from an instructor

baffled: very confused

exhortations: strong recommendation, urging someone to do something

grounding: basic understanding

sourcing: looking for, locating

coined: invented

denote: mean, stand for

synonym: word with similar or the same meaning

ibid: same as the previous reference

inferencing: when meaning is unclear, looking at evidence and reaching a conclusion

academic discourse: academic language and communication

construe: analyze and understand

information literacy: ability to find and use information

The term 'patchwriting' was **coined** by Howard in 1992 to **denote** 'copying from a source text and then deleting some words, altering grammatical structures, or plugging in one-for-one **synonym**-substitutes' (Howard, 1992:233). While some assessors judge this to be a form of plagiarism, Howard argues that it should instead be considered a 'valuable composing strategy' enabling the novice writer's 'manipulation of new ideas and vocabulary' in an unfamiliar discourse (**ibid**). This view of patchwriting as a learning strategy is confirmed in Pecorari's (2003) study of postgraduate student writing. Investigating the influence of mother tongue, Keck (2006) found that L2 writers were more likely than native speakers to use 'Near Copy' as a textual borrowing strategy. However, she also noted that both L1 and L2 undergraduates made significant use of 'minimal revision' paraphrase in their writing (Keck, 2006:275–6). This may be partly due to confusion over what constitutes acceptable paraphrase (Zimitat, 2008). Yet native English writers may, like users of English as an Additional Language (EAL), lack the vocabulary, background knowledge, **inferencing** ability and fluency with **academic discourse** to **construe** complex texts 'in their own words'.

Higher Education Institutions have numerous ways of helping students develop their **information literacy** and academic writing skills. In addition to course guidance documents and academic writing tuition …, many institutions have developed online tutorials on academic writing from sources, and some are commercially available.

One tool which is becoming widely adopted in teaching academic writing is the text-matching software Turnitin, which compares uploaded text with documents in its database (including webpages, academic articles and previously uploaded student papers), then generates an 'Originality Report' highlighting potentially copied material, linked by colour-coding to its possible source.

References

Badge, J.L. and Scott, J. (2009). *Dealing with plagiarism in the digital age.* Available at: http://evidencenet.pbworks.com/Dealing-with-plagiarism-in-the-digital-age (Accessed: 23 June 2011).

Bartlett, J. and Miller, C. (2011). *Truth, lies and the internet: a report into young people's digital fluency.* Available at: http://www.demos.co.uk (Accessed: 23 July 2013).

Ellery, K. (2008). 'An investigation into electronic-source plagiarism in a first-year essay assignment', *Assessment and Evaluation in Higher Education,* 33(6), pp. 607–617.

Harwood, N. and Petric, B. (2012). 'Performance in the citing behavior of two student writers', *Written Communication,* 29(1), pp. 55–103.

Howard, R.M. (1992). 'A plagiarism pentimento'. *Journal of Teaching Writing,* 11(2), pp. 233–245.

Howard, R.M., Serviss, T. and Rodrigue, T.K. (2010). 'Writing from sources, writing from sentences', *Writing & Pedagogy,* 2(2), pp. 177–192.

iParadigms (2012). *The Sources in Student Writing – Higher Education.* Turnitin White Paper. Available at: http://www.turnitin.com (Accessed: 18 July 2013).

Jamieson, S. and Howard, R.M. (2011b). 'Unravelling the citation trail', *Project Information Literacy Smart Talk,* no. 8. The Citation Project, August 15, 2011. Available at: http://citationproject.net (Accessed: 17 July 2013).

Judd, T. and Kennedy, G. (2011). 'Expediency-based practice? Medical students' reliance on Google and Wikipedia for biomedical enquiries', *British Journal of Educational Technology*, 42(2), pp. 351–360.

Keck, C. (2006). 'The use of paraphrase in summary writing: a comparison of L1 and L2 writers', *Journal of Second Language Writing*, 15, pp. 261–278.

Pecorari, D. (2003). 'Good and original: plagiarism and patchwriting in academic second-language writing', *Journal of Second Language Writing*, 12, pp. 317–45.

Zimitat, C. (2008). 'A student perspective of plagiarism', in Roberts, T. (2008) *Student plagiarism in an online world: problems and solutions*. New York: Hershey, pp. 10–22.

Excerpts from Bailey, C., & Challen, R. (2015). Student perceptions of the value of Turnitin text-matching software as a learning tool. *Practitioner Research in Higher Education*, 9(1), 38–51.

TASK 3 GUESS THE MEANING FROM CONTEXT

Read the following sentences and phrases from the Bailey and Challen article, and focus on the words in bold. First, find the sentence or phrase in the text; then look at the surrounding text to try to guess the meaning. Write what you think the words mean (if you are sure) or might mean (if you are not sure). See the example below.

Novice writers may find themselves engaging in a '**hollow simulacrum of research**'. [LINES 20–22]

What do you think it means? Novice writers may find themselves engaging in an *empty and unsatisfactory imitation of research*.

Which words give you clues? The next sentence begins with the defining words "This can include." Then it refers to "falsification of references, copy-pasting citations to sources the student has not read," and "quote-mining."

1. Academic writing is **a challenging venture**. [LINE 2]

   What do you think it means? _____

   _____

   Which words give you clues? _____

   _____

2. It is of crucial importance that we correctly represent and **attribute each other's views**. [LINES 8–9]

   What do you think it means? _____

   _____

   Which words give you clues? _____

   _____

3. However, a key function of student writing is assessment of **said knowledge and skills**. [LINES 14–15]

   What do you think it means? _____

   _____

Which words give you clues? _____

_____

4. Turnitin is commonly employed **to detect inappropriate textual borrowing**. [LINES 28–29]

What do you think it means? _____

_____

Which words give you clues? _____

_____

5. Keck (2006) found that **L2 writers** were more likely than native speakers to use 'Near Copy' as a textual borrowing strategy. [LINES 61–63]

What do you think it means? _____

_____

Which words give you clues? _____

_____

Inference

In the margin of the Bailey and Challen article, inference is defined as "looking at evidence and reaching a conclusion when meaning is unclear." As a reader, you need to infer meaning when a writer's idea is not completely clear to you. You may understand the words but struggle to fully understand the writer's broader opinion, claim, or purpose in making the statement. Consider the following example:

> Baffled by sometimes inexplicable and apparently contradictory exhortations to read more widely yet be selective, to 'use your own words and ideas' yet provide a citation for every statement, novice writers may find themselves engaging in a 'hollow simulacrum of research'. [LINES 17–22]

Problem: Even if you understand the individual words, the authors' stance (their opinion of students who do unsatisfactory research) is not clearly stated. If the authors' purpose had been to state their position explicitly, they could have done so as follows:

> Novice writers may **have no option but to engage** in a "hollow simulacrum of research." (sympathetic)

> Novice writers may **try to deceive their instructors by engaging** in a "hollow simulacrum of research." (unsympathetic)

However, because the stance is unclear, the reader has to infer it by looking at the evidence and reaching a conclusion.

Question: Do you think the authors are being sympathetic toward students or critical of them?

Inference: The authors seem sympathetic because they explain that students are baffled by being asked to do things that are inexplicable and contradictory, and that this contradiction may be the reason—at least in part—for their unsuccessful attempts at research.

TASK 4 INFER THE MEANING

Look at each of the following quotations from the article, and read the problem that requires you to infer meaning. Then answer the question that follows. Compare the inferred meanings with a partner before writing your answers.

1. While students are likely to access increasingly authoritative sources as they progress through their studies, Judd and Kennedy found that even in their final year students were relying on Google and Wikipedia 41% of the time, and only 40% of the sources they accessed via Google were classified by the authors as highly reliable. [LINES 40–44]

   Problem: The authors' purpose in citing these statistics is not clear.

   Question: What can you infer from the statistics about the authors' opinion of final-year students?

   Inference: _____

   _____

   _____

   _____

2. A further finding of the Citation Project is that a high proportion of citations were to the first page of a source (46%) or to the first three pages (77%). Most of the citations were quotations, sentence-level paraphrase or patchwriting. [LINES 49–52]

   Problem: The authors' purpose in including these findings is not clearly stated.

   Question: Do these specific findings of the Citation Project portray students in a positive or negative light? Explain your answer.

   Inference: _____

   _____

   _____

   _____

3. While some assessors judge this to be a form of plagiarism, Howard argues that it should instead be considered a 'valuable composing strategy' enabling the novice writer's 'manipulation of new ideas and vocabulary' in an unfamiliar discourse. [LINES 56–59]

   Problem: The authors are presenting two opposing views without explicitly stating their own stance.

   Question: Do the authors give more emphasis to one idea than to the other, thus giving a clue to their stance? Consider what you studied in Chapter 3 about emphasizing information in complex sentences.

   Inference: _____

   _____

   _____

   _____

4. One tool which is becoming widely adopted in teaching academic writing is the text-matching software Turnitin, which compares uploaded text with documents in its database (including webpages, academic articles and previously uploaded student papers), then generates an 'Originality Report' highlighting potentially copied material, linked by colour-coding to its possible source. [LINES 75–80]

Problem: The authors do not indicate whether they support using Turnitin.

Question: In their description of Turnitin, do the authors give any indication whether they support or oppose its use in higher education?

Inference: _____

_____

_____

_____

ACTIVE AND CRITICAL READING

PLAGIARISM IN THE MUSIC INDUSTRY

You are going to read an online article on plagiarism in the music industry.

TASK 5 EXPLORE THROUGH DISCUSSION

Discuss the following question in groups: Why do laws and rules about plagiarism exist?

Online Sources

Online, non-peer-reviewed articles are usually written in a less formal style. The style is a reflection of the genre, the aim to attract a broad audience, as well as the personal preferences of the writer. Such articles can provide useful background knowledge about a subject, especially if it is topical and no reliable peer-reviewed books or articles are available.

There are two important challenges to consider when you refer to online articles in your academic writing: reliability and style shift.

Reliability

If you look for sources using an Internet search engine, you will find many different types of articles:

- newspaper and magazine articles
- articles and documents from governmental and non-governmental organizations
- blogs
- peer-reviewed journal articles

You can find different information in different sources, but if you want to use information, ideas, or statistics from any of these sources, you need to be sure that what you are reading is reliable.

MORE RELIABLE

- Peer-reviewed books and articles

  For a source to be considered reliable, it should be peer-reviewed, which means it has been assessed by academic experts and editors. As the peer-review process takes time, it is not always possible to find peer-reviewed articles or books on very recent topics.

- News media

  Newspaper articles are reviewed by editors but rarely by academic experts. News media sources vary considerably in terms of reliability. Some serious news organizations are trustworthy and reliable because professional journalists verify their sources; other organizations—for example, many tabloid newspapers—do not hold their writers to the same standards.

- Websites, blogs, and wikis

  You can find useful information, especially statistics and information about policies, on the websites of governmental and non-governmental organizations. The information is not usually reviewed by peers or editors, and you will often find different views on a topic depending on the type of organization, so you need to read critically.

  Popular websites, blogs, and wikis can give you a good idea of the general debate around a topic, but they are not considered reliable due to the lack of peer review and editorial control of their content.

LESS RELIABLE

Reliability Checklists

Use the following checklists to assess the reliability of different sources.

Academic books and articles are the most reliable sources. Nonetheless, some are more reliable than others. Consider the following criteria when using academic books and articles:

☐ Has the book or article been reviewed by expert peers?

☐ Does the book or article contain in-text citations and references?

☐ Is the publisher a recognized academic publisher?

☐ Has the book or article been cited by other academic publications?

And for articles only:

☐ Is the journal linked to recognized academic databases?

☐ Does the journal appear regularly?

☐ Does the journal have an editor and an editorial board of academics?

If the answer to any of these questions is no, the book or article may be less reliable.

News media are useful sources for up-to-date information on a broad range of topics. There are many different news media—some reliable, and some not. Consider the following criteria when using news media:

☐ Does the newspaper or news website seem serious?

☐ Is the language and style formal?

☐ Are opinions and statistics attributed to reliable sources?

☐ Are opinions and claims balanced, and supported with evidence?

If the answer to any of these questions is no, the news source is not reliable.

Websites, blogs, and wikis can provide useful background information about a topic, but they are not always reliable. Consider the following criteria if you intend to cite such sources:

☐ Is the source a recognized governmental or non-governmental organization?

☐ Does the content have an author, date, in-text citations, and a reference list?

☐ Is the style of writing formal and academic?

☐ Is the tone serious and the site devoid of flashy colours and advertisements?

If the answer to any of these questions is no, the site is not reliable.

Find reproducible checklists in the online Documents.

TASK 6 ASSESS RELIABILITY

Look at the article below, an online news article, and assess its reliability by answering the questions in the news media checklist. Discuss your answers in small groups.

Style Shift

The next article is from an online news source and is written in a style that is wholly appropriate for the genre: it does not follow the formal citation and referencing rules required for academic texts, and it is engaging, informal, and conversational. However, this style is not appropriate for academic writing.

In Effective Writing Style on pages 89 and 90, you will practise shifting from informal to formal style. Later in the chapter, you will write a 200-word response paper in which you summarize the main ideas of the article below and respond to them with your personal opinions and impressions. As you write, you will need to shift the style to formal academic English.

TASK 7 READ AND TAKE NOTES

Read the article below on plagiarism in the music industry. As you read, take notes on the following:

- main information and ideas
- whether you think the information and claims are reliable
- your personal response to the article (whether you agree or disagree, whether you are convinced, surprised, etc.)
- examples of informal style that you will need to shift to formal academic English

You will refer to these notes later when you write the response paper.

Here's What Makes a Song a Ripoff, according to the Law: How You Think about Music ≠ How the Courts Think about Music

by Reggie Ugwu

Music is art, and art is for people—not lawyers. But musicians have long relied on the law to protect their creations. For nearly two centuries, courts in the United States have heard cases from songwriters seeking to defend their compositions from thieves, cheats, and liars **of all stripes**. It's a trad-
5 ition that continues today—with recent disputes between Tom Petty and Sam Smith (settled amicably out of court) and the Marvin Gaye family and Robin Thicke, Pharrell Williams, T.I., et al (currently at trial)—putting the modern music industry on high alert.

In those cases, and in most disputes alleging copyright **infringement** of a
10 musical composition, a few **perennial** questions arise: When can a person be said to *own* something like a **chord progression** or **melody**? And in a world where everyone is inspired by someone else, where is the line between plagiarism and influence? To help us answer these questions in plain English, we spoke to Paul Fakler, a **veteran** copyright lawyer with a specialty in music
15 law, of the law firm Arent Fox.

What we learned **underscores** the gap between how casual music fans think about music, and how it's treated as a matter of law. . . .

Music compositions, like other forms of creative expression, are protected by copyright under the law. Under the Copyright Act of 1976, which took
20 effect in 1978, anytime a person writes or records an original piece of music, a copyright automatically exists. Registration with the U.S. Copyright Office is optional, but does come with certain benefits in the event of an infringe-ment **dispute**. Copyrighted elements of a musical composition can include melody, chord progression, rhythm, and **lyrics**—anything that reflects a
25 "**minimal spark**" of creativity and originality.

"It really doesn't have to be a whole lot," said Fakler. "If a single chord pro-gression were **elaborate** enough and **unconventional** enough, it could be protected."

One important instance where copyright doesn't apply is public domain. If
30 a song was published prior to 1923, it is considered to be in the public domain and is not protected. Federal law says that creative works, including music compositions, enter the public domain after the life of the creator plus 70 years. . . . Copyright is designed to prevent people from copying a creative work, or specific elements **thereof**, without permission.

35 Disputes over music copyrights are very common, but often don't **go to trial**. If you've ever listened to a song and thought it sounded a lot like another, older song, you probably weren't alone. It's a **truism** of popular music that everyone is influenced by their **predecessors** (and, often, **contemporaries**), and perceived similarities between songs often lead to disputes.

---

ripoff: bad imitation

Tom Petty, Marvin Gaye (d. 1984), Robin Thicke, Pharrell Williams, and T.I. are American musicians; Sam Smith is a British musician.

of all stripes: of all sorts

infringement: illegal act

perennial: recurring, happening again and again

chord progression: series of musical chords

melody: tune

veteran: highly experienced

underscores: highlights

dispute: disagreement

lyrics: words to a song

minimal spark: very small amount

elaborate: detailed, complex

unconventional: not usually done

The federal law mentioned here is US law; other countries have different copyright terms.

thereof: of this or that

go to trial: go to court

truism: something that is obviously true

predecessors: people before us

contemporaries: people living at the same time

murky: unclear (negative connotation)

the latter: the second of two examples

litigation: legal action

juries: groups of people who decide a verdict

stigmas: shame

duplicitous: dishonest

belligerent: aggressive

tort: act that is legally wrong

defendant: person in court accused of a crime

parties: groups (litigants and defendants)

on someone's radar: that has come to someone's attention

subconsciously: without realizing

hallmark: main feature

40 "In songwriting, you're always building on what came before you, and the line between influence and copying can be a **murky** one," said Fakler.

As was the case with Tom Petty and Sam Smith, in which **the latter**'s "Stay With Me" was alleged to infringe on the former's "I Won't Back Down," most disputes are settled privately out of court. Fakler says that's because 45 **litigation** is expensive, **juries** are unpredictable, and there are **stigmas** that can stick to both sides: The accused can get labeled as unoriginal or **duplicitous**, and the accuser can be viewed as greedy or **belligerent**.

In the event of a trial, the person claiming infringement (the plaintiff) has to prove two things: "access" and "substantial similarity." Copyright infringe- 50 ment is what's called a "strict liability **tort**," which means the **defendant** doesn't have to have intended to infringe to be found guilty. To prove guilt, the plaintiff must only demonstrate that the defendant had access to the allegedly infringed song, and that the two songs in question have substantial similarity.

55 Access is a question of whether the defendant ever actually heard, or could reasonably be presumed to have heard, the plaintiff's song at some point before creating the allegedly infringing song. Though not always easy to prove, courts often consider whether a relationship existed between the two **parties** and how well known the plaintiff's song is generally.

60 In the famous 1976 case *Bright Tunes Music v. Harrisongs Music*, the late Beatles member George Harrison was found to have infringed on The Chiffons' hit "He's So Fine" with his own solo song "My Sweet Lord" in part because The Chiffons' song was so popular that there was little doubt whether Harrison had been exposed to it. The judge concluded that even though there 65 was no evidence that "He's So Fine" had been **on Harrison's radar**, he had likely heard the song and internalized it "**subconsciously**."

In the case of Robin Thicke and "Blurred Lines," by contrast, there was never any question of access, since Thicke admitted on his own that his song was inspired by Marvin Gaye's "Got 70 to Give It Up."

Substantial similarity is a question of whether or not the average listener can tell that one song has been copied from the other. This is the "ordinary observer test," what Fakler calls "the **hallmark** of copyright infringement." The more elements 75 two works have in common, the more likely they are to be ruled substantially similar. Proving substantial similarity in music cases is complicated by the fact that all songs carry two kinds of copyright, for composition and sound recording, that have to be evaluated independently. ...

80 Because most people can't read music, it's actually pretty hard for the average juror to tell whether two songs have substantial similarities or not. Given the unreliability of sound recordings and performances in cases where compositions are in dispute, musicologists are often called as expert witnesses to

walk jurors through: explain to members of the jury

cut to the chase: deal quickly with the main issue

attorneys: lawyers

incurred: suffered or experienced

85 **walk jurors through** sheet music. A musicologist for the plaintiff will underscore the similarities between the two songs as written, while the defendant's musicologist will stress the differences. "With novels and movies, it's often easier for jurors to sort of **cut to the chase** and tell whether the thing has been copied or not," said Fakler. "Music cases quickly turn into a battle of 90 the experts." If accused of infringement, a person can use several specific defenses to try to beat the claim. . . .

Being found guilty of copyright infringement often comes with serious damages. Copyright infringement in music cases can easily cost the infringer millions of dollars in damages—plus **attorneys**' fees in some instances— 95 which can be calculated based on a variety of factors, including the degree of infringement and the financial losses **incurred**. The plaintiff may also seek what's called "injunctive relief" and block the record label from further distribution and sale of the infringing song(s).

Though most people, artists included, like to think of their favorite songs as 100 unique, copyright forces us to ask tough questions about the true nature of creativity, community, and commerce. "Nothing is completely original," Fakler said. "We're all standing on the shoulders of giants."

Excerpts from Ugwu, R. (2015, March 6). Here's what makes a song a ripoff, according to the law: How you think about music ≠ how the courts think about music. *BuzzFeed*. Retrieved from http://www.buzzfeed.com/reggieugwu/what-the-law-says-about-music-plagiarism#.mgqoM2dQP

EFFECTIVE WRITING STYLE

SHIFTING STYLE

The Ugwu article is written according to the genre features of an online persuasive text, which is targeting quite a broad readership, including non-expert readers. To make such texts accessible and engaging for as broad an audience as possible, writers often mix informal online writing styles with more formal academic styles. For example, in the text above, Ugwu uses several less formal, conversational words and phrases to catch his readers' attention.

TASK 8 IDENTIFY INFORMAL STYLE

Scan the article above for language that you think is not appropriate style for academic writing, and which will require a shift in style when you write the response paper. Underline as many examples as you can in five minutes; then discuss your answers in pairs.

TASK 9 SHIFT FROM INFORMAL TO FORMAL STYLE

In the sentences on the next page (taken from the Ugwu article), the phrases in bold are examples of less formal style that would not normally be used in formal academic writing. Match each sentence to one or more of the following descriptions of informal style, and write the corresponding letter(s) under the sentence. Then rewrite the sentence to make it more in line with formal academic writing.

Descriptions of informal style:

a) use of short simple words (e.g., *look into* instead of *investigate*)

b) conversational language (e.g., a phrase normally used in spoken, but not written English)

c) use of simple quantifiers (e.g., *a lot of, lots of, loads of*)

d) addressing the reader as *you*

e) use of coordinators at the beginning of sentences (e.g., *and, but, so*)

f) contractions (e.g., *doesn't, don't* instead of *does not, do not*)

1. **But** musicians have long relied on the law to protect their creations.

   Letter(s): _____

   _____

2. **It's** a tradition that continues today.

   Letter(s): _____

   _____

3. **"It really doesn't have to be a whole lot,"** said Fakler.

   Letter(s): _____

   _____

4. If **you've** ever listened to a song and thought it sounded **a lot** like another, older song, **you** probably weren't alone.

   Letter(s): _____

   _____

5. "In songwriting, **you're** always building on what came before **you** . . .," said Fakler.

   Letter(s): _____

   _____

6. Because most people **can't** read music, **it's** actually **pretty hard** for the average juror to **tell** whether two songs have substantial similarities or not.

   Letter(s): _____

   _____

7. "With novels and movies, **it's** often easier for jurors to **sort of cut to the chase** and **tell** whether **the thing** has been copied or not," said Fakler.

   Letter(s): _____

   _____

REPORTING VERBS

Academic writers use a range of reporting verbs when they refer to others' ideas and arguments. Different reporting verbs have different meanings and functions, which reflect the writer's view of the information being cited.

Reporting Different Types of Information

You can use reporting verbs in different tenses. In most cases, tenses have little effect on the meaning of reporting verbs. You can also use reporting verbs in the active or passive voice without changing the meaning.

The following are some examples taken from, or referring to, the two articles in this chapter.

Reporting Factual Information

Reporting Verbs	Examples
say	Ugwu (2015) **says** that music compositions, like other forms of creative expression, are protected by copyright under the law.
state	Bailey and Challen (2015) **state** that higher education institutions help students develop their academic writing in many ways.
	As stated by Bailey and Challen (2015), higher education institutions help students develop their academic writing in many ways.

Reporting Arguments

Reporting Verbs	Examples
argue	Ugwu (2015) **argues** that the general public and courts do not listen to music in the same way.
claim maintain support the view that	**It is claimed by** Ugwu (2015) that the general public and courts do not listen to music in the same way.
suggest imply	Bailey and Challen (2015) **suggest** that some students may be confused by what is not acceptable in paraphrasing.

Reporting Opposition to Arguments

Reporting Verbs	Examples
challenge	Howard (1992) **challenges** the view that patchwriting should be understood as intentional plagiarism.
question disagree	The view that patchwriting should be understood as intentional plagiarism **is questioned by** Howard (1992).
	In Ugwu (2015), Fakler **questions** whether any musical work can be completely original.

Using Present and Past Tenses with Reporting Verbs

As a general rule of thumb, use the present tense for reporting verbs even if the article you are referring to was written in the past. If you use the past tense, sometimes the tense will affect the meaning. Specifically, if you are referring to primary research (for which data are collected and analyzed, for example, in an experiment), using a different tense can change the meaning or emphasis.

No Change in Meaning (General Ideas)

> In Ugwu (2015), Fakler **says** that is because litigation is expensive, juries are unpredictable, and there are stigmas that can stick to both sides.

The present tense works well for an argument that still stands at the time of writing, as in the example above.

> "In songwriting, you're always building on what came before you, and the line between influence and copying can be a murky one," **said** Fakler (as cited in Ugwu, 2015).

The past tense works well here because the writer is citing Fakler's exact words and using a narrative style.

Change in Meaning (Primary Research)

If the reporting verbs (and other descriptive verbs) that refer to primary research are in the past tense, this can suggest that the findings are limited to one particular study.

> Judd and Kennedy **found** that even in their final year students **were relying** on Google and Wikipedia 41% of the time, and only 40% of the sources they **accessed** via Google **were classified** by the authors as highly reliable.

On the other hand, if the reporting verbs (and other descriptive verbs) that refer to primary research are in the present tense, this can suggest that the findings are generalizable, which means they can be applied beyond the limits of the study to broader populations. Consider this example (not based on the chapter articles):

> Piaget (1952) **argues** that children **learn** by "assimilating" information from the environment.

The present tense here (for the reporting verb *argues* and the verb *learn*) suggests the writer thinks Piaget's findings are generalizable, which indeed they are: when his studies were replicated with different groups, his original findings were confirmed.

Adding Your Own Opinion with Adverbs

You can express your opinion about information you are citing by adding an adverb such as *interestingly*, *mistakenly*, *wrongly*, *correctly*, or *rightly* before the reporting verb.

> In Ugwu (2015), Fakler **interestingly** questions whether any musical work can ever be completely original.

(The writer thinks Fakler's idea is interesting.)

Howard (1992) **wrongly** challenges the view that patchwriting should be understood as intentional plagiarism.

(The writer thinks Howard's idea is wrong.)

Ugwu (2015) **correctly** states that copyright does not apply in the public domain.

(The writer thinks Ugwu's statement is correct.)

TASK 10 PRACTISE USING REPORTING VERBS

Use reporting verbs to fill in the blanks in the following sentences about the two articles in this chapter. Use a verb that matches the meaning as closely as possible. There may be more than one correct answer.

1. Ugwu (2015) _____ that musicians rely on the law to protect their musical compositions.

2. The view that patchwriting constitutes plagiarism is _____ by Howard (1992). (Use the passive voice.)

3. In Ugwu (2015), Fakler _____ that no musical work is completely original.

4. Bailey and Challen (2015) _____ that the difference between paraphrasing and patchwriting might be confusing for some students.

5. Ugwu (2015) _____ _____ that musicians rely on the law to protect their musical compositions. (I agree with his statement.)

6. In Ugwu (2015), Fakler _____ _____ that no musical work is completely original. (I disagree with his argument.)

7. In Ugwu (2015), Fakler _____ concludes by _____ we are all standing on the shoulders of giants. (I think his idea is interesting.)

EXTEND YOUR ACADEMIC VOCABULARY

Extend your knowledge of key vocabulary from this chapter.

allegedly	**denote**	incur
attribute	discourse	infringe
critically	**incidence**	underscore

*Words in bold type are AWL entries.

Practise Chapter 4 vocabulary online.

REFERENCE LISTS IN APA AND MLA STYLES

In Chapter 3, you were directed to Appendices 2 and 3 on APA and MLA citation styles. To write APA- or MLA-style reference list entries for the two articles in this chapter, you should use the formats below.

Scholarly Journal Article

APA Format

Surname, Initial. (year). Title of article. *Title of Journal, volume number*(issue number), page numbers. doi:xxxxx

MLA Format

Surname, Name. "Title of Article." *Title of Journal*, vol. xx, no. xx, year, pp. xxx–xxx.

A Page on a Website

APA Format

Surname, Initial. (year, Month day). Title of document. [*Title of Site.*] Retrieved from URL

MLA Format

Surname, Name. "Title of Document." *Title of Site*, Sponsor or publisher, date of publication [if available], URL. Accessed date.

TASK 11 WRITE APA AND MLA REFERENCE LIST ENTRIES

Write reference list entries for the two articles in this chapter, following either the APA or MLA format above.

1. _____
   _____
   _____
   _____
   _____

2. _____
   _____
   _____
   _____

> Learn more about APA and MLA reference lists in Appendices 2 and 3.

STANDING ON THE SHOULDERS OF GIANTS

TASK 12 DISCUSS

1. The Ugwu article contains the phrase *standing on the shoulders of giants*, which was also the opening quotation in this chapter. Answer the following related questions in small groups:

   a) What do you think *standing on the shoulders of giants* means?

   b) Why do you think Ugwu closed the article with this quotation?

   c) Does it help you to do academic writing when you "stand on the shoulders of giants"?

2. Look back at the exploratory writing you did for Task 1: What is academic integrity, and what is plagiarism? Are there any ideas or key concepts you have learned in this chapter that have changed your initial understanding?

RELATIVE CLAUSES

A relative clause defines or gives extra (non-defining) information about a thing or idea in a nearby independent clause. Defining and non-defining clauses are also called *restrictive* and *non-restrictive* clauses. A relative clause can begin with any of the following common relative pronouns (the context in which they are used is in parentheses):

- *which* (a thing)
- *that* (a thing or person)
- *who(m)* (a person)
- *whose* (possessive form)
- *what* (the thing that)
- *when* (time)
- *where* (place)
- *why* (reason)

In the following examples from the Ugwu article, focus on the relative clauses in italics.

Defining Relative Clauses

> Copyrighted elements of a musical composition can include melody, chord progression, rhythm, and lyrics—anything *that reflects a "minimal spark" of creativity and originality.*

The relative clause *that reflects a "minimal spark" of creativity and originality* is defining because it tells us *which specific things*. Without this information, the idea in the independent clause would not be complete.

Do not set off defining relative clauses with commas. Use *that* to define things; however, note that in British English, it is common to use *which* in defining relative clauses.

Non-Defining Relative Clauses

> Under the Copyright Act of 1976, *which took effect in 1978*, any time a person writes or records an original piece of music, a copyright automatically exists.

The relative clause *which took effect in 1978* is non-defining. It does not tell us which Copyright Act; it is giving extra, non-essential information about it. Without the non-defining relative clause, the idea in the independent clause would still be complete.

In non-defining relative clauses, use *which*, and set off the clause with commas. It is incorrect to use *that* in non-defining relative clauses.

TASK 13 IDENTIFY RELATIVE CLAUSES

In the following sentences from the Ugwu article, focus on the relative clauses in italics. Indicate whether they are defining or non-defining.

		Defining	Non-Defining
1	One important instance *where copyright doesn't apply* is public domain.		
2	As was the case with Tom Petty and Sam Smith, *in which the latter's "Stay With Me" was alleged to infringe on the former's "I Won't Back Down,"* most disputes are settled privately out of court.		
3	Copyright infringement is what's called a "strict liability tort," *which means the defendant doesn't have to have intended to infringe to be found guilty*.		
4	This is the "ordinary observer test," *what Fakler calls "the hallmark of copyright infringement."*		
5	Given the unreliability of sound recordings and performances in cases *where compositions are in dispute*, musicologists are often called as expert witnesses to walk jurors through sheet music.		

TASK 14 ADD RELATIVE CLAUSES

Complete the following sentences with a defining or non-defining relative clause. Follow the prompts in parentheses. Remember to set off non-defining relative clauses with commas.

1. Plagiarism _____ is sometimes unintentional. (non-defining / a thing / use *refer*)

2. Today, most universities provide software _____. (defining / a thing / use *detect*)

3. He's the person _____. (defining / a person / use *write*)

4. She's the person _____. (defining / possessive / use *essay* and *win an award*)

5. Effective paraphrasing is _____. (defining / the thing that / use *many students* and *find challenging*)

6. Thirty years ago _____ most students wrote assignments by hand. (non-defining / time / use *be* and *no Internet*)

7. I need somewhere quiet _____. (defining / place / use *can study*)

Do Unit 4: Relative Clauses in the Handbook, pp. 343–348.

8. I was never told _____. (defining / reason / use *get a C grade*)

THE WRITING PROCESS

EXTENDED WRITING: RESPONSE PAPERS

What Is a Response Paper?

A response paper is a type of essay that requires you to respond to one or more texts. Usually, you must complete some or all of the following tasks:

- show that you have understood the text as a whole
- identify the author's main claim(s) and the main idea(s) in the text
- show how the ideas interrelate
- assess the validity of the author's supporting reasons, examples, and evidence
- assess the importance of the text and topic
- show how the text fits into a broader debate
- present a balanced opinion of the ideas in the text (strengths and weaknesses, whether you agree or disagree)
- consider counter-arguments to the ideas in the text
- look for what might be missing in the text

Style in Response Papers

Response papers involve a combination of summarizing, evaluating, and arguing. To write in an appropriate style, do the following:

- Write in formal academic language (shift style if the original text is less formal).
- Balance objective language (to highlight main ideas) and subjective language (to argue).
- Use a range of reporting verbs.
- If appropriate in your subject area, use personal language to present your opinion, e.g., *I believe, in my opinion.*

The Response Paper Writing Process

The following are five common stages in the process of writing a response paper. You have already completed stages 1 and 2 for the response paper you will write in Task 15.

Stage 1: **Skim the Text**

Read the text for gist, highlight or underline the main ideas, and write notes in the margin.

Stage 2: **Read the Complete Text**

Follow up the skimming with a detailed reading of the text. Add to your notes as you read if you find other important information to include in your response paper.

Stage 3: **Decide on Your Structure**

There are different ways to structure a response paper. You can follow the original structure of the text or use a thematic structure based on relevant topics.

Stage 4: **Start Writing**

Once you have gone through the three stages above, it is time to start writing.

4.1 **Write the opening sentence.** Include the following information in the first sentence of the response paper (if the information is available):

- the title of the article
- the author's name
- the name and date of the publication
- the main topic

> In the article "Here's What Makes a Song a Ripoff, according to the Law," published on *BuzzFeed* March 6, 2016, author Reggie Ugwu discusses plagiarism in the music industry.

4.2 **Write the next sentences.** State the main argument or idea of the article, and present your initial response to it. A good way to do this is to look at your notes for the first paragraph(s) of the article and paraphrase the main argument, with or without a direct quotation.

agree!
musicians and the law

NB: shift informal style

Music is art, and art is for people—not lawyers. But musicians have long relied on the law to protect their creations. For nearly two centuries, courts in the United States have heard cases from songwriters seeking to defend their compositions from thieves, cheats, and liars of all stripes. It's a tradition that continues today—with recent disputes between Tom Petty and Sam Smith (settled amicably out of court) and the Marvin Gaye family and Robin Thicke, Pharrell Williams, T.I., et al (currently at trial)—putting the modern music industry on high alert.

In those cases, and in most disputes alleging underline{copyright infringement} of a musical composition, a few perennial questions arise: When can a person be said to *own* something like a chord progression or melody? And in a world where everyone is inspired by someone else, underline{where is the line between plagiarism and influence}? To help us answer these questions in plain English, we spoke to Paul Fakler, a veteran copyright lawyer with a specialty in music law, of the law firm Arent Fox. What we learned underscores underline{the gap between how casual music fans think about music, and how it's treated as a matter of law.}

Example of a paraphrase:

> The author begins with a paradox, arguing that music should be for people, not lawyers, while recognizing that musicians often resort to the law to protect their work. After highlighting copyright infringement as central to plagiarism disputes in the music industry, Ugwu points to two central concepts in such disputes: contested ownership and the fine line between influence and plagiarism.

Example with a direct quotation:

> The author begins with a paradox, arguing that music should be for people, not lawyers, while recognizing that musicians often resort to the law to protect their work. After highlighting copyright infringement as central to plagiarism disputes in the music industry, Ugwu asks two questions that are central to such disputes: "When can a person be said to *own* something like a chord progression or melody? And in a world where everyone is inspired by someone else, where is the line between plagiarism and influence?" (para. 2).

Since the response paper is focusing on a single article, and since the date and author are introduced in the opening sentence, it is not necessary to use in-text citations every time the author is mentioned, e.g., Ugwu (2015). When you quote the article directly, include an in-text citation stating the paragraph number, e.g., (para. 2). Use direct quotations sparingly, for example, for ideas that are key to the response and which you could not express as effectively in your own words.

4.3 Write the rest of the response paper. After writing the introductory sentences of the paper, write the remaining sections or paragraphs according to the structure you chose in stage 3. Your decision on the number of paragraphs to write will depend on the required length of the paper, the structure you have chosen, and the number of main themes you have identified. Make sure to finish the paper with an appropriate concluding sentence so that it does not end too abruptly.

Stage 5: Edit Your Work

After you have finished writing your first draft, edit your work for accuracy and variety of language and for accurate representation of ideas and information. After self-editing, ask a peer to review your work.

A RESPONSE PAPER

TASK 15 WRITE A RESPONSE PAPER

Write a 200-word response paper on Reggie Ugwu's article, "Here's What Makes a Song a Ripoff, according to the Law." Follow the five stages you just studied, and use your margin notes from Task 7. Remember to use appropriate reporting verbs to attribute the ideas to their sources. When paraphrasing, be sure to change the vocabulary and grammar enough to avoid patchwriting. Write the paper in a formal academic style, changing the less formal language as needed. You do not have to include citations (APA or MLA) in this task.

Peer Review

When you have finished the first draft of your paper in Task 15, use the Response Paper Review Sheet to first do a review of your own work. Then ask two peers to review your work, also using the Review Sheet. Compare your self-evaluation with the peer review and look for similarities, differences, and areas to improve.

Find the Response Paper Review Sheet in the online Documents.

Identify useful criticism and recommendations in the reviews; revise and edit your response paper accordingly.

ESSAY SECTIONS: PARAGRAPHS, INTRODUCTIONS, AND CONCLUSIONS

CHAPTER 5

PRESENTING COHERENT ARGUMENTS

> It's not bragging if you can back it up.
>
> Muhammad Ali

In Part 2, you will learn techniques to write paragraphs, introductions, and conclusions for different kinds of academic writing. In each of these essay sections, you are presenting key arguments to your readers and trying to convince them. Arguments need to be clear and coherent, well written, convincing, and backed up with reasons, examples, and evidence. In this way, you can show confidence in your arguments and persuade your readers.

In this chapter, you will:

- read a newspaper article that discusses rehabilitation and punishment in prisons
- review shifting styles between formal and informal
- learn how to support arguments with reasons, examples, and evidence
- study personal and impersonal language of opinion
- learn to avoid logical fallacies based on cause and effect
- study rules on how to use commas correctly
- write two opinion paragraphs

TASK 1 EXPLORE THROUGH DISCUSSION

Which is more important in academic writing: effective language or convincing arguments?

Discuss this question in small groups.

THE ROLE OF PRISONS: TO REHABILITATE OR PUNISH?

In societies around the world, politicians and government officials are faced with this question when dealing with people who break laws and go to prison. Should prisons focus on punishment, create harsh living conditions, and make convicts repay their debt to society in discomfort? Or should prisons be more like schools, with a focus on education, counselling, and preparing convicts for a successful reintroduction to society after their release?

At the heart of this debate is the question of blame and responsibility. Does the responsibility for committing crimes lie solely with the individuals who make the decision to break society's rules? Or is society also partly to blame due to social inequality? This discussion has a long history and continues to generate controversy today.

TASK 2 EXPLORE THROUGH WRITING

The following quotation is attributed to the Ancient Greek philosopher Aristotle (384–322 BCE):

"Poverty is the parent of crime."

Take five minutes to write as much as you can about the following questions:

1. What do you consider the main idea of the quotation?

2. Do you agree with this main idea? Why or why not?

THE ROLE OF PRISONS: THE SWEDISH MODEL

Read the following article, written by Erwin James for the *Guardian* newspaper in the UK. James, now a journalist, served 20 years of a life sentence before being released in 2004.

TASK 3 TAKE NOTES

As you read, take notes on the following points:
- the main idea of each paragraph
- arguments that convince you
- arguments that do not convince you

You will refer back to your notes later in the chapter, when you write two opinion paragraphs.

'Prison is not for punishment in Sweden. We get people into better shape'

With prisoner numbers falling and jails closing, Swedish criminal justice works, says director-general Nils Öberg

by Erwin James

deprived of: prevented from having

probation: supervised period outside prison, usually with restrictions

penal reform: improvement of the prison system

stark contrast: clear and striking contrast

mothballed: no longer in use but kept ready for possible future needs

reoffending rates: rates of prisoners committing new crimes after release from prison

rehabilitation: education, training, and counselling to prepare criminals for a crime-free life

undertaken: carried out

psychiatric problems: mental health problems

sentences: periods of imprisonment

window of opportunity: short period during which to take advantage of something

convicted: found guilty by a court

"Our role is not to punish. The punishment is the prison sentence: they have been **deprived of** their freedom. The punishment is that they are with us," says Nils Öberg, director-general
5 of Sweden's prison and **probation** service.

Öberg, 54, is giving the annual Longford lecture on **penal reform** in London tomorrow, where he will explain how, in **stark contrast** to the UK, Sweden is closing prisons and reducing
10 the prison population.

Since 2004, Swedish prisoner numbers have fallen from 5,722 to 4,500 out of a population of 9.5 million, and last year four of the country's 56 prisons were closed and parts of other jails **mothballed**. In contrast, the prison population in England
15 and Wales is 85,000 out of a population of 57 million.

With **reoffending rates** at about 40%—less than half of those in the UK and most other European countries—does he attribute this success to the country's effective policies on prisoner **rehabilitation**? "We obviously believe that it is part of the explanation; we hope we are doing something right. But
20 it's going to be very difficult to prove that scientifically. We are increasing our efforts all the time," he says.

Last year a "national client survey" of several thousand Swedish prisoners was **undertaken** in order to identify the issues that have affected their criminal behaviour. "The survey did not bring up any surprises, but it gave
25 us confirmation of what we have learned from experience—that it is not one problem that our clients face, but two or more, sometimes as many as seven or eight different ones, including perhaps drugs, alcohol and **psychiatric problems**. And these problems did not just appear overnight. These are things that have developed over years. Most of the **sentences** in this country
30 are relatively short. The **window of opportunity** that we have to make a change is very small, so we need to start from day one. Our strategy is to cover the whole range of problems, not just the one problem."

Unlike England and Wales, where since 2004 anyone **convicted** by the courts is categorised as an offender, the implication in the Swedish model is that
35 sentenced individuals are still primarily regarded as people with needs, to be assisted and helped. As well as having rehabilitation at the heart of its penal policy, the other huge difference between the Swedish and UK approaches is the role of politicians.

Chris Grayling, the justice secretary, has recently introduced **measures** that
amount to "a **ramped-up** political emphasis on punishment rather than real
rehabilitation" in prison regimes, according to Juliet Lyon, director of the
Prison Reform Trust. These include forcing prisoners to wear uniform,
banning books being sent to prisoners, and turning off cell lights at 10:30 p.m.
in young offender institutions.

Öberg says: "A politician who tried something like that in Sweden would be
thrown out of office. It would be a **breach of our constitution**—in our system
that is the forbidden area. When we exercise authority over individuals, a
politician cannot interfere with the administration process. In reality, there
is a dialogue—politicians will tell me and my colleagues what they expect

and we will do our best to achieve those goals. We have a very clear **division
of labour** between the government and public administration.

"An individual politician cannot **interfere with** the running of our business.
The government sets goals in a yearly letter of intent, and then the responsibility for the work is entirely ours."

But what about public opinion in Sweden? Is there less desire for **retribution**
than in the UK? "There is a lot of anger among the Swedish public when it
comes to crime and criminals," says Öberg. "But, regardless of what public
opinion may be at any one time, whatever you do in the justice sector, you
have to take a long-term perspective. You cannot try something one day and
then change it to something else the next day—that would be completely
useless. The system in our sector is set up to implement long-term strategies

and **stick to** them."

He adds, however, that the country's well-educated population appreciates
that almost all prisoners will return to society. "So when you go into a political
dialogue, there is a fair amount of understanding that the more we can do
during this small window of opportunity when people are deprived of their
liberty, the better it will be in the long run."

Is he hoping his Longford lecture will provide some helpful advice that may
assist the UK government with its prison difficulties, ranging from overcrowding,

staff shortages and a 69% increase last year in **self-inflicted death**?

"I'm very excited to be giving the lecture. But I will be very careful about
giving anybody any advice. We can try to share our experiences and perhaps
inspire each other a little bit, recognising that the preconditions for carrying
out our work are very, very different.

My ambition is to try to tell a story about how we have come to the conclusions
that we have, and explain why we have made the choices that we have made.
It has to do with whether you decide to use prison as your first option or as a
last resort, and what you want your probation system to achieve. Some people

have to be **incarcerated**, but it has to be a goal to get them back out into
society in better shape than they were when they came in."

James, E. (2014, November 26). Prison is not for punishment in Sweden. We get people into better
shape. *The Guardian*. Retrieved from http://www.theguardian.com/society/2014/nov/26/
prison-sweden-not-punishment-nils-oberg

TASK 4 DEFEND YOUR ARGUMENTS

1. Refer to your notes from Tasks 2 and 3. Select three main arguments that you feel strongly about (they may be arguments with which you agree or disagree), and write them below. Even if you are confident of your argument, back it up with at least one reason and one example from your existing knowledge.

Argument 1: _____

_____

Reasons: _____

_____

Examples: _____

_____

Argument 2: _____

_____

Reasons: _____

_____

Examples: _____

_____

Argument 3: _____

_____

Reasons: _____

_____

Examples: _____

_____

2. In groups of two or three, present your arguments, with the backup, to each other. Try to convince the others to agree with your point of view.

EFFECTIVE WRITING STYLE

SHIFTING STYLE

In the article above, the styles of language used by journalist Erwin James and interviewee Nils Öberg are different. As a journalist for the *Guardian*, a serious British newspaper, James's writing is characterized by formal language that would be appropriate for academic writing. In contrast, Öberg's language is more conversational, as would be expected in the context of an interview.

TASK 5 SHIFT STYLE FROM CONVERSATIONAL TO FORMAL

If you were to directly quote language from the Öberg interview excerpts in a formal academic writing task, you would not need to shift style because direct quotation requires you to use exactly the same words as the source. If, however, you decided to paraphrase the excerpts, you would need to shift style.

Below is a selection of quotations by Öberg; words and phrases in bold are more appropriate for conversational English. Rewrite each statement, changing the words and phrases in bold to a more formal style, suitable for academic writing.

1. The survey did not **bring up** any surprises.

   _____

2. These are **things** that have developed over years.

   _____

3. A politician who tried something like that in Sweden would be **thrown out of** office.

   _____

   _____

4. There is **a lot of** anger among the Swedish public **when it comes to** crime and criminals.

   _____

   _____

5. The system in our sector is **set up** to implement long-term strategies and **stick to** them.

   _____

   _____

6. So when you **go into** a political dialogue, . . .

   _____

7. We can try to share our experiences and perhaps inspire each other **a little bit**, recognising that the preconditions for **carrying out** our work are **very, very** different.

   _____

   _____

   _____

8. Some people have to be incarcerated, but it has to be a goal to **get them back out into** society in better shape than they were when they **came in**.

   _____

   _____

TASK 6 FIND EQUIVALENT PHRASAL VERBS

In spoken academic English—for example, in oral presentations—speakers often mix formal and less formal English. In such cases, they tend to use phrasal verbs more often than when writing. The excerpts below are from the James article. Imagine you are doing an oral presentation. To strike a balance between conversational and formal academic vocabulary, reword the excerpts, replacing each verb in bold with the equivalent phrasal verb.

1. They have **been deprived of** their freedom.

   _____

   _____

2. Since 2004, Swedish prisoner numbers have **fallen** from 5,722 to 4,500 out of a population of 9.5 million.

   _____

   _____

3. Last year a "national client survey" of several thousand Swedish prisoners was **undertaken** in order to **identify** the issues that have affected their criminal behaviour.

   _____

   _____

4. The implication in the Swedish model is that sentenced individuals are still primarily **regarded** as people with needs.

   _____

   _____

5. Chris Grayling, the justice secretary, has recently **introduced** measures that . . .

   _____

   _____

6. He adds, however, that the country's well-educated population appreciates that almost all prisoners will **return** to society.

   _____

   _____

7. Is he hoping his Longford lecture will provide some helpful advice that may **assist** the UK government with its prison difficulties?

   _____

   _____

DEVELOPING ARGUMENTS

The most important goal of writing effective paragraphs is to present convincing arguments to your reader.

Supporting Your Arguments

When you state arguments in your writing, show evidence of critical thinking as well as your knowledge of the broader scholarly debates around your topic as follows:

- Avoid presenting opinions as facts.
- Support your arguments with reasons, examples, and evidence.
- Consider counter-arguments and other positions in the scholarly debate.
- Bring in ideas from reliable sources.
- Shift from a starting opinion to a broader, informed position.

Avoid Presenting Opinions as Facts

The example below is an opinion presented as a fact.

> The role of prisons is to rehabilitate people, not just to punish them.

If you present opinions as facts, your arguments lack credibility. One way to avoid this is to use language that makes it clear to the reader this is your personal opinion, not a factual statement. Depending on the subject area and expectations of your reader, you can decide to use either personal or impersonal language for this purpose.

Personal Language

In my opinion,	
I believe that	the role of prisons is to rehabilitate people, not just to punish them.
My personal view is that	

Impersonal Language

It could be argued that	
It is evident that	the role of prisons is to rehabilitate people,
Clearly/Evidently/	not just to punish them.
Without doubt,	
The role of prisons is clearly/evidently/ undoubtedly	to rehabilitate people, not punish them.

With the additional language, it is now clear to the reader that this argument is an opinion, not a fact. However, as long as it remains unsupported, it may not be accepted as a convincing argument.

Support Your Arguments with Reasons, Examples, and Evidence

Add a reason to your argument so that your reader understands why you are taking this stance.

Add a Reason

> I believe that the role of prisons is to rehabilitate people, not just to punish them. This is because policies that promise to get tough on crime often focus on political and economic factors rather than on helping prisoners reintegrate into society after serving their sentences.

The argument is improved because the reader now has an idea of the writer's reason for taking this stance. However, the argument can be made even stronger by adding an example.

Add an Example

> For example, if a prisoner serves a 10-year sentence in a punishment-oriented environment and is released back into society without accommodation, a job, or training skills for employability, that offender is highly likely to reoffend after release and return to prison.

The argument is now more credible because the writer has provided a reason and given an example that relates to, and clarifies, the reasoning. To improve the argument even further, the writer can back up the example with reliable evidence.

Add Evidence

> In this regard, a study of post-prison recidivism in 2002 across France found that 59% of former convicts were reconvicted within five years of their release, and 80% of them were reincarcerated (Kensey & Benaouda, 2011, as cited in Monnery, 2015). With reference to stricter prison regimes and recidivism, Chen and Shapiro (2007) found that harsher prisons in the US "do not reduce post-release criminal behavior, and may even increase it" (p. 24).

With the addition of evidence to the reason and example, the argument becomes more credible and is more likely to convince the reader.

Consider Counter-Arguments and Evaluate Evidence

You can do more to strengthen your argument. First, consider counter-arguments, that is, ideas that those opposed to your stance would present.

Counter-Arguments

All arguments have counter-arguments. The following are two counter-arguments to the stance taken above—arguments that people with an opposing view might hold:

- The purpose of prisons should be to punish offenders, not to rehabilitate them.
- Taxpayers should not have to pay for expensive rehabilitation programs in prisons.

If you consider counter-arguments, you show your reader that you are aware of the position of your own argument within a broader scholarly debate and that you are able to consider the issue from multiple perspectives.

Evaluate the Evidence

You should also critically evaluate the evidence you have brought in to support your argument, and recognize any possible weaknesses or inconsistencies. The first evidence cited seems factual and reliable. The authors of the second study mentioned (Chen and Shapiro) are suggesting that stricter prison regimes do not reduce post-release criminality and that they may even make the situation worse. In each case, many factors could be related to reoffending, such as socio-economic status, gender, level of education, living conditions, family support, mental illness, and addiction. Moreover, the relevance of studies from France and the US to the writer's context should be considered.

Include what you see as main counter-arguments and a critical evaluation of the statistics before moving on to a closing argument:

> Opponents of rehabilitation-focused detention may call into question such statistics and would argue that taxpayers should not have to pay for expensive rehabilitation programs in prisons. Admittedly, behind these statistics lies a range of factors that relate to post-release criminal behaviour, including socio-economic status, gender, level of education, living conditions, family support, mental illness, and addiction. The relevance of statistics from studies in France and the US should also be considered with regard to Canadian prisons, where the contexts are different.

Present a Final Position

A closing argument is a repositioning of the original argument in light of the stages below:

- Start with an argument.
- Back it up with reasons, examples, and evidence.
- Consider counter-arguments.
- Critically evaluate the evidence.
- End with a final position.

Your final position shows in-depth understanding of your argument, consideration of other perspectives, and critical evaluation. It should offer the reader a more developed, contextualized adaptation of the initial argument. With a final position added, the entire text of the above argument would be as follows:

Initial argument
Reason

Example

I believe that the role of prisons is to rehabilitate people, not just to punish them. This is because policies that promise to get tough on crime often focus on political and economic factors rather than on helping prisoners reintegrate into society after serving their sentences. For example, if a prisoner serves a 10-year sentence in a punishment-oriented environment and is released back into society without accommodation, a job, or training skills for employability, that offender is highly likely to reoffend after release and return to prison.

Evidence	In this regard, a study of post-prison recidivism in 2002 across France found that 59% of former convicts were reconvicted within five years of their release, and 80% of them were reincarcerated (Kensey & Benaouda, 2011, as cited in Monnery, 2015). With reference to stricter prison regimes and recidivism, Chen and Shapiro (2007) found that harsher prisons in the US "do not reduce post-release criminal behavior, and may even increase it" (p. 24). Opponents of
Counter-arguments	rehabilitation-focused detention may call into question such statistics and would argue that taxpayers should not have to pay for expensive rehabilitation programs in prisons. Admittedly, behind these statistics lies a range of factors
Critical evaluation	that relate to post-release criminal behaviour, including socio-economic status, gender, level of education, living conditions, family support, mental illness, and addiction. The relevance of statistics from studies in France and the US should also be considered with regard to Canadian prisons, where the contexts are
Final position	different. Recidivism rates are clearly too high in many countries around the world. Although many social reasons outside the prison context may affect reoffending rates, I believe that a greater emphasis on rehabilitation through education, counselling, and employment training will enable some, but not all, ex-convicts to integrate more effectively back into society upon release.

References

Chen, M., & Shapiro, J. (2007). Do harsher prison conditions reduce recidivism? A discontinuity-based approach. *American Law and Economics Review, 9*(1), 1–29. Retrieved from http://www.jstor.org.proxy.lib.sfu.ca/stable/42705508

Monnery, B. (2015). The determinants of recidivism among ex-prisoners: A survival analysis on French data. *European Journal of Law and Economics, 39*(1), 37–56.

TASK 7 SHIFT FROM AN INITIAL ARGUMENT TO A FINAL POSITION

First, read the example below. Then read initial arguments 1 and 2 that follow and go through the stages to develop a final position. For this task, you do not need to find evidence to support your arguments.

Initial argument: Poverty is the main cause of crime. To make societies safer, governments should give poor communities more money to address this root cause of crime.

Add a reason: The crime rate in poor neighbourhoods is higher because poor people are more likely to be unemployed, and unemployed people are more likely to commit crimes.

Add an example: A typical example would be a young person living in a poor neighbourhood, surrounded by gang and drug culture, with few work or educational opportunities. If this young person has dropped out of school and sees no opportunities to progress economically through legal means, it is quite possible that he or she will resort to illegal means of making money.

Consider counter-arguments: Opponents might argue that poverty is a factor in crime, but not the causal factor. There are many people living in poverty in the world today, with little access to quality education and jobs. Most of them do not resort to crime to better themselves. From this perspective, responsibility lies with the individual, not in social conditions such as poverty.

Final position: Few would dispute the fact that crime is related to poverty. The question, then, is whether poverty causes crime. I would argue that there is a clear cycle of poverty and crime since this cycle is rarely seen in richer neighbourhoods. I therefore believe poverty is the key underlying causal factor in crime. Responsibility lies with government *and* the individual to break this vicious circle.

1. **Initial argument:** Sentencing juveniles to life imprisonment without parole is never justifiable.

   Add a reason in favour of the statement: Those opposed to life imprisonment without parole for juveniles convicted of the most serious crimes would argue that _____

   _____

   _____

   Add an example: For example, _____

   _____

   _____

   _____

   Consider counter-arguments: However, people who support life imprisonment without parole for violent juvenile offenders would disagree, arguing that _____

   _____

   _____

   _____

   _____

   Final position: _____

   _____

   _____

   _____

   _____

2. **Initial argument:** Mandatory sentencing requires judges to impose minimum sentences for certain crimes. It is wrong because it takes away the judge's discretion. The final decision on a sentence should always lie with a judge.

   Add a reason in favour of the statement: Those opposed to mandatory sentencing would argue that _____

   _____

   _____

Add an example: For example, _____

_____

_____

_____

Consider counter-arguments: However, people who support mandatory sentencing may counter that _____

_____

_____

_____

_____

Final position: _____

_____

_____

_____

_____

LANGUAGE OF OPINION

To develop arguments in academic writing, you need to be able to express your opinion, agree, and disagree, using personal or impersonal language. Your choice of form to use will depend primarily on common practice in your subject area. Another important issue for consideration is correct usage. While some phrases may have more or less the same meaning, they may be used with different grammatical structures. Some phrases can be followed by more than one structure, while others cannot. Compare the following examples of personal and impersonal language, and note the accompanying structures.

Personal Language

Examples		Structure
Expressing Your Opinion in General		
I believe (that) **I think (that)** **In my opinion,** **I would argue/claim/maintain/ suggest that**	the purpose of prison should be rehabilitation.	Independent clause
I believe in **I favour / am in favour of**	rehabilitation in prisons / the rehabilitation of prisoners / rehabilitating prisoners.	Noun phrase / gerund

A gerund is a verb + *ing* that functions as a noun in a sentence, for example, "I am in favour of *recycling*."

Examples		Structure
Agreeing		
I agree (that) **I support the view that** **I concur with the view that**	the purpose of prison should be rehabilitation.	Independent clause
I support	rehabilitation in prisons / the rehabilitation of prisoners / rehabilitating prisoners.	Noun phrase / gerund
Disagreeing		
I disagree (that) **I disagree with the view that** **I challenge/contest the view that**	the purpose of prison should be rehabilitation.	Independent clause
I am against **I oppose / am opposed to**	rehabilitation in prisons / the rehabilitation of prisoners / rehabilitating prisoners.	Noun phrase / gerund

Impersonal Language

Examples		Structure
Expressing Your Opinion in General		
It is evident/clear/obvious that **There is no/little doubt that** **Few would argue with the view that**	the purpose of prison should be rehabilitation.	Independent clause
Clearly / Obviously / Undoubtedly / Without doubt,	the purpose of prison is rehabilitation.	Independent clause
Few would argue against	rehabilitation in prisons / the rehabilitation of prisoners / rehabilitating prisoners.	Noun phrase / gerund
The purpose of prison is **clearly / obviously / undoubtedly / without doubt** rehabilitation.		Independent clause
Agreeing		
The view that prisons are for rehabilitation **should be supported**.		Passive-voice sentence
The view that prisons are for rehabilitation **is correct**.		*Be* + adjective
Disagreeing		
Rehabilitation in prisons / The rehabilitation of prisoners / Rehabilitating prisoners **should be opposed/challenged/contested**. **The view that** prisons are for rehabilitation **should not be supported**.		Passive-voice sentence
The view that prisons are for rehabilitation **is questionable / not correct**.		*Be* + adjective

TASK 8 COMPLETE PARAGRAPHS OF OPINION

Use the selected phrases of opinion, agreement, and disagreement to fill in the blanks in the paragraphs below. The phrases you use should match the grammatical structure. They should also match the overall opinion of the writer, who is in favour of prisons promoting rehabilitation without being too comfortable for inmates.

1. **Personal language:**

- am in favour of
- challenge the view that
- clearly
- few would argue with the view that
- should not, in my opinion, be

There is _____ divided opinion on whether prisons are for rehabilitation or punishment. Although I _____ the rehabilitation of prisoners, I _____ prison life should be comfortable and relaxing for all inmates. _____ many criminals need to be punished and that society needs to be protected from violent offenders. In sum, prisons _____ totally rehabilitation-oriented.

2. **Impersonal language:**

- should be supported
- should not be
- the view that . . . is questionable
- there is little doubt that
- without doubt

There is _____ divided opinion on whether prisons are for rehabilitation or punishment. The rehabilitation of prisoners _____ _____; however, _____ prison life should be comfortable and relaxing for all inmates _____. _____ many criminals need to be punished and that society needs to be protected from violent offenders. In sum, prison _____ totally rehabilitation-oriented.

EXTEND YOUR ACADEMIC VOCABULARY

Extend your knowledge of key vocabulary from this chapter.

believe	contest	oppose
challenge	**evident**	question
concur	favour	suggest

*Words in bold type are AWL entries.

My eLab

Practise Chapter 5 vocabulary online.

LOGICAL FALLACIES

A logical fallacy is a claim that is not logical and that weakens or nullifies the argument. Logical fallacies show a lack of critical thinking and should be avoided. There are many different kinds of logical fallacies; in this book, you will study four:

- misrepresentations of causal relations
- incorrect generalizations
- misrepresentations of others' opinions and actions
- other fallacies based on weak reasoning

Learning to recognize logical fallacies in the texts you read and to avoid them in your writing will make your arguments more convincing.

Logical Fallacies of Cause and Effect

Below are four examples of logical fallacies based on misrepresentations of causal relations.

a) **Post hoc fallacy:** The post hoc fallacy misrepresents chronological sequence as causality. In other words, it is based on an assumption that because *a* occurred before *b*, *a* caused *b* to happen. Accordingly, other causal factors are not considered.

b) **Slippery slope:** The slippery slope fallacy is a specific kind of post hoc fallacy. It is based on the assumption that if one thing *a* (often bad) happens, it will inevitably lead to a series of even worse things *x*, *y*, and *z*.

c) **Single cause:** The single cause fallacy, also known as *causal reductionism*, involves attributing the effect of something to one single cause *a* when multiple other causes *x*, *y*, and *z* are also at work.

d) **Wrong direction:** The wrong direction fallacy confuses cause and effect by identifying the cause as the effect, and the effect as the cause.

TASK 9 IDENTIFY LOGICAL FALLACIES

Read the following statements that exemplify logical fallacies of cause and effect. Then match them to the descriptions you have just read. Write the corresponding letter next to the statement.

		Description
1	Newly released prisoners will reoffend within six months if they cannot find work.	
2	We have to get tough on plagiarism! If we don't punish students who plagiarize, they will go on to cheat when they take other courses and in their future careers.	
3	The inability to use numbers causes dementia later in life.	
4	The new prisoner rehabilitation workshop was a resounding success, and it led to a 50% reduction in post-release reoffending.	

TASK 10 ANALYZE WAYS TO AVOID LOGICAL FALLACIES

In the article about Sweden's prison system, both the author, Erwin James, and the interviewee, Nils Öberg, use careful language to avoid expressing logical fallacies based on cause and effect. They do this as a rhetorical strategy to make their arguments more convincing.

Analyze the following two excerpts from the article, underlining language that is used to avoid any of the four logical fallacies you have just studied. Then write which logical fallacy you think Öberg is avoiding, and why.

1. With reoffending rates at about 40% . . . does he attribute this success to the country's effective policies on prisoner rehabilitation? "We obviously believe that it is part of the explanation; we hope we are doing something right. But it's going to be very difficult to prove that scientifically. We are increasing our efforts all the time," he says. [LINES 16–21]

    _____

    _____

    _____

2. Last year a "national client survey" of several thousand Swedish prisoners was undertaken in order to identify the issues that have affected their criminal behaviour. "The survey did not bring up any surprises, but it gave us confirmation of what we have learned from experience—that it is not one problem that our clients face, but two or more, sometimes as many as seven or eight different ones, including perhaps drugs, alcohol and psychiatric problems. And these problems did not just appear overnight. . . . Our strategy is to cover the whole range of problems, not just the one problem." [LINES 22–32]

    _____

    _____

TASK 11 READ CRITICALLY

Answer the following questions about more excerpts from the article that show careful use of language to present convincing arguments.

1. Last year a "national client survey" of several thousand Swedish prisoners was undertaken in order to identify the issues that have affected their criminal behaviour. "The survey did not bring up any surprises, but it gave us confirmation of what we have learned from experience—that it is not one problem that our clients face, but two or more." [LINES 22–26]

    Question: Why do you think the journalist places quotation marks around the term *national client survey*?

    _____

    _____

    _____

    _____

2. Chris Grayling, the justice secretary, has recently introduced measures that amount to "a ramped-up political emphasis on punishment rather than real rehabilitation" in prison regimes, according to Juliet Lyon, director of the Prison Reform Trust. *These include forcing prisoners to wear uniform, banning books being sent to prisoners, and turning off cell lights at 10:30 p.m. in young offender institutions.* [LINES 39–44]

Question: How might the measures highlighted in italics relate to the logical fallacies you have studied?

_____

_____

_____

_____

3. But what about public opinion in Sweden? Is there less desire for retribution than in the UK? "There is a lot of anger among the Swedish public when it comes to crime and criminals," says Öberg. "But, regardless of what public opinion may be at any one time, whatever you do in the justice sector, you have to take a long-term perspective. You cannot try something one day and then change it to something else the next day—that would be completely useless. The system in our sector is set up to implement long-term strategies and stick to them." [LINES 55–62]

> Learn more about the ad populum fallacy in Chapter 7, p. 164.

Question: There is a logical fallacy called the *ad populum fallacy*, which involves stating that an argument should be accepted because it has popular support in society, without considering broader factors. Where does Öberg address this logical fallacy in the excerpt above, and do you agree with him?

_____

_____

_____

4. Is he hoping his Longford lecture will provide some helpful advice that may assist the UK government with its prison difficulties, ranging from overcrowding, staff shortages and a 69% increase last year in self-inflicted death?

"I'm very excited to be giving the lecture. But I will be very careful about giving anybody any advice. We can try to share our experiences and perhaps inspire each other a little bit, recognising that the preconditions for carrying out our work are very, very different." [LINES 68–74]

Question: Öberg recognizes that "the preconditions for carrying out our work are very, very different." How does this statement strengthen his final position?

Find supplementary reading, writing, and critical-thinking activities online.

_____

_____

_____

Munroe, R. (*n.d.*). Correlation [Web comic]. *xkcd.* Retrieved from https://xkcd.com/552/

TASK 12 INTERPRET HUMOUR ABOUT LOGICAL FALLACIES

The comics opposite refer to correlation and causality, which you studied in Chapter 2. Read the comics and answer the questions below. Then discuss your answers in pairs.

'Football has ruined money'

Best of Matt. (2016, March 31). *The Telegraph.* Retrieved from http://www.telegraph.co.uk/news/2016/03/31/best-of-matt/

1. Why does the student in the first comic say "Well, maybe" instead of "Yes, it did!" in the final frame? What is the humorous message?

_____

_____

_____

_____

2. How does the statement "Football has ruined money" relate to the logical fallacies you have studied? How is it humorous?

_____

_____

_____

_____

EFFECTIVE SENTENCE STRUCTURE

PUNCTUATION: COMMAS

See Unit 3, p. 336, in the Handbook for a definition of independent clauses.

Commas are used in sentences primarily for three reasons:

1. for adding extra, non-defining information to an independent clause (The information can be added before, inside, or after the independent clause.)
2. for coordination
3. for separating two or more adjectives or adverbs

The following example sentences are taken from the James article and exemplify these three uses of commas.

Adding Extra, Non-Defining Information to an Independent Clause

Before the Independent Clause

• An introductory phrase:

Since 2004, Swedish prisoner numbers have fallen from 5,722 to 4,500 out of a population of 9.5 million.

In contrast, the prison population in England and Wales is 85,000 out of a population of 57 million.

- An introductory dependent clause:

  Whatever you do in the justice sector, you have to take a long-term perspective.

  When we exercise authority over individuals, a politician cannot interfere with the administration process.

Within the Independent Clause

- A conjunctive adverb:

  He adds**, however,** that the country's well-educated population appreciates that almost all prisoners will return to society.

- A noun phrase:

  Chris Grayling, **the justice secretary,** has recently introduced measures that . . .

After the Independent Clause

- A noun phrase:

  Our strategy is to cover the whole range of problems**, not just the one problem**.

- A verb phrase:

  "We are increasing our efforts all the time**," he says**.

- A participle phrase:

  We can try to share our experiences and perhaps inspire each other a little bit**, recognising that the preconditions for carrying out our work are very, very different**.

No comma is required for defining information.

> A politician **who tried something like that in Sweden** would be thrown out of office.

Coordination

Before the "FANBOYS" Coordinators in Compound Sentences

Compound sentences are made up of two independent clauses joined by a coordinator (*for, and, nor, but, or, yet, so*).

- *and*

  The government sets goals in a yearly letter of intent**, and** then the responsibility for the work is entirely ours.

  Since 2004, Swedish prisoner numbers have fallen from 5,722 to 4,500 out of a population of 9.5 million, **and** last year four of the country's 56 prisons were closed and parts of other jails mothballed.

- *but*

  Some people have to be incarcerated**, but** it has to be a goal to get them back out into society in better shape than they were when they came in.

  The survey did not bring up any surprises, **but** it gave us confirmation of what we have learned from experience.

- *so*

  The window of opportunity that we have to make a change is very small**, so** we need to start from day one.

Between the Items in Lists of Three or More Things

> These include [1] <u>forcing prisoners to wear uniform</u>**,** [2] <u>banning books being sent to prisoners</u>**, and** [3] <u>turning off cell lights at 10:30 p.m. in young offender institutions</u>.

No comma is required when two things are joined by a coordinator.

> We have a very clear division of labour between the <u>government</u> **and** <u>public administration</u>.

No comma is required before the coordinator in lists of three or more things in British and other varieties of English.

> It is not one problem that our clients face, but two or more, sometimes as many as seven or eight different ones, including perhaps <u>drugs</u>, <u>alcohol</u> **and** <u>psychiatric problems</u>.

Here, the author did not use a comma before the coordinator, while in the previous example, he did. Either form is acceptable, but writers should avoid inconsistency.

Separating Adjectives or Adverbs

- Adjectives that belong to the same category (e.g., opinion, shape, colour) and come before the noun:

> Prisoners are now expected to live in a **harsher, more punitive** environment.

- Adverbs:

> We can try to share our experiences and perhaps inspire each other a little bit, recognising that the preconditions for carrying out our work are **very, very** different.

TASK 13 ADD COMMAS

The following are sentences about the James article, with the commas removed. Add commas where required. Then identify each comma according to its function: addition of non-defining information (ND), coordination (C), or separation of adjectives or adverbs (S).

Type of Comma

1. Journalist Erwin James interviewed Nils Öberg director-general of Sweden's prison and probation service.   _____

2. Öberg gave the Longford Lecture in London where he talked about Sweden's focus on rehabilitation in prisons.   _____

3. In recent years Sweden's prison population has fallen.   _____

4. However that of the UK which is becoming less focused on rehabilitation has increased.   _____

5. Regarding the causal effect of rehabilitation on reoffending Öberg accepts that it is difficult to prove scientifically.   _____

6. Swedish prisoners who were surveyed faced problems including drug addiction alcohol dependence and mental illness.   _____

Do the section on commas in Unit 5 of the Handbook, pp. 349–353.

7. In Sweden the government minister states its annual goals in a letter and the prison authorities are responsible for implementing the policies. _____

8. Öberg promotes a supportive educational focus in prisons. _____

▮ WRITE, REVISE, AND EDIT ▮

PARAGRAPHS OF OPINION

TASK 14 WRITE TWO PARAGRAPHS

Write two paragraphs about rehabilitation versus punishment in prisons. Refer back to the exploratory writing you did for Task 2 and the notes you took about the newspaper article for Task 3.

In the first paragraph, present the arguments that supporters of a rehabilitation approach would use. In the second paragraph, write about arguments that would be put forward by people in favour of punishment.

In each paragraph, include your personal opinion and end with a final position. Support your opinions with reasons and examples based on your personal knowledge and with what you have written and read in this chapter.

Checklist for Revising and Editing

In groups of three, review each other's paragraphs for the following:

☐ Clear opinion: Are the writer's opinions easy to understand?

☐ Supporting reasons and examples: Does the writer support arguments with adequate and convincing reasons and examples?

☐ Shift from opinion to final position: Is there a development from the first opinion to the final position?

☐ Avoiding logical fallacies: Does the writer use language effectively to avoid logical fallacies?

☐ Use of commas: Are commas used correctly and consistently?

CHAPTER 6

PARAGRAPHS

> Words create sentences; sentences create paragraphs;
> sometimes paragraphs quicken and begin to breathe.
>
> Stephen King

Writing effective paragraphs is an essential skill for academic success. To convince your readers, your paragraphs should be well organized and should convey well-supported, coherent arguments that catch your readers' attention. As novelist Stephen King implies, good paragraphs can come alive for your readers and engage their minds.

In this chapter, you will:

- read excerpts from articles about fair trade and slow food
- learn six key aspects of effective paragraphs
- study APA and MLA in-text citation styles
- study linking words: conjunctive adverbs
- learn to avoid logical fallacies based on generalization
- study participle phrases
- rewrite and revise the two paragraphs you wrote in Chapter 5

TASK 1 EXPLORE THROUGH DISCUSSION

Do you support spending a little extra on products such as coffee and bananas to allow small-scale farmers in the developing world to receive a fair price for their products? Do you make an effort to buy locally produced food?

Take five minutes to discuss these questions in pairs.

PARAGRAPHS

Fair Trade and Slow Food

The paragraphs you will read in this chapter come from articles about fair trade and slow food, which are movements that promote ethical trade and farming practices in communities around the world.

Fair trade aims to support local farmers and their employees in developing countries by ensuring that farmers receive fair prices for their products, and their employees, fair wages. To do this, consumers pay more than the mass-market price for products such as coffee, chocolate, and bananas.

Slow food emerged as a movement in Italy in response to the spread of fast food. The slow food movement promotes ethical eating by supporting local producers, organic food production, and consumer awareness of food production methods, quality, and taste.

What Is a Paragraph?

A paragraph is a group of sentences with a focus on one topic. Although some definitions state that a paragraph can be formed by one sentence, single-sentence paragraphs are generally discouraged in academic writing.

Paragraphs are written in different ways depending on the subject area and text type. However, there are some important common features of good paragraphs that will help you get your ideas across effectively:

- topic sentences
- paragraph unity
- paragraph coherence
- paragraph cohesion
- concluding sentences
- support for arguments

Topic Sentences

Most paragraphs in academic English have a topic sentence, which guides readers by highlighting the main focus of the paragraph. A good topic sentence gives your reader an idea of the general topic of your essay or essay section, and of the specific focus of your paragraph.

Position in the Paragraph

It is common practice in academic English to begin paragraphs with a topic sentence. In this way, the reader knows from the outset what the paragraph will be about. This approach is a feature of writing *deductive paragraphs*. If you write paragraphs deductively, you begin each one by stating its specific focus in the topic sentence and then follow up with examples and discussion.

A less common way of writing paragraphs in academic English is to write *inductive paragraphs*, which begin with general discussion and examples and finish with the specific topic sentence. Generally speaking, most English-speaking instructors in "Western" higher education are more familiar with deductive paragraphs; some may respond negatively to student work that is written inductively.

TASK 2 IDENTIFY THE GENERAL TOPIC AND SPECIFIC FOCUS

Identify the general topic and specific focus in the topic sentences below. Highlight the general topic, and underline the specific focus.

> Another important factor in the debate on fair trade versus free trade is the effects on small farmers in developing countries.

1. It has been argued that fair trade benefits local producers in the following ways.

2. When it comes to people buying fair trade products, three key factors have been shown to determine consumer choice.

3. The role of intermediaries is perhaps the main problem in the chain from fair trade producer to supermarket consumer.

4. Fair trade farming as a development strategy has had particular success with some small-scale coffee producers in Nicaragua.

5. Many studies have shown, however, that the benefits of fair trade certification for local farmers are limited due to administrative costs.

TASK 3 COMPLETE TOPIC SENTENCES

The two paragraphs for this task are from a chapter in an academic text about the fairness of fair trade products. The topic sentences have been removed. First, read the title, which shows the general topic of the excerpt. Then read the paragraph and decide what the specific focus is. Finally, complete the topic sentences.

1.
Fairness of Fair Trade Product Markets

Perhaps the most likely motivation for fair trade products _____
_____
_____

To determine fair prices, Fairtrade International develops agreements with producer organizations, not individuals, and calculates the price minimum 'on the basis of production and broader reproduction costs', among other things (Wilkinson 2007, 222). By raising the price received by low-wage farmers, inequality is diminished somewhat and farmers will earn more and live better. Thus, fair trade products are fairer because they can ensure a higher price is paid to the commodity producers, which will in turn reduce the inequality. However, to determine if low wages and inequality are unfair, as discussed in the scenarios above, it makes sense to evaluate how the inequality arises.

2.

Fairness of Fair Trade Product Markets

Perhaps the best candidate for unfairness in international commodity markets is _____

_____

The supply chain for fair trade products is often described like an hourglass, in which many producers on one end supply many consumers on the other end, but the product must pass through the hands of a small number of wholesale intermediaries. In the coffee industry, for example, from the early 1990s, four transnational companies—Nestlé, Phillip Morris, Sara Lee and Procter & Gamble—accounted for more than 60 per cent of coffee sales in the major consuming markets. Among the coffee importing companies, five major ones, Neumann Gruppe, Volcafe, ED&F Man, Ecom Agroindustrial and Goldman Sachs controlled 40 per cent of the coffee market (Talbot 2004).

Excerpts from Suranovic, S. (2015). The meaning of fair trade. In L. T. Raynolds, & E. A. Bennett (Eds.), *Handbook of research on fair trade* (pp. 45–60). Cheltenham, UK: Edward Elgar.

Paragraph Unity

Achieving paragraph unity means that you keep to a single subject in your paragraph, that is, the specific topic highlighted in your topic sentence. If you wish to write about a new subject, you should start a new paragraph.

TASK 4 FIND LACK OF UNITY

In the two paragraphs below from an article about slow food, sentences have been added to break the paragraph unity. Read each paragraph and <u>underline</u> the intruding sentence(s).

1.

The Origin and Principles of Slow Food

One of the most well-known ethical food organizations in the world is Slow Food. Now a global phenomenon, Slow Food was born from the passion for food (and politics) by the inhabitants of a small town in Italy (Bra) (Petrini & Padovani, 2005) as a type of opposition to fast food culture and also to establish a relationship between nature, pleasure and tradition. Slow Food had its genesis in the creation in 1986 of the association called "Arcigola", which formed in reaction to the methanol crisis of that year and the perceived diffusion of fast foods in Italy. Its main promoter, the journalist Carlo Petrini, wanted to advance Italian quality wines and local simple dishes which he saw as being under threat. So-called Slow Food has been criticized as being far from slow in many cases, as restaurants and food producers take advantage of the movement for a quick profit. Petrini created two important food guides: "Osterie d'Italia" and "Vini d'Italia". The Slow Food organization was officially created in Paris in 1989.

2.

Introduction

Consumers in general understand that ethical food choices are good not just for society, but for themselves and their families (Context Marketing, 2010). The growing awareness of consumers has provoked an increase of the demand for ethical foods, resulting in demand in the organic and fair-trade market. In particular, the sector is estimated to account for 5%–10% of the total food and beverage trade globally (Sarkar, 2014). However, it has been argued that tourist locations have not done enough to attract the ethical food market. The UK, Western Europe, the USA and Canada have dominated the ethical food market for the last decade, accounting for 97% of organic and fair-trade sales. In emerging markets such as India and China, the growth of ethical food and drink sales is predicted to increase in the next few years (Clarke, 2012).

Excerpts from Viassone, M., & Grimmer, M. (2015). Ethical food as a differentiation factor for tourist destinations: The case of "Slow Food." *Journal of Investment and Management*, 4(1-1), 1–9. doi:10.11648/j.jim.s.2015040101.11

Paragraph Coherence

When you write paragraphs, it is important to write coherently. Coherence in paragraphs means that ideas are ordered in a logical way, not randomly. There are many ways to order ideas in paragraphs, including the following:

- Chronological: order your ideas according to a sequence in time.
- General to specific: begin with a broad idea and shift to narrower or more specific ideas and examples.
- Listing: present a concept, and then list examples.
- Multiple lenses: look at an issue from various angles, including pros and cons.
- Combined approach: combine two or more of the above approaches.

TASK 5 IDENTIFY COHERENCE STRATEGIES

Read the following paragraphs and identify which of the above coherence strategies have been used by the authors.

1.

Introduction

The political effectiveness of unfair trade allegations as a rhetorical device is bolstered by several factors. First, virtually everyone supports fairness; no one can reasonably argue that *unfair* policies are acceptable and so there is never opposition to fairness in principle. Second, fairness is a multifaceted concept that can take on different meanings. This implies that a group of people, all in support of fairness, may actually be supporting different notions of fairness simultaneously. Third, most people instinctively and strongly respond to situations they interpret as unfair. For these reasons, if you can convince someone that something is unfair, then you may also convince them to support actions or policies that will protect against or eliminate the unfairness.

Excerpt from Suranovic, S. (2015). The meaning of fair trade. In L. T. Raynolds, & E. A. Bennett (Eds.), *Handbook of research on fair trade* (pp. 45–60). Cheltenham, UK: Edward Elgar.

Coherence strategy: _____

2.

Slow Food Revisited

Weismantel's (2004) "Society of the Quarter" feature about Slow Food, published in this journal, details the origin of the Slow Food movement, beginning with its founding in Italy in 1986 as a response to, and backlash against, the spread of U.S.-based fast food chains. Under the leadership of its charismatic founder and president, Carlo Petrini, Slow Food spread across Europe during the 1990s, focusing largely on gastronomy and local food traditions (Slow Food, n.d.). A U.S. chapter commenced in 2000. The Slow Food International website drew greater international attention to the movement with its 2001 launch, marking the beginning of a period of growth of the Slow Food movement and expansion of its mission. As Slow Food has gained members and chapters worldwide, its members have carried out a range of projects connecting food to environmental responsibility, cultural preservation, and gustatory enjoyment.

Excerpt from Page, J. R. (2012). Slow food revisited. *Journal of Agricultural & Food Information, 13*(1), 2–6. doi:10.1080/10496505.2012.639684

Coherence strategy: _____

3.

Mind the Fair Trade Gap

The most obvious problem is that this labelling scheme costs money. Flocert, a certification body set up by the Fairtrade Labelling Organization, charges farmer co-operatives €538 merely to apply for certification, plus an initial audit fee of €1,466 even for a small co-op. Cynics might suspect bureaucratic bloat but the costs may well be real. It cannot be cheap to check pay and conditions in some remote Peruvian coffee plantation. But every euro spent on certification is a euro that the farmer cannot spend on his family. And larger co-operatives from richer, better-connected countries are more likely to find it worthwhile to pay for certification. For this reason, economist and fair trade critic Ndongo Sylla says that fair trade benefits "the rich". That seems too strong; but it is certainly a challenge for the fair trade model to reach the poorest.

Excerpt from Harford, T. (2015, May 29). Mind the fair trade gap. *FT Magazine*. Retrieved from https://next.ft.com/content/fc9a2e14-03e1-11e5-a70f-00144feabdc0

Coherence strategy: _____

4.

Mind the Fair Trade Gap

In 2001, the world price of coffee sank to its lowest ebb for decades, threatening dreadful hardship for the often-poor farmers who grow the sainted berry. It was also around that time that fair trade coffee seemed to come of age, with a common certification mark launched in 2002, and the product becoming a familiar sight in supermarkets and coffee chains. The premise

of fair trade is that the disparity between poor coffee farmers and prosperous drinkers presents both a problem and an opportunity. The problem is that farmers often live a precarious existence: geographically isolated and growing a crop with a volatile price. The opportunity is that many western consumers care about the earnings and conditions of the people who grow their coffee, and have some money to spare if only it might reach those people.

Excerpt from Harford, T. (2015, May 29). Mind the fair trade gap. *FT Magazine*. Retrieved from https://next.ft.com/content/fc9a2e14-03e1-11e5-a70f-00144feabdc0

Coherence strategy: _____

_____

Paragraph Cohesion

Cohesion and coherence are closely linked. Writing cohesively means holding ideas and arguments together by using effective linking words that help the reader understand the relationships between ideas, and the transitions from one idea to the next. In Appendix 1, you will find a broad range of linking words, from coordinators (e.g., *and*, *but*, *so*) and subordinators (e.g., *although*, *unless*, *while*) to conjunctive adverbs (e.g., *however*, *therefore*, *moreover*) and linking words for enumerating (e.g., *first*, *second*, *third*).

TASK 6 COMPLETE PARAGRAPHS TO CREATE COHESION

In the following two paragraphs from the Suranovic article (see p. 128 for the full source), the linking words or phrases that give the text cohesion are missing. Without looking at the complete versions above, fill in the blanks with one of the words or phrases given (explanations on usage are in parentheses).

1. Use the following words and phrases:
   - first (enumerating)
   - for these reasons (describing effects or results)
   - second (enumerating)
   - third (enumerating)
   - this implies that (possible meaning of previous idea)

Introduction

The political effectiveness of unfair trade allegations as a rhetorical device is bolstered by several factors. _____, virtually everyone supports fairness; no one can reasonably argue that *unfair* policies are acceptable and so there is never opposition to fairness in principle. _____, fairness is a multifaceted concept that can take on different meanings. _____ a group of people, all in support of fairness, may actually be supporting different notions of fairness simultaneously. _____, most people instinctively and strongly respond to situations they interpret as unfair. _____, if you can convince someone that something is unfair, then you may also convince them to support actions or policies that will protect against or eliminate the unfairness.

2. Use the following words and phrases:
   - as discussed . . . above (restating an earlier statement)
   - by raising (showing how something that follows was done)
   - however (introducing contrast)
   - perhaps (tentatively introducing an idea)
   - thus (as a result)
   - to determine (showing the purpose of something that follows)
   - which will (giving extra information about a previous idea or argument)

Fairness of Fair Trade Product Markets

_____ the most likely motivation for fair trade products is the income inequalities that arise from the very low prices and wages paid to workers who produce the basic commodities. _____ fair prices, Fairtrade International develops agreements with producer organizations, not individuals, and calculates the price minimum 'on the basis of production and broader reproduction costs', among other things (Wilkinson 2007, 222). _____ the price received by low-wage farmers, inequality is diminished somewhat and farmers will earn more and live better. _____, fair trade products are fairer because they can ensure a higher price is paid to the commodity producers, _____ in turn reduce the inequality. _____, to determine if low wages and inequality are unfair, _____ in the scenarios _____, it makes sense to evaluate how the inequality arises.

Concluding Sentences

It is not necessary to write a concluding sentence for every paragraph, especially if your paragraphs end smoothly, that is, coherently and cohesively. However, if you find that some of your paragraphs are ending rather abruptly, it is a good idea to add a concluding sentence. You can write concluding sentences in many ways, including the following:

- Give a final opinion: end with a final opinion on the subject discussed in the paragraph.
- Present a final example: end with the final item in a list of examples.
- Provide a synthesis of ideas: end with a new idea that encompasses the overall focus of the paragraph.
- Provide a thematic transition to the next paragraph: end with a sentence containing keywords that relate to the focus of the next paragraph.

TASK 7 IDENTIFY TYPES OF CONCLUDING SENTENCES

In the paragraphs below, the concluding sentences are in italics. Identify the type of concluding sentence used in each paragraph.

1.

Perhaps the most likely motivation for fair trade products is the income inequalities that arise from the very low prices and wages paid to workers who produce the basic commodities. To determine fair prices, Fairtrade International develops agreements with producer organizations, not individuals, and calculates the price minimum 'on the basis of production and broader reproduction costs', among other things (Wilkinson 2007, 222). By raising the price received by low-wage farmers, inequality is diminished somewhat and farmers will earn more and live better. Thus, fair trade products are fairer because they can ensure a higher price is paid to the commodity producers, which will in turn reduce the inequality. **[a]** *However, to determine if low wages and inequality are unfair, as discussed in the scenarios above, it makes sense to evaluate how the inequality arises.*

Perhaps the best candidate for unfairness in international commodity markets is the concentration of market power among intermediaries (Nicholls and Opal 2005). The supply chain for fair trade products is often described like an hourglass, in which many producers on one end supply many consumers on the other end, but the product must pass through the hands of a small number of wholesale intermediaries. In the coffee industry, for example, from the early 1990s, four transnational companies—Nestlé, Phillip Morris, Sara Lee and Procter & Gamble—accounted for more than 60 per cent of coffee sales in the major consuming markets. **[b]** *Among the coffee importing companies, five major ones, Neumann Gruppe, Volcafe, ED&F Man, Ecom Agroindustrial and Goldman Sachs controlled 40 per cent of the coffee market (Talbot 2004).*

Excerpt from Suranovic, S. (2015). The meaning of fair trade. In L. T. Raynolds, & E. A. Bennett (Eds.), *Handbook of research on fair trade* (pp. 45–60). Cheltenham, UK: Edward Elgar.

a) Type of concluding sentence: _____

b) Type of concluding sentence: _____

2.

Food and diet trends come and go, but the Slow Food movement (http://slowfood.com) endures, gaining even greater traction throughout the world in the past decade. Slow Food's staying power may be a product of its mission to promote good, clean, and fair food for all, integrating an appreciation for the pleasure to be found in food's flavors and culture with a sense of environmental and social responsibility (Slow Food, n.d.). By drawing attention to the environmental and economic effects of food production, this mission helps to counter accusations of elitism lobbed toward an organization that, early on, was considered by critics to be merely a gourmet dining club (Andrews, 2008, p. 45). *By focusing on issues such as the working conditions of producers and healthy food access for the poor, Slow Food remains relevant and attracts new members during a global recession.*

Excerpt from Page, J. R. (2012). Slow food revisited. *Journal of Agricultural & Food Information, 13*(1), 2–6. doi:10.1080/10496505.2012.639684

Type of concluding sentence: _____

3.

Unlike a taxi driver or a waiter, you can't just tip the guy who grew your coffee. The fair trade answer to the conundrum is a labelling scheme: an inspector verifies that all is well on the farm, with good conditions and a higher price paid for coffee; this information is conveyed to consumers by way of a recognisable trademark, the most famous of which is the Fairtrade logo. It's an appealing idea—a voluntary scheme that helps people who want to help people. (Or rather, several voluntary schemes: there is more than one fair trade label, alongside diverse certification schemes such as Organic or Rainforest Alliance.) Who wouldn't want a better deal for farmers who are poor and work hard? **[a]** *But there are problems with the idea too.*

The most obvious problem is that this labelling scheme costs money. Flocert, a certification body set up by the Fairtrade Labelling Organization, charges farmer co-operatives €538 merely to apply for certification, plus an initial audit fee of €1,466 even for a small co-op. Cynics might suspect bureaucratic bloat but the costs may well be real. It cannot be cheap to check pay and conditions in some remote Peruvian coffee plantation. But every euro spent on certification is a euro that the farmer cannot spend on his family. And larger co-operatives from richer, better-connected countries are more likely to find it worthwhile to pay for certification. For this reason, economist and fair trade critic Ndongo Sylla says that fair trade benefits "the rich". **[b]** *That seems too strong; but it is certainly a challenge for the fair trade model to reach the poorest.*

Excerpt from Harford, T. (2015, May 29). Mind the fair trade gap. *FT Magazine.* Retrieved from https://next.ft.com/content/fc9a2e14-03e1-11e5-a70f-00144feabdc0

a) Type of concluding sentence: _____

b) Type of concluding sentence: _____

TASK 8 COMPLETE CONCLUDING SENTENCES

Complete the concluding sentence in each of the following paragraphs.

1. **a)** Write a thematic transition from the first to the second paragraph.

   b) Write a final opinion.

Slow Food

The Slow Food movement is not just about eating slowly; it also relates to good and clean food. Agrillo, Milano, Roveglia, and Scaffidi (2015) highlight two subjective factors in their definition of good food. The first is taste, which relates to the subjective senses of the individual; the second is what they refer to as good knowledge of local culture, environment, and history of communities and their culinary practices. The role of promoting these values falls to local organizations called *convivia*, established to educate people of all ages about "how food is produced and its production origins" and to instill "an appreciation of food culture and flavors" (Page, 2012, p. 3). *Clearly, the mission of slow food is to encourage lifestyles that promote good and clean food; however,*

_____

_____

Ethical eating is a concept that is key to the philosophy and practices of a slow food lifestyle, at home and while travelling. In their study of ethical food as a factor in tourists' choice of holiday destinations, Viassone and Grimmer (2015) provide a useful overview of the key ethical dimensions of slow food. The authors offer a description of ethical eating framed around supply and consumption. In this sense, it could be argued that consumers become the agents of change every time they make a food choice. This idea of ethical agency relates to everyday interactions with food and the food industry. An example is the shopper who faces the decision to buy either a cheap mass-produced, ready-made meal for microwaving or fresh local ingredients to cook the same meal from scratch. *The slow food choice must be, without doubt,*

_____

References

Agrillo, C., Milano, S., Roveglia, P., & Scaffidi, C. (2015, December). *Slow food's contribution to the debate on the sustainability of the food system.* Paper presented at the 148th Seminar of the European Association of Agricultural Economists (No. 229276), The Hague, The Netherlands.

Page, J. R. (2012). Slow food revisited. *Journal of Agricultural & Food Information, 13*(1), 2–6. doi:10.1080/10496505.2012.639684

Viassone, M., & Grimmer, M. (2015). Ethical food as a differentiation factor for tourist destinations: The case of "Slow Food." *Journal of Investment and Management, 4*(1-1), 1–9. doi:10.11648/j.jim.s.2015040101.11

2. Write a synthesis of ideas.

Fair Trade

Many fair trade producers face problems and disincentives that limit their productivity and profitability. It has been suggested that the most unfair aspect of fair trade may be the amount of power that intermediaries have in the route from farm to consumer (Suranovic, 2015). Suranovic provides the helpful image of an hourglass, "in which many producers on one end supply many consumers on the other end, but the product must pass through the hands of a small number of wholesale intermediaries" (p. 54). Moreover, the author points to government and agencies regulating fair trade as another bottleneck in the flow between producer and consumer. According to Harford (2015), labelling is also a major problem for many farmers due to cost. In his *Financial Times* article on fair trade becoming a victim of its own success, Harford explains that the Fairtrade Labelling charges are €538 for the application fee in addition to initial auditing fees of €1,466. *It is evident that* _____

_____

References

Harford, T. (2015, May 29). Mind the fair trade gap. *FT Magazine*. Retrieved from https://next.ft.com/content/fc9a2e14-03e1-11e5-a70f-00144feabdc0

Suranovic, S. (2015). The meaning of fair trade. In L. T. Raynolds, & E. A. Bennett (Eds.), *Handbook of research on fair trade* (pp. 45–60). Cheltenham, UK: Edward Elgar.

Support for Arguments

In Chapter 5, you studied the importance of backing up arguments with reasons, examples, and evidence. Support for arguments is an important focus when you read and write paragraphs. When you critically engage with other writers' paragraphs, evaluate the effectiveness of their supporting ideas and evidence. When you write your own paragraphs, remember that your reader will engage critically with your writing in the same way.

The supporting reasons and examples you provide will allow your reader to understand how and why you construct a particular argument. However, it is equally, if not more, important to bring in evidence (e.g., arguments and statistics) from experts in the field, using an appropriate citation style such as APA or MLA. In this way, you can position your argument in the broader scholarly community and write more convincingly.

In the excerpts you have read in this chapter, the authors bring in supporting evidence in different ways, for different purposes, and with different citation techniques. In the following activities, you will analyze these techniques.

APA AND MLA IN-TEXT CITATION STYLES

In Chapter 4, you studied how to write APA and MLA reference list entries for a journal article and a page on a website. In this chapter, the focus is on APA and MLA in-text citations. Full information on APA and MLA citation styles can be found in Appendices 2 and 3.

To avoid plagiarism, in-text citations should be included any time you paraphrase or directly quote others' ideas, statistics, or creative works. Each in-text citation should correspond directly with a full entry at the end of the essay in the References (APA) or Works Cited (MLA). In-text citations may be positioned before or after the information cited. The formats for APA and MLA are different.

APA Format

In-text citations are most commonly positioned in two ways in APA format:

- before the information being cited, which places emphasis on the author
- after the information being cited, which places emphasis on the information

Consider the following examples:

1. **Suranovic (2015) suggests** that the most unfair aspect of fair trade may be the amount of power that intermediaries have in the route from farm to consumer.

2. **According to Suranovic (2015), / It is suggested by Suranovic (2015) that** the most unfair aspect of fair trade may be the amount of power that intermediaries have in the route from farm to consumer.

3. **Suranovic (2015) suggests** that the most unfair aspect of fair trade may be the amount of power that intermediaries have because "the product must pass through the hands of a small number of wholesale intermediaries" **(p. 54)**.

See Chapter 4, p. 91, for examples of reporting verbs used in citation phrases.

In example 1, the in-text citation is placed before the information being cited. The author's surname, *Suranovic*, is followed by the year of publication in parentheses and the reporting verb *suggests*. The author's surname functions as the subject of the verb. When you cite in this way, you emphasize the author more than the information.

In example 2, the citation phrases also include the author's surname and the year of publication. As in example 1, there is more emphasis on the author than on the information because the citation phrase precedes the information.

Example 3 contains a direct quotation, which is incorporated grammatically in the sentence and set off with double quotation marks. For direct quotations, you must place the page number(s) in parentheses after the quotation (as above), followed by a period if the quotation comes at the end of the sentence.

Now consider the following example:

It has been suggested that the most unfair aspect of fair trade may be the amount of power that intermediaries have in the route from farm to consumer **(Suranovic, 2015)**.

In this example, the in-text citation is placed in parentheses after the information cited. The author's surname is followed by a comma and the year of publication. When you cite in this way, you emphasize the information more than the author.

MLA Format

In-text citations are positioned similarly in MLA format:

- before the information being cited, which places emphasis on the author
- after the information being cited, which places emphasis on the information

Consider the following examples:

1. **Suranovic suggests** that the most unfair aspect of fair trade may be the amount of power that intermediaries have in the route from farm to consumer **(54)**.

2. **According to Suranovic, / It is suggested by Suranovic that** the most unfair aspect of fair trade may be the amount of power that intermediaries have in the route from farm to consumer **(54)**.

3. **Suranovic suggests** that the most unfair aspect of fair trade may be the amount of power that intermediaries have because "the product must pass through the hands of a small number of wholesale intermediaries" **(54)**.

In example 1, the in-text citation is placed before the information being cited. The author's surname is the subject of the reporting verb *suggests*. The page number is positioned after the cited information. When you cite in this way, you emphasize the author more than the information. Note that MLA in-text citations do not require publication dates.

In example 2, the citation phrases include the author's surname. As in example 1, there is more emphasis on the author than on the information.

Example 3 contains a direct quotation, which is incorporated grammatically in the sentence and set off with double quotation marks. For direct quotations, you must place the page number(s) in parentheses after the quotation, followed by a period if the quotation comes at the end of the sentence.

Now consider the following example:

> It has been suggested that the most unfair aspect of fair trade may be the amount of power that intermediaries have in the route from farm to consumer **(Suranovic 54)**.

In this example, the in-text citation is placed in parentheses after the information cited. The author's surname is followed by the page where the information can be found. There is no comma separating the author and page, and no year. When you cite in this way, you emphasize the information more than the author.

TASK 9 ANSWER QUESTIONS ABOUT CITATION PRACTICES

The following are excerpts from the model paragraphs in Task 8. Answer the questions that follow each excerpt.

1. **Agrillo, Milano, Roveglia, and Scaffidi (2015) highlight** two subjective factors in their definition of good food. The first is taste, which relates to the subjective senses of the individual; the second is what they refer to as good knowledge of local culture, environment, and history of communities and their culinary practices. The role of promoting these values falls to local organizations called *convivia*, established to educate people of all ages about **"how food is produced and its production origins"** and to instill **"an appreciation of food culture and flavors" (Page, 2012, p. 3)**.

a) In the first citation, of Agrillo et al.'s work, which is given more emphasis: the authors or the information?

_____

b) In the quotation from Page's work, why are the surname, year, and page number included in parentheses?

_____

_____

2. Clearly, the mission of slow food is to encourage lifestyles that promote good and clean food; however, slow food living also promotes food that is fair **(Page, 2012)**, which has clear ethical implications.

Why is the citation *(Page, 2012)* not placed at the end of the sentence?

_____

_____

_____

_____

3. In their study of ethical food as a factor in tourists' choice of holiday destinations, **Viassone and Grimmer (2015) provide** a useful overview of the key ethical dimensions of slow food.

Why is the citation phrase written with *provide* instead of *provides*?

_____

_____

4. It has been suggested that the most unfair aspect of fair trade may be the amount of power that intermediaries have in the route from farm to consumer **(Suranovic, 2015)**. **Suranovic provides** the helpful image of an hourglass, "in which many producers . . . supply many consumers . . ."

Why does the citation phrase in the second sentence, *Suranovic provides*, not include the year of publication?

_____

_____

5. **According to Harford (2015)**, labelling is also a major problem for many farmers due to cost. In his *Financial Times* article on fair trade becoming a victim of its own success, **Harford explains** that the Fairtrade Labelling charges are €538 for the application fee in addition to initial auditing fees of €1,466.

Why does the citation phrase in the second sentence, *Harford explains*, have no year or page number(s) in parentheses?

_____

_____

_____

TASK 10 CHANGE CITATIONS TO APA OR MLA FORMAT

The following excerpts are from the Suranovic article, "The Meaning of Fair Trade." The author uses a citation style known as Chicago, with different formatting from APA and MLA styles. Rewrite the sentences, using either APA or MLA format.

1. To determine fair prices, Fairtrade International develops agreements with producer organizations, not individuals, and calculates the price minimum **'on the basis of production and broader reproduction costs', among other things (Wilkinson 2007, 222).**

   _____

   _____

   _____

   _____

   _____

2. Perhaps the best candidate for unfairness in international commodity markets is the concentration of market power among the intermediaries **(Nicholls and Opal 2005)**.

   _____

   _____

   _____

3. Among the coffee importing companies, five major ones, Neumann Gruppe, Volcafe, ED&F Man, Ecom Agroindustrial and Goldman Sachs controlled 40 per cent of the coffee market **(Talbot 2004)**.

   _____

   _____

   _____

TASK 11 THINK CRITICALLY ABOUT CITATIONS

1. Reread the Suranovic excerpt in question 1 of Task 5 (pp. 129–130). There are no in-text citations in the paragraph. Is this acceptable? Why or why not?

   _____

   _____

2. Read the two excerpts below from Harford's *Financial Times* article, "Mind the Fair Trade Gap," in which the author cites statistics from the Fairtrade Labelling Organization and includes a direct quotation from fair trade critic Ndongo Sylla. Why are there no in-text citations in the excerpts? Does their absence constitute plagiarism?

   The most obvious problem is that this labelling scheme costs money. Flocert, a certification body set up by the Fairtrade Labelling Organization, charges farmer co-operatives €538 merely to apply for certification, plus an initial audit fee of €1,466 even for a small co-op. . . . For this reason, economist and fair trade critic Ndongo Sylla says that fair trade benefits "the rich". That seems too strong; but it is certainly a challenge for the fair trade model to reach the poorest.

_____

_____

_____

_____

CONJUNCTIVE ADVERBS

Conjunctive adverbs are used to join ideas and arguments in different clauses and sentences. An easy way to remember the functions of conjunctive adverbs is to think of them as different ways to express addition (as an alternative to *and*), contrast (as an alternative to *but*), or cause and effect (as an alternative to *so*).

Conjunctive adverbs can be positioned at the beginning of sentences, in the middle, or at the end. A full list and description of conjunctive adverbs can be found in Appendix 1.

TASK 12 IDENTIFY THE MEANING OF CONJUNCTIVE ADVERBS

Read the following excerpts from paragraphs in this chapter. Write whether the conjunctive adverbs in bold are used for addition, contrast, or cause and effect.

1. By raising the price received by low-wage farmers, inequality is diminished somewhat and farmers will earn more and live better. **Thus**, fair trade products are fairer because they can ensure a higher price is paid to the commodity producers, which will in turn reduce the inequality. **However**, to determine if low wages and inequality are unfair, as discussed in the scenarios above, it makes sense to evaluate how the inequality arises.

   Thus _____
   However _____

2. **Moreover**, the author points to government and agencies regulating fair trade as another bottleneck in the flow between producer and consumer.

   Moreover _____

TASK 13 SHIFT STYLE

In less formal writing styles, it is common to use coordinators such as *and*, *but*, and *so* instead of conjunctive adverbs. Rewrite the following sentences from paragraphs in this chapter by replacing the coordinators in bold with conjunctive adverbs. Refer to Appendix 1 to select appropriate conjunctive adverbs.

1. It cannot be cheap to check pay and conditions in some remote Peruvian coffee plantation. **But** every euro spent on certification is a euro that the farmer cannot spend on his family. **And** larger co-operatives from richer, better-connected countries are more likely to find it worthwhile to pay for certification.

    _____

    _____

    _____

2. The political effectiveness of unfair trade allegations as a rhetorical device is bolstered by several factors. First, virtually everyone supports fairness; no one can reasonably argue that _unfair_ policies are acceptable **and so** there is never opposition to fairness in principle.

    _____

    _____

    _____

EXTEND YOUR ACADEMIC VOCABULARY

Extend your knowledge of key vocabulary from this chapter.

arise	key	multifaceted
bolster	mark	**phenomenon**
ebb	mere(ly)	provoke

*Words in bold type are AWL entries.

My eLab

Practise Chapter 6 vocabulary online.

CRITICAL THINKING

LOGICAL FALLACIES

Logical Fallacies Based on Generalization

Generalization means making a statement and attributing it to all members of a group. In academic writing, this type of generalization is acceptable as long as the writer provides convincing statistical evidence to show that the statement is reliable. Without such supporting evidence, generalizations may be read as logical fallacies.

Below are three related examples of logical fallacies based on incorrect generalization.

a) **Generalization without evidence:** This type of generalization involves making a statement about all members of a group of things or people without evidence, as if the statement were a fact. This is a mistake of logic.

b) **Hasty generalization:** The "hasty generalization" fallacy occurs when someone reaches a conclusion prematurely, without enough evidence. The speaker or writer typically reacts to something he or she has observed, or to limited evidence, and quickly draws a conclusion, without considering broader evidence.

c) **Stereotype:** A stereotype fallacy is a specific kind of generalization about all members of a group of people. Such statements are judgmental, unrepresentative, and unsupported by evidence.

TASK 14 IDENTIFY LOGICAL FALLACIES

Read the following statements that exemplify logical fallacies of generalization. Then match them to the descriptions you have just read. Write the corresponding letter next to the statement.

		Description
1	Men are no good at multitasking.	
2	I visited Vancouver in Canada last winter, and it didn't snow a single day. I told my friends in England that the winters in Canada aren't as cold as people make out.	
3	Smart phones today are built to last for only two years.	

TASK 15 ANALYZE WAYS TO AVOID LOGICAL FALLACIES

In the example paragraphs in this chapter, the authors write carefully to avoid making logical fallacies based on generalization. This makes their arguments and ideas more convincing to the reader.

Analyze the excerpts below, <u>underlining</u> language that is used to avoid any of the three logical fallacies you have just studied. Then write which logical fallacy you think the authors are avoiding, why, and whether they succeed.

1. From Suranovic, 2015: Perhaps the most likely motivation for fair trade products is the income inequalities that arise from the very low prices and wages paid to workers who produce the basic commodities.

   _____

   _____

   _____

2. From Viassone and Grimmer, 2015: One of the most well-known ethical food organizations in the world is Slow Food.

   _____

   _____

   _____

3. From Viassone and Grimmer, 2015: Consumers in general understand that ethical food choices are good not just for society, but for themselves and their families (Context Marketing, 2010).

   _____

   _____

   _____

4. From Harford, 2015: Cynics might suspect bureaucratic bloat but the costs may well be real.

_____

_____

_____

5. From Suranovic, 2015: First, virtually everyone supports fairness; no one can reasonably argue that *unfair* policies are acceptable and so there is never opposition to fairness in principle.

_____

_____

_____

6. From Suranovic, 2015: Third, most people instinctively and strongly respond to situations they interpret as unfair.

Find supplementary reading, writing, and critical-thinking activities online.

_____

_____

_____

EFFECTIVE SENTENCE STRUCTURE

PARTICIPLE PHRASES

Participle phrases (also called *participle clauses*) add to the information in independent clauses in the same way that relative clauses do. Participle phrases function as reduced relative clauses. In this sense, they add an economical style, as well as variety, to writing.

The following example from the Suranovic article illustrates how the relative clause (in italics) can be reduced to a participle phrase (in bold).

> Thus, fair trade products are fairer because they can ensure a higher price is paid to the commodity producers, *which will in turn reduce the inequality.*   (relative clause)

> Thus, fair trade products are fairer because they can ensure a higher price is paid to the commodity producers, in turn **reducing the inequality**.   (participle phrase)

Present and Past Participle Phrases

The difference between present and past participle phrases does not relate to time. Present participle phrases are used as an alternative for clauses in the active voice, and past participle phrases, as an alternative for clauses in the passive voice.

Present Participle Phrases

> Thus, fair trade products are fairer because they can ensure a higher price is paid to the commodity producers, in turn **reducing the inequality**.

Form: In the present participle phrase (in bold), the present participle is formed by adding *ing* to the verb *reduce*: *reducing*.

Concept: In this example, the present participle phrase means "which in turn reduces / will reduce the inequality."

Time idea: present or future

Corresponding active-voice clause: This reduces / will reduce the inequality.

Past Participle Phrases

The role of promoting these values falls to local organizations called *convivia*, **established to educate people of all ages about "how food is produced and its production origins."**

Form: In the past participle phrase (in bold), the past participle form of the verb is used: *established*.

Concept: In this example, the past participle phrase means "which were established to . . ."

Time idea: past

Corresponding passive-voice clause: They were established to . . .

TASK 16 IDENTIFY PARTICIPLE PHRASES

<u>Underline</u> the participle phrases in the following sentences from the example paragraphs in this chapter. Decide whether the participle phrase is replacing a clause in the active or passive voice and whether it contains a present or past participle. Then state the time idea.

1. In 2001, the world price of coffee sank to its lowest ebb for decades, threatening dreadful hardship for the often-poor farmers who grow the sainted berry.

   ☐ active voice ☐ passive voice ☐ present participle ☐ past participle

   Time idea: _____

2. Under the leadership of its charismatic founder and president, Carlo Petrini, Slow Food spread across Europe during the 1990s, focusing largely on gastronomy and local food traditions.

   ☐ active voice ☐ passive voice ☐ present participle ☐ past participle

   Time idea: _____

3. Flocert, a certification body set up by the Fairtrade Labelling Organization, charges farmer co-operatives €538 merely to apply for certification, plus an initial audit fee of €1,466 even for a small co-op.

   ☐ active voice ☐ passive voice ☐ present participle ☐ past participle

   Time idea: _____

4. The growing awareness of consumers has provoked an increase of the demand for ethical foods, resulting in demand in the organic and fair-trade market.

☐ active voice ☐ passive voice ☐ present participle ☐ past participle

Time idea: _____

TASK 17 WRITE PARTICIPLE PHRASES

The following sentences, from the example paragraphs in this chapter, contain relative clauses (in italics). Reduce the relative clauses by changing them to participle phrases. Decide whether the participle phrase is replacing a clause in the active or passive voice and whether it contains a present or past participle. Then state the time idea.

1. Perhaps the most likely motivation for fair trade products is the income inequalities *that arise from the very low prices and wages* paid to workers who produce the basic commodities.

_____

☐ active voice ☐ passive voice ☐ present participle ☐ past participle

Time idea: _____

2. Perhaps the most likely motivation for fair trade products is the income inequalities that arise from the very low prices and wages paid to workers *who produced the basic commodities.*

_____

☐ active voice ☐ passive voice ☐ present participle ☐ past participle

Time idea: _____

3. Slow Food had its genesis in the creation in 1986 of the association called "Arcigola", *which formed in reaction to the methanol crisis of that year and the perceived diffusion of fast foods in Italy.*

_____

☐ active voice ☐ passive voice ☐ present participle ☐ past participle

Time idea: _____

4. Slow Food had its genesis in the creation in 1986 of the association called "Arcigola", *which was formed in reaction to the methanol crisis of that year and the perceived diffusion of fast foods in Italy.*

Do Unit 6: Participle Phrases in the Handbook, pp. 358–363.

_____

☐ active voice ☐ passive voice ☐ present participle ☐ past participle

Time idea: _____

SEMICOLONS

Semicolons are used in the same way as periods to separate two independent clauses, especially when the clauses contain closely related ideas. The semicolon, sometimes followed by a conjunctive adverb, cues the reader that the next idea is related. Consider these examples from paragraphs in this chapter:

> First, virtually everyone supports fairness**;** no one can reasonably argue that *unfair* policies are acceptable.

> Clearly, the mission of slow food is to encourage lifestyles that promote good and clean food**; however**, slow food living also promotes food that is fair.

Normally, commas are used to separate three or more items in a list, as you saw in Chapter 5. However, if one or more of the items in the list contains a comma, then the items are separated by semicolons.

> The challenges facing the fair trade movement are as follows: expensive registration costs, which disadvantage poor farmers**;** excessive profits for intermediaries**;** and unstable product prices in world markets, which fluctuate regularly.

Do the section on semicolons in Unit 5 of the Handbook, pp. 354–357.

TASK 18 ADD SEMICOLONS

The following sentences are written without semicolons. Identify any places where commas or periods should be replaced with semicolons, and rewrite the sentences.

1. Journalist Tim Harford, writing for the *Financial Times*, describes how fair trade may have become the victim of its own success. He sees labelling costs as the major problem for small-scale farmers.

_____

_____

_____

2. Suranovic (2015) describes the power of intermediaries as the main example of unfairness in fair trade. The hourglass metaphor illustrates the unfair practices in the path from farm to supermarket.

_____

_____

_____

3. Possible solutions to this unfairness would include reducing the power of intermediaries, guaranteeing stable minimum prices for producers, and reducing registration costs for small-scale farmers.

_____

_____

_____

4. Possible solutions to this unfairness would include the following: reducing the power of intermediaries, who make large profits in the supply chain, guaranteeing stable minimum prices for producers who are suffering financial hardship, and reducing registration costs for small-scale farmers, which could lead to greater uptake from producers.

_____

_____

_____

_____

▬▬▬ REVISE AND EDIT ▬▬▬

PARAGRAPHS OF OPINION

In Chapter 5, you developed your notes and wrote two paragraphs about rehabilitation versus punishment in prisons: the arguments that supporters of a rehabilitation focus would use, and those often adopted by people in favour of punishment.

TASK 19 IMPROVE YOUR PARAGRAPHS

Analyze the paragraphs, and rewrite them according to the features of paragraph writing that you have studied in this chapter:

• topic sentences
• paragraph unity
• paragraph coherence
• paragraph cohesion
• concluding sentences
• support for arguments

Search for reliable sources to back up your arguments and opinions and include them in the paragraphs, using APA or MLA citation style.

Checklist for Revising and Editing

In pairs, review and edit each other's paragraphs for the following:

☐ key features studied in this chapter

☐ effective, grammatical incorporation of sources

☐ correct use of APA or MLA citation style

☐ correct punctuation, with particular attention to commas and semicolons

☐ well-formed relative clauses and participle phrases

CHAPTER 7

INTRODUCTIONS IN ACADEMIC WRITING

Introduction: a thing preliminary to something else, especially an explanatory section at the beginning of a book, report, or speech: *Your talk will need an introduction that states clearly what you are talking about and why.*

Oxford Dictionary

There is no single way to write an introduction in academic writing. Introductions are written differently depending on who your readers are, what kind of text you are writing, and why you are writing—your audience, genre, and purpose. Moreover, some shorter forms of writing—for example, response paragraphs—do not require introductions. Nonetheless, there are some common features of writing academic introductions; these features, and how different writers apply them, are the focus of this chapter.

In this chapter, you will:
- learn common features of writing introductions
- study different strategies for writing thesis statements
- read and analyze introductions from articles about international business leadership across cultures
- learn to avoid logical fallacies based on others' actions and ideas
- identify linking words and phrases in introductions
- review the passive voice and personal versus impersonal language
- write an introduction

TASK 1 EXPLORE THROUGH WRITING

Write an introduction to the two paragraphs on rehabilitation versus punishment in prisons that you have been working on in the last two chapters. Take 10 minutes. With a partner, read each other's writing and comment on how the information has been organized.

INTRODUCTIONS IN ACADEMIC WRITING

Most introductions in academic writing perform the following functions:

- provide general background information about the topic
- add specific information about the focus of the essay
- guide the reader by explaining how the essay will be organized
- give an indication of the writer's position on the topic

An Information Funnel: Shift from General to Specific

One of the most common features of introductions in many different types of academic writing is a shift from general to specific, as illustrated in Figure 1.

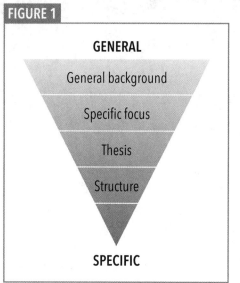

FIGURE 1

GENERAL

General background

Specific focus

Thesis

Structure

SPECIFIC

The introduction begins with general background information about the topic. It then shifts gradually by adding information of relevance to the specific focus of the essay. The introduction becomes more specific with a thesis statement, which presents the writer's main focus, purpose, or stance, followed by an explanation of how the essay is organized. Alternatively, some writers explain the organization of the essay before presenting the thesis statement.

Business Leadership across Cultures

In the academic fields of management, business, and leadership, there is a long tradition of research that looks at how local cultures interact with dominant international cultures. Due to the many effects of globalization, the local-global relationship in international business leadership has become more complex. As a result, a number of studies have aimed to challenge the dominance of Western business leadership practices in other parts of the world, for example, in Asia and Africa. The introductions in this chapter relate to this focus in the field.

Model Introduction on Business and Leadership across Cultures

Read the model introduction below.

Recent Perspectives on Business and Leadership across Cultures: The West, Asia, and Africa

[1] Today's globalizing world is characterized by changing time-space relations (Giddens, 1984), **neoliberalism**, mobility of people and resources, new technologies, and growing trading blocs. [2] In the contexts of global change, international business leaders face many challenges in their work, such as understanding local cultures, finding common goals across cultures, and carrying out successful transactions through partnerships. [3] Sophisticated strategies are especially required when leaders engage in contexts that bring together partners with

neoliberalism: free-market business model

different philosophical traditions and forms of knowledge making, for example, in business between Asia, Africa, and the West.

[4] Recent research has focused on different aspects of the business leadership **nexus** between China and the West: for example, how three leading Chinese philosophies—Daoism, Confucianism, and Legalism—can **complement** Western-influenced leadership in China (Ma & Tsui, 2015), and the need for Chinese approaches to **stem** the shift of Chinese leaders toward Western practices (Li, 2016). [5] Kim and Moon (2015) focus on leadership and Corporate Social Responsibility (CSR), comparing CSR in Asia (from Pakistan eastward to Japan) and Western CSR, while the determinants for success in business leadership and the role of women leaders in China, India, and Singapore are discussed in Peus, Braun, and Knipfer (2015). [6] A recent study has also highlighted the need to promote indigenous African forms of knowledge to meet the needs of the African workforce, addressing the growth in Asia-Africa relations (Kamoche, Siebers, Mamman, & Newenham-Kahindi, 2015).

[7] In this article, business leadership strategies for collaboration between Asia, Africa, and the West will be analyzed, focusing primarily on recent perspectives that have been brought into the field of international business leadership. [8] In the following sections, a brief history of international business leadership approaches will be presented, followed by an in-depth analysis of recent literature focusing on research between Asia, Africa, and the West, before a discussion and conclusions. [9] It will be argued that **binary** cross-cultural strategies are inadequate to promote successful relationships between leaders across cultures for two reasons. [10] First, the fluidity brought about by globalization means that the local-global/here-there view of leadership is no longer valid. [11] Second, the **hegemony** of Western business practices **skews** the two-way understanding of leadership practices in favour of the West, at the expense of local knowledge and practice, which may have a long-term negative effect on **sustainable** business success.

nexus: connection or relationship between two or more things

complement: go well with or improve

stem: counter or reduce the flow of something negative

binary: made up of two parts or opposites

hegemony: dominance (social, cultural, economic) of one thing over another

skews: distorts or changes so as to make inaccurate

sustainable: that can be maintained

TASK 2 ANALYZE THE TEXT

1. In the model introduction above, the writer shifts from general to specific. Identify the sentences that perform the following functions of introductions. Write the sentence number(s) next to the corresponding function.

		Sentence(s)
a)	Provide general background information	
b)	Begin a gradual shift from general to specific	
c)	Briefly review key literature	
d)	Transition to the specific focus of the essay	
e)	Describe the organizational structure of the essay	
f)	Provide a thesis statement	

2. In Chapter 2, and in Unit 2 of the Handbook, you studied how writers shift from general to specific by using general and specific noun phrases. Reread the first and last paragraphs of the model introduction, focusing on the noun phrases. Do they mirror the general-to-specific shift in the introduction? Explain your answer.

_____

_____

_____

WRITING INTRODUCTIONS

Six Stages of Writing an Introduction

The following is a breakdown of the six stages of writing an introduction as exemplified in the model introduction. Remember: the model serves to illustrate the common features of introductions in academic writing; it is not intended as a model to follow exactly for writing introductions in all subject areas. As you will see in this chapter, authors select and organize these stages of writing introductions quite differently.

Stage 1: Provide General Background Information

Sentence 1 provides general background information on the topic of the essay: recent perspectives on business and leadership across cultures in Asia, Africa, and the West. The sentence makes no specific reference to any of the keywords in the title of the essay; rather, it sets the scene or background context for the essay. The writer is also attempting to catch the interest of the reader by showing the breadth and global scope of the topic. Many writers skip this most general of sentences and begin with a more specific focus as in stage 2.

Stage 2: Begin a Gradual Shift from General to Specific

Sentences 2 and 3 provide a gradual shift to the specific focus of the essay. In sentence 2, the writer achieves this by introducing keywords from the title: *business*, *leaders*, and *cultures*. Sentence 3 goes on to mention the scope of the essay: Asia, Africa, and the West. It also introduces topics that will be addressed: strategies, philosophical traditions, and knowledge.

Stage 3: Briefly Review Key Literature

In sentences 4 to 6, the writer briefly reviews key texts of importance to the essay, using APA citation style (see Chapter 6, p. 137, and Appendix 2). The citations allow the writer to position the essay in a current body of scholarly literature. They are ordered to show existing research on leadership in Western-Chinese contexts, broader Asian contexts, and then African-Western-Asian contexts. This order reflects the essay title and may also reflect the order of the upcoming essay sections.

Stage 4: State the Specific Focus of the Essay

Sentence 7 marks the completion of the shift from general to specific by describing the specific focus of the essay, that is, recent perspectives on international business leadership in Asia, Africa, and the West.

Stage 5: Describe the Organizational Structure of the Essay

Sentence 8 gives an overview of the organizational structure of the essay: a brief history, detailed analysis, discussion, and then conclusions.

Stage 6: Provide a Thesis Statement

The thesis statement in an introduction may be made up of one or more sentences and can come before or after the description of the organizational structure of the essay. In the model introduction, the writer chooses to close with a three-sentence thesis statement: he presents an argument (binary approaches are inadequate) in sentence 9 and then expands briefly on the argument in the following two sentences by providing further explanation (binary approaches are inadequate due to globalization and Western dominance). The thesis statement makes the writer's opinion clear to the reader from the outset, but without diminishing the reader's need to continue reading to learn more.

Thesis Statements

Most introductions to academic writing include a type of thesis statement in which the writer presents a central idea (or ideas), purpose(s), or argument(s) to frame the text. The thesis statement is like the beginning of a thread of guiding concepts that will run through the writing.

The following are three common strategies for writing thesis statements. The examples given are written using personal and impersonal language, and active and passive voice, all of which you will review later in the chapter.

Present an Argument

> I will argue / It will be argued that traditional cross-cultural perspectives on business leadership are inadequate for fostering sustainable success in partnerships between Asia, Africa, and the West. (explicit)

If you have a clear and strong argument, you can let your readers know from the outset. The example above is a very direct, explicit way to guide your reader. Alternatively, you can present a more implicit argument in a thesis statement.

> In today's globalized world, fostering sustainable success in partnerships between Asia, Africa, and the West is highly complex, requiring multilayered strategies. (implicit)

Here, the writer states the same idea but in a less argumentative, direct manner. This style leaves the reader with more questions about the writer's overall position on the topic.

State Your Purpose or Goal

> In my analysis of business leadership strategies across Asia, Africa, and the West, I aim to contribute to the debate on promoting Asian and African philosophies in the international business world as a counterbalance to Western practices, thus giving more power and recognition to the values of local workforces.

Here, the writer is presenting more of a broad social goal than an opinion. By stating this in the introduction, the writer invites the reader to frame the upcoming discussion and analysis around this goal.

Ask Questions

> What, then, are the benefits of Western leadership models in Asian and African contexts? Do these models allow for alternative local perspectives that have long histories in local business contexts?

Some writers present questions in their introductions with the intention of answering the questions either through the discussion or at the end of the essay. One critique of this type of thesis statement is that it lacks stance: your reader receives no indication of your position on the topic.

The three strategies above are the most common methods for writing thesis statements. It is also common for writers to write a compound thesis statement, which combines aspects of two or more strategies, for example, a thesis statement that presents an opinion and a goal.

Some academic writing does not require a thesis statement. For example, a student may write an assignment on an experiment or lab work that simply requires a detailed description of the process. Alternatively, if an assignment on an experiment or lab work requires detailed analysis, the thesis statement would normally be presented as a hypothesis.

TASK 3 ANALYZE THE THESIS STATEMENT

Look back at the thesis statement in the model introduction (you identified it in Task 2). Which of the three strategies for writing thesis statements is or are employed?

_____

Different Ways of Introducing

As stated above, academic introductions are written differently due to a number of factors, including the following:

- the specific ways of writing in different subject areas (genre)
- the expectations and requirements of readers (audience)
- the reason for writing a text (purpose)
- the style and individual preference of the writer

The example introductions that you will analyze in the next section are all from articles in the field of international business leadership, yet there are notable differences in how the authors organize their information.

ACTIVE AND CRITICAL READING

The following introductions are taken from the articles cited in the model introduction. Read the title of each introduction to get an idea of the specific focus of the article. Next, read the complete text. Then answer the questions that follow to analyze the structure, content, and language of the text.

INTRODUCTION 1

Traditional Chinese Philosophies and Contemporary Leadership

by Li Ma and Anne S. Tsui

[1] Traditional philosophical and cultural roots influence the thought patterns and behaviors of all citizens in a community including its leaders (Parsons & Shils, 1951). [2] Hence, leadership practices would reflect unique cultural **idiosyncrasies** even though in a rapidly changing context, multiple forces could shape the behavior of its people. [3] For example, in China, it has been shown that leadership behaviors reveal cultural, political and economic influences (Fu & Tsui, 2003). [4] Due to global competition and Western education, many Chinese business leaders have adopted Western management practices (Tsui, Wang, Xin, Zhang, & Fu, 2004). [5] Though most scholarly studies of leadership in China have relied on Western leadership theories (Zhang, Chen, Chen, & Ang, 2014), there are also studies **invoking** the deep Chinese philosophical thoughts such as Confucianism or Daoism in explaining possible patterns of contemporary Chinese leadership behaviors (Fu, Tsui, Liu, & Li, 2010; Jing & Van de Ven, 2014). [6] Further, it has been documented that Chinese philosophies, especially Confucianism, greatly impact leaders in the **Chinese diaspora**, and have done so for many years (Chai & Rhee, 2010). [7] Clearly, traditional philosophies are still part of the **cultural fabric** in China today. [8] In this paper, we seek to understand the ideas underlying three major traditional Chinese philosophical **schools**—Daoism (also spelled *Taoism*), Confucianism, and Legalism—which have an explicit discourse on leadership. [9] We identify their parallels in the major leadership theories in the Western literature, and analyze, through published reports of interviews with fifteen successful Chinese business leaders, how current Chinese leadership practices may reflect these traditional philosophies.

[10] Our work **diverges** from most (cross-)cultural leadership analyses that often use culture as a **moderating variable** or contextual factor. [11] Instead we investigate culture's main effects by examining how the three traditional Chinese philosophies treat leadership. [12] Our choice of these three philosophies

idiosyncrasies: characteristic, individual ways of behaving

invoking: referring to (to gain support)

Chinese diaspora: Chinese people living outside their homeland

cultural fabric: basic cultural structure of a society

schools: groups of people/ philosophers/academics sharing common beliefs

diverges: moves in a different direction

moderating variable: factor that lessens an impact

contemporary: today or in recent times

core ideas: key ideas

propositions: points or concepts to consider for discussion

was influenced by a recent survey of traditional values in a sample of more than two thousand Chinese (Pan, Rowney, & Peterson, 2012). **[13]** The factor analysis results showed that Chinese people combine Buddhism and Daoism, probably because both are characterized by action avoidance. **[14]** In addition, they consider Confucianism, Legalism, and the Art of War as separate types. **[15]** While Daoism, Confucianism, and Legalism provide extensive discussion on managing people and leading the state, the Art of War focuses on competition such as in business strategy or marketing, and is thus less relevant to the purpose of the current paper. **[16]** Though relatively less known than Daoism and Confucianism, Legalism—with emphasis on rules, systems of rewards and punishment, and preservation of power—was a very important stream of traditional Chinese thinking. **[17]** It was a widely adopted practice in Chinese leadership for centuries and, as we will show, is still the major form of leadership practices in **contemporary** China.

[18] We first introduce the **core ideas** of the three traditional Chinese philosophical schools, focusing on content relevant to leadership. **[19]** We then link each school to current leadership theories and summarize our ideas in **propositions**. **[20]** We further aim to detect the influence of these traditional philosophical schools in the leadership practices of contemporary Chinese business leaders. **[21]** Drawing on articles that reported interviews of fifteen business leaders, we code their leadership behaviors according to the school they exemplify. **[22]** We use these fifteen cases to illustrate, rather than as a test of, the propositions. **[23]** Finally, we discuss how traditional culture could be a rich source of understanding for future leadership research in China and beyond.

Excerpt from Ma, L., & Tsui, A. S. (2015). Traditional Chinese philosophies and contemporary leadership. *The Leadership Quarterly, 26*(1), 13–24. doi:10.1016/j.leaqua.2014.11.008

TASK 4 READ CRITICALLY

1. Highlight the keywords from the title of the article that you find in sentences 1 to 3. What do you notice about the order of these words?

   _____

   _____

2. The purpose of sentence 4 is to:

   ☐ highlight a problem that underpins the focus of the authors.

   ☐ present an explicit argument.

3. Sentence 5 is a complex sentence that begins with a dependent clause and ends with an independent clause. In light of what you have learned about emphasis in the clauses of complex sentences, what does this sentence imply to you about the authors' stance?

_____

_____

_____

_____

4. The function of sentences 6 and 7 is to:

☐ present an implicit argument as a thesis statement.

☐ justify the selection of the topic by showing it is historically and currently important in China.

5. a) Which sentences complete the shift from general to specific by describing the specific focus of the article?

_____

b) Describe this focus in your own words.

_____

_____

_____

_____

_____

6. The function of sentences 10 and 11 is to:

☐ position the authors' specific perspective on the subject in the broader field.

☐ refer to the structure of the article.

7. The function of sentences 12 to 17 is to:

☐ argue that the three philosophies are superior to Western philosophies for business leadership in China.

☐ give a brief overview of the three philosophies before the detailed discussion in the article.

8. Sentences 18 to 23 set out the structure and aims of the article. Where does the authors' stance come in?

_____

_____

INTRODUCTION 2

corporate: relating to a large corporation or group

supersede: take the place of

renders: causes to become

consequential: important

dispersion: scattering or spreading widely

universalistic: that can be applied everywhere

posit: suggest for discussion

convergence: coming together

thesis: statement presented for discussion

persistence: continuation in spite of difficulties

inter-cultural: between cultures

cross-vergence: interaction across many different groups or cultures

intra-national: within nations

variance: change or difference

indigenous: originating in a particular place

Understanding the Varieties of Chinese Management: The ABCD Framework

by Xin Li

[1] Pope & Meyer (2015) envisage the rise of a global or universal **corporate** organization that 'tends to **supersede** national business contexts' (p. 174) or at least **renders** 'the national institutional environment as less **consequential**' (p. 176), due to the globalization of economy and business education, consequences of which include **dispersion** of enterprise ownership, adoption of best practices, and emergence of **universalistic** principles of management such as CSR. [2] In so doing, they **posit** a **convergence thesis**, namely, ultimately, business organizations around the globe will converge to or should follow the organizational form of such a universalistic corporation.

[3] My purpose here is to make a counter-argument to Pope & Meyer's (2015) convergence thesis. [4] My counter-argument has two components, one being the **persistence** of **inter-cultural cross-vergence**, the other being **intra-national variance**, both of which make their convergence thesis problematic. [5] The aim of my analysis is to stimulate discussion and debate in a relatively new area of study, i.e., Chinese **indigenous** management research, rather than to provide definitive general conclusions.

Excerpt from Li, X. (2016, June). *Understanding the varieties of Chinese management: The ABCD framework.* Paper presented at the Seventh Biennial International Association for Chinese Management Research Conference, Hangzhou, China.

TASK 5 READ CRITICALLY

1. Which of the following organizational structures describes Introduction 2?

☐ **Organizational Structure 1**

a) Describe a theory or approach.

b) Focus on the key idea of that approach.

c) State your purpose.

d) Briefly summarize your counter-position to the approach.

e) End with a broad aim.

☐ **Organizational Structure 2**

a) Challenge a theory or approach.

b) Challenge the key idea of that approach.

c) State your purpose.

d) Briefly summarize your counter-position.

e) End with a narrow aim.

2. In sentence 5, the author states the following: "The aim of my analysis is to stimulate discussion and debate in a relatively new area of study, i.e., Chinese indigenous management research, rather than to provide definitive general conclusions."

How does this statement affect your expectations of the rest of the article?

_____

INTRODUCTION 3

Dynamics of Corporate Social Responsibility in Asia: Knowledge and Norms

by Rebecca Chunghee Kim and Jeremy Moon

[1] This article aims to capture the recent dynamics of Corporate Social Responsibility (CSR) in Asia, particularly since the turn of the twenty-first century. [2] Following a discussion of the comparative contexts for CSR in Asia and the West, both broadly understood, it examines research on CSR in management since the **turn of the century** and compares the findings with a more Western investigation of CSR research (Lockett *et al*, 2006). [3] This includes insights into the changing **salience** of CSR in Asia research, as well as the nature of knowledge (empirical: quantitative or qualitative; theoretical: non-**normative** or normative). [4] It extends the research of Lockett *et al* by expanding the concept of 'focus' from simply issue (social, environmental, ethical and **stakeholder**) to include 'geographical region' (East Asia, South Asia, South East Asia) and 'forms of institutionalization' (by regulation and organization).

[5] A key finding is both the relative domination and relative decline of ethical norms as an institutional focus for CSR in Asia, particularly when contrasted with its more modest status (31 per cent) in Western CSR research (Lockett *et al*, 2006). [6] **Accordingly**, a closer analysis of ethical norms in Asian CSR is provided, giving special attention to the place of 'community' as a prime CSR stakeholder, in contrast to the West, where it is rather more seen as one among several stakeholders. [7] The concluding discussion focuses on what unites and **distinguishes** CSR across Asia; and on what unites and distinguishes Asian CSR from Western and other CSRs.

[8] By Asia we refer to the countries from Pakistan moving eastwards to Japan, north of Australasia and south of the former USSR. [9] This definition is close to Witt and Redding's (2013, p. 265) definition of 'the landmass from India to Japan' and the analysis of geographical focus in our CSR in Asia research includes Afghanistan, Bangladesh, Burma (Myanmar), China, India, Indonesia, Japan, Korea, Malaysia, Taiwan, Pakistan, the Philippines, Singapore, Sri Lanka, Thailand and Vietnam.

Excerpt from Kim, R. C., & Moon, J. (2015). Dynamics of corporate social responsibility in Asia: Knowledge and norms. *Asian Business & Management, 14*(5), 349–382. doi:10.1057/abm.2015.15

turn of the century: period around the end of one century and the beginning of the next

salience: importance or relevance

normative: following norms or expected behaviour

stakeholder: person or group who is affected by or has invested in something

accordingly: therefore

distinguishes: shows to be different

TASK 6 READ CRITICALLY

1. Does the article shift from general to specific?

_____

_____

2. What are the functions of sentences 5 to 7?

_____

_____

_____

_____

INTRODUCTION 4

On Becoming a Leader in Asia and America: Empirical Evidence from Women Managers

by Claudia Peus, Susanne Braun, and Kristin Knipfer

innovative: using new ideas

determinants: causal factors

flourished: succeeded or developed well

facets: aspects

[1] Asian economies have become increasingly important global players (Cappelli, Singh, Singh, & Useem, 2010), and Singapore's economy is one of the most **innovative** (The Global Innovation Index, 2012) and competitive (Global Competitiveness Report, 2012–2013) economies worldwide. [2] As a result, there is a necessity to learn more about the way business works in Asia, particularly with regard to leadership, one of the major **determinants** of organizational success (Hogan & Kaiser, 2005).

[3] Although cross-cultural leadership research has **flourished** in recent years (e.g., House, Dorfman, Javidan, Hanges, & de Luque, 2014; House, Hanges, Javidan, Dorfman, & Gupta, 2004; Javidan, Dorfman, Howell, & Hanges, 2010), the clear demand for cross-cultural analyses of leadership persists (e.g., Bryman, 2004; Gardner, Lowe, Moss, Mahoney, & Cogliser, 2010; Lau, 2002). [4] In particular, more research on the specific **facets** of leadership in India (e.g., Palrecha, Spangler, & Yammarino, 2012), China (e.g., Chan, Huang, Snape, & Lam, 2013), and Singapore (e.g., Toor & Ofori, 2009) has been called for. [5] Furthermore, even though leader emergence has received attention in recent years (Javidan & Carl, 2005), the emergence of women leaders has been understudied in general (Gardner et al., 2010), and in cross-cultural leadership research in particular (Bullough, Kroeck, Newburry, Kundu, & Lowe, 2012).

[6] Thus, the purpose of this research is to investigate how women emerge as leaders in China, India, and Singapore, and how the success factors and barriers compare to those reported by women leaders in the U.S. [7] Second, this research aims at analyzing how women in these countries lead and whether their leadership styles are more similar among Asian countries than between Asia and the U.S.

Excerpt from Peus, C., Braun, S., & Knipfer, K. (2015). On becoming a leader in Asia and America: Empirical evidence from women managers. *The Leadership Quarterly, 26*(1), 55–67. doi:10.1016/j.leaqua.2014.08.004

TASK 7 READ CRITICALLY

1. Do the authors make a shift from general to specific or from specific to general in the introduction?

_____

_____

2. In which sentences do the authors justify their work by highlighting the need for research in their specific area?

_____

_____

3. Sentences 3 to 5 provide a brief overview of related research. How are the citations ordered?

_____

_____

4. Which sentences explicitly describe the specific focus and aims of the article?

_____

_____

INTRODUCTION 5

The Dynamics of Managing People in the Diverse Cultural and Institutional Context of Africa

by Ken Kamoche, Lisa Qixun Siebers, Aminu Mamman, and Aloysius Newenham-Kahindi

[1] The management and organisation literature often characterises managing in Africa as "the challenge of" and rarely do scholars look to the continent for **novel** ideas, inspiration, best practice or theoretical **insights**. [2] Yet, in the last five years or so, the African organisational landscape has **witnessed** substantial transformation and renewal. [3] While challenges of course remain, we now have a better understanding of the nature, scope and extent of management practices and the role of theory in **unpacking** these practices than we did a decade ago (e.g. Newenham-Kahindi *et al.*, 2013). [4] Examples of the **emergent** literature in specific African countries include the relationship between **human resource management** (HRM) in Mozambique and business systems theory (Wood *et al.*, 2011), human resource practices in

novel: new

insights: understanding

witnessed: undergone

unpacking: making easy to understand

emergent: new and still in development

human resource management: engaging employees and developing systems to manage people in an organization

mergers and acquisitions: combining companies and taking over others

appropriation: using someone else's idea or possession (often without permission)

labour force: workforce

embedded: fixed as an integral part

derive meaning: obtain meaning

eschew: avoid

foster: promote

corpus: body or collection of works

and so forth: et cetera

warrant: justify

dissemination: spreading (knowledge)

entrepreneurship: ability to do business

business ethics: principles about what is morally acceptable in business

poverty alleviation: poverty reduction

viable organisations: organizations that can succeed

mergers and acquisitions in the Nigerian banking sector (Gomez *et al.*, 2012), cultural influences in small and medium sized enterprises in Kenya (Jackson *et al.*, 2008), the processes of knowledge **appropriation** amongst foreign banks in Tanzania (Kamoche and Newenham-Kahindi, 2012), and challenges associated with skill shortages and talent management in South Africa (Horwitz, 2013).

[5] This emergent literature highlights the diversity of management approaches, the role of multinational firms, the changing employment relationship, as well as advancing new theoretical insights. [6] Nevertheless, much remains to be done to develop indigenous forms of knowledge which are relevant to Africa and which address the needs of the African **labour force**. [7] Studies that merely describe and characterise HRM practices, or simply replicate western studies do little to advance knowledge. [8] The same applies to those studies in which the purpose is to collect African samples with little thought to the unique circumstances of those samples and the context within which they are **embedded** and from which they **derive meaning**. [9] A similar phenomenon has been observed in the Asian context whereby the "exploitation" or "refinement" of western theories generates only modest contributions to knowledge and does not substantially advance understanding of phenomena in under-researched contexts (Leung, 2009; Li and Tsui, 2002). [10] Scholars engaging organisational phenomena in Africa need to **eschew** such approaches if we are to gain a deep understanding of the management of people and organisations in the emerging economies of Africa.

[11] We argue that there is a need for a shift in emphasis to **foster** research that is not only committed to analysing how the diverse African context shapes current thinking and practice in the management of people and organisations (Kamoche *et al.*, 2004), but also how this in turn contributes to the "mainstream" **corpus** of knowledge. [12] Hence, scholars need to go beyond the topics that have characterised debate so far, for example, comparative analysis of practices at the cross-cultural, cross-sectoral or cross-national levels, the relationship between HRM practices and organisational performance **and so forth**. [13] Issues that **warrant** further attention today include the creation, **dissemination** and appropriation of knowledge, talent management, human resource capabilities for innovation and **entrepreneurship**, ethical and strategic leadership, sustainability and **business ethics** and the Africa-Asia nexus. [14] These topics have significant implications for the continued creation of a highly skilled African workforce, employment creation and **poverty alleviation**, the fostering of **viable organisations** that contribute to economic development, as well as the scope for Africans to realise meaningful benefits from the engagement with foreign investors and multinational firms.

Excerpt from Kamoche, K., Siebers, L. Q., Mamman, A., & Newenham-Kahindi, A. (2015). The dynamics of managing people in the diverse cultural and institutional context of Africa. *Personnel Review*, 44(3), 330–345. doi:10.1108/PR-01-2015-0002

TASK 8 READ CRITICALLY

1. Which sentences provide a brief overview of examples of recent related research?

   _____

2. In sentence 7, the authors state the following: "Studies that merely describe and characterise HRM practices, or simply replicate western studies do little to advance knowledge."

   How do you interpret this statement?

   _____

TASK 9 FIND THESIS STATEMENTS

In the example introductions, the authors present arguments and goals in different ways, and not always in a single-sentence thesis statement. Reread each introduction and underline what you consider to be the thesis statement.

Facts and Gaps in Introductions

In introductions, it is common to make factual statements as part of the shift from general to specific. Writers use various techniques when they present facts, to support their statements and to avoid being challenged by readers. Many writers also use the introduction to highlight gaps in the research, thereby showing that they have an original contribution to make to scholarship.

TASK 10 IDENTIFY WAYS TO SUPPORT FACTUAL STATEMENTS

Look at the four sentences below from Introduction 1. What techniques do the authors use to avoid making factual statements that could be challenged by a reader?

1. Traditional philosophical and cultural roots influence the thought patterns and behaviors of all citizens in a community including its leaders (Parsons & Shils, 1951).

   _____

2. Hence, leadership practices would reflect unique cultural idiosyncrasies even though in a rapidly changing context, multiple forces could shape the behavior of its people.

   _____

3. Further, it has been documented that Chinese philosophies, especially Confucianism, greatly impact leaders in the Chinese diaspora, and have done so for many years (Chai & Rhee, 2010).

   _____

4. The factor analysis results showed that Chinese people combine Buddhism and Daoism, probably because both are characterized by action avoidance.

TASK 11 IDENTIFY WAYS TO HIGHLIGHT GAPS

In Introduction 5, the authors give considerable attention to what is lacking in existing research and the need to shift direction. Read the introduction again and highlight any language they use to achieve this.

■ CRITICAL THINKING ■

LOGICAL FALLACIES

Logical Fallacies Based on Others' Actions and Ideas

Another group of logical fallacies to avoid are those that misrepresent or misuse the actions and ideas of others. This occurs when a speaker or writer incorrectly or inappropriately brings others into his or her arguments to strengthen the point.

Below are three examples of logical fallacies based on others' actions and ideas.

a) Ad hominem fallacy: The ad hominem fallacy involves trying to win an argument by attacking one's opponent rather than his or her argument.

b) Ad populum fallacy: The ad populum fallacy occurs when someone emphasizes popular support for an idea rather than focusing on arguments that can prove the idea to be right or wrong.

c) Straw man fallacy: The straw man fallacy occurs when someone misrepresents an opponent's argument to make the person seem weak and then criticizes his or her argument for being weak. In this way, the opponent becomes easy to knock down, like a straw man.

TASK 12 IDENTIFY LOGICAL FALLACIES

Read the following statements that exemplify logical fallacies based on others' actions and ideas. Then match them to the descriptions you have just read. Write the corresponding letter next to the statement.

		Description
1	Sixty percent of respondents in a recent survey expressed support for a new oil pipeline to south coast refineries. It's time we stopped talking and got on with implementation.	
2	The head of the South Coast Pipeline Commission graduated with a degree in English Literature. He is not qualified to decide on this environmental issue from an objective, scientific point of view.	
3	The head of the South Coast Pipeline Commission is happy to destroy the local flora and fauna with this new pipeline. Such a lack of concern for the environment is unacceptable.	

TASK 13 ANALYZE WAYS TO AVOID LOGICAL FALLACIES

In the example introductions, the authors are careful to avoid making logical fallacies based on others' actions and ideas. Answer the following questions to explain how the authors achieve this.

1. In Introduction 2, the author, Li, critiques the work of Pope and Meyer (2015). How does the author avoid the ad hominem fallacy?

   _____

   _____

   _____

   _____

   _____

2. In Introduction 1, Ma and Tsui highlight the socio-cultural role of traditional Chinese philosophies despite the current popularity of Western business practices in China. Explain why the authors do not need to avoid the ad populum logical fallacy.

   _____

   _____

   _____

▍VOCABULARY▍

LINKING WORDS

See Chapter 6, pp. 131–132, and Appendix 1 to learn more about linking words.

When authors write introductions to academic articles, they need to create cohesion between many different ideas, describe general and specific information, state aims, give opinions, and define concepts, to name but a few requirements. In the example introductions, the authors use a wide range of linking words and phrases to make their texts cohesive.

TASK 14 FIND THE LINKING WORDS

Read the list of linking functions below. Then scan the example introductions again to find words or phrases that perform these functions. Write two or three examples of linking words or phrases beside each function.

1. Explain the focus [TEXTS 1, 2, 3] _____

2. Exemplify [TEXTS 2, 5] _____

3. Enumerate [TEXTS 1, 4] _____

4. Express addition (and) [TEXT 1]_____

5. Express contrast (*but*) [TEXTS 1, 5] _____

6. Express an effect (*so*) [TEXTS 2, 4, 5] _____

7. Define [TEXT 3] _____

8. Introduce an argument, opinion, purpose, or aim [TEXTS 2, 3, 4, 5] _____

_____

EXTEND YOUR ACADEMIC VOCABULARY

Extend your knowledge of key vocabulary from this chapter.

binary	foster	posit
complement	**insight**	render
diverge	**invoke**	salience
facet	normative	unpack

*Words in bold type are AWL entries.

Practise Chapter 7 vocabulary online.

EFFECTIVE SENTENCE STRUCTURE

REVIEW OF THE PASSIVE VOICE

Do Unit 7: The Passive Voice in the Handbook, pp. 364–369 (if you have not already done it).

In Chapter 2, you analyzed how the passive voice was used in an article on scientific research, and practised writing sentences in the passive voice.

TASK 15 ANALYZE USE OF THE PASSIVE VOICE

Refer to the model introduction, on pages 150 and 151, to answer the following questions.

1. List the verbs in the passive voice in the final paragraph.

_____

_____

2. Why do you think the writer used the passive voice rather than the active voice for these sentences?

_____

_____

3. Why do you think the writer used agentless passives (passive-voice sentences with no stated agents)?

_____

_____

REVIEW OF PERSONAL VERSUS IMPERSONAL LANGUAGE

In Chapter 1, you learned about using or avoiding personal language, and you practised four strategies to make writing less personal.

TASK 16 MAKE SENTENCES LESS PERSONAL

Look at the following sentences from Introduction 1, which are written with appropriate personal language in the active voice. If you are writing for an instructor or in a subject area that discourages personal language, you may need to use impersonal and passive-voice sentences instead of personal and active-voice sentences. For practice, rewrite the following sentences to make them less personal.

1. Our work diverges from most (cross-)cultural leadership analyses that often use culture as a moderating variable or contextual factor.

   _____

   _____

2. We first introduce the core ideas of the three traditional Chinese philosophical schools, focusing on content relevant to leadership.

   _____

   _____

3. We then link each school to current leadership theories and summarize our ideas in propositions.

   _____

   _____

4. We further aim to detect the influence of these traditional philosophical schools in the leadership practices of contemporary Chinese business leaders.

   _____

   _____

   _____

5. Finally, we discuss how traditional culture could be a rich source of understanding for future leadership research in China and beyond.

   _____

   _____

My eLab

Find supplementary reading, writing, and critical-thinking activities online.

AN INTRODUCTION

TASK 17 WRITE AN INTRODUCTORY PARAGRAPH

In Chapter 6, you rewrote and revised two paragraphs on the topic of rehabilitation versus punishment in prisons. As part of that task, you added reliable academic sources to support the ideas in the paragraphs, using APA or MLA citation style.

Reread the introduction you wrote for the exploratory writing task at the beginning of this chapter (Task 1, p. 149). Based on what you have learned, develop your exploratory writing into an introductory paragraph. Give an indication of your stance, that is, the way you are leaning in the debate.

Checklist for Revising and Editing

In pairs, revise and edit each other's work, addressing the following questions:

☐ Does the introduction have a clear organizational structure, for example, general to specific, or other?

☐ Does the introduction match the context of the paragraphs?

☐ Is your stance evident to the reader?

☐ Does the introduction have an effective thesis statement?

☐ Does the introduction guide the reader as to the organization of the following paragraphs?

☐ Are active- and passive-voice sentences used correctly?

☐ Is there a broad and effective range of linking words to add cohesion?

CHAPTER 8

CONCLUSIONS IN ACADEMIC WRITING

> **If one thinks, one must reach conclusions.**
>
> Helen Keller

The best way to begin studying conclusions in academic writing is to think of the conclusion as a mirror to the introduction: many introductions shift from general to specific; many conclusions shift from specific to general. Your introduction gives your reader a first impression of you and your work; your conclusion gives a final impression. In academic writing, conclusions should reflect, reinforce, and conclude the argumentation and findings of an essay or article, even if this might involve challenging generally accepted ideas.

In this chapter, you will:

- learn common features of writing conclusions
- read and analyze conclusions from articles about international business leadership across cultures
- study synonyms
- learn how to avoid gender-exclusive language
- study how to use colons and apostrophes correctly
- review relative clauses and participle phrases
- learn to avoid logical fallacies based on weak reasoning
- write a conclusion

TASK 1 EXPLORE THROUGH WRITING

Write a conclusion to the text on rehabilitation versus punishment in prisons that you have been working on in the last three chapters. Take 10 minutes. With a partner, read each other's writing and comment on how the information has been organized.

CONCLUSIONS IN ACADEMIC WRITING

As was the case with the introductions you studied in Chapter 7, there is no single correct way to write a conclusion. Writers organize and present concluding information in different ways depending on the genre, audience, and purpose. However, not all articles and essays have a section titled "Conclusion." Sometimes they have a concluding section embedded in a section of another name, for example, "Discussion."

There are some features of writing good conclusions that are present in most concluding sections, regardless of the name and format; these features, and how different writers apply them, are the focus of this chapter.

Most conclusions in academic writing perform the following functions:

- briefly summarize the focus and main arguments of the essay
- synthesize the arguments by bringing the threads of the essay together into one coherent concept
- provide a final answer and end the discussion
- provide a general closing statement

A Reverse Funnel: Shift from Specific to General

One of the most common features of conclusions in many different types of academic writing is a shift from specific to general, as illustrated in Figure 1.

The conclusion begins with a summary of the specific content covered in the essay or article. After the summary, the synthesis brings together the various threads of the essay or article into one coherent closing concept. Next, the writer provides a final answer to the question being addressed, or a final solution to the given problem, before completing the shift from specific to general with a general closing statement.

FIGURE 1

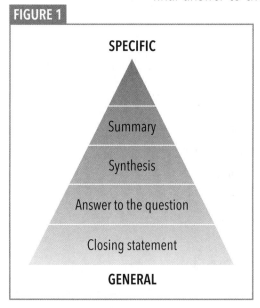

Conclusions: Business Leadership across Cultures

The conclusions in this chapter match the introductions you studied in Chapter 7 on management, business, and leadership. After analyzing a model conclusion, you will study the conclusions from four of the five Chapter 7 articles to see how the authors incorporated the above features of writing conclusions in different ways.

Model Conclusion on Business and Leadership across Cultures

Read the model conclusion on the next page.

Recent Perspectives on Business and Leadership across Cultures: The West, Asia, and Africa

[1] In the above sections, a number of recent perspectives on business leadership strategies between Asia, Africa, and the West have been analyzed. [2] It was argued that new multi-faceted, intercultural strategies embracing difference are required to promote success in business leadership. [3] Two key factors were highlighted as **underpinning** the new analytic lenses: globalization and the hegemonic dominance of Western business practices around the world. [4] Together, these two factors were often seen as central to the relegation of local knowledge and practices to positions of secondary importance, and behind the need for crossvergence strategies. [5] In short, I strongly advocate Guo's (2015) and Li's (2016) support for crossvergence as it offers a definitive way forward for international business leaders by overcoming the limitations of two alternative lenses: cultural universalism and coming together across cultures (convergence), and moving in opposite cultural directions (divergence). [6] As stated by Guo (2015), crossvergence of influences and business ideology can bring about a new system of independent cultural values, which find representation on multiple levels of business leadership. [7] A crossvergence perspective is not only a lens that reflects the **multipolarity** of the international world of business; it is also a practical business strategy that can help a business leader's process of decision-making across diverse cultures. [8] In the next 20 years, business success and international cooperation will depend on leaders who have an in-depth understanding of these complexities.

underpinning: supporting as a foundation

multipolarity: having many centres of power and influence

TASK 2 ANALYZE THE TEXT

In the model conclusion above, the writer shifts from specific to general. Identify the sentences that perform the following functions of conclusions. Write the sentence number(s) next to the corresponding function.

		Sentence(s)
1	Briefly summarize the focus and main arguments of the essay	
2	Synthesize the arguments by bringing the threads of the essay together into one concept	
3	Provide a final answer and end the discussion	
4	Provide a general closing statement	

WRITING CONCLUSIONS

Four Stages of Writing a Conclusion

The following is a breakdown of the four stages of writing a conclusion as exemplified in the model conclusion. As was the case with the model introduction in Chapter 7, the model conclusion shows several common features of conclusions in academic writing but is not intended as a model to follow exactly. In the example conclusions that follow, you will see that authors select and adapt these features quite differently.

Stage 1: Briefly Summarize the Focus and Main Arguments

Sentences 1 to 3 summarize the focus on business leadership between Asia, Africa, and the West. Sentence 1 marks the shift from the main body of the essay to the conclusion by specifically stating the main topic and focus, that is, the strategies analyzed. This sentence mirrors the sentence in the introduction that refers to the organizational structure of the essay. Sentence 2 summarizes the main argument, the need for new strategies, while sentence 3 highlights two underlying factors: globalization and Western dominance.

Stage 2: Synthesize by Bringing the Essay Threads Together into One Concept

Sentence 4 provides a synthesis of the focus and main arguments by bringing the essay threads together into one overall concept around which the essay will conclude: crossvergence strategies. The writer can thus focus the rest of the conclusion around this central concept rather than around the different threads. The synthesis in a conclusion often highlights a central interrelationship, dilemma, challenge, or theme that has run through the essay, and may mirror and develop the idea put forward in the thesis statement in the essay introduction.

Stage 3: Provide a Final Answer and End the Discussion

In sentences 5 to 7, the writer provides a final answer to the issue, problem, or question that was set out in the introduction, that is, that binary cross-cultural strategies are inadequate to promote successful relationships between leaders across cultures due to the dominance of Western business practices in today's globalized world. Sentence 5 is an explicit statement of support for crossvergence, which two expert authors advocate. In sentences 6 and 7, the writer expands on this statement by providing more details and then closes the discussion.

Stage 4: Provide a General Closing Statement

Sentence 8 marks the completion of the shift from specific to general, closing the paragraph with a broad statement about the future of the subject. This sentence, which refers to future cooperation, mirrors the focus of the first sentence of the introduction, in which the writer introduced the topic in the most general sense.

Different Ways of Concluding

As in writing introductions, the ways writers choose to present their conclusions may differ according to genre, audience, purpose, and individual preference.

███████████ **ACTIVE AND CRITICAL READING** ███████████

The following are four of the five conclusions that match the introductions you read on business leadership in Chapter 7. As you will see, the authors include most of the concluding functions present in the model conclusion but organize them in different ways. Read the title above each conclusion, which indicates the specific focus of the article. Next, read the complete text. Then answer the questions that follow to analyze the structure, content, and language of the text.

CONCLUSION 1

In the article by Ma and Tsui (2015), the following conclusion is presented after a section titled "Discussion," which also includes detailed analysis of their main questions.

Traditional Chinese Philosophies and Contemporary Leadership

by Li Ma and Anne S. Tsui

Conclusion

[1] In this article, we introduce three major Chinese philosophical schools and show how they relate to modern leadership theories. [2] We also analyze the leadership behaviors of fifteen highly successful Chinese business leaders revealing the cultural-philosophical roots of their leadership practices. [3] Legalism dominates in an unsurprising **alignment** with modern management emphasizing order, control, reliability, predictability, and professionalism. [4] However, leader **integrity**, **benevolence**, trust in followers, and empowerment are also important, suggesting the influence of Confucianism and Daoism. [5] We hope that this study has illustrated the intellectual value of digging deep into the cultural fabric of a society to understand the multiple sources influencing contemporary leaders' beliefs, values, and actions.

Excerpt from Ma, L., & Tsui, A. S. (2015). Traditional Chinese philosophies and contemporary leadership. *The Leadership Quarterly, 26*(1), 13–24. doi:10.1016/j.leaqua.2014.11.008

---

alignment: correspondence with

integrity: honesty and trustworthiness

benevolence: kindness and generosity to others

TASK 3 READ CRITICALLY

1. In which sentence(s) do the authors summarize the specific focus of the article?

_____

2. In which sentence(s) do the authors stress the importance of the three Chinese philosophies that were the focus of the article?

_____

3. In which sentence(s) do the authors provide a general closing statement?

_____

CONCLUSION 2

In the article by Li (2016), the following conclusion is presented after a five-page section that analyzes different kinds of Chinese management.

Understanding the Varieties of Chinese Management: The ABCD Framework

by Xin Li

Conclusion

[1] Above, I have argued that Pope & Meyer's (2015) convergence thesis is too optimistic to be realistic. [2] Two counterarguments are raised, one being inter-cultural cross-vergence, the other being intra-national variance. [3] For the latter point, I show the varieties of Chinese management and the underlying Chinese traditional philosophy. [4] The 2x2 scheme indicates that, as there are varieties of philosophical elements and corresponding **management modes** available, companies and their management teams have much freedom to select and **configure** their idiosyncratic management models. [5] As a consequence, there is little possibility that all business organizations will converge to the so-called global or universal corporate organization as Pope & Meyer (2015) predict, although this is not to deny that the universal corporate organization can also be a choice among many that can be chosen by some or many firms around the globe.

management modes: forms of management

configure: arrange something for use

Excerpt from Li, X. (2016, June). _Understanding the varieties of Chinese management: The ABCD framework._ Paper presented at the Seventh Biennial International Association for Chinese Management Research Conference, Hangzhou, China.

TASK 4 READ CRITICALLY

1. How does Li's sentence 1 differ from Ma and Tsui's sentence 1?

_____

_____

2. Which two concluding functions does the author combine in sentence 5?

_____

3. Does the conclusion shift from specific to general?

_____

_____

4. Sentence 5 lacks precision. Rewrite the sentence to make it clearer and more readable.

_____

_____

_____

_____

CONCLUSION 3

In Kim and Moon's (2015) article, there is a three-page section titled "Discussion and Conclusions." At the end of this section, the authors present certain concluding remarks, in which they analyze the limitations of their study.

Dynamics of Corporate Social Responsibility in Asia: Knowledge and Norms

by Rebecca Chunghee Kim and Jeremy Moon

[1] Clearly our study has several limitations. [2] First, our analysis based primarily on titles, keywords and abstracts of journal papers is always going to miss some of the **nuance** of methodology, argument and conclusions that single papers possess. [3] This is the nature of quantitative bibliographic research. [4] However, in the case of the role of ethics and community in CSR Asia we have **striven** to **interrogate** the deeper meanings of these CSR values and practices. [5] Second, the comparison with Western CSR literature is based on data which are not strictly comparable in terms of time or sources, though in the absence of strictly comparable data, this offers a place to start. [6] Third, inferences about how research reflects practice must be very **cautious**. [7] Certainly it is likely that there are **lag effects** between practices and research, suggesting that some conclusions about the research do not take account of how CSR organization and regulation through non-ethical modes may understate developments in the field.

[8] **Notwithstanding** these limitations, our contributions are clear. [9] First, we have set **benchmarks** for analysis of CSR in Asia research for **temporal** and national comparisons. [10] Second, we have confirmed what might well have been imagined, that in Asian CSR, ethical norms play a very important role, and we have comprehensively illustrated this with respect to the treatment of 'community' in Asian CSR …. [11] Moreover, we have detailed these in order to identify specific ethical **orientations** with expectations of business. [12] Third, we have also extended the field of analysis of CSR knowledge by introducing two additional dimensions to the question of 'focus' in research. [13] In addition to examining the 'issue' focus, we also analyzed the 'geographic' and

nuance: subtle meaning

striven: made a great effort

interrogate: investigate

cautious: careful

lag effects: differences caused by passing time

notwithstanding: in spite of

benchmarks: reference points by which other things can be measured

temporal: relating to time

orientations: interests or beliefs

'institutional' focuses, which give additional insights into our understanding of CSR knowledge. [14] Finally, our paper offers a challenge to CSR in Asia researchers to **deploy** and build on our comparative framework, and to engage in more **non-normative theoretical research**, particularly around conceptualization and explanation.

[15] In sum, we suggest that CSR in Asia is both a distinctive emerging research agenda inside Asia and also partly connected with the wider international CSR research arena. [16] While we emphasize the importance of ethical norms underpinning Asian business, we also note that this is **in relative decline** in CSR research. [17] Does this mean that implicit CSR is being **eroded** and explicit CSR is on the rise? [18] Or will CSR in Asia **entail** a more complex mix of implicit and explicit **drivers** and behaviours? [19] How can we explain business' critical role in the 'community', which we suggest as a prime stakeholder in Asian CSR? [20] As discussed, there are multiple reasons for CSR in Asia, and we need to have further exploration on their interactions. [21] There is also a need to reveal how Asia pursues the balance between the impact of national political, cultural and ethical norms on CSR and international CSR institutions and systems. [22] We hope the findings of this article address gaps in our understanding of Asian CSR dynamics and inform further research agendas in what is **indubitably** a growing field of Asian business and management research.

Excerpt from Kim, R. C., & Moon, J. (2015). Dynamics of corporate social responsibility in Asia: Knowledge and norms. *Asian Business & Management*, *14*(5), 349–382. doi:10.1057/abm.2015.15

TASK 5 READ CRITICALLY

1. In sentence 4, do the authors state an argument or restate an aim?

   _____

2. In sentences 8 to 13, do the authors summarize or synthesize?

   _____

3. In sentence 15, do the authors summarize or synthesize?

   _____

4. In sentences 17 to 19, the authors ask questions. Are these questions that they will answer in the remainder of the conclusion, or food for thought for the reader?

   _____

5. Which sentence rounds off the article with a general closing statement? How do the authors achieve this?

   _____

   _____

Recognizing Limitations

In the first paragraph of Conclusion 3, authors Kim and Moon mention the limitations of their study.

TASK 6 DISCUSS LIMITATIONS

1. Look again at sentences 1 to 7 of their conclusion. Describe each limitation using as many of your own words as possible.

   Limitation 1: _____

   _____

   _____

   Limitation 2: _____

   _____

   _____

   Limitation 3: _____

   _____

   _____

2. Why do you think the authors mention the limitations of their work? Does it weaken their argument? Why or why not?

   _____

   _____

   _____

3. Read the sentences that follow each statement of limitation. How do the authors develop the discussion around each limitation?

   Limitation 1 (developed in sentences 3 and 4): _____

   _____

   _____

   _____

   Limitation 2 (developed in the second part of sentence 5): _____

   _____

   _____

   _____

   Limitation 3 (developed in sentence 7): _____

   _____

   _____

   _____

CONCLUSION 4

In Peus et al.'s (2015) article, the following concluding section comes at the end of a four-page Results section in which the findings of the study are presented around key themes. There is no separate section titled "Conclusion."

On Becoming a Leader in Asia and America: Empirical Evidence from Women Managers

by Claudia Peus, Susanne Braun, and Kristin Knipfer

Future Research

validate: support, show to be true

longitudinal: research characterized by observations over time

subordinates: employees with less power

[1] Future research is necessary to **validate** our findings. [2] In a next step quantitative and in particular **longitudinal** analyses seem fruitful as they enable an analysis of developments concerning the social structures of Asian countries (Sun & Wang, 2009) as well as potential changes in gender stereotypes (Duehr & Bono, 2006) and their impact on leadership. [3] Further, in correspondence with an increasing shift from leaders' perspectives to an integration of leader and follower perspectives in organizations (e.g., Peus, Braun, & Frey, 2012), future studies should incorporate **subordinates'** perceptions of women managers in their cultural contexts.

criteria: principles or standards used to judge something or someone (Note that the singular form is *criterion*.)

mentoring systems: systems to help less experienced colleagues

pursue: aim to achieve (a career)

enact: perform, practise

inspires: makes others want to do something

Practical Implications

[4] Despite the above stated limitations, our research makes substantial contributions to cross-cultural perspectives on women's advancement to leadership positions and their leadership behavior. [5] First, practitioners, who are in charge of evaluating and selecting managers in organizations, should be aware that gender stereotypes still negatively influence evaluations of women and attitudes toward women in leadership positions (Heilman, 2012). [6] Therefore leadership assessments "must be conducted in a structured manner, primarily based on behavioral **criteria**" (Peus et al., 2012, p. 106). [7] Second, our findings emphasize that access to role models is necessary to encourage and guide women across countries. [8] Hence, the implementation of professional **mentoring systems** is likely to be useful. [9] Third, much more emphasis must be put on family-friendly policies through corporate and political regulations that enable women to **pursue** managerial careers and fulfill their caregiver roles at the same time (Peus & Traut-Mattausch, 2008).

[10] In short, due to the global shift in economic power toward Asia on the one hand and the increase in female leaders on the other hand, a deeper understanding of the way women reach leadership positions in Asia and the way they **enact** leadership is necessary. [11] We hope that this article represents an important first step in this direction and **inspires** future research.

Excerpt from Peus, C., Braun, S., & Knipfer, K. (2015). On becoming a leader in Asia and America: Empirical evidence from women managers. *The Leadership Quarterly, 26*(1), 55–67. doi:10.1016/j.leaqua.2014.08.004

TASK 7 READ CRITICALLY

1. Which two of the following three functions do the authors perform in sentences 4 to 9?

   ☐ Refer in general to the future

   ☐ State the achievements of the research and article

   ☐ Make recommendations for leaders

2. Sentences 10 and 11 complete the shift from specific to general. Explain how the authors achieve this shift in the two sentences.

   _____

   _____

VOCABULARY

SYNONYMS

Synonyms are words that have the same meaning or that are very close in meaning. You should use synonyms to paraphrase others' words and to improve the variety of your writing.

TASK 8 FIND SYNONYMS

The words in bold in the following phrases are from the model conclusion on page 171. Use your own knowledge, a dictionary, or a thesaurus to find at least three synonyms for each word or phrase in bold. Remember: many words have multiple meanings; choose synonyms that have a similar or the same meaning in the given context.

1. Intercultural strategies **embracing** difference

   _____

2. The new analytic **lenses**

   _____

3. These two factors were often seen as **central** to the relegation of local knowledge.

   _____

4. These two factors were often seen as central to the **relegation** of local knowledge.

   _____

5. I strongly **advocate** the lens of crossvergence.

_____

6. Crossvergence of influences and business ideology can **bring about** a new system of independent cultural values.

_____

TASK 9 SELECT SYNONYMS

The sentences and phrases below are from Conclusion 4; each contains a word in bold. Look at the four synonyms that follow, and indicate which is _furthest_ in meaning from the word in bold.

1. Longitudinal analyses seem **fruitful** as they enable an analysis of developments concerning the social structures of Asian countries.

☐ effective ☐ efficient ☐ plentiful ☐ useful

2. . . . as well as **potential** changes in gender stereotypes . . .

☐ future ☐ possible ☐ potent ☐ probable

3. Our research makes **substantial** contributions to cross-cultural perspectives on women's advancement to leadership positions and their leadership behavior.

☐ eminent ☐ important ☐ meaningful ☐ significant

4. Our research makes substantial contributions to cross-cultural perspectives on women's **advancement** to leadership positions and their leadership behavior.

☐ advocacy ☐ growth ☐ promotion ☐ rise

5. Our findings **emphasize** that access to role models is necessary to encourage and guide women across countries.

☐ affirm ☐ expose ☐ highlight ☐ stress

EXTEND YOUR ACADEMIC VOCABULARY

Extend your knowledge of key vocabulary from this chapter.

configure	entail	**perspective**
criteria	**notwithstanding**	**validate**
enact	nuance	

*Words in bold type are AWL entries.

Practise Chapter 8 vocabulary online.

AVOIDING GENDER-EXCLUSIVE LANGUAGE

In recent years, many colleges and universities have adopted policies requiring students to avoid gender-exclusive language, that is, language that excludes groups on the basis of their gender. The following two examples illustrate gender-exclusive and gender-inclusive language:

See Unit 2, p. 329, of the Handbook to review the use of *the* in general noun phrases.

1. In today's globalized world, the company CEO must accept that part of **his** role is to promote intercultural understanding. (gender-exclusive)

2. In today's globalized world, company CEOs must accept that part of **their** role is to promote intercultural understanding. (gender-inclusive)

In example 1, *the company CEO* refers in general to all company CEOs. However, the following possessive adjective *his* is unacceptable in academic English because it is gender-exclusive. It implies that all company CEOs are men, thus excluding women CEOs.

In contrast, example 2 is acceptable because the language is gender-inclusive: *company CEOs* is followed by the possessive adjective *their*, which includes both genders.

Example 2 could also be written with alternative gender-inclusive language as follows:

In today's globalized world, the company CEO must accept that part of **his or her** role is to promote intercultural understanding.

In today's globalized world, the company CEO must accept that part of **her or his** role is to promote intercultural understanding.

In today's globalized world, the company CEO must accept that part of **his/her** role is to promote intercultural understanding.

In today's globalized world, the company CEO must accept that part of **her/his** role is to promote intercultural understanding.

TASK 10 ANALYZE TEXT FOR GENDER-INCLUSIVE LANGUAGE

Read the following excerpts from the articles by Xin Li (author of Conclusion 2) and by Li Ma and Anne Tsui (authors of Conclusion 1), and answer the questions that follow.

1. For example, any waiter or waitress who is responsible for a table of customers has the power to waive the entire bill of his or her table if he or she finds the customers at his or her table are dissatisfied with anything related to the meal and service. [Li, 2016, p. 8]

   a) How does the author avoid gender-exclusive language in the excerpt?

b) The excerpt language is rather repetitive. Rewrite the excerpt to make it more readable.

_____

_____

_____

2. Mr. Nie Shengzhe, the founder of the company, is deeply influenced by both Confucianism and Western ways of management. **He** instills four core values into his company, i.e., 'honesty, integrity, hardworking and love for the others'. [Li, 2016, p. 8]

Is the use of the pronoun _he_ gender-exclusive? Is it acceptable? Why or why not?

_____

_____

_____

3. Daoism teaches leaders to avoid useless and counterproductive actions. One of the most famous sayings on leadership from _Dao De Jing_ is "Governing a large state is like cooking a [pot of] small fish" (Lynn, 1999, p. 164), which "means no stirring. Action results in much harm, but quietude results in the fulfillment of authenticity. Thus the larger the state, the more its ruler should practice quietude, for only then can **he** widely obtain the hearts/minds of the mass of common folk" (Lynn, 1999, p. 164). [Ma & Tsui, 2015, pp. 14–15]

Is the use of the pronoun _he_ gender-exclusive? Is it acceptable? Why or why not?

_____

_____

_____

4. In a sharp departure from Daoism, Confucius praised the ethic of hard work. He said that even when situations are not ideal, noble people must work hard and loyally, pursuing work as a noble purpose in itself, even if they know they cannot achieve their objectives. [Ma & Tsui, 2015, p. 16]

How do the authors avoid gender-exclusive language in the excerpt?

_____

_____

TASK 11 REWRITE SENTENCES, USING GENDER-INCLUSIVE LANGUAGE

The following sentences contain problems in the references to gender. Rewrite the sentences as necessary.

1. Discuss the role of the manager in transnational corporations and the priorities he should have with regard to intercultural awareness in the workplace.

_____

_____

2. Managers in large companies should always be aware of his or her employees' family needs.

_____

_____

3. This essay has discussed the role of the middle manager in terms of their role in organizational cultures.

_____

_____

Rules regarding the use of *their* as a gender-neutral term to refer to people in general are changing, and some writers now use *their* to refer to singular noun phrases such as *the middle manager*. However, many instructors will consider such usage incorrect.

▌EFFECTIVE SENTENCE STRUCTURE▐

COLONS AND APOSTROPHES

Colons

In the conclusions in this chapter, colons are used to introduce examples and lists at the end of an independent clause:

> Two key factors were highlighted as underpinning the new analytic lenses**:** globalization and the hegemonic dominance of Western business practices around the world.

However, do not use a colon to introduce a list or examples that are incorporated grammatically into the sentence:

> Two key factors that were highlighted as underpinning the new analytic lenses **were** globalization and the hegemonic dominance of Western business practices around the world.

Colons were also used elsewhere in the articles to introduce direct quotations at the end of an independent clause:

> One company leader . . . specifically stated his understanding of virtue and selflessness**:** "You must manage your own needs and refrain from greed." [Ma & Tsui, 2015, p. 22]

However, do not use a colon to introduce a direct quotation that is incorporated grammatically into the sentence:

> Therefore leadership assessments "must be conducted in a structured manner, primarily based on behavioral criteria."

TASK 12 ADD COLONS

In the following sentences adapted from the example conclusions, there are no colons. Add colons where required. Not all the sentences require colons.

1. The lens of crossvergence put forward by Guo (2015) and Li (2016) overcomes the limitations of two alternative lenses cultural universalism (convergence) and moving in opposite cultural directions (divergence).

2. A crossvergence perspective is a lens that reflects the multipolar nature of the international world of business and a practical business strategy.

3. Legalism emphasizes order, control, reliability, predictability, and professionalism.

4. Legalism emphasizes important aspects of successful leadership order, control, reliability, predictability, and professionalism.

Apostrophes

Apostrophes are used mainly for possessives (showing that something belongs to someone or to something else) and contractions (short forms such as *doesn't* instead of *does not*). The conclusions in this chapter contain several examples of apostrophes used with possessives. The position of the apostrophe depends on whether the noun it is added to is singular or plural, as illustrated below.

Add a possessive apostrophe and an *s* to a singular noun:

> A crossvergence perspective is not only a lens that reflects the multipolarity of the international world of business; it is also a practical business strategy that can help **a business leader's process** of decision-making across diverse cultures.

Place a possessive apostrophe after the *s* of a plural noun:

> We hope that this study has illustrated the intellectual value of digging deep into the cultural fabric of a society to understand the multiple sources influencing **contemporary leaders' beliefs**, values, and actions.

Add a possessive apostrophe and an *s* to a plural noun not ending in *s*:

> Our research makes substantial contributions to cross-cultural perspectives on **women's advancement** to leadership positions.

TASK 13 ADD APOSTROPHES

Add the missing apostrophes to the following sentences adapted from the conclusions in this chapter. Explain your placement of the apostrophe in each case.

1. There is an urgent need to meet employees intrinsic and extrinsic needs.

_____

_____

2. I strongly support Guos (2015) and Lis (2016) stance on crossvergence.

_____

_____

3. I believe that Pope and Meyers (2015) convergence thesis is too optimistic.

_____

_____

4. A business leaders role should be to respect both organizational and national cultures.

_____

_____

Do Unit 8: Colons and Apostrophes in the Handbook, pp. 370–378.

REVIEW OF RELATIVE CLAUSES AND PARTICIPLE PHRASES

In Chapter 4 and in Unit 4 of the Handbook, you studied defining and non-defining relative clauses, including how relative clauses are expressed differently in different forms of English (for example, in North American varieties of English versus British English). In Chapter 6 and in Unit 6 of the Handbook, you learned how present and past participle phrases are reduced forms of relative clauses. Refer to these sections as necessary to do the review exercises below.

TASK 14 IDENTIFY RELATIVE CLAUSES AND PARTICIPLE PHRASES

The following sentences from the model conclusion on page 171 include relative clauses and participle phrases (in italics). Identify the relative clauses as defining or non-defining, and the participle phrases as present or past participle phrases.

1. It was argued that new multifaceted, intercultural strategies *embracing difference* are required to promote success in business leadership.

_____

2. As stated by Guo (2015), crossvergence of influences and business ideology can bring about a new system of independent cultural values, *which find representation on multiple levels of business leadership*.

_____

3. A crossvergence perspective is not only a lens **[a]** *that reflects the multipolarity of the international world of business*; it is also a practical business strategy **[b]** *that can help a business leader's process of decision-making across diverse cultures*.

a) _____

b) _____

4. In the next 20 years, business success and international cooperation will depend on leaders *who have an in-depth understanding of these complexities*.

_____

TASK 15 ANALYZE RELATIVE CLAUSES AND PARTICIPLE PHRASES

The following sentences from two of the example conclusions contain relative clauses or participle phrases (in italics). Read the sentences and answer the questions that follow.

1. Note the absence of commas before the italicized phrases in the following examples from Conclusion 1:

   1. We also analyze the leadership behaviors of fifteen highly successful Chinese business leaders *revealing the cultural-philosophical roots of their leadership practices.*

   2. Legalism dominates in an unsurprising alignment with modern management *emphasizing order, control, reliability, predictability, and professionalism.*

   a) Do you find the sentences easy to understand? Why or why not?

   _____

   _____

   _____

   _____

   b) Now add a comma before the phrases. Are the sentences easier to understand with commas? Do you think the original sentences were incorrect?

   _____

   _____

   _____

   _____

   _____

2. Focus on the relative pronouns in the following examples from Conclusion 3:

   1. The comparison with Western CSR literature is based on data *which are not strictly comparable in terms of time or sources.*

   2. We also analyzed the 'geographic' and 'institutional' focuses, *which give additional insights into our understanding of CSR knowledge.*

   3. We have confirmed *what might well have been imagined.*

   a) Compare the use of *which* in examples 1 and 2. Are they both grammatically correct? What does *which* refer to in each sentence?

   _____

   _____

   _____

   _____

   b) In example 3, what are the function and meaning of the word *what*?

   _____

LOGICAL FALLACIES

Logical Fallacies Based on Weak Reasoning

Another group of logical fallacies to avoid are those that are based on what can best be described as weak reasoning. Below are three examples of such fallacies.

a) Red herring fallacy: The red herring fallacy involves distracting your reader or listener by bringing in an irrelevant example or argument.

b) False dichotomy fallacy: The false dichotomy fallacy involves presenting your reader or listener with a situation or problem and then putting forward two opposite ideas (*a* or *b*) as the only possible solutions or conclusions, without accepting a compromise between the two extremes.

c) Circular logic fallacy: When someone makes a circular logic fallacy, he or she presents an argument or idea and then backs it up with the same argument or idea.

TASK 16 IDENTIFY LOGICAL FALLACIES

Read the following statements that exemplify logical fallacies based on weak reasoning. Then match them to the descriptions you have just read. Write the corresponding letter next to the statement.

		Description
1	Business leaders in Western countries should improve their awareness of local business practices in African and Asian countries, which in turn may lead to increased profitability in the future. If business leaders fail to become more internationally minded in their practices, their profit margins may fall in years to come.	
2	It is time to decide. Business leaders in Africa and Asia must decide either to adapt to Western business practices and succeed or to reject them and fail.	
3	I agree with the view that bonus payments to top Western business leaders in the financial field are disproportionately high and should be regulated by governments. As they say, money corrupts, so more money will corrupt more.	

TASK 17 ANALYZE WAYS TO AVOID LOGICAL FALLACIES

In the conclusions in this chapter, the authors are careful to avoid making logical fallacies based on weak reasoning. Read the following two examples, and answer the questions to explain how the authors achieve this.

1. In short, I strongly advocate Guo's (2015) and Li's (2016) support for cross-vergence as it offers a definitive way forward for international business leaders by overcoming the limitations of two alternative lenses: cultural universalism and coming together across cultures (convergence), and moving in opposite cultural directions (divergence).

   In this excerpt from the model conclusion, which logical fallacy does the writer avoid, and how?

2. In sum, we suggest that CSR in Asia is both a distinctive emerging research agenda inside Asia and also partly connected with the wider international CSR research arena. While we emphasize the importance of ethical norms underpinning Asian business, we also note that this is in relative decline in CSR research. Does this mean that implicit CSR is being eroded and explicit CSR is on the rise? Or will CSR in Asia entail a more complex mix of implicit and explicit drivers and behaviours? How can we explain business' critical role in the 'community', which we suggest as a prime stakeholder in Asian CSR? As discussed, there are multiple reasons for CSR in Asia, and we need to have further exploration on their interactions.

After summing up and highlighting the relative decline in the focus on ethical norms in CSR research, Kim and Moon (2015) introduce three questions in the excerpt above. Are these questions red herrings? Why or why not?

My eLab

Find supplementary reading, writing, and critical-thinking activities online.

_____

_____

WRITE, REVISE, AND EDIT

A CONCLUSION

TASK 18 WRITE A CONCLUSION

In Chapter 7, you wrote an introduction to the two paragraphs you wrote previously on the pros and cons of rehabilitation versus punishment in prisons. Reread the conclusion you wrote for the exploratory writing task at the beginning of this chapter (Task 1, p. 169). Based on what you have learned, develop your exploratory writing into a concluding paragraph. Include the functions of conclusions that you have studied in the order that works best for your text.

Checklist for Revising and Editing

In pairs, revise and edit each other's work, addressing the following questions:

☐ Does the conclusion have a clear organizational structure, for example, specific to general, or other?

☐ Does the conclusion match the paragraphs and introduction?

☐ Does the conclusion begin by summarizing and then synthesizing?

☐ Does the conclusion give a final answer to the question, argument, or problem?

☐ Does the conclusion have a general closing statement?

☐ Are relative clauses, participle phrases, colons, and apostrophes used correctly?

CHAPTER 9

REVIEW AND CONSOLIDATION

> Twice and thrice over, as they say, good is it to repeat and review what is good.
>
> Plato

This chapter will help you consolidate your learning from Chapters 1 to 8 before you go on to study specific writing forms in Part 3.

In this chapter, you will begin by reviewing the main content from Chapters 1 to 8:

- the writing and research processes
- active and critical reading skills
- bringing in others' ideas
- developing arguments and paragraphs
- writing introductions and conclusions

Next, you will do consolidation tasks for the following three features of successful academic writing:

- critical thinking: avoiding logical fallacies, checking the reliability of sources, and inferring meaning
- effective writing style: using APA and MLA citation styles, shifting style, using and avoiding personal language, and paraphrasing
- vocabulary: language of attribution, reporting verbs, and reference words

You will end the chapter by writing, revising, and editing a 700- to 1,000-word research essay related to one of the topics you read about in Chapters 1 to 8.

TASK 1 EXPLORE THROUGH WRITING

What do you need to review and practise most to improve your writing?

Take five minutes to answer the question. In small groups, read each other's writing.

CONTENT OVERVIEW

The Writing Process

Chapter 1 focused on the writing process as a sequence of seven stages. Each of these stages involves different forms of cognitive and critical engagement as you create the final written product.

1. Understand your audience, genre, and purpose.
2. Find your focus and task, question and subquestions.
3. Gather ideas in free writing, concept maps, and linear notes.
4. Form an outline.
5. Add research through reading and note taking.
6. Write the essay sections.
7. Edit and review your work for coherence, cohesion, accuracy, and style.

The Research Process

In Chapter 2, you studied the reasons for doing research, and explanations of empirical, non-empirical, quantitative, qualitative, and mixed-method research. This was followed by the explanation and analysis of 10 common stages of the research process:

1. Find a research problem or question.
2. State the purpose and/or goals.
3. Review relevant literature.
4. Adopt a theoretical position.
5. State a hypothesis.
6. Select a research methodology.
7. Collect data.
8. Code and analyze the data.
9. Present and evaluate results and conclusions.
10. Disseminate the research.

Active and Critical Reading Skills

In Chapter 3, you learned that effective academic writing requires effective active and critical reading. Accordingly, you studied the following:

- the difference between active and critical reading
- reading around a text
- skimming a text
- scanning for specific information
- annotation

You also learned the difference between patchwriting and paraphrasing, and studied the five stages of the summary-writing process. You completed the chapter by writing a 200-word summary.

Bringing in Others' Ideas

Chapter 4 focused on incorporating the ideas of other writers into your own work, with a specific focus on the following important aspects:

- academic integrity
- avoiding plagiarism
- common knowledge
- acknowledging sources
- techniques for writing from sources

At the end of the chapter, you studied the five stages of writing a response paper and then applied them in a 200-word response paper.

Developing Arguments

In Chapter 5, you studied techniques to strengthen your arguments in ways that reveal critical thinking and convince your reader:

- Avoid presenting opinions as facts.
- Support your arguments with reasons, examples, and evidence.
- Consider counter-arguments and other positions in the scholarly debate.
- Bring in ideas from reliable sources.
- Shift from a starting opinion to a broader, informed position.

Paragraphs

The focus of Chapter 6 was six key aspects of writing effective paragraphs:

- topic sentences
- paragraph unity
- paragraph coherence
- paragraph cohesion
- concluding sentences
- support for arguments

Through analyzing different writers' paragraphs, you learned that paragraphs are written in different ways depending on the subject area and the type of text.

Introductions

In Chapter 7, you studied six stages of writing introductions. Central to these six stages was a shift from general to specific:

1. Provide general background information.
2. Begin a gradual shift from general to specific.
3. Briefly review key literature.
4. State the specific focus of the essay.

5. Describe the organizational structure of the essay.

6. Provide a thesis statement.

You then analyzed several example introductions and learned that writers present these common features in different ways: they select some but not all of the stages, order them differently, and do not always shift from general to specific.

Conclusions

Chapter 8 focused on conclusions, presenting the image of a reverse funnel in which the conclusion mirrored the introduction by shifting from specific to general in four stages:

1. Briefly summarize the focus and main arguments of the essay.

2. Synthesize by bringing the essay threads together into one concept.

3. Provide a final answer and end the discussion.

4. Provide a general closing statement.

Again, through analyzing example conclusions, you found that writers select some but not all of the stages, order them differently, and do not always shift from specific to general. Moreover, some of the examples were from articles that did not contain a section titled "Conclusion."

CRITICAL THINKING

CONSOLIDATION TASKS

Logical Fallacies

In Chapters 5 to 8, you studied logical fallacies based on the following:

- misrepresentations of cause and effect
- incorrect generalizations
- misrepresentations of others' actions and ideas
- weak reasoning

You also analyzed the techniques that different writers use to avoid making logical fallacies in their argumentation.

TASK 2 IDENTIFY LOGICAL FALLACIES

Read the statements on the next page and identify the fallacy in each. Write the type of fallacy (choose from the following list) and explain why it weakens the writer's argument.

Misrepresenting cause and effect: post hoc, slippery slope, single cause, wrong direction

Generalization: generalization without evidence, hasty generalization, stereotype

Misrepresenting others' actions and ideas: ad hominem, ad populum, straw man

Weak reasoning: red herring, false dichotomy, circular logic

1. After being vaccinated at elementary school, my son lost his interest in music and art, and his grades went down. These vaccinations should be stopped.

   Logical fallacy: _____

   Explanation: _____

   _____

   _____

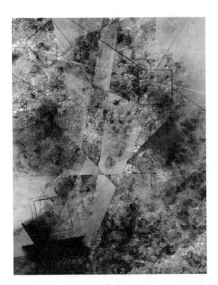

2. After one hour at the Tate Modern art gallery in London, I reached the conclusion that modern art should not qualify as art.

   Logical fallacy: _____

   Explanation: _____

   _____

   _____

3. When asked in opinion polls, most people in this country support the reduction of income tax. I believe the government should respect their wishes.

   Logical fallacy: _____

   Explanation: _____

   _____

   _____

4. I strongly support the introduction of nutritious lunches to our schools to send young people a clear message about healthy eating. If we can change the menu to healthy options, we will raise the profile of well-balanced diets.

   Logical fallacy: _____

   Explanation: _____

   _____

   _____

TASK 3 AVOID LOGICAL FALLACIES

The following sentences are written carelessly, which could lead to accusations that the writer is presenting logical fallacies. Identify the logical fallacy in each statement, and then rewrite the sentence so that it presents a sound argument.

1. Consumers understand that the fair trade label means paying extra to support small-scale producers.

   Logical fallacy: _____

   Rewrite: _____

   _____

2. Last year's survey of thousands of Swedish prisoners found that a large number of offenders came from broken families. Strategies are needed, therefore, to promote supportive families if we want to reduce crime.

Logical fallacy: _____

Rewrite: _____

_____

_____

_____

3. The majority of transnational corporations in China have Western-trained managers and directors; other Asian countries should aim to match China in this respect.

Logical fallacy: _____

Rewrite: _____

_____

_____

4. Business leaders in Africa should either adopt Western business approaches or promote local practices if they want to develop and succeed. Alternative options that take the best from both approaches are unrealistic in today's globalized world.

Logical fallacy: _____

Rewrite: _____

_____

_____

_____

Inferring Meaning

In Chapter 3, you practised the critical reading skill of inferring meaning when a writer's idea is not explicitly stated or understandable.

TASK 4 INFER THE MEANING

Read the statements below and the problems and questions that follow. To answer the questions, you will need to infer meaning.

1. While many business leaders from Europe and North America have advanced qualifications from reputable universities and business schools, it could be argued that these qualifications are less useful if the leaders' training has not addressed issues of cultural convergence, divergence, and crossvergence in business relations with Africa and Asia.

Problem: The writer is presenting two opposing views without explicitly stating his or her own stance.

Question: Does the writer give more emphasis to one idea than to the other, thus giving a clue to his or her stance?

Inference: _____

_____

_____

_____

2. Compare two versions of the same finding:

a) The report found that, on average, Western transnational corporations with mission statements supporting "local engagement" succeeded in hiring 32% local staff for management positions in Africa.

   Problem: The writer's purpose in including this finding is not clearly stated.

   Question: Does this specific finding portray Western transnational corporations in a positive or negative light? Explain your answer.

   Inference: _____

   _____

b) The report found that, on average, Western transnational corporations with mission statements supporting "local engagement" hired less than one third of local staff for management positions in Africa.

   Problem: The writer's purpose in including this finding is not clearly stated.

   Question: Does this specific finding portray Western transnational corporations in a positive or negative light? Explain your answer.

   Inference: _____

   _____

Reliability of Sources

In Chapter 4, you read about the importance of using reliable academic sources. You then practised applying criteria for assessing the reliability of an online news article.

TASK 5 SEARCH FOR SOURCES AND ASSESS RELIABILITY

Later in this chapter, you will write a research essay on one of the following topics that you read about in Chapters 1 to 8:

- college writing
- research methodology or homeopathy
- self-driving cars
- plagiarism in the music industry
- rehabilitation versus punishment in prisons
- fair trade
- slow food
- business leadership

You can also find a reproducible copy of the checklists in the online Documents.

To begin the writing process, choose one of the topics and do a keyword search for relevant sources on a general search engine and on an academic search engine. Choose two sources from each search engine and assess their reliability, using the reliability checklists on pages 85 and 86.

EFFECTIVE WRITING STYLE

CONSOLIDATION TASKS

APA and MLA Citation Styles

From Chapters 3 to 8, you studied APA and MLA citation styles, specifically, how to format references, where to place in-text citations in a sentence, and how the positioning can emphasize the author or the information. You also analyzed example sentences that had no in-text citations, or parts of the citation missing, and rewrote sentences written in another citation style.

TASK 6 CHANGE TO APA OR MLA STYLE

Correct and rewrite the sentences below, which are adapted from Chapter 6 texts. For MLA, if you do not know the required page numbers, write XX in their place.

1. Wilkinson (2007: 222) explains that Fairtrade International sets fair prices with producer organizations rather than individual producers mainly according to "production and broader reproduction costs."

   _____

   _____

   _____

   _____

2. Agrillo, Milano, Roveglia, & Scaffidi (2015) argues that taste and local knowledge are the main factors of importance in the slow food movement. Agrillo, Milano, Roveglia, & Scaffidi also analyze the development of slow food around the world today. (ibid) Page explains that local organizations called *convivia* take on the role of educating people about "how food is produced and its production origins, as well as instilling an appreciation of food culture and flavors." (2012, pp. 3).

   _____

   _____

   _____

   _____

   _____

   _____

Shifting Style

In Chapters 1 to 8, you studied how to shift style from semi-formal to formal if you bring information from newspaper and online articles into your writing, and from conversational to formal if you bring in information from interview excerpts. You learned that direct quotations should remain in the original form, while paraphrases require a shift to more formal written style.

TASK 7 SHIFT STYLE

The sentences below contain words and phrases that are commonly used in less formal English. <u>Underline</u> the examples of less formal English. Then rewrite each sentence in a style that is more suitable for academic writing.

1. The report on violent crime brought up important issues related to rehabilitation and funding and came up with some interesting conclusions.

   _____

   _____

2. Prison directors were asked to come up with responses for their institutions and to do away with ineffective initiatives.

   _____

   _____

3. They were asked not to go against government policy in the media and to hold on for six months before implementing changes.

   _____

   _____

4. Managers were required to pick out the three major problems their prisons faced and to run them by their directors.

   _____

   _____

5. The report made loads of recommendations to cut costs.

   _____

6. If you want to prevent prisoners from reoffending after release, they've got to be trained while they're locked up.

   _____

   _____

7. The committee will review the main findings of the report and its specific recommendations carefully and as fast as they can.

   _____

   _____

8. The report received lots of criticism from opponents.

_____

_____

Using and Avoiding Personal Language

You have learned that personal language does not in itself make writing informal; you also studied how the use of personal or impersonal language can depend on practices in different subject areas, readers' expectations, and your own personal preference. In many subject areas, especially scientific subjects, the use of personal language is discouraged due to the belief that it makes writing seem less objective and scientific; in other subject areas, personal language is encouraged.

TASK 8 MAKE SENTENCES LESS OR MORE PERSONAL

Rewrite the following sentences, using impersonal language (1 and 2) and personal language (3 and 4).

1. In this essay, I have discussed the challenges that car manufacturers face in using artificial intelligence in self-driving cars. I argued that it will be many years before autonomous vehicles replace human drivers.

_____

_____

_____

2. I contend that rather than investing vast sums of money in autonomous vehicles, car manufacturers should focus more on developing electric and hybrid vehicles.

_____

_____

3. The following section will introduce the terms *self-driving car* and *autonomous vehicle*. Key terminological distinctions will then be highlighted.

_____

_____

4. It has been suggested that autonomous vehicle technology has the potential to dominate the market within 15 years.

_____

_____

Paraphrasing

As part of the Chapter 3 focus on bringing others' ideas into your writing, you analyzed examples of paraphrasing and patchwriting. You then practised writing effective paraphrases by changing vocabulary, grammar, and sentence structure, to make the writing your own.

TASK 9 PARAPHRASE A PARAGRAPH

Paraphrase the following paragraph. Remember to keep the meaning as close as possible to the original.

Autonomous systems in cars can currently take over several driving functions in certain circumstances. However, a main challenge for autonomous vehicle technology is harsh weather, especially snowy, wintry conditions, in which visibility may be limited. Even though many people use the terms interchangeably, autonomous cars are not synonymous with driverless cars. While there is much talk in the media about driverless cars becoming market leaders, many feel that such talk is wildly optimistic.

_____

_____

_____

_____

_____

_____

VOCABULARY

CONSOLIDATION TASKS

Language of Attribution

Language of attribution is the language you use to make it clear to your reader _who thinks what_, and to avoid being accused of plagiarism for appropriating others' ideas and presenting them as your own.

TASK 10 LOCATE LANGUAGE OF ATTRIBUTION

Underline the language of attribution in the paragraph below.

Washington Post journalist Brian Fung believes that autonomous vehicles will face their biggest test when they are operated in icy and wet winter conditions. With regard to a timeline, researchers working the field have suggested that it could take a minimum of 10 years for driverless cars to have the ability to drive in all types of weather. Striking a more optimistic tone, Tesla chief executive Elon Musk has claimed that the forward radar in Tesla autonomous cars is already capable of functioning properly in fog and snow. A recent Google report stated that, during test drives in bad weather, its autonomous car had the capacity to pull over and wait for the weather to change. To sum up, in my opinion, there are still more cons than pros, and bad weather poses the greatest challenge to the new technology.

Reporting Verbs

Reporting verbs are used in different tenses, and in the active and passive voice, to refer to others' ideas. Using different reporting verbs can indicate your stance on the information you cite. It is a common feature of academic writing to use reporting verbs in the present tense when citing others' work. For empirical studies, using the past tense to cite the findings can suggest the findings are limited to the particular study in question; using the present tense to refer to empirical studies can indicate the findings are generalizable, that is, applicable in broader contexts or to a broader population beyond the parameters of the study.

TASK 11 ADD REPORTING VERBS

Add reporting verbs to the sentences below, following the prompts in parentheses.

1. Ugwu (2015) _____ that music compositions, like other forms of creative expression, are protected by copyright under the law. (factual information)

2. Ugwu (2015) _____ that the general public and courts do not listen to music in the same way. (argument)

3. Bailey and Challen (2015) _____ that some students _____ be confused by what is not acceptable in para-phrasing. (tentative argument)

4. The view that patchwriting should be understood as intentional plagiarism _____ Howard (1992). (Howard disagrees.)

5. In their study, Judd and Kennedy _____ that even in their final year, students were relying on Google and Wikipedia 41% of the time. (findings limited to one empirical study)

6. Piaget (1952) _____ that children learn by "assimilating" information from the environment. (argument, generalizable finding)

7. Ugwu (2015) _____ that musicians rely on the law to protect their compositions. (factual information that you agree with)

8. In Ugwu (2015), Fakler _____ that no musical work is completely original. (argument that you disagree with)

Anaphoric and Cataphoric Reference Words

In Chapter 3, you studied how reference words (*it, this, these, those*) are used to refer back to previous information (anaphoric reference) or forward to upcoming information (cataphoric reference). You learned that the use of such reference words adds cohesion to your writing and can make it more readable by allowing you to avoid repetition of words and phrases.

Read the paragraph below, which refers to the Marshall et al. (2015) article you read about on pages 22 and 23. Identify the reference words in bold as anaphoric or cataphoric, and explain what they refer to.

Sense of Belonging and First-Year Academic Literacy

It is not always easy for students to begin their first year of university. In fact, **it** can be quite a daunting transition. **For this reason**, many institutions begin the academic year with events that aim to help students develop a sense of belonging. Equally, many first-year courses attempt to promote a sense of belonging in their curriculum. Marshall, Zhou, Gervan, and Wiebe (2012) analyzed the factors affecting the sense of belonging of first-year students taking an academic literacy course called ALC. Participants described their sense of belonging to the university as being affected by interacting with peers, making new friends, interacting with faculty and advisers, living in residence, and having a manageable course load. **This** suggests that belonging is a complex, multifaceted phenomenon. **Those** who described a lack of sense of belonging to the university linked it to two of **these** factors (interacting with peers and not making friends) as well as to the size of the campus and concerns about maintaining GPA (Marshall et al., 2012).

1. **It** is not always easy for students to begin their first year of university.

   ☐ anaphoric ☐ cataphoric

   Reference: _____

2. In fact, **it** can be quite a daunting transition.

   ☐ anaphoric ☐ cataphoric

   Reference: _____

3. **For this reason**, many institutions begin the academic year with events that aim to help students develop a sense of belonging.

   ☐ anaphoric ☐ cataphoric

   Reference: _____

4. **This** suggests that belonging is a complex, multifaceted phenomenon.

   ☐ anaphoric ☐ cataphoric

   Reference: _____

   _____

5. **Those** who described a lack of sense of belonging to the university linked it to two of these factors . . .

   ☐ anaphoric ☐ cataphoric

   Reference: _____

6. Those who described a lack of sense of belonging to the university linked it to two of **these** factors . . .

☐ anaphoric ☐ cataphoric

Reference: _____

_____

WRITE, REVISE, AND EDIT

A RESEARCH ESSAY

TASK 13 WRITE A RESEARCH ESSAY

In Chapters 1 to 8, you studied different aspects of writing and research. From Chapters 5 to 8, you practised the writing process for a research essay on the topic of rehabilitation versus punishment in prisons, writing the introduction, main body paragraphs, and conclusion, and doing peer review for each part.

To conclude Part 2, write an original research essay on one of the following topics you have read about:

- college writing
- research methodology or homeopathy
- self-driving cars
- plagiarism in the music industry
- rehabilitation versus punishment in prisons
- fair trade
- slow food
- business leadership

Find detailed rules and formats for APA and MLA citation styles in Appendices 2 and 3.

Choose your own specific focus and type of essay (e.g., argument, comparative, problem-solution, cause and effect, or a combination of these essay types). The essay should be 700 to 1,000 words in length and should contain accurate in-text citations and a complete list of references following APA, MLA, or another citation style recommended by your instructor.

As necessary, refer back to the seven stages of the writing process (Chapter 1) and the 10 stages of the research process (Chapter 2).

TASK 14 REVISE AND EDIT YOUR ESSAY

Find the Research Essay Review Sheet in the online Documents.

When you have written your first complete draft of the essay, go through one stage of revision and editing, using the Research Essay Review Sheet. First, do a detailed self-evaluation of your work, focusing on the criteria on the review sheet and filling in the sections with your own observations about your writing. Next, ask two peers to review your work, using copies of the same sheet. Compare your self-evaluation with the two peer reviews before you make final revisions to improve the essay.

© **ERPI** Reproduction prohibited

WRITING FOR DIFFERENT ACADEMIC PURPOSES

CHAPTER 10

DESCRIBING PROCESSES AND STATISTICAL DATA

Facts are stubborn things, but statistics are pliable.

Mark Twain

Your ability to persuade your reader and develop an authoritative voice as a writer in your subject area depends on many factors. One of these factors is the ability to show a clear understanding of processes and statistical data. Describing processes requires detailed and accurate description of their stages and steps. Equally, when you write about statistics, you need to write with precision. Your ability to do so will depend not only on the language you use for this purpose but also on your ability to engage critically with statistical data.

In this chapter, you will:

- read and analyze texts on the topics of 3D printing and air pollution
- learn how to describe processes and statistical data
- study vocabulary to describe statistics
- critically engage with statistical data
- study subject-verb agreement
- review strategies for improving writing style
- write a process paragraph based on a diagram illustrating sources of pollution
- write a paragraph based on two bar charts presenting statistical data on air emissions

TASK 1 EXPLORE THROUGH DISCUSSION

Discuss the quotation above, attributed to American novelist Mark Twain. How do you understand the quotation, and do you agree with the main idea?

DESCRIBING PROCESSES

You may be required to study, understand, and describe many different processes on academic courses—for example, how a machine works, the steps of a laboratory experiment, or the stages of a management model. In doing so, your role as a writer is to read, observe, and provide accurate, detailed description. Describing processes is a kind of expository writing, that is, writing that describes, illustrates, and informs.

From Photocopies to Printed Objects

Printing has developed rapidly in recent years due to technological advances. While traditional printing involved transferring two-dimensional images onto paper or other surfaces, using ink or toner in a copier, today three-dimensional objects can be copied by 3D printers. The applications of this new technology range from copying machine components and other metal and plastic objects to the "printing" of body parts in the field of regenerative science.

The following text is an encyclopedia entry on 3D printing, published online by Britannica.com.

three-dimensional: having length, width, and depth

fabricating: producing

cross sections: inside layers, as if cut open

sequentially: in a particular order

analogous: similar

fusing: joining together (often by heating and melting)

binding: fastening (in this case, a solid mass)

prototypes: first models or designs

mold patterns: shaped containers for pouring liquid into to solidify

apparatus: equipment for a specific task

patented: officially registered to give sole rights to one producer

generic label: label referring to a whole group

successive: following one after another

3D Printing

3D printing, in full **three-dimensional** **printing**, in manufacturing, any of several processes for **fabricating** three-dimensional objects by layering two-dimensional **cross sections sequentially**, one on top of another. The process is **analogous** to the **fusing** of ink or toner onto paper in a printer
5 (hence the term *printing*) but is actually the solidifying or **binding** of a liquid or powder at each spot in the horizontal cross section where solid material is desired. In the case of 3D printing, the layering is repeated hundreds or thousands of times until the entire object has been finished throughout its vertical dimension. Frequently, 3D printing is employed in quickly turning
10 out plastic or metal **prototypes** during the design of new parts, though it also can be put to use in making final products for sale to customers. Objects made in 3D printing range from plastic figurines and **mold patterns** to steel machine parts and titanium surgical implants. An entire 3D printing **apparatus** can be enclosed in a cabinet roughly the size of a large kitchen
15 stove or refrigerator.

The term *3D printing* originally designated a specific process **patented** as 3DP by scientists at the Massachusetts Institute of Technology (MIT) in 1993 and licensed to several manufacturers. Today the term is used as a **generic label** for a number of related processes. Central to all of them is computer-
20 aided design, or CAD. Using CAD programs, engineers develop a three-dimensional computer model of the object to be built up. This model is translated into a series of two-dimensional "slices" of the object and then into instructions that tell the printer exactly where to solidify the starting material on each **successive** slice.

dispensed: given out in controlled portions

array: set of objects arranged in a specific pattern

nozzles: short tubes that control the flow of a substance

unconsolidated: not joined together

mock-ups: models, usually of the same size as the final product

sintering: creating a mass through heat without melting

electron: negatively charged particle in all atoms

alloys: mixtures of two or more metals

polymer: type of chemical compound including many synthetic and natural substances (e.g., plastics, proteins)

ultraviolet: invisible rays of light

additive: made through adding parts or components

subtractive: made through taking away parts or components

foundry: factory where objects are made from melted metal

milling: grinding or crushing solids into powder

25 In most processes the starting material is a fine plastic or metal powder. Typically, the powder is stored in cartridges or beds from which it is **dispensed** in small amounts and spread by a roller or blade in an extremely thin layer (commonly only the thickness of the powder grains, which can be as small as 20 micrometres, or 0.0008 inch) over the bed where the part is being
30 built up. In MIT's 3DP process this layer is passed over by a device similar to the head of an ink-jet printer. An **array** of **nozzles** sprays a binding agent in a pattern determined by the computer program, then a fresh layer of powder is spread over the entire build-up area, and the process is repeated. At each repetition the build-up bed is lowered by precisely the thickness of
35 the new layer of powder. When the process is complete, the built-up part, embedded in **unconsolidated** powder, is pulled out, cleaned, and sometimes put through some post-processing finishing steps.

The original 3DP process made mainly rough **mock-ups** out of plastic, ceramic, and even plaster, but later variations employed metal powder as
40 well and produced more-precise and more-durable parts. A related process is called selective laser **sintering** (SLS); here the nozzle head and liquid binder are replaced by precisely guided lasers that heat the powder so that it sinters, or partially melts and fuses, in the desired areas. Typically, SLS works with either plastic powder or a combined metal-binder powder; in the
45 latter case the built-up object may have to be heated in a furnace for further solidification and then machined and polished. These post-processing steps can be minimized in direct metal laser sintering (DMLS), in which a high-power laser fuses a fine metal powder into a more-solid and finished part without the use of binder material. Yet another variation is electron beam
50 melting (EBM); here the laser apparatus is replaced by an **electron** gun, which focuses a powerful electrically charged beam onto the powder under vacuum conditions. The most-advanced DMLS and EBM processes can make final products of advanced steel, titanium, and cobalt-chromium **alloys**.

Many other processes work on the building-up principle of 3DP, SLS, DMLS,
55 and EBM. Some use nozzle arrangements to direct the starting material (either powder or liquid) only to the designated build-up areas, so that the object is not immersed in a bed of the material. On the other hand, in a process known as stereolithography (SLA), a thin layer of **polymer** liquid rather than powder is spread over the build area, and the designated part
60 areas are consolidated by an **ultraviolet** laser beam. The built-up plastic part is retrieved and put through post-processing steps.

All 3D printing processes are so-called **additive** manufacturing, or additive fabrication, processes—ones that build up objects sequentially, as opposed to casting or molding them in a single step (a consolidation process) or cutting
65 and machining them out of a solid block (a **subtractive** process). As such, they are considered to have several advantages over traditional fabrication, chief among them being an absence of the expensive tooling used in **foundry** and **milling** processes; the ability to produce complicated, customized parts on short notice; and the generating of less waste. On the other hand, they
70 also have several disadvantages; these include low production rates, less precision and surface polish than machined parts, a relatively limited range

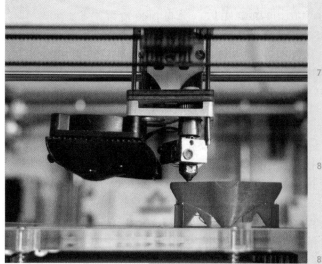

of materials that can be processed, and severe limitations on the size of parts that can be made inexpensively and without **distortion**. For this reason, the principal market of 3D printing is in so-called rapid prototyping—that is, the quick production of parts that eventually will be mass-produced in traditional manufacturing processes. Nevertheless, commercial 3D printers continue to improve their processes and **make inroads** into markets for final products, and researchers continue to experiment with 3D printing, producing objects as **disparate** as automobile bodies, concrete blocks, and edible food products.

The term *3D bioprinting* is used to describe the application of 3D printing concepts to the production of biological **entities**, such as tissues and organs. Bioprinting is based largely on existing printing technologies, such as ink-jet or laser printing, but makes use of "bioink" (suspensions of living cells and **cell growth medium**), which may be prepared in **micropipettes** or similar tools that serve as printer cartridges. Printing is then controlled via computer, with cells being deposited in specific patterns onto **culture plates** or similar sterile surfaces. Valve-based printing, which enables fine control over cell **deposition** and improved preservation of cell **viability**, has been used to print human **embryonic stem cells** in preprogrammed patterns that facilitate the cells' aggregation into **spheroid** structures. Such human tissue models generated through 3D bioprinting are of particular use in the field of regenerative medicine.

3D printing. (2016, January 26). In *Encyclopædia Britannica*. Retrieved from https://www.britannica.com/technology/3D-printing

distortion: change in desired shape or form

make inroads: increase in presence and influence

disparate: different from each other

entities: things existing independently

cell growth medium: liquid or solid substance for growing cells

micropipettes: very narrow glass tubes for transferring liquids in experiments

culture plates: small dishes used to grow cells in experiments

deposition: placing on a specific surface

viability: ability to survive

embryonic stem cells: basic human cells, found in embryos, that can develop into other types of cell

spheroid: shaped like a sphere

TASK 2 ANALYZE THE STYLE

The text above is written in a style that is appropriate for an encyclopedia entry describing a complex process. Which of the following descriptions best match the style of the text? Check all appropriate answers.

1. Subjective language that includes personal opinions ☐

2. Objective language that is mainly descriptive ☐

3. Personal language with pronouns such as *I*, *you*, and *we* ☐

4. Impersonal language, including the passive voice ☐

5. Informal language with few technical terms ☐

6. Formal academic language with many technical terms ☐

Road Transport Emissions: The Process

The following diagram is from a guide written by the European Environment Agency, titled *Explaining Road Transport Emissions*. The guide describes emissions cycles, presents statistical data, and explains the need for regulation to improve local environments.

FIGURE 1 THE EMISSIONS CYCLE

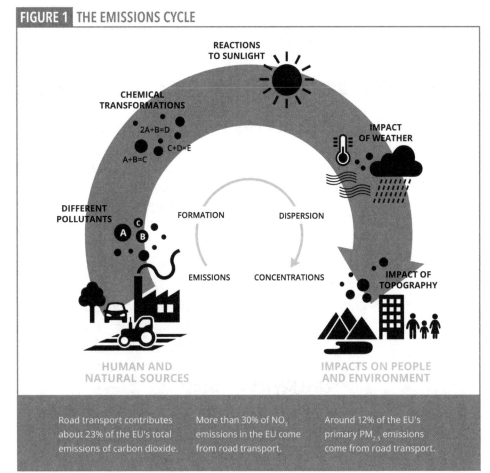

REACTIONS TO SUNLIGHT

CHEMICAL TRANSFORMATIONS

2A+B=D

C+D=E

A+B=C

DIFFERENT POLLUTANTS

A C B

FORMATION

DISPERSION

EMISSIONS

CONCENTRATIONS

IMPACT OF WEATHER

IMPACT OF TOPOGRAPHY

HUMAN AND NATURAL SOURCES

IMPACTS ON PEOPLE AND ENVIRONMENT

Road transport contributes about 23% of the EU's total emissions of carbon dioxide.

More than 30% of NO_x emissions in the EU come from road transport.

Around 12% of the EU's primary $PM_{2.5}$ emissions come from road transport.

European Environment Agency. (2016). *Explaining road transport emissions: A non-technical guide*. Copenhagen: EEA.

topography: features of an area of land, such as mountains, lakes, and rivers

NO_x: nitrogen oxides

$PM_{2.5}$: fine particulate matter, e.g., particles from fuel combustion

TASK 3 DESCRIBE A PROCESS

Complete the sentences below to describe the emissions cycle illustrated in Figure 1. Follow the prompts in parentheses, and write the sentences in an appropriate style for this genre of expository writing. Where possible, include the key technical terms from Figure 1: *emissions*, *formation*, *dispersion*, and *concentrations* (as nouns or other parts of speech).

1. Human and natural sources cause _____

   _____.

   (Begin with a general statement that links the sources to impacts.)

2. The different pollutants gather _____

   _____.

   (Explain that the pollutants change in the air.)

3. The chemical formations are _____

   _____.

   (Explain that sunlight interacts with the pollutants; use the passive voice.)

4. The pollutants are further _____

   _____.

   (Explain the effect of weather and topography on the pollutants; use the passive voice.)

ACTIVE AND CRITICAL READING

ENGAGING WITH DATA

Another important skill in successful academic writing is engaging with data presented in graphs, tables, charts, diagrams, and illustrations. You may study and analyze data in an article you are reading, or you may be writing about data that you have collected for a research project. In either case, it is important to do the following:

- Select key information: concentrate on information that is related to your specific focus.
- Represent information accurately: interpret the statistics correctly and avoid changing their meaning.
- Engage critically with information: think critically as you read and write.

Select Key Information

As you read, highlight or underline information that is related to your specific focus. Be careful and selective; look for the following:

- the purpose of presenting the data
- main trends and general findings in the data
- highs and lows in the data
- specific reference to changes over time

The text below provides statistical data on air pollutants in European countries, and an explanation of the data. Read the text and do the tasks that follow.

Air Pollution Statistics

[1] Air pollution caused by human activities, including industrial and energy production, the burning of fossil fuels and increased use of certain types of transport, causes serious health problems for hundreds of thousands of Europeans every year. [2] Environmental damage such as acidification, **eutrophication**, tropospheric (ground-level) **ozone** and reduced air quality, especially in urban areas, can be a local as well as a **transboundary** problem as air pollutants are transported in the atmosphere and harm human health and the environment elsewhere.

eutrophication: excessive growth of plants such as algae in lakes and rivers due to fertilizer runoff

ozone: toxic O_3 gas in the atmosphere

transboundary: across boundaries

FIGURE 2 EMISSIONS OF AIR POLLUTANTS, EU-28, 1990-2013

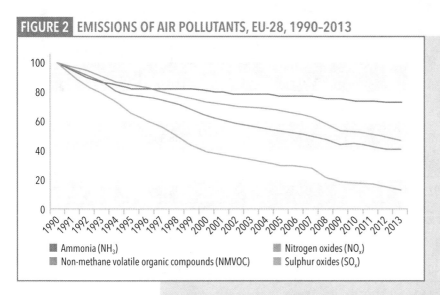

■ Ammonia (NH₃)
■ Non-methane volatile organic compounds (NMVOC)
■ Nitrogen oxides (NOₓ)
■ Sulphur oxides (SOₓ)

Main Statistical Findings

[3] From 1990 to 2013 the EU-28 recorded reductions in emissions of all air pollutants considered in this article (see Figure 2). [4] The biggest fall was reported for sulphur oxides (SO_x) which between 1990 and 2013 decreased by 86.7%, followed by non-methane volatile organic compounds (NMVOCs) which declined by nearly 60%. [5] Nitrogen oxides (NO_x) stood at 53.5% of their 1990 levels (a decrease of roughly 46.5%); while the smallest decrease was reported for ammonia (NH_3), emissions of which fell only by 27% by 2013.

[6] In 2013 emissions of ammonia (NH_3) in the EU-28 stood at 3 847 870 tonnes, NMVOCs at 7 004 930 tonnes, nitrogen oxides (NO_x) at 8 176 454 tonnes and sulphur oxides (SO_x) at 3 429 764 tonnes (see Table 1). [7] The biggest emitters of ammonia in 2013 in the EU-28 were France with 18.7% of the EU total, followed by Germany with 17.4% and Italy with 10.5%. [8] The NMVOC emissions were highest in Germany, Italy, France and the United Kingdom—each with double-digit shares of the EU total. [9] Nitrogen oxides (NO_x) were emitted the most in Germany (15.5% of the EU total), the United Kingdom (12.5%), and France (12.1%). [10] Regarding sulphur oxides (SO_x), unlike the other pollutants, the biggest emitter was a country from Eastern Europe: Poland with 24.7% of the EU total, followed by Germany with 12.1% and the United Kingdom with 11.5%.

Excerpt from Eurostat. (2016, October 19). Air pollution statistics. *Statistics Explained*. Retrieved from http://ec.europa.eu/eurostat/statisticsexplained/index.php/Air_pollution_statistics

TABLE 1 EMISSIONS OF AIR POLLUTANTS BY COUNTRY, IN TONNES, 2013

	NH₃ (Ammonia)	NOₓ (Nitrogen Oxides)	NMVOC (Non-Methane Volatile Organic Compounds)	SOₓ (Sulphur Oxides)
EU-28	3 847 870	8 176 454	7 004 930	3 429 764
Belgium	62 233	207 680	137 430	45 558
Bulgaria	30 497	122 573	88 832	193 966
Czech Republic	68 500	181 094	136 397	137 915
Denmark	74 320	123 865	114 431	13 643
Germany	670 849	1 269 182	1 138 241	416 214
Estonia	11 303	29 721	32 931	36 500
Ireland	107 758	79 064	90 001	25 393

	NH₃ (Ammonia)	NOₓ (Nitrogen Oxides)	NMVOC (Non-Methane Volatile Organic Compounds)	SOₓ (Sulphur Oxides)
Greece	60 570	238 621	144 765	152 327
Spain	379 308	812 152	550 801	287 128
France	718 133	989 521	758 380	218 785
Croatia	33 729	55 749	46 072	16 378
Italy	402 230	820 574	905 539	145 054
Cyprus	4 756	16 164	6 681	13 766
Latvia	14 707	34 044	87 448	1 502
Lithuania	40 410	46 166	63 394	18 928
Luxembourg	4 573	31 434	7 650	1 580
Hungary	81 243	120 567	120 400	29 309
Malta	1 586	4 872	3 318	5 028
Netherlands	133 801	239 619	149 682	29 926
Austria	66 249	162 317	126 341	17 245
Poland	263 402	798 233	635 776	846 845
Portugal	49 111	161 476	169 630	42 276
Romania	165 147	218 823	322 953	202 676
Slovenia	17 451	42 893	33 324	11 294
Slovakia	25 245	79 582	63 204	53 208
Finland	37 283	144 877	94 558	47 377
Sweden	52 168	125 915	173 756	26 785
United Kingdom	271 309	1 019 674	802 997	393 158
Iceland	5 337	20 775	5 402	72 563
Liechtenstein	174	704	417	28
Norway	27 239	154 437	133 737	17 038
Switzerland	61 690	72 304	84 139	10 207
Turkey	1 089 748	1 047 000	868 184	1 939 104

TASK 4 ANALYZE THE TEXT

Complete the following paragraphs to describe the functions of the sentences in the Eurostat text.

Figure 2

Sentences 1 and 2 set _____

_____ .

Sentence 3 presents _____.

Sentence 4 begins with _____, followed by
_____. Sentence 5 shows
_____ in descending order.

Table 1

Sentence 6 gives _____.

Sentence 7 shows _____ in descending order.

Sentences 8 to 10 show _____
_____.

TASK 5 LOCATE KEY INFORMATION

Locate the sentences in the Eurostat text where you found the following key information.

		Sentence(s)
1	The purpose of presenting the data	
2	Main trends and general findings in the data	
3	Highs and lows in the data	
4	Specific references to changes over time	

VOCABULARY

DESCRIBING DATA

TASK 6 IDENTIFY USEFUL VOCABULARY

List the phrases used to describe the following aspects of the data in the Eurostat text.

Fixed Percentages

1. Sentence 5: _____
_____

Polluting Emissions Falling

2. Sentence 3: _____

3. Sentence 4: _____
_____

4. Sentence 5: _____
_____
_____

Highest Percentages

5. Sentence 7: _____

_____

6. Sentence 8: _____

_____

7. Sentence 9: _____

_____

8. Sentence 10: _____

_____

Representing Information Accurately

It is important to represent information accurately and precisely when you describe statistical data. You should use appropriate vocabulary to convey the exact nature of the statistics, including increases, decreases, fluctuations, highs, lows, and changes over time. The following words and phrases are commonly used to describe statistical data with precision. Note that the examples are not intended to represent the tables and figures in this chapter.

Increases and Decreases

Part of Speech	Vocabulary	Examples
Increases		
Nouns	*increase* *climb* *growth* *rise* **jump* **surge*	There was **an increase / a climb / growth / a rise** in the figure for total emissions for all countries. There was a notable **jump/surge** in carbon emissions worldwide from 2000 to 2010.
Verbs	*increase* *climb* *go up* *grow* *rise* **jump* **rocket* **shoot up* **soar* **surge*	The figure for total emissions **increased / climbed / went up / grew / rose** in three of four countries. The total figure for carbon emissions **jumped / rocketed / shot up / soared / surged** worldwide from 2000 to 2010.
Decreases		
Nouns	*decrease* *decline* *drop* *fall* **plunge* **slump*	There was a **decrease/decline/drop/fall** in the figure for total emissions for all countries. The **plunge/slump** in sulphur oxide emissions was particularly encouraging.

Part of Speech	Vocabulary	Examples
Verbs	*decrease* *decline* *drop* *fall* *go down* **plummet* **plunge* **sink*	The figure for total emissions **decreased / declined / dropped / fell / went down** in most countries. The figure for sulphur oxide emissions **plummeted/ plunged/sank** during the same period.
Increases and Decreases		
Add adjectives	*gradual* *moderate* *slight* *slow* *steady* *dramatic* *rapid* *sharp* *significant* *steep* *sudden*	There was a **gradual/moderate/slight/slow/ steady** increase in CO_2 emissions. There was a **gradual/moderate/slight/slow/ steady** decrease in ammonia emissions. There was a **dramatic/rapid/sharp/significant/ steep/sudden** increase in acidification. There was a **dramatic/rapid/sharp/significant/ steep/sudden** decrease in sulphur oxide emissions.
Add adverbs	*gradually* *moderately* *slightly* *slowly* *steadily* *dramatically* *rapidly* *sharply* *significantly* *steeply* *suddenly*	The percentage increased **gradually/moderately/ slightly/slowly/steadily**. CO_2 emissions decreased **gradually/moderately/ slightly/slowly/steadily**. Air pollution increased **dramatically/rapidly/ sharply/significantly/steeply/suddenly**. Sulphur oxide emissions decreased **dramatically/ rapidly/sharply/significantly/steeply/suddenly**.

An asterisk (*) indicates an extreme increase or decrease.

Change and Stability

Vocabulary	Examples
Change	
fluctuate (verb)	The figure for CO_2 emissions **fluctuated** between 1990 and 2000.
fluctuation (noun)	There was **a fluctuation** in the figure for CO_2 emissions between 1990 and 2000.
Change over Time	
increase twofold/threefold (verb) *twofold/threefold increase* (noun)	The percentage **increased twofold/threefold**. Figure X shows **a twofold/threefold increase** in percentage.
double/treble/quadruple (verb) *double / twice / two times*	The percentage **doubled/trebled/quadrupled**. The percentage for 2016 **is double / twice / two times** that of 2012.

Vocabulary	Examples
Stability	
remain constant / stable / steady / the same / unchanged	Nitrogen oxide emissions **remained constant / stable / steady / the same / unchanged**.
stay constant / stable / steady / the same / unchanged	Nitrogen oxide emissions **stayed constant / stable / steady / the same / unchanged**.
stabilize	Nitrogen oxide emissions **stabilized**.

Highs and Lows in the Data

Vocabulary	Examples
Highs	
peak	In 2013, emissions of ammonia **peaked**.
reach a high/peak	In 2013, emissions of ammonia **reached a high/peak**.
reach their highest level/point/ percentage	In 2013, emissions of ammonia **reached their highest level/point/percentage**.
rise to their highest level/point/ percentage	In 2013, emissions of ammonia **rose to their highest level/point/percentage**.
Lows	
fall to a low / a low point	In 2013, NMVOC emissions **fell to a low / a low point**.
reach a low / a low point	In 2013, NMVOC emissions **reached a low / a low point**.
reach their lowest level/point/ percentage	In 2013, NMVOC emissions **reached their lowest level/point/percentage**.

TASK 7 DESCRIBE STATISTICAL DATA

Complete the sentences below to describe the statistical data in Figure 2 and Table 1 on pages 211 and 212. Follow the prompts in parentheses, and write the sentences in an appropriate style for this genre of expository writing.

Figure 2

1. Between 1990 and 2013, _____.

   (Describe a fall in percentage terms; include an adverb.)

2. During the same period, the most dramatic fall was in emissions of _____

   _____.

   (Describe the fall in percentage terms.)

3. Between 1994 and 2000, emissions of ammonia _____.

   (Describe whether emissions rose, fell, or did both.)

Table 1

4. In 2013, the highest emitter of ammonia was _____

   _____.

   (Compare the highest and lowest emitters of ammonia; include the number of tonnes.)

5. Nitrogen oxide emissions in Belgium were _____

_____

_____ .

(Compare nitrogen oxide emissions in Belgium and the UK; state the difference in terms of a fraction, percentage, or multiple.)

EXTEND YOUR ACADEMIC VOCABULARY

Extend your knowledge of key vocabulary from this chapter.

additive	**decline**	**fluctuate**
analogous	diagnose	generic
array	disparate	slight
as such	**dramatic**	**successive**

*Words in bold type are AWL entries.

My eLab

Practise Chapter 10 vocabulary online.

CRITICAL THINKING

ENGAGING CRITICALLY WITH STATISTICAL DATA

As well as selecting key information and representing that information accurately, it is important to engage critically with statistical data by analyzing and evaluating information as you read and write. Figure 2 and Table 1 on pages 211 and 212 are from a reputable European Union organization. Nonetheless, it is still possible to read such sources with a critical eye, weighing factors that could affect the reliability of the statistics, such as inconsistencies in the collection and analysis of data.

TASK 8 THINK CRITICALLY ABOUT FIGURE 2 AND TABLE 1

Look again at Figure 2 and Table 1 on pages 211 and 212. List below any factors to consider when assessing the reliability of the statistics.

_____

_____

_____

_____

_____

Statistics in News Media

When you read statistics in news reports, it is important to read critically and assess the reliability of the statistics and the resulting claims made by the media. This is especially the case when reading sensational stories in popular tabloid newspapers. The following is an example from the British tabloid *Daily Mail*, in which the headline claims that modern life is killing children.

Modern Life Is KILLING Children: Gadgets, Pollution and Pesticides Are Blamed as Cancer Rates Soar 40 per cent in Just 16 Years

by Simon Holmes

Pollution, pesticides and fast food is killing our children with new government statistics revealing that the number of youngsters diagnosed with cancer has risen by 40% over the past 16 years.

Analysis compiled by researchers from the charity Children with Cancer UK found new cases of cancer in young people rose by 1,300 every year since statistics were last compiled in 1998.

The charity found this is most evident in colon cancer which has increased by 200% and thyroid cancer which has seen its cases doubled during the 18 years since the last report was released.

Although researchers can attribute some of the rise to improvements in cancer diagnoses and more screening, they admit the majority is probably caused by environmental factors.

Alasdair Philips, science adviser at Children with Cancer UK told Sky News that there seems to be 'a correlation between the lifestyle of young people.'

'They tend to be doing a lot less exercise and there's also a lot of fast food being eaten, which is fine in moderation, but we know they do contain cancer giving substances,' he said. . . .

Excerpt from Holmes, S. (2016, September 4). Modern life is killing children: Gadgets, pollution and pesticides are blamed as cancer rates soar 40 per cent in just 16 years. *MailOnline*. Retrieved from http://www.dailymail.co.uk/news/article-3773015/KILLING-children-gadgets-pollution-pesticides-blamed-cancer-rates-soar-40-cent-just-16-years.html

TASK 9 ENGAGE CRITICALLY WITH MEDIA STATISTICS

Answer the following questions about the headline and excerpt from the *Daily Mail* article.

1. In what ways does the headline fail to match the content of the article in terms of causality and correlation?

   _____

   _____

   _____

2. How does the mismatch between the headline and content affect you as a critical reader? Are you convinced?

_____

_____

3. Find the grammatical errors in the first and third paragraphs of the text, and correct them below. How might the grammatical inaccuracy affect readers' inclination to be persuaded by the arguments?

_____

_____

_____

_____

_____

_____

_____

_____

_____

EFFECTIVE SENTENCE STRUCTURE

SUBJECT-VERB AGREEMENT

All complete sentences in academic writing should have a subject, and a verb (or verbs) that corresponds with the subject. This feature of sentences is called _subject-verb agreement_. The most important aspect of this feature is making sure that singular and plural verbs agree with singular and plural subjects, respectively. Several additional rules of usage are explained in detail in Unit 10 of the Handbook.

TASK 10 IDENTIFY THE SUBJECTS AND CORRESPONDING VERBS

The following excerpts are taken from the _Encyclopædia Britannica_ entry on 3D printing. Underline the subject(s) and highlight the corresponding verb(s) in each excerpt. One excerpt lacks a subject and corresponding verb.

1. **3D printing**, in full **three-dimensional printing**, in manufacturing, any of several processes for fabricating three-dimensional objects by layering two-dimensional cross sections sequentially, one on top of another.

2. The process is analogous to the fusing of ink or toner onto paper in a printer.

3. Objects made in 3D printing range from plastic figurines and mold patterns to steel machine parts and titanium surgical implants.

4. In most processes the starting material is a fine plastic or metal powder.

5. An array of nozzles sprays a binding agent in a pattern determined by the computer program.

6. A thin layer of polymer liquid rather than powder is spread over the build area.

Do Unit 10: Subject-Verb Agreement in the Handbook, pp. 385–390.

7. Such human tissue models generated through 3D bioprinting are of particular use in the field of regenerative medicine.

REVIEW OF SENTENCE FRAGMENTS AND PUNCTUATION

TASK 11 ANALYZE A SENTENCE FRAGMENT

The opening sentence of the *Encyclopædia Britannica* entry is a sentence fragment because it lacks a subject and a corresponding verb:

> **3D printing**, in full **three-dimensional printing**, in manufacturing, any of several processes for fabricating three-dimensional objects by layering two-dimensional cross sections sequentially, one on top of another.

Is the usage appropriate for this type of text? Explain why or why not.

_____

_____

_____

TASK 12 CORRECT PUNCTUATION

The Eurostat article is not punctuated consistently according to the rules of academic writing that you have studied in this book. Read the following sentences from the article and add, change, or delete punctuation where necessary.

1. From 1990 to 2013 the EU-28 recorded reductions in emissions of all air pollutants considered in this article.

2. The biggest fall was reported for sulphur oxides (SO_x) which between 1990 and 2013 decreased by 86.7%, followed by non-methane volatile organic compounds (NMVOCs) which declined by nearly 60%.

3. Nitrogen oxides (NO_x) stood at 53.5% of their 1990 levels (a decrease of roughly 46.5%); while the smallest decrease was reported for ammonia (NH_3), emissions of which fell only by 27% by 2013.

EFFECTIVE WRITING STYLE

REWRITING FOR IMPROVED STYLE

In previous chapters, you analyzed the style of different texts and did practice activities to improve the style of your academic writing, ranging from avoiding contractions and addressing the reader as *you* to using more academic vocabulary and more varied sentence structure. In this chapter, you will review the earlier tasks on effective style by analyzing sentences from one of the texts in this chapter and rewriting them in a different, improved style.

TASK 13 REVIEW EFFECTIVE STYLE

The excerpts below are from the *Encyclopædia Britannica* entry on 3D printing. Read each excerpt and the explanation that follows. Then rewrite the sentence(s) in a different style according to the explanation.

1. Objects made in 3D printing range from plastic figurines and mold patterns to steel machine parts and titanium surgical implants. An entire 3D printing apparatus can be enclosed in a cabinet roughly the size of a large kitchen stove or refrigerator.

   Explanation: The two sentences do not flow well. Improve the flow by connecting them with a conjunctive adverb.

   _____

   _____

   _____

   _____

2. Typically, the powder is stored in cartridges or beds from which it is dispensed in small amounts and spread by a roller or blade in an extremely thin layer (commonly only the thickness of the powder grains, which can be as small as 20 micrometres, or 0.0008 inch) over the bed where the part is being built up.

   Explanation: The sentence is too long and contains too much information. Improve the clarity by separating it into two or more sentences.

   _____

   _____

   _____

   _____

3. The original 3DP process made mainly rough mock-ups out of plastic, ceramic, and even plaster, but later variations employed metal powder as well and produced more precise and more durable parts.

   Explanation: This is a compound sentence, with two independent clauses joined by the coordinator *but*. Improve the style by replacing *but* with a subordinator, thus creating a complex sentence.

   _____

   _____

   _____

   _____

4. Yet another variation is electron beam melting (EBM); here the laser apparatus is replaced by an electron gun, which focuses a powerful electrically charged beam onto the powder under vacuum conditions.

Explanation: The style is repetitive because previously in the same paragraph, the writer also uses a semicolon followed by the word *here*. Improve the style by avoiding the repeated form.

_____

_____

_____

_____

5. As such, they are considered to have several advantages over traditional fabrication, chief among them being an absence of the expensive tooling used in foundry and milling processes; the ability to produce complicated, customized parts on short notice; and the generating of less waste.

Explanation: The advantages are correctly separated by semicolons because one of the examples includes a comma. However, the exemplification is rather confusing. Improve the style by rewriting the sentence, using *the following*.

Find supplementary reading, writing, and critical-thinking activities online.

_____

_____

_____

_____

▌WRITE, REVISE, AND EDIT

TWO EXPOSITORY PARAGRAPHS

TASK 14 WRITE A PROCESS PARAGRAPH

Write a process paragraph to describe the pollution cycle as illustrated in the diagram on the next page, published by the New South Wales government in Australia. Follow this method:

1. Begin with an introductory sentence describing the focus and purpose of the diagram and identifying its source.

2. Continue with a selective sentence-by-sentence description of the most salient parts of the process, following the order of the cycle from the bottom left upward and then down the right side.

FIGURE 3 SOURCES OF POLLUTION

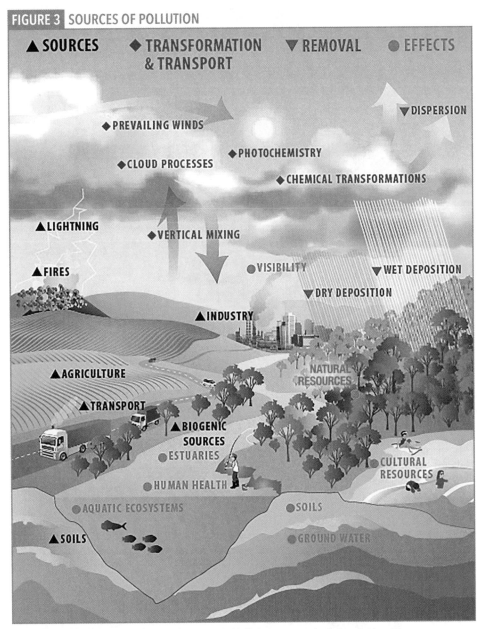

▲ SOURCES   ◆ TRANSFORMATION & TRANSPORT   ▼ REMOVAL   ● EFFECTS

◆ PREVAILING WINDS

◆ PHOTOCHEMISTRY

◆ CLOUD PROCESSES

◆ CHEMICAL TRANSFORMATIONS

▼ DISPERSION

▲ LIGHTNING

◆ VERTICAL MIXING

▲ FIRES

● VISIBILITY

▼ WET DEPOSITION

▼ DRY DEPOSITION

▲ INDUSTRY

▲ AGRICULTURE

NATURAL RESOURCES

▲ TRANSPORT

▲ BIOGENIC SOURCES

● ESTUARIES

CULTURAL RESOURCES

● HUMAN HEALTH

● AQUATIC ECOSYSTEMS

● SOILS

▲ SOILS

● GROUND WATER

aquatic ecosystems: communities of interdependent plants and organisms living in water

estuaries: points where rivers flow into the sea

biogenic: produced by living things

prevailing winds: frequent winds in an area

photochemistry: chemical reactions caused by light

New South Wales Environment Protection Authority. (n.d.). *Various sources of pollution*. Retrieved from http://www.epa.nsw.gov.au/air/

TASK 15 WRITE A PARAGRAPH DESCRIBING DATA

Write a paragraph to describe the data on human versus natural emissions in the bar charts on the next page. This data is also from the New South Wales government in Australia. Follow this method:

1. Begin with an introductory sentence describing the focus and purpose of the data and identifying the data source.

2. Next, write a sentence describing any overall trends you can find.

3. Continue with a selective sentence-by-sentence description of the most salient data, comparing amounts, ranking emissions from high to low, or other.

FIGURE 4 HUMAN VERSUS NATURAL EMISSIONS, SYDNEY (AUSTRALIA), 2008

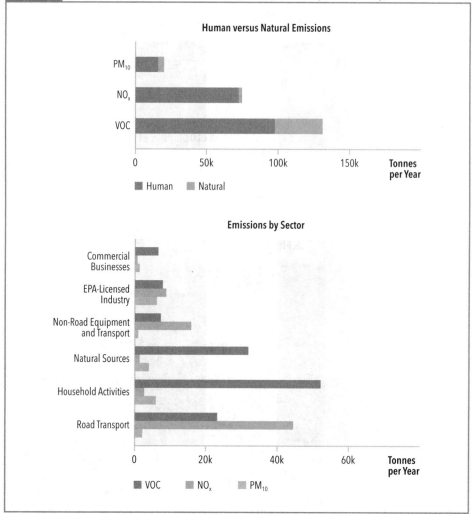

New South Wales Environment Protection Authority. (n.d.). *Air emissions in my community web tool*. Retrieved from http://www.epa.nsw.gov.au/air/airemissionsinmycommunity.htm

PM_{10}: particulate matter with a diameter of 10 micrometres or less

k: thousands

EPA: Environment Protection Authority

Checklist for Revising and Editing

Use the checklist below to revise and edit the sentences in your paragraphs. First, check your own writing for these features. Then, in groups of three, review each other's paragraphs, using the same checklist. Add comments as necessary.

☐ The text contains objective, descriptive language.

☐ The language is impersonal.

☐ The passive voice is used appropriately.

☐ The style is formal and academic (in this case, non-technical style is acceptable).

☐ Paragraphs are coherent and cohesive.

☐ The grammar is accurate.

Identify useful criticism and recommendations in the reviews of your work; revise and edit your paragraphs accordingly.

CHAPTER 11

WRITING ARGUMENTS IN ESSAYS

> Cell phones are so convenient that they're an inconvenience.
>
> Haruki Murakami

In recent years, cellphones, or *mobile phones*, have become an essential communication tool and social accessory, revolutionizing the ways that people organize their daily lives. One area where the role of cellphones is controversial is in higher education classrooms, where they can be a convenience to some and an inconvenience to others, to borrow the terms of novelist Haruki Murakami. Therein lies the controversy. Addressing controversy and presenting a position on controversial topics is a key skill in successful academic writing. This chapter focuses on argumentative writing and builds on Chapter 5, in which you studied how to present coherent and convincing arguments.

In this chapter, you will:

- practise techniques for effective keyword searches
- identify stance, opinion, and relevance in abstracts
- guess vocabulary meaning from context
- form and analyze outlines for argumentative essays
- describe the genre features of an academic blog
- write about statistical data
- consider including your life experience in essays
- study language of exemplification
- study conditional sentences
- write an argumentative essay

TASK 1 EXPLORE THROUGH DISCUSSION

In small groups, discuss the convenience and inconvenience of cellphones for learning in higher education.

PRE-READING RESEARCH SKILLS

Cellphone or *cell phone*? *Smartphone* or *smart phone*? The spelling of terms for recent technology often varies depending on the source or dictionary you refer to.

Cellphones as Tools for Learning in Higher Education

Many studies in recent years have analyzed the pros and cons of cellphone use in higher education classrooms. The effects of texting, Twitter, and message content on student learning were examined by Kuznekoff, Munz, and Titsworth (2015) while Katz and Lambert (2016) analyzed how the removal of students' cellphones from classrooms affected learning. In a naturalistic study of student learning, Tossell, Kortum, Shepard, Rahmati, and Zhong (2015) studied students' use of smart phones to achieve their educational goals, and Yaman, Şenel, and Yeşilel (2015) focused on English language learners, exploring the extent to which they used their smart phones for language learning purposes.

At the heart of this body of literature lies the following question: Do the potential benefits of learning with cellphones in higher education classrooms outweigh the drawbacks that come with students' constant connection to social networking sites and other distracting means of digital communication? In this chapter, you will work on the key stages of constructing a successful argumentative research essay that addresses this question. A good starting point in this process is to do keyword searches, using academic search engines to find relevant sources.

Strategies for Keyword Searches

Part of the process of positioning your arguments within the broader scholarly literature, including finding sources to support your arguments, involves performing targeted keyword searches, using academic search engines. To do effective searches, there are several issues and strategies to consider.

General Topic and Specific Focus

Before you begin your search, it is advisable to decide on your *general topic* and to narrow down the *specific focus*. The essay you will write in this chapter requires you to weigh the arguments for and against the use of cellphones in higher education classrooms. You could state your general topic and specific focus as follows:

General topic: Mobile technology and learning in higher education

Specific focus: Does allowing the use of cellphones in class enhance or hinder learning?

Keywords

Once you have decided on the general topic and specific focus of your essay, select the main keywords for your search. The following kinds of keywords can help you find relevant sources: keywords from your essay title—or from your general topic and specific focus—and synonyms of those keywords.

TASK 2 SELECT KEYWORDS

Select the keywords that you would use for a search on the general topic and specific focus stated on the opposite page.

_____

Synonyms

In addition to the keywords above, you will find more results by using synonyms for your search. For example, instead of searching with the keyword _higher education_, you could try with the synonyms _post-secondary education_, _tertiary education_, _college_, and _university_.

TASK 3 SELECT SYNONYMS

Select synonyms that you could use in addition to the keywords you selected for Task 2.

_____

_____

_____

_____

_____

And versus *Or*

The most common way to join your keywords and synonyms is to use _and_ or _or_. If you searched for "cellphones _or_ higher education," your search results would include articles that focus on cellphones, higher education, or both. If, however, you searched for "cellphones _and_ higher education," you would receive a smaller, more focused number of results. In this case, the search engine would provide a list of sources that focused exclusively on both cellphones and higher education.

TASK 4 EXPERIMENT WITH *AND* VERSUS *OR*

Compare the results for searches that combine your keywords and synonyms, first using _and_, then using _or_. What do you notice?

_____

Quotation Marks

The use of quotation marks will also affect the results provided by a search engine. For example, if you search for _the effects of mobile phones on college learning_ without quotation marks, you will obtain results that include combinations of these keywords in any order. If, however, you do the same search with quotation marks—"_the effects of mobile phones on college learning_"—you will receive a much narrower and more specific list of results. This is because the search engine will limit the results to sources that contain the words in quotation marks in exactly the same order.

TASK 5 COMPARE SEARCHES WITH AND WITHOUT QUOTATION MARKS

Compare the results for searches that combine your keywords and synonyms with and without quotation marks. What do you notice?

ACTIVE AND CRITICAL READING

LOCATING STANCE, OPINION, AND RELEVANCE IN ABSTRACTS

> Review Chapter 1, p. 18, and Chapter 2, p. 33, to identify the following in an abstract: the main question, subquestions, background, research methods, results, and conclusion.

When you are doing argumentative writing, it is necessary to find reliable sources that support and challenge arguments. If your search yields reliable academic journal articles, you can usually find an indication of the authors' stance and opinion, and of the relevance of the article to your task, in the abstract.

In the following abstract of an article about cellphone use in higher education, the authors' stance and opinion have been highlighted in italics.

You Can Lead a Horse to Water but You Cannot Make Him Learn: Smartphone Use in Higher Education

by Chad C. Tossell, Philip Kortum, Clayton Shepard, Ahmad Rahmati, and Lin Zhong

Abstract

[1] Smartphone technology is penetrating world markets and becoming ubiquitous in most college settings. [2] This study takes a naturalistic approach to explore the use of these devices to support student learning. [3] Students that had never used a smartphone were recruited to participate and reported on their expectations of the value of smartphones to achieve their educational goals. [4] Instrumented iPhones that logged device usage were then distributed to these students to use freely over the course of 1 year. [5] After the study, students again reported on the actual value of their smartphones to support their educational goals. [6] *We found that students' reports changed substantially before and after the study; specifically, the utility of the smartphone to help with education was perceived as favorable prior to use, and then, by the end of the study, they viewed their phones as detrimental to their educational goals.* [7] *Although students used their mobile device for informal learning and access to school resources according to the logged data, they perceived their iPhones as a distraction and a competitor to requisite learning for classroom performance.*

Excerpt from Tossell, C. C., Kortum, P., Shepard, C., Rahmati, A., & Zhong, L. (2015). You can lead a horse to water but you cannot make him learn: Smartphone use in higher education. *British Journal of Educational Technology*, 46(4), 713–724. doi:10.1111/bjet.12176

TASK 6 GUESS THE MEANING FROM CONTEXT

In Chapter 1, you studied four strategies for learning vocabulary. One of these strategies was guessing the meaning from context. Guess the meaning of the following words and phrases by looking at the surrounding text for clues; then write the words that provided clues. If you already know the meaning of the word, define it and find the surrounding words that give clues as to its meaning. You may also consider English words that share the same root.

1. ubiquitous [sentence 1]: _____

   Clues: _____

   _____

2. naturalistic approach [sentence 2]: _____

   Clues: _____

   _____

3. instrumented iPhones [sentence 4]: _____

   Clues: _____

   _____

4. logged [sentence 4]: _____

   Clues: _____

   _____

5. detrimental [sentence 6]: _____

   Clues: _____

   _____

6. distraction [sentence 7]: _____

   Clues: _____

   _____

7. requisite [sentence 7]: _____

   Clues: _____

   _____

Identifying Stance and Opinion in Abstracts

In sentences 6 and 7 of the abstract opposite, the authors state that students' perceptions of smart phone use in class shifted during the study from favourable to detrimental, with students eventually viewing their phones as having a negative effect on academic success. These two sentences at the end of the abstract present readers with the overall position of the article: that cellphones can have a negative effect on learning. Accordingly, it can be assumed that the article will provide useful data and arguments to support a stance against cellphone use in higher education classrooms.

The following abstracts are from the other three journal articles cited in the introduction on page 226. Read each abstract and answer the questions about stance and opinion that follow.

tweets: messages sent on Twitter

Mobile Phones in the Classroom: Examining the Effects of Texting, Twitter, and Message Content on Student Learning

by Jeffrey H. Kuznekoff, Stevie Munz, and Scott Titsworth

[1] This study examined mobile phone use in the classroom by using an experimental design to study how message content (related or unrelated to class lecture) and message creation (responding to or creating a message) impact student learning. [2] Participants in eight experimental groups and a control group watched a video lecture, took notes, and completed tests of student learning. [3] The control and relevant message groups earned a 10–17% higher letter grade, scored 70% higher on recalling information, and scored 50% higher on note-taking than students who composed **tweets** or responded to irrelevant messages. [4] Sending/receiving messages unrelated to class content negatively impacted learning and note-taking, while related messages did not appear to have a significant negative impact.

Excerpt from Kuznekoff, J. H., Munz, S., & Titsworth, S. (2015). Mobile phones in the classroom: Examining the effects of texting, Twitter, and message content on student learning. *Communication Education*, 64(3), 344–365. doi:10.1080/03634523.2015.1038727

TASK 7 READ CRITICALLY

1. Which sentences indicate stance and opinion?

   _____

2. How do you interpret the authors' position on the topic?

   _____

   _____

A Happy and Engaged Class without Cell Phones? It's Easier Than You Think

by Louise Katz and Warren Lambert

Abstract

positive reinforcement: providing rewards for desired behaviour

endorsed: supported

[1] Although there have been many suggestions for incorporating cell phone use into classroom activities, there have been few suggestions for removing cell phone use from the classroom. [2] This article presents an easy-to-implement method using **positive reinforcement** that effectively removes cell phones from the classroom in a way that is highly **endorsed** by students and that greatly fosters

student engagement, class participation, and a focused and respectful classroom atmosphere. [3] In a **quasi-experiment**, we found significant correlations between giving up cell phones and students' test grades, overall grade point average (GPA), semester's GPA, and attendance. [4] Rate of improvement of higher and lower participators suggested that better students were more likely to give up their cell phones to earn an extra point toward their final course grade.

Excerpt from Katz, L., & Lambert, W. (2016). A happy and engaged class without cell phones? It's easier than you think. *Teaching of Psychology*, *43*(4), 340–345. doi:10.1177/0098628316662767

quasi-experiment: experiment without random selection

TASK 8 READ CRITICALLY

1. Which sentences indicate stance and opinion?

   _____

2. How do you interpret the authors' position on the topic?

   _____

   _____

   _____

Exploring the Extent to Which ELT Students Utilise Smartphones for Language Learning Purposes

by Ismail Yaman, Müfit Şenel, and Deren Başak Akman Yeşilel

advent: coming or arrival

in the realm of: in the area of

to this end: to achieve this aim

[1] The **advent** of smartphones has had dramatic influences on our daily lives and has rendered human beings 'walking computers'. [2] This holds important reflections **in the realm of** language learning, as well as in many other areas. [3] This study aimed to explore the extent to which English Language Teaching (ELT) students utilise smartphones for language learning purposes. [4] **To this end**, a 25-item questionnaire was administered to 120 Grade Three and Four ELT students at Ondokuz Mayis University in Turkey. [5] Following the questionnaire, a follow-up oral interview was conducted with 29 of the participants on a voluntary basis in order to further investigate their perceptions of smartphones. [6] The statistical analysis of the participants' responses to the items in the questionnaire clearly shows that smartphones are actively used for language learning purposes. [7] In particular, their contribution to the development of vocabulary skills is frequently reported, which is also verified by the answers given during the interview. [8] The analysis regarding the 'gender' and 'length of the students' possession of a smartphone' variables does not yield any statistically significant effect on the degree to which students utilise smartphones for language learning purposes. [9] Given the fact that almost all students have a personal smartphone, and use it very often, and considering the findings of this study, it is suggested that students be encouraged to utilise the **invaluable** language learning opportunities offered by smartphones when put to **conscious use**.

invaluable: very useful

conscious use: deliberate use for a specific purpose

Excerpt from Yaman, I., Şenel, M., & Yeşilel, D. B. A. (2015). Exploring the extent to which ELT students utilise smartphones for language learning purposes. *South African Journal of Education*, *35*(4), 01–09. doi:10.15700/saje.v35n4a1198

TASK 9 READ CRITICALLY

1. Which sentences indicate stance and opinion?

_____

2. How do you interpret the authors' position on the topic?

_____

_____

THE WRITING PROCESS

FORMING OUTLINES FOR ARGUMENTATIVE ESSAYS

Forming an Outline

After you select a range of relevant sources and take notes, you need to organize these notes and your emerging ideas into an effective outline. Your essay outline should be coherent, that is, organized logically. Two common formats for organizing ideas in an outline for an argumentative essay are *for-then-against* and *thematic* outlines. Each format organizes three types of information in different ways:

1. the pros (arguments showing the benefits of using cellphones in class)
2. the cons (arguments showing the drawbacks of using cellphones in class)
3. your position in the debate (whether you are for, against, or somewhere in between)

For-Then-Against Outlines

In a for-then-against outline, the arguments in favour and against, and your opinion, are organized and presented in separate sections. The arguments in each section should be ordered coherently, for example, from abstract to concrete, from general to specific, or according to themes.

TASK 10 ORGANIZE INFORMATION COHERENTLY

The pros and cons below are listed randomly in note form. In the corresponding boxes in the for-then-against outline that follows, organize the arguments in a logical order by selecting themes and grouping the arguments accordingly. Add any arguments of your own.

Pros and Cons of Cellphone Use in Higher Education Classes

Pros	Cons
• Instant access to information • Need to embrace technology rather than reject it • Need to incorporate students' world into classes • Clear guidelines re. appropriate use can be given • Provides access to new forms of learning	• Can distract learners • Can disrupt a class and other students visually and by sound • Can make cheating easier • Results in poor note taking • Can be divisive in group work if not all students have smart phones

Pros	Cons
• Can foster collaboration among groups	• Classes encouraging cellphone use can emphasize socio-economic disparity
• A lot of curricula now made cellphone-friendly	• Traditional forms of learning are not necessarily bad
• Students can use educational apps	
• Young students are used to mental multi-tasking	• Students may waste time playing games or going on social media
• Useful for taking quick and accurate notes	• Results in poor concentration and focus
• Students can send information to absent classmates	• Sometimes teachers should step back and consider new technology critically
• Students can keep up to date with world events	• Encourages learning with a short attention span
• Students can check meaning, grammar, spelling	• Photographic notes result in poor retention and internalization of information
• Many students have cellphones so they should be used	• Need to encourage students to break free from their cyberworld and focus in class

A For-Then-Against Outline

Introduction
• **General background information:** statistics on cellphone ownership, general statement about learning changing with technology
• **Shift to specifics:** cellphones in classes in higher education, pros and cons, research is ongoing and divided
• **Essay organization:** will look at pros and cons, give my opinion, then conclude
• **Thesis statement:** indicate stance for or against

Pros
_____
_____
_____
_____
_____
_____
_____
_____
_____
_____
_____
_____
_____
_____
_____
_____
_____

Cons
_____
_____
_____
_____
_____
_____
_____
_____
_____
_____
_____
_____
_____
_____
_____
_____
_____
_____
_____

My Position
_____
_____
_____

Conclusion

- **Summary of main points:** looked at pros and cons, gave my opinion
- **Synthesis:** weighing pros and cons depends on contexts: institution, teacher, course content, students
- **Final answer:** overall, benefits outweigh drawbacks (in favour), or drawbacks outweigh benefits (against); expand on reasons why
- **General closing statement:** refer to the future and the need to adapt classrooms to accommodate technological advances

TASK 11 COMPLETE AND ANALYZE THE OUTLINE

1. Add your current position on the subject in the My Position box. Note: Your final position may change after writing the essay sections and engaging with the ideas and arguments more deeply.

2. Look at the for-then-against outline as a whole. Write what you consider to be its strengths and weaknesses, and describe the ordering principles you followed for the Pros and Cons boxes.

   Strengths: _____

   _____

Weaknesses: _____

_____

_____

Ordering principles: _____

_____

_____

TASK 12 MATCH ARGUMENTS AND COUNTER-ARGUMENTS

1. Look again at the two boxes in which you organized your arguments for and against the use of cellphones in higher education classes. Match arguments in the Pros box with their counter-arguments in the Cons box by labelling pairs with matching numbers. See the example below.

Pros	Cons
① Need to embrace technology rather than reject it	① Sometimes teachers should step back and consider new technology critically

2. How might the organization of arguments and counter-arguments in separate essay sections affect the coherence of the essay?

_____

_____

Thematic Outlines

It is also possible to organize your arguments thematically. In a thematic outline, the pros, cons, and your personal opinions or position are presented together in sections organized according to relevant themes. As an illustration, in the main body sections of the thematic outline below, the same arguments as in Task 10 have been reorganized under three themes: keeping up with technology, convenience and inconvenience, and effects on student learning.

A Thematic Outline

> The introduction and conclusion would be the same in a thematic organization as in a for-then-against essay structure.

Keeping Up with Technology	
Pros	• Need to embrace technology rather than reject it • Need to incorporate students' world into classes • Provides access to new forms of learning • Many students have cellphones so they should be used • A lot of curricula now made cellphone-friendly • Students can use educational apps • Clear guidelines re. appropriate use can be given
Cons	• Sometimes teachers should step back and consider new technology critically • Need to encourage students to break free from their cyberworld and focus in class • Traditional forms of learning are not necessarily bad • Classes encouraging cellphone use can emphasize socio-economic disparity

Convenience and Inconvenience	
Pros	• Instant access to information • Students can keep up to date with world events • Students can check meaning, grammar, spelling • Students can send information to absent classmates
Cons	• Can disrupt a class and other students visually and by sound • Can distract learners • Can make cheating easier

My Opinion and Personal Experience

Effects on Student Learning	
Pros	• Young students are used to mental multi-tasking • Useful for taking quick and accurate notes • Can foster collaboration among groups
Cons	• Results in poor concentration and focus • Students may waste time playing games or going on social media • Encourages learning with a short attention span • Results in poor note taking • Photographic notes result in poor retention and internalization of information • Can be divisive in group work if not all students have smart phones

My Opinion and Personal Experience

TASK 13 ANALYZE THE THEMATIC OUTLINE

What are the advantages and disadvantages of organizing the outline thematically?

ACTIVE AND CRITICAL READING

AN ACADEMIC BLOG

An Academic Blog on Mobile Devices in Higher Education

The following text is from *The Teaching Professor Blog*, written by Maryellen Weimer.

How Concerned Should We Be about Cell Phones in Class?

by Maryellen Weimer, PhD

As faculty, it seems we are very concerned about cell phones in the classroom. Articles about the problem are popping up everywhere in the pedagogical literature, and they often are the "most-read" and "most-commented" articles listed on various websites. Is student use of electronic devices that pressing of a pedagogical problem? I've been wondering if our focus on it isn't becoming excessive.

No question, it's a vexing problem. Research makes it abundantly clear that students can't multitask, despite their beliefs to the contrary. Even a casual observation of them texting in class while they're supposed to be listening and taking notes makes it clear that it's the listening and note-taking that are getting short shrift. The question is, to what extent is this a problem for teachers and students?

Does the use of the devices make it harder for other students to focus on learning tasks? More than 60% of a diversified student cohort said it does, according to a recent survey. However, 80% of that cohort reported using their cell phones at least once a period, with 75% saying that doing so was either acceptable or sometimes acceptable. So apparently from the student perspective, we're not talking about a disruption they consider serious. Perhaps that's because 92% of those in this survey didn't believe that using their phones had negative effects.

Does the use of devices disrupt the teacher? It can. We also care that students aren't engaging with the material when they're on their phones, and we have leadership responsibility for the classroom environment. Both of those are justified concerns, but does some of our agitation grow out of personal offense? Students aren't listening to us, and that's rude. Should we be taking this personally? People everywhere are paying more attention to their devices than to those around them.

I also wonder if it isn't getting under our skin because most of our policies really aren't working all that well. Students in the survey didn't rate a university policy, a syllabus policy, a glare from the teacher, and a public reprimand as all that effective. Forty percent of the students said they would still text in class even after a teacher reprimand. What did stop them from texting, they said, was a confrontational action—the teacher took their device, lowered their grade, or removed them from the classroom. Researchers didn't ask what those confrontations did to/for the learning environment and the ongoing teacher-student relationships within that class.

Are we failing to see that in some ways this isn't about the devices, but rather about power? When there's a policy against using phones in class and students use them anyway, that says something about how powerful we are, or

in this case, aren't. It feels like we should be doing something, but we're
45 justifiably reluctant to make the big power moves that fix the problem when
there's such a high risk of collateral damage.

Some faculty report success with redirecting use of these devices—the "if
you can't beat 'em, join 'em" solution. Students are encouraged to search for
material, look things up, or use their phones as clickers. Okay, that works,
50 but you can't have students constantly looking things up throughout an
entire class. Even when given the opportunity, is everybody searching for
what you've asked them to find?

And is the smell of hypocrisy in the air? In conference sessions, professional
development workshops, faculty meetings, and academic gatherings of vari-
55 ous sorts, faculty are on their devices. Of course, it isn't just faculty using
devices at all sorts of questionable times. Everybody is.

Lots of points, but here's the bottom line: I think we can make the use of
electronic devices more important than it merits. Yes, it compromises student
learning and we have a responsibility to make sure students understand
60 what they're doing, but is it our job to prevent it? If we get too focused on
the problem, then isn't that taking away time we could be using to shape our
content in interesting ways and to devise activities that so effectively engage
students they forget to check devices? I know it's a radical thought, but as
one of my colleagues wondered, maybe the best policy here is no policy—but
65 instead regular conversations about what learning requires.

Reference

Berry, M. J. and Westfall, A., (2015). Dial D for distraction: The making and breaking of
cell phone policies in the college classroom. *College Teaching 63*(2), 62–71.

Weimer, M. (2015, October 14). How concerned should we be about cell phones in class? [Web log
post]. Retrieved from http://www.facultyfocus.com/articles/teaching-professor-blog/
how-concerned-should-we-be-about-cell-phones-in-class/

TASK 14 ASSESS THE RELIABILITY OF THE BLOG

In Chapter 4, you saw checklists to assess the reliability of sources. Popular websites, blogs, and wikis were placed at the bottom of the list in terms of reliability,
due to a lack of peer review and editorial control over what is published.

Look again at the blog above. Would you use the arguments presented in the
blog in your essay? Do you think the blog is a reliable academic source?

_____

_____

_____

_____

TASK 15 ADD ARGUMENTS TO YOUR OUTLINE

Add any new arguments from the blog to your thematic outline on page 236.

ACADEMIC BLOGS

In earlier chapters, you studied various aspects of genre: understanding genre in Chapter 1, comparing formal and less formal genres in Chapter 3, and shifting styles when bringing in information from less formal genres in Chapter 4. In each case, you were required to consider genre features, that is, the specific ways of writing associated with different genres.

TASK 16 DESCRIBE THE GENRE FEATURES OF AN ACADEMIC BLOG

Describe the stylistic features of this genre that differ from academic journal articles and underline examples in the text.

_____

_____

_____

_____

REVIEW: DESCRIBING STATISTICAL DATA

In Chapter 10, you studied vocabulary to describe statistical data from tables, graphs, and charts, and you wrote a paragraph about data in two bar charts that compared human and natural air emissions.

TASK 17 PRACTISE WRITING ABOUT STATISTICAL DATA

Write a paragraph to describe the data in Table 1 from the Yaman, Şenel, and Yeşilel article (see the abstract on p. 231). The table presents participants' responses to 25 questions about their use of smart phones for learning; the first 12 responses are shown below. The respondents, all English-language learners, ranked each answer according to a Likert scale ranging from 1 (strongly disagree) to 5 (strongly agree).

TABLE 1 FREQUENCY ANALYSIS OF THE PARTICIPANTS' RESPONSES TO THE ITEMS IN THE QUESTIONNAIRE

		1	2	3	4	5
1	The advent of smartphones has contributed significantly to my language learning process.	1.7% 2	10% 12	32.5% 39	41.7% 50	14.2% 17
2	I intentionally use my smartphone for language learning purposes.	5.8% 7	15.8% 19	18.3% 22	48.3% 58	11.7% 14
3	I use the voice recorder of my smartphone to record the lessons and be able to listen to them at a later time.	25% 30	34.2% 41	11.7% 14	20% 24	9.2% 11
4	I generally look up unknown lexical items in my mobile dictionary.	1.7% 2	1.7% 2	3.3% 4	25% 30	68.3% 82
5	The non-stop advancement of technology brings unique opportunities for me to develop foreign language skills.	3.3% 4	8.3% 10	21.7% 26	50% 60	16.7% 20

		1	2	3	4	5
6	I do not like using my smartphone for language learning purposes.	47.5% 57	29.2% 35	13.3% 16	6.7% 8	3.3% 4
7	I use my smartphone to take photos and videos of important classwork in my language classes.	2.5% 3	12.5% 15	14.2% 17	36.7% 44	34.2% 41
8	Having a smartphone enables me to learn English whenever and wherever I want without any limitation.	4.2% 5	7.5% 9	16.7% 20	49.2% 59	22.5% 27
9	Having a smartphone saves a considerable amount of time in my studies of the English language.	3.3% 4	8.3% 10	25.8% 31	45% 54	17.5% 21
10	Various applications offered by the smartphones generally distract me from focusing on my English-related studies.	6.7% 8	35.8% 43	30% 36	18.3% 22	9.2% 11
11	Having a smartphone is a real problem preventing my concentration on my English-related school studies.	20.8% 25	37.5% 45	21.7% 26	13.3% 16	6.7% 8
12	Smartphones are undoubtedly among the most important tools in terms of access to information.	0% 0	6.7% 8	16.7% 20	42.5% 51	34.2% 41

CRITICAL THINKING

BRINGING IN LIFE EXPERIENCE

In Chapter 2, you studied the research process and how personal philosophical beliefs about knowledge, behaviour, and society are central to understanding the differences between quantitative and qualitative research processes. In several chapters, you also practised changing writing styles from personal to impersonal, and vice versa. One question that relates to all of these issues is whether writers should bring personal life experience into their writing. In some cases, it is appropriate, for example, if you are writing a reflection essay or personal response essay. For most other forms of writing, you should avoid referring to personal life experience.

Why to Avoid Mentioning Personal Life Experience

The first reason relates to the purpose of most academic writing, which is to show your knowledge of a subject and to enter an ongoing scholarly debate. Unless you are an expert in the subject about which you are writing, your life experience lacks academic credibility: personal experience cannot be checked in a reference list in the same way that academic references can be verified.

However, if the guidelines for a writing task explicitly state that personal life experience is required or acceptable, then it can be included. In such cases, a brief anecdote can provide interesting contextual background to your thoughts and arguments; equally, describing an event or experience in your life can contribute to an essay in which you are applying theory to real-life contexts. If you do refer to personal life experience, no citations or reference list entries are required.

Find supplementary reading, writing, and critical-thinking activities online.

TASK 18 ADD YOUR PERSONAL LIFE EXPERIENCE

In the upcoming writing task, you will be asked to include personal life experience where relevant. To prepare for the task, add some examples to the thematic outline on page 236.

EXEMPLIFICATION

One of the main ways to support your arguments and make them more credible is to provide examples. When writers exemplify (give examples), they commonly use the following phrases:

- *for example*
- *for instance*
- *namely*
- *such as*

The following excerpts, from two of the articles cited in this chapter, show how the authors use *for example* to exemplify.

engrossed: very interested and paying full attention

> Indeed, face-to-face interaction among students appears to have diminished. **For example,** students frequently are observed to be individually **engrossed** in their cell phones before class, and that traditional time for talking with and getting to know classmates, a valuable part of the college experience, has been replaced by silence. (Katz & Lambert, 2016, p. 340)

sic: word used to indicate that a copied word or phrase is incorrect in some way

> Depending upon the responses of the participants regarding the future of smartphones, it can be said that most believe that smartphones will consolidate their place in everyday life. Student 1, **for example,** states "smartphones will become an indispensable part of human's daily life" **[*sic*]**. (Yaman et al., 2015, p. 6)

In the first excerpt, the phrase *for example* is used after a period and followed by a comma and an independent clause:

> **For example,** students frequently are observed to be . . .

In the second excerpt, the phrase *for example* is inserted into the independent clause and set off by commas:

> Student 1**, for example,** states "smartphones will become . . ."

Rules for Structure and Punctuation

When you use language of exemplification, there are rules to follow regarding grammatical structure and punctuation.

For Example and *For Instance*

For example and *for instance* can be used interchangeably and in different positions in a sentence.

When *for example* or *for instance* comes before an independent clause (underlined), a period or semicolon precedes the phrase, and a comma follows it:

> Cellphones also cause problems in classes. **For example,** they can distract other students.

> Cellphones also cause problems in classes**; for instance,** they can distract other students.

When *for example* or *for instance* is inserted into an independent clause, commas set off the inserted phrase:

> They can**, for example,** <u>distract other students</u>.

When *for example* or *for instance* comes before a dependent clause (1) or a noun phrase (2), the exemplifying phrase is set off by commas:

1. Cellphones can cause problems**, for instance,** when they distract others.
2. Cellphones have several advantages**, for example,** convenience and portability.

Namely

Namely is used to give precise information about something mentioned in the previous clause. It can be followed by an independent clause (1), a dependent clause (2), or a noun phrase (3).

1. Mobile devices have one key drawback**; namely,** they often distract other students.
2. Mobile devices have one key drawback**, namely,** when they distract others.
3. Mobile devices have one key drawback**, namely,** their short lifespan.

In sentence 1, a semicolon precedes *namely*, which is followed by a comma and an independent clause. In sentences 2 and 3, *namely* is followed by a dependent clause and noun phrase, respectively, and set off by commas.

Such As

The phrase *such as* is also used to exemplify, but it can be followed by noun phrases only. The punctuation depends on whether the exemplifying phrase is defining or non-defining.

1. Mobile devices such as cellphones and tablets can help students learn.
2. New software, such as educational apps, is increasingly used in class.

In sentence 1, *such as* defines two specific types of mobile devices that can help students learn, and therefore requires no punctuation. In sentence 2, *such as* is non-defining (it gives an example without defining the software), so the phrase is set off by commas.

TASK 19 ANALYZE THE USE OF *SUCH AS*

1. Does sentence 1 above state that all mobile devices can help students learn or that only two types can? Explain your answer.

   _____

2. Does sentence 2 state that new software in general is increasingly used in class or that just one type (educational apps) is used?

   _____

   _____

TASK 20 PRACTISE USING EXEMPLIFYING PHRASES

Fill in the blanks in the following sentences with an appropriate exemplifying phrase. Add correct punctuation.

1. Technological advances _____ wireless communication should be embraced by colleges.

2. There is a major problem with cellphones in class _____ students who use them often have reduced attention spans.

3. Cellphones allow for quick learning _____ through note taking and fact checking.

m-learning: mobile learning

4. M-learning has been embraced by local colleges _____ five institutions have already collaborated on new m-learning programs.

5. Students can _____ use mobile devices for research.

EXTEND YOUR ACADEMIC VOCABULARY

Extend your knowledge of key vocabulary from this chapter.

collaboration	embrace	result in
considerable	endorse	ubiquitous
disrupt	invaluable	

*Words in bold type are AWL entries.

Practise Chapter 11 vocabulary online.

EFFECTIVE SENTENCE STRUCTURE

CONDITIONAL SENTENCES

Do Unit 11: Conditional Sentences in the Handbook, pp. 391–398.

When writers present, support, and defend arguments, they often use conditional sentences to describe things that could have been different in the past, or real and hypothetical possibilities in the present and future. Before doing the task that follows, study Unit 11: Conditional Sentences in the Handbook to learn about *zero*, *first*, *second*, and *third* conditionals, and *mixed* conditionals.

TASK 21 ANALYZE CONDITIONAL SENTENCES

The following sentences are from two of the articles cited in this chapter. Read each sentence and answer the questions that follow about the time idea and concept.

1. However, if they are made aware of its benefits in detail, including which applications to choose, they can integrate this 'magic' tool into their learning process in a far more motivated and conscious way. (Yaman et al., 2015, p. 8)

a) Is the time idea past or any time? _____

b) Is the concept a factual reality or a hypothetical reality? _____

c) Is the sentence a zero or second conditional? _____

2. We propose that even if students are responding to messages from others, if that activity is related to class content, those students will take better-quality notes than students responding to unrelated content. (Kuznekoff et al., 2015, p. 351)

a) Is the time idea present or present to future? _____

b) Is the concept a real possibility or a hypothetical reality? _____

c) Is the sentence a first or second conditional? _____

3. If the act of using mobile phones was itself distracting, and presumably detrimental to learning, we would see all groups that used mobile devices having lower scores, which we did not find. (Kuznekoff et al., 2015, p. 360)

a) Is the time idea past or present to future? _____

b) Is the concept a real possibility or a hypothetical reality? _____

c) Is the sentence a first or second conditional? _____

WRITE, REVISE, AND EDIT

AN ARGUMENTATIVE ESSAY

TASK 22 WRITE AN ARGUMENTATIVE ESSAY

Write a four-page, double-spaced argumentative essay on the pros and cons of using cellphones in higher education classrooms. Decide whether to use a for-then-against or thematic outline. Add research from reliable academic sources, and bring in your personal experience if it helps you put forward an argument.

Checklist for Revising and Editing

Use the checklist below to do a self-evaluation of your essay. Then, in groups of three, review each other's essays, following the Research Essay Review Sheet you used in Chapter 9. Make any necessary revisions.

☐ Coherent arguments are supported with reasons, examples, and reliable evidence.

My eLab 📁

Find the Research Essay Review Sheet in the online Documents.

☐ The writer's opinions and final position are clear and convincing.

☐ Personal experience, if present, is appropriate and helps develop arguments.

☐ Examples are introduced effectively and accurately.

CHAPTER 12

MAKING COMPARISONS

Even if one is interested only in one's own society, which is one's prerogative, one can understand that society much better by comparing it with others.

Peter L. Berger

In everyday life, people make many comparisons as they engage in conversations with friends. In academic writing, making comparisons involves complex comparative analysis, such as looking for similarities and differences and comparing like with like. It is part of an interaction with an expert, in which you seek recognition for your work. As stated by sociologist Peter L. Berger, comparing your own society (and your research or ideas) is enriching and enhances understanding and awareness. This is the case if you are writing a comparative essay or doing comparative analysis as part of another type of essay.

In this chapter, you will:

- compare nuclear power with solar and wind power
- read texts to find inference, stance, and bias
- study comparative analysis
- form and analyze outlines for comparative essays
- analyze effective comparative paragraphs
- review shifting style from informal to formal
- study language of comparison
- study parallel structure in sentences
- write a comparative research essay or two comparative paragraphs

TASK 1 EXPLORE THROUGH WRITING

Would you prefer to live next door to a nuclear power station or a large wind farm?

Take five minutes to answer the question, explaining your choice. In small groups, read each other's writing and add comments.

NUCLEAR VERSUS SOLAR AND WIND: THE ONGOING DEBATE

There has been much debate in the media and in academic circles about the role of nuclear power as a source of energy, particularly with regard to safety, effectiveness, carbon emissions, and climate change. A large amount of literature can be found on the topic, ranging from academic studies that contain highly technical language and complex data to argument pieces in newspapers and blogs, which are often one-sided.

Inference and Stance

Read the following introduction to a book chapter on nuclear power and sustainable energy. Answer the questions on inference and stance that follow.

Second Life or Half-Life? The Contested Future of Nuclear Power and Its Potential Role in a Sustainable Energy Transition

by M. V. Ramana

Introduction

Can nuclear power be part of a transition to a more sustainable energy future? This question has been debated for some time now without any consensus emerging. Most scholars agree that in comparison with **fossil fuels**, nuclear
5 power generation results in a low level of carbon dioxide emissions even after taking into account emissions associated with different steps in the nuclear fuel chain. Given the great concern about climate change and the need to reduce carbon dioxide emissions, the low emission level is the main reason that nuclear power has entered the debate about sustainable energy. Some
10 others add other sustainability indicators, and nuclear power is good on some of them; examples include ozone depletion and photochemical smog (Stamford and Azapagic 2011). The points of disagreement about the sustainability of nuclear power are often related to some well-known problems associated with the technology: the production of radioactive waste, the potential
15 for catastrophic accidents, and the linkage with nuclear weapons. Those who argue for considering nuclear power a sustainable source of energy claim that these problems can be controlled, especially through the use of newer reactor designs, and in any case **pale in comparison** to the dangers posed by climate change (Adamantiades and Kessides 2009; Duffey 2005; Omoto
20 2005; Sailor et al. 2000). Opponents see these problems as not going away anytime soon and argue against thinking of nuclear power as a sustainable source of energy (Mez 2012; Smith 2006; Sovacool 2011).

This chapter takes a **different tack** and addresses this question by examining the future prospects of nuclear power around the world and the main chal-
25 lenges that confront an expansion of nuclear reactor construction. These suggest that although nuclear power is going to remain part of electricity generation in several countries, its future is highly contested. If this contest

fossil fuels: fuels such as gas and coal formed in the earth over millions of years from dead plants and animals

pale in comparison: seem unimportant when compared to something else

different tack: different direction

© **ERPI** Reproduction prohibited

results in future nuclear growth being significantly limited, then it reduces the desirability of a nuclear solution to climate change, which requires a very rapid and drastic reduction in emissions, and this has relevance for the question of whether nuclear power can be a part of a sustainable energy future.

If anyone were to have been in doubt that reliance on nuclear energy is contested, those doubts would surely have vanished in 2011 after the multiple accidents at the Fukushima Daiichi nuclear power plant. The accident set off widespread protests, and opinion polls around the world showed declining support for the construction of new nuclear reactors (Ramana 2011). There was also, however, a significant effort mounted by the nuclear industry and various governments that support nuclear power to **shore up support** for the technology. As this chapter demonstrates, those efforts have had mixed success, leading to future prospects for nuclear power showing dramatically wide geographical variations. At the same time, a number of factors, including mounting costs and intense competition from other sources of electricity generation such as natural gas and renewable technologies, have **propelled** a decline in the share of nuclear energy in the world's power production.

This chapter begins with a brief overview of the present state of nuclear energy around the world as well as future projections by the International Atomic Energy Agency (IAEA) as well as by various national governments; these point to an energy technology struggling to maintain a significant market share. This is followed by a short examination of the economics of nuclear energy and other social challenges to nuclear power. The chapter continues with an overview of the different strategies used by the nuclear industry to promote reactor construction, before concluding with some thoughts on how nuclear power might or might not play a role in the transition to a sustainable energy future.

shore up support: increase support to stop something from falling

propelled: forced or moved forward

References

Adamantiades, A., & Kessides, I. (2009). Nuclear power for sustainable development: Current status and future prospects. *Energy Policy, 37*(12), 5149–5166. doi:10.1016/j.enpol.2009.07.052

Duffey, R. B. (2005). Sustainable futures using nuclear energy. *Progress in Nuclear Energy, 47*(1–4), 535–543.

Mez, L. (2012). Nuclear energy–Any solution for sustainability and climate protection? *Energy Policy, 48*, 56–63.

Omoto, A. (2005). Nuclear power for sustainable development and relevant IAEA activities for the future. *Progress in Nuclear Energy, 47*(1–4), 16–26.

Ramana, M. V. (2011). Nuclear power and the public. *Bulletin of the Atomic Scientists, 67*(4), 43–51.

Sailor, W. C., Bodansky, D., Braun, C., Fetter, S., & van der Zwaan, B. (2000). A nuclear solution to climate change? *Science, 288*, 1177–1178.

Smith, B. (2006). *Insurmountable risks: The dangers of using nuclear power to combat global climate change.* Takoma Park: IEER Press.

Sovacool, B. K. (2011). *Contesting the future of nuclear power: A critical global assessment of atomic energy.* Hackensack: World Scientific.

Stamford, L., & Azapagic, A. (2011). Sustainability indicators for the assessment of nuclear power. *Energy, 36*(10), 6037–6057.

Excerpt from Ramana, M. V. (2016). Second life or half-life? The contested future of nuclear power and its potential role in a sustainable energy transition. In T. Van de Graaf et al. (Eds.), *The Palgrave handbook of the international political economy of energy* (pp. 363–396). London: Palgrave Macmillan.

TASK 2 INFER MEANING AND IDENTIFY STANCE

The author's stance is not explicitly stated in the Ramana introduction. As a result, the reader needs to infer meaning. Do you think the author is for or against nuclear power? Analyze the balance of information in each paragraph and write what you feel the author's overall stance may be. Explain your reasons with examples from the text.

Paragraph 1: _____

_____

Paragraph 2: _____

_____

Paragraph 3: _____

_____

Paragraph 4: _____

_____

Overall stance: _____

_____

The Case for Nuclear Power

The following excerpt is from an academic article in which the authors present the case for nuclear power as an effective and safe alternative to energy generated from fossil fuels.

TASK 3 HIGHLIGHT ARGUMENTS

As you read, use one colour to highlight the arguments in favour of nuclear power, and another colour to highlight those against.

Nuclear Energy in Focus

by Barry W. Brook and Corey J. A. Bradshaw

MCDMA: multicriteria decision-making analysis

nuclear fission: nuclear reaction that occurs when an atom is split

contentious: likely to cause disagreement

lingering: slow to disappear

An outcome of the **MCDMA** that might surprise many is how well nuclear energy emerged from these overall ranked-and-weighted comparisons. Given the hostility toward **nuclear fission** by most environmental NGOs (e.g., Greenpeace's energy plan described in the previous section rejects outright
5 any use of nuclear), we decided to focus more deeply here on the pros and cons of this particularly **contentious** energy option. . . .

Nuclear-power advocates have fought an enduring battle to present this energy source as clean, safe, and sustainable. Today, a mix of **lingering** myths and half-truths continue to influence people's thinking on nuclear power
10 (Blees 2008), whereas proponents of other low-carbon energy-production types typically do not admit to the difficulties of large-scale use of these

qualms: worries or doubts

technologies (Trainer 2012). Common **qualms** about nuclear energy are that uranium supplies will soon run out, long-lived radioactive waste needs isolation for 100,000 years, large amounts of greenhouse gases are produced over the full nuclear cycle, development is too slow and costly, and large-scale deployment increases the risk of nuclear war. Crises such as the one at the Fukushima Daiichi nuclear plant (a 1960s vintage reactor) in Japan in 2011, triggered by a massive earthquake and tsunami, **amplified** people's concerns (Hong et al. 2013*b*). Yet, given the urgency of the global environmental challenges we must deal with in the coming decades, closing off our option on nuclear energy may be dangerously shortsighted.

amplified: increased

In 2010, nuclear energy was used to generate commercial electricity in 31 countries, provided 74% of total supply in France, and contributed 2,628 **terawatt** hours (TWh; IEA 2013). Based on life-cycle emissions intensities for nuclear (20 t CO_2-e TWh^{-1}) and coal (>1,000 t CO_2-e TWh^{-1}) power, this is an effective saving of at least 2.4 billion tons of carbon dioxide annually, as well as avoidance of a toxic **brew** of heavy metals, black carbon, sulfates, and numerous other aerosols (Kharecha & Hansen 2013). **Foregoing** nuclear power therefore means overlooking an already large global contributor to low-carbon electricity, especially given its use as a direct substitute for coal. Currently, only hydroelectricity displaces more fossil-fuel energy than nuclear power (3,490 TWh), but it is geographically dependent on the distribution of waterways.

terawatt: unit of power equal to one trillion watts

brew: mixture

foregoing: giving up something you like or need

Nuclear power is deployed commercially in countries whose joint energy intensity is such that they collectively constitute 80% of global greenhouse-gas emissions. If one adds to this tally those nations that are actively planning nuclear deployment or already have scientific or medical research reactors, this figure rises to over 90% (Brook & Lowe 2010). As a consequence, displacement of fossil fuels by an expanding nuclear-energy sector would not lead to a large increase in the number of countries with access to nuclear resources and expertise. Nuclear weapons proliferation is a complex political issue, with or without commercial nuclear power plants, and is under strong international oversight (Blees 2008).

Today, over 70 so-called generation III reactors are under construction, including 29 in energy-hungry China (www.world-nuclear.org/info/Current-and-Future-Generation/Nuclear-Power-in-the-World-Today), attesting to its price competitiveness with other energy sources in the appropriate economic and regulatory environments (Nicholson et al. 2011). In terms of future costs and build times, the standardized, compact, passive-safety blueprints of next-generation nuclear power plants (generation IV small modular reactors)—designed to be built in assembly-line factories and shipped as complete units to a site—have the potential to be transformative in an industry that has, in the past, been **plagued** by **regulatory ratcheting** and legal challenges against one-off designs (Cohen 1990). France, which built 59 large reactors in 22 years (1978 to 1999) to **alleviate**

plagued: negatively affected over a period of time

regulatory ratcheting: increasing regulations step by step

alleviate: reduce the severity

its oil dependence, using generation II standardized designs, is a real-world
60 illustration of what can be achieved quickly with nuclear deployment under
favorable sociopolitical circumstances (Mackay 2008). To date, there have
been no accidents or deaths at any of the French plants, despite nuclear
power providing >75% of the nation's electricity supply for decades. . . .

thorium: radioactive
chemical element

The IFR [integral fast reactor], and other generation IV designs that use
65 **thorium** (Hargraves 2012), offer a realistic future for nuclear power as a
major source of sustainable, carbon-free energy for global civilization; there
are sufficient fuel resources to last for millions of years (Lightfoot et al. 2006).
At present, uranium remains cheap and policies for treating **actinide** wastes
(e.g., direct geological disposal vs. recycling) are **in limbo** in most countries.
70 However, if nuclear power were to be deployed on a large scale, such recycling
would become essential.

actinide: radioactive metal

in limbo: in a state of
inaction and uncertainty

For many countries—including most high energy-consuming nations in East
Asia and Western Europe with little spare land and already high population
densities—the options for massive expansion of renewable energy alterna-
75 tives are heavily constrained (Trainer 2010; Hong et al. 2013a). But making
a case for a major role for nuclear fission in a future sustainable energy mix
does not mean arguing against energy efficiency and renewable options.
Under the right circumstances, these alternatives might also make important
contributions (Mackay 2008; Nicholson 2012). Ideally, all low-carbon energy
80 options should be free to compete on a fair and **level playing field** against
a range of sustainability criteria . . . so as to maximize displacement of fossil
fuels (one of the key goals for effective biodiversity conservation). Ultimately,
as the urgency of climate-change mitigation and land sparing mounts and
requirements for sustainable growth in developing economies and replace-
85 ment of ageing infrastructure in the developed world come to the fore,
pragmatic decisions on the viability of all types of nonfossil-fuel energy
technologies will have to be made on a **nonprejudicial** basis.

level playing field:
situation allowing fair
competition

nonprejudicial: fair for all

References

Blees T. 2008. *Prescription for the planet: The painless remedy for our energy & environmental crises.* BookSurge, Charleston, South Carolina.

Brook BW, Lowe I. 2010. Nuclear power: Yes or no? *Physics World* October 2010:24–25.

Cohen BL. 1990. *The nuclear energy option.* Plenum Press, New York.

Hargraves R. 2012. *Thorium: Energy cheaper than coal.* CreateSpace Publishing, Scotts
Valley, CA.

Hong S, Bradshaw CJA, Brook BW. 2013a. Evaluating options for sustainable energy mixes
in South Korea using scenario analysis. *Energy* **52**:237–244.

Hong S, Bradshaw CJA, Brook BW. 2013b. Evaluating options for the future energy mix
of Japan after the Fukushima nuclear crisis. *Energy Policy* **56**:418–424.

IEA (International Energy Agency). 2013. International Energy Agency: World energy
outlook 2013. Available from http://www.iea.org/weo/ (accessed 21 March 2014).

Kharecha PA, Hansen JE. 2013. Prevented mortality and greenhouse gas emissions from
historical and projected nuclear power. *Environmental Science and Technology*
47:4889–4895.

Lightfoot HD, Manheimer W, Meneley DA, Pendergast D, Stanford GS. 2006. Nuclear fission fuel is inexhaustible. Pages 39–46 available from http://www.mcgill.ca/files/gec33/Nuclear FissionFuelisInexhaustibleIEEE.pdf. 2006 IEEE EIC Climate Change Conference, Vol. 1 and 2.

Mackay D. 2008. Sustainable energy—without the hot air. Cavendish Laboratory, Cambridge. Available from http://www.withouthotair.com.

Nicholson M. 2012. *The power maker's challenge*. Springer-Verlag, London.

Nicholson M, Biegler T, Brook BW. 2011. How carbon pricing changes the relative competitiveness of low-carbon baseload generating technologies. *Energy* **36**:305–313.

Trainer T. 2010. Can renewables etc. solve the greenhouse problem? The negative case. *Energy Policy* **38**:4107–4114.

Trainer T. 2012. A critique of Jacobson and Delucchi's proposals for a world renewable energy supply. *Energy Policy* **44**:476–481.

Excerpts from Brook, B. W., & Bradshaw, C. J. A. (2015). Key role for nuclear energy in global biodiversity conservation. *Conservation Biology*, *29*(3), 702–712. doi:10.1111/cobi.12433

TASK 4 COMPARE ARGUMENTS FOR AND AGAINST

1. Compare the number of ideas you highlighted in the two colours. Do the authors present a balanced discussion, or is their approach unbalanced?

   _____

   _____

2. Does lack of balance in a text represent bias? Why or why not?

   _____

   _____

3. Do you think the authors' arguments are reliable enough to use in an academic essay requiring a balanced comparison of pros and cons? Why or why not?

   _____

   _____

The Case for Renewable Energy

Now read an abridged version of an article written by Mark Diesendorf, an associate professor in environmental studies at the University of New South Wales, in Australia.

dispelling the myths: making untrue beliefs go away

spurious: based on weak logic or false ideas

shills: (rare) paid spokespersons

hurdle: obstacle

refute: prove wrong

ultimately doomed: that will eventually die

Renewable Energy versus Nuclear: Dispelling the Myths

by Mark Diesendorf

Don't believe the **spurious** claims of nuclear **shills** constantly doing down renewables, writes Mark Diesendorf. Clean, safe renewable energy technologies have the potential to supply 100% of the world's electricity needs—but the first **hurdle** is to **refute** the deliberately misleading myths designed to
5 promote the politically powerful but **ultimately doomed** nuclear industry.

Nuclear energy and renewable energy (RE) are the principal competitors for low-carbon electricity in many countries. As RE technologies have grown in volume and investment, and become much cheaper, nuclear **proponents** and **deniers of climate science** have become deniers of RE. The strategies and tactics of RE deniers are very similar to those of climate science deniers. To create uncertainty about the ability of RE to power an industrial society, they **bombard** decision-makers and the media with negative myths about RE and positive myths about nuclear energy, attempting to turn these myths into **conventional wisdom**.

In responding to the climate crisis, few countries have the economic resources to expand investment substantially in both nuclear and RE. This is demonstrated in 2016 by the UK government, which is offering huge long-term subsidies to nuclear while severely cutting existing short-term subsidies to RE.

This article, a **sequel** to one **busting** the myth that we need **baseload power stations** such as nuclear or coal, examines critically some of the other myths about nuclear energy and RE. It offers a resource for those who wish to question these myths. The myths discussed here have been drawn from comments by nuclear proponents and RE opponents in the media, articles, blogs and on-line comments.

Myth 1: Baseload power stations are necessary to supply baseload demand

. . . Underlying this claim are three key assumptions. First, that baseload power is actually a good and necessary thing. In fact, what it really means is too much power when you don't want it, and not enough when you do. What we need is flexible power (and flexible demand too) so that supply and demand can be matched instant by instant.

The second assumption is that nuclear power is a reliable baseload supplier. In fact it's no such thing. All nuclear power stations are subject to **tripping out** for safety reasons or technical faults. That means that an electricity system that includes a 3.2GW nuclear power station needs at least 3.2GW of expensive 'spinning reserve' that can be called in at a moment's notice.

The third is that the only way to supply baseload power is from baseload power stations, such as nuclear, coal and gas, designed to run **flat-out** all the time whether their power is actually needed or not. That's wrong too.

Myth 2: There is a renaissance in nuclear energy

Global nuclear electricity production in terawatt-hours per year (TWh/y) peaked in 2006. The percentage contribution of nuclear energy to global electricity peaked at 17.5% in 1993 and declined to under 11% in 2014. Nowadays annual global investment in nuclear is exceeded by investment in each of wind and solar.

Over the past decade the number of global start-ups of new nuclear power reactors has been approximately balanced by the number of closures of existing reactors. . . .

Myth 3: Renewable energy is not ready to replace fossil fuels, and nuclear energy could fill the (alleged) gap in low-carbon energy supply

Most existing nuclear power reactors are classified as Generation 2 and are widely regarded as **obsolete**. The current generations of new nuclear power stations are classified as Generation 3 and 3+. Only four Generation 3 reactors have operated, so far only in Japan, and their performance has been poor. No Generation 3+ reactor is operating, although two are under construction in Europe, four in the USA and several in China.

All are behind schedule and over-budget—the incomplete European reactors are already triple their budgeted prices. Not one Generation 4 power reactor—e.g. **fast breeder, integral fast reactor (IFR), small modular reactor**—is commercially available. So it can be argued that modern nuclear energy is not ready.

On the other hand, wind and solar are both growing rapidly and are still becoming cheaper. Large wind and solar farms can be planned and built in 2–3 years (compared with 10–15 years for nuclear) and are ready now to replace fossil and nuclear electricity. . . .

Renewables could be scaled up long before nuclear

Computer simulation models and growing practical experience suggest that electricity supply in many regions, and possibly the whole world, could transition to 100% renewable energy (RE). Most of the RE technologies are commercially available, affordable and environmentally sound. There is no fundamental technical or economic reason for delaying the transition.

The pro-nuclear and anti-RE myths disseminated by nuclear proponents and supporters of other **vested interests** do not **stand up to examination**. Given the **political will**, RE could be **scaled up** long before Generation 3 and 4 nuclear power stations could make a significant contribution to electricity supply.

Excerpts from Diesendorf, M. (2016, April 19). Renewable energy versus nuclear: Dispelling the myths. *The Ecologist*. Retrieved from http://www.theecologist.org/News/news_analysis/2987577/renewable_energy_versus_nuclear_dispelling_the_myths.html

obsolete: out of date and no longer usable

fast breeder, integral fast reactor (IFR), small modular reactor: types of nuclear reactors

The article goes on to list and refute what the author sees as 12 additional myths.

vested interests: groups with a financial interest in something

stand up to examination: convince when analyzed

political will: political desire

scaled up: increased

TASK 5 COMPARE ARGUMENTS FOR AND AGAINST

1. a) Reread the article and highlight the ideas the author presents in favour of and against nuclear power in two different colours.

   b) Compare the numbers of ideas you highlighted in the two colours. Does the author present a balanced discussion, or is his approach unbalanced?

2. Which of the two articles, the Brook and Bradshaw or the Diesendorf article, do you find more biased? Is one more reliable than the other? Explain your reasons.

_____

_____

3. If you had to choose one side of the argument over the other, which would you choose? Explain your reasons.

_____

_____

CRITICAL THINKING

COMPARATIVE ANALYSIS

The following is a definition of comparative analysis from a business dictionary.

> The item-by-item comparison of two or more comparable alternatives, processes, products, qualifications, sets of data, systems, or the like. In accounting, for example, changes in a financial statement's items over several accounting periods may be presented together to detect the emerging trends in the company's operations and results. See also _comparability analysis_.
>
> http://www.businessdictionary.com/definition/comparative-analysis.html

Comparing Like with Like versus Apples and Oranges

One of the main tenets of comparative analysis is to compare like with like. In other words, researchers should compare and contrast the same things in each case, rather than comparing different things ("apples and oranges").

TASK 6 DISCUSS HOW TO COMPARE LIKE WITH LIKE

In small groups, discuss the following question:

If you compare nuclear energy with solar and wind power, how can you compare like with like rather than apples and oranges?

THE WRITING PROCESS

FORMING OUTLINES FOR COMPARATIVE ESSAYS

Comparative essays are commonly organized in two ways: via a _case-by-case_ or a _thematic_ outline. In this section, you will study two ways to organize information for the following essay question:

Compare and contrast nuclear power with solar and wind power in terms of the reduction of global warming, risks to the environment, and cost. Include your personal opinion as to which energy forms should be promoted by governments.

Case-by-Case Outlines

In the case-by-case outline below, each case is organized in a separate essay section: nuclear power and then solar and wind power. In each section, information is organized according to themes: the reduction of global warming, risks to the environment, and cost. These sections are followed by a section that highlights the main similarities and differences and presents the writer's personal opinion.

A Case-by-Case Outline

Introduction
• **General background information:** information on climate change, energy sources, divided opinions
• **Shift to specifics:** nuclear power, solar and wind power – fewer carbon emissions; ongoing debate about which should be promoted
• **Essay organization:** will look at nuclear power, then solar and wind power; give my opinions; then conclude
• **Thesis statement:** indicate stance for or against

Nuclear Power
Reduction of global warming _____
_____
_____
Risks to the environment _____
_____
_____
Cost _____
_____
_____

Solar and Wind Power
Reduction of global warming _____
_____
_____
Risks to the environment _____
_____
_____
Cost _____
_____
_____

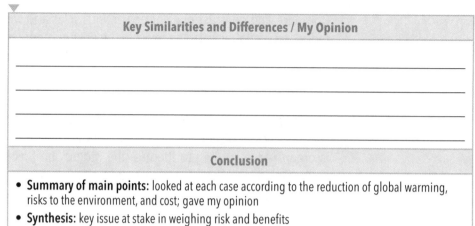

Key Similarities and Differences / My Opinion

Conclusion

- **Summary of main points:** looked at each case according to the reduction of global warming, risks to the environment, and cost; gave my opinion
- **Synthesis:** key issue at stake in weighing risk and benefits
- **Final answer:** overall, benefits of nuclear outweigh risks, or risks of nuclear outweigh benefits; expand on reasons why
- **General closing statement:** refer to the future and the need to continue to provide safe energy

TASK 7 ANALYZE AND COMPLETE THE OUTLINE

1. The themes in the above outline are the reduction of global warming, risks to the environment, and cost. Why do you think the themes are presented in this order?

2. Add the points you highlighted for Tasks 3 and 5 under each theme.

Thematic Outlines

The above arguments can also be organized thematically with the two cases presented together in the same section under key themes. Each thematic section would also include a summary of the main similarities and differences as well as the writer's personal opinion.

TASK 8 REORGANIZE INFORMATION COHERENTLY

Reorganize the information from the case-by-case outline above in the thematic outline below under the three themes: the reduction of global warming, risks to the environment, and cost.

A Thematic Outline

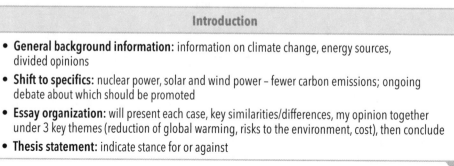

Introduction

- **General background information:** information on climate change, energy sources, divided opinions
- **Shift to specifics:** nuclear power, solar and wind power – fewer carbon emissions; ongoing debate about which should be promoted
- **Essay organization:** will present each case, key similarities/differences, my opinion together under 3 key themes (reduction of global warming, risks to the environment, cost), then conclude
- **Thesis statement:** indicate stance for or against

Reduction of Global Warming		
Nuclear power _____		
_____		
Solar and wind power _____		
_____		
Key similarities and differences / My opinion _____		
_____		

Risks to the Environment		
Nuclear power _____		
_____		
Solar and wind power _____		
_____		
Key similarities and differences / My opinion _____		
_____		

Cost		
Nuclear power _____		
_____		
Solar and wind power _____		
_____		
Key similarities and differences / My opinion _____		
_____		

Conclusion

- **Summary of main points:** presented each case, key similarities/differences, my opinion together under 3 key themes (reduction of global warming, risks to the environment, cost)
- **Synthesis:** key issue at stake in weighing risks and benefits
- **Final answer:** overall, benefits of nuclear outweigh risks, or risks of nuclear outweigh benefits; expand on reasons why
- **General closing statement:** refer to the future and the need to continue to provide safe energy

TASK 9 COMPARE THE OUTLINES

What are the pros and cons of each outline?

_____

_____

_____

_____

_____

Effective Comparative Paragraphs

Comparative paragraphs can be written in different ways, depending on the essay outline. Case-by-case outlines require paragraphs that list key aspects, ideas, or arguments in separate sections. The following two paragraphs exemplify different techniques for following a thematic outline, in which comparisons are made in the same section.

TASK 10 ANNOTATE COMPARATIVE PARAGRAPHS

Paragraphs 1 and 2 below compare and contrast nuclear and solar power in terms of their effects on local environments. Each effect is highlighted in bold. As you read, make a note in the margin when each new effect is introduced. Label the effects of nuclear power N1, N2, N3, and the effects of solar power S1, S2, S3.

1. Impacts of Nuclear Power and Solar Power on Local Environments

An important area of comparison between nuclear power and solar power is how each energy source affects local environments. The effects of nuclear power on local environments are numerous and detrimental. **First, materials such as uranium require mining, which has many negative impacts on local flora and fauna, including humans.** The mines not only take up land, they also damage the land, require access routes, and cause increased local traffic and air pollution. **A second aspect of nuclear energy that affects local environments negatively is the use of water,** which is drawn in great quantities from local water sources. This places a strain on local water supplies; moreover, radioactive water needs to be stored and then released back into local environments. **Another negative impact is decommissioning.** Once uranium mines are no longer in use, the complex process of decommissioning has inevitable consequences for local environments, which can never fully return to their previous states. In contrast, solar power has comparatively few negative impacts on local environments. **One impact to consider is the high number of heliostats required to generate enough power to become financially viable, which takes up a large area of land.** Inevitably, this land is affected as a result of the construction and maintenance required for effective power generation. Granted, a large solar power plant may take up as much land as a nuclear power plant, or even more. Nonetheless, the potential for radioactive contamination is absent. **Water use is another important factor to consider.** While it is necessary to draw from local water sources during the construction phases of solar power, much less water is required during operation, and the water used does not come into contact with dangerous radiation. **Finally, when solar plants require decommissioning, local environments are also affected negatively.** Facilities need to be dismantled, local access routes returned to their natural state, and waste removed safely. In comparison with nuclear decommissioning, however, the negative impacts are fewer and less severe.

2. Impacts of Nuclear Power and Solar Power on Local Environments

An important area of comparison between nuclear power and solar power is how each energy source affects local environments. The effects of nuclear power on local environments are numerous and detrimental. **First, materials such as uranium require mining, which has many negative impacts on local flora and fauna, including humans.** The mines not only take up land, they also damage the land, require access routes, and cause increased local traffic and air pollution. **Equally, many heliostats are required to generate enough solar power to become financially viable, which takes up a large area of land.** Inevitably, this land is affected as a result of the construction and maintenance required for effective power generation. Granted, a large solar power plant may take up as much land as a nuclear power plant, or even more. Nonetheless, the potential for radioactive contamination is absent. **A second aspect of nuclear energy that affects local environments negatively is the use of water**, which is drawn in great quantities from local water sources. This places a strain on local water supplies; moreover, radioactive water needs to be stored and then released back into local environments. **It is also necessary to draw from local water sources during the construction phases of solar power** although much less water is required during operation. More importantly, the water used for solar power does not come into contact with dangerous radiation. **Another negative impact of nuclear power stations is decommissioning.** Once uranium mines are no longer in use, the complex process of decommissioning has inevitable consequences for local environments, which can never fully return to their previous states. Admittedly, **when solar plants require decommissioning, local environments are also affected negatively.** Facilities need to be dismantled, local access routes returned to their natural state, and waste removed safely. Nevertheless, in comparison with nuclear decommissioning, the negative impacts are fewer and less severe.

Reference (for paragraphs 1 and 2)

Pfenninger, S., & Keirstead, J. (2015). Comparing concentrating solar and nuclear power as baseload providers using the example of South Africa. *Energy, 87*, 303–314. doi:10.1016/j.energy.2015.04.077.

TASK 11 COMPARE PARAGRAPH STRUCTURE

1. Look at your margin notes. Match the paragraphs to the following structures.

   N1 + N2 + N3, followed by S1 + S2 + S3: _____

   N1 + S1, followed by N2 + S2, followed by N3 + S3: _____

2. Which structure do you think allows for more effective comparative analysis? Explain why.

   _____

   _____

REVIEW SHIFTING STYLE

In Chapters 4, 5, and 6, you practised shifting from informal to formal style. In the Diesendorf article, the author uses some aspects of informal style to engage the reader. While this may be appropriate for the semi-formal style the author is employing, in most academic writing, it is advisable to use more formal alternatives, unless you are quoting the author's words directly.

TASK 12 REWRITE THE SENTENCES

Rewrite the following sentences from the Diesendorf article to add formality.

1. Don't believe the spurious claims of nuclear shills constantly doing down renewables, writes Mark Diesendorf.

    _____

    _____

2. In fact, what it really means is too much power when you don't want it, and not enough when you do.

    _____

    _____

3. That's wrong too.

    _____

My eLab

Find supplementary reading, writing, and critical-thinking activities online.

4. So it can be argued that modern nuclear energy is not ready.

    _____

VOCABULARY

LANGUAGE OF COMPARISON

There are two main types of language of comparison: words and phrases that highlight similarities and those that highlight differences. The following are common phrases used to compare and contrast in academic writing.

Describing Similarities

Expressions	Examples
both a and b	**Both** nuclear power **and** wind power have negative effects on local environments.
neither a nor b	**Neither** solar power **nor** wind power **is** 100% environmentally friendly.
like	**Like** solar power, wind power has a low carbon footprint.

With *neither–nor*, the verb agrees with the nearer noun.

Expressions	Examples
similar to	Solar power **is similar to** wind power **in that** it is a renewable source of energy. Solar power **is similar to** wind power **in its** low carbon footprint.
similarly equally	Wind power has a low carbon footprint. **Similarly/Equally,** solar power has low emissions.
the same	Solar power has a low carbon footprint. **The same can be said for** wind power. Solar power has a low carbon footprint. **The same applies to** wind power.
also the case	Solar power has a low carbon footprint. **This is also the case with** wind power.
another case in point	Solar power has a low carbon footprint. Wind power **is another case in point**.

Describing Differences

Expressions	Examples
compared to in comparison unlike	**Compared to/with** nuclear power, solar power has minimal environmental impact. **In comparison to/with** nuclear power, solar power has minimal environmental impact. **Unlike** nuclear power, solar power has minimal environmental impact.
however nevertheless nonetheless (conjunctive adverbs)	Wind power has a low carbon footprint. **However/Nevertheless/Nonetheless,** many communities do not want wind turbines in their area.
but yet (coordinators)	Wind power has a low carbon footprint**, but** coal-fired power stations emit large quantities of carbon dioxide into the atmosphere. (contrast) Wind turbines have a low carbon footprint**, yet** many communities do not want them in their area. (contrast – can have an idea of stronger contrast than *but*)
while whereas (subordinators)	**While** wind power has a low carbon footprint, coal-fired power stations emit large quantities of carbon dioxide into the atmosphere. Wind power has a low carbon footprint **while/whereas** coal-fired power stations emit large quantities of carbon dioxide into the atmosphere.
the same (with negative)	Coal and gas-fired power stations emit large amounts of CO_2 into the atmosphere. **The same cannot be said of** nuclear energy. Coal and gas-fired power stations emit large amounts of CO_2 into the atmosphere. **The same does not apply to** nuclear energy.
the difference	**The difference between** nuclear power and solar power **is most evident in** their environmental impacts. **The main difference / One of the main differences between** nuclear power and solar power is their environmental impacts.
distinguishing	**A key distinguishing feature between** nuclear power and solar power is their environmental impacts.

Note that a comma is required in the first example with *while* because the dependent clause comes first, but not in the second example, where the dependent clause comes second.

TASK 13 PRACTISE USING EXPRESSIONS OF COMPARISON

Fill in the blanks in the sentences below with expressions of comparison.

1. _____ solar power _____ wind power have relatively low carbon footprints.

2. Wind power has a low carbon footprint, _____ coal-fired power stations.

3. _____ solar power _____ wind power provides quick financial returns.

4. Wind power has a low carbon footprint _____ coal-fired power stations are major producers of greenhouse gases.

5. Solar power provides slow financial returns. _____ wind power.

6. Wind power has a low carbon footprint. _____ coal-fired power stations.

7. Solar power _____ wind power _____ it provides slow financial returns.

EXTEND YOUR ACADEMIC VOCABULARY

Extend your knowledge of key vocabulary from this chapter.

address	**impact**	refute
admittedly	misleading	subject to
dispel	numerous	viable
hurdle	proponent	

*Words in bold type are AWL entries.

My eLab

Practise Chapter 12 vocabulary online.

© **ERPI** Reproduction prohibited

EFFECTIVE SENTENCE STRUCTURE

PARALLEL STRUCTURE

Parallel structure (also referred to as *parallelism*) means that a writer uses the same types of words and phrases in a list or a series of examples. Not only does the use of parallel structure add cohesion to sentences, it can also accord equal importance to ideas. The following sentence from the Ramana introduction (see p. 246) illustrates parallel structure (key phrases are in bold):

The points of disagreement about the sustainability of nuclear power are often related to some well-known problems associated with the technology: **the production of radioactive waste**, **the potential for catastrophic accidents**, and **the linkage with nuclear weapons**.

The sentence has parallel structure because each of the three problems is described in a noun phrase. If the same sentence were written as follows, the structure would no longer be parallel:

The points of disagreement about the sustainability of nuclear power are often related to some well-known problems associated with the technology: **the production of radioactive waste**, **the linkage with nuclear weapons**, and **catastrophic accidents may occur**.

The structure is no longer parallel because the first and second problems are noun phrases (*the production of radioactive waste* and *the linkage with nuclear weapons*) while the third problem is a clause (*catastrophic accidents may occur*).

TASK 14 CORRECT THE SENTENCES

The following sentences are from the texts in this chapter. They have been rewritten in ways that remove their parallel structure. Without looking at the original texts, rewrite the sentences so that they have parallel structure.

1. [Comparative analysis is the] item-by-item comparison of two or more comparable alternatives, processes, products, qualifications, how people understand sets of data, systems, or the like.

   _____

   _____

2. The uranium mines not only take up land, they also damage the land and require access routes, and local traffic and air pollution increase.

   _____

   _____

3. Facilities need to be dismantled, local access routes returned to their natural state, and people have to remove waste safely.

   _____

   _____

Do Unit 12: Parallel Structure in the Handbook, pp. 399–402.

A COMPARISON

TASK 15 WRITE AN ESSAY OR TWO PARAGRAPHS

Option 1: Write a research essay in response to the essay question you have been working on in this chapter:

Compare and contrast nuclear power with solar and wind power in terms of the reduction of global warming, risks to the environment, and cost. Include your personal opinion as to which energy forms should be promoted by governments.

Use correct APA or MLA citation style to incorporate information and to write a reference list (APA) or list of works cited (MLA).

Option 2: Write two paragraphs that compare nuclear power with solar and/or wind power. Refer to the articles in this chapter. Include your opinion in each paragraph. Use correct APA or MLA citation style to incorporate information and to write a reference list (APA) or list of works cited (MLA).

Checklist for Revising and Editing

Find the Comparative Essay Review Sheet in the online Documents.

Option 1: First, use the checklist below to do a self-evaluation of your essay. Make any necessary revisions. Then do peer review in groups of three, using the Comparative Essay Review Sheet.

Option 2: Use the checklist below to do a self-evaluation of your paragraphs. Then make any necessary revisions.

- [ ] Effective case-by-case or thematic structure
- [ ] Accurate comparison of like with like
- [ ] Clear and convincing opinions
- [ ] Variety of sentence types and vocabulary

CHAPTER 13

WRITING ABOUT PROBLEMS AND SOLUTIONS

> The death of a language is not only a tragedy for those directly involved but also an irretrievable cultural loss for the rest of the world.
>
> Rodger Doyle

Analyzing problems, suggesting solutions, and evaluating the solutions you put forward are important in many forms of academic writing. In a criminology essay, for example, the analysis of problems and solutions is often central to forming a position in a debate; in a business essay, a writer may be required to suggest solutions to a problem that is affecting profit margins; or in a lab report, a writer may need to mention problems that arose during the experimentation process, explaining how these problems were solved. In the fields of Indigenous studies, anthropology, and applied linguistics, the problem of language loss is a topic that has been discussed in depth, with different authors offering different approaches to solving the problem.

In this chapter, you will:

- read about the problem of language loss
- improve your writing style when defining and classifying
- identify problems and solutions in abstracts
- analyze articles for problems, solutions, and evaluation
- study language of problems, solutions, and evaluation
- study modal auxiliary verbs for expressing likelihood and obligation
- write an essay on problems and solutions

TASK 1 EXPLORE THROUGH DISCUSSION

What are the main linguistic minority groups in the countries you have lived in? How do their languages differ from the majority language(s) of those countries?

Discuss these questions in small groups.

LANGUAGE LOSS

Language loss refers to the loss of minority languages, usually the result of younger generations shifting to another, more widely spoken language such as English. There are 7,097 living languages in the world today with over 6.5 billion speakers (https://www.ethnologue.com/statistics). According to Ethnologue, over 30% of these languages are either threatened with extinction or in the process of dying due to the lack of intergenerational transmission. Many of these endangered languages are Indigenous languages spoken by communities that are socially and economically marginalized and often geographically isolated. It is possible that in the next 50 years, many of these endangered languages will die out unless measures are taken to protect them and increase the number of speakers. One strategy that has been successful in reversing language loss in Indigenous communities, and which should continue to succeed in the future, is the setting up of "language nests." In language nests, young children spend time with community elders who speak to them in the community's Indigenous language while the children are still young enough to learn it through immersion.

Protection or Survival of the Fittest?

TASK 2 DISCUSS

Discuss the following statement in small groups:

Governments should take special measures to protect endangered minority languages. Language survival should not be determined by social Darwinism, that is, "survival of the fittest."

Take notes on the main ideas you discuss. You will refer to these notes later in the chapter.

DEFINITIONS AND CLASSIFICATIONS

The above introduction began with a defining sentence: "Language loss refers to the loss of minority languages, usually the result of younger generations shifting to another, more widely spoken language such as English."

While most readers will understand the meanings of the words *language* and *loss*, the writer provides a defining sentence to explain how the term is used in the specific field of study. In other cases, definitions of academic terms may be shorter (a word in parentheses) or longer (a whole paragraph).

Words and Different Meanings

A technical term may have a generally recognized meaning as well as a meaning specific to a subject area. One such example is the word *significant*. In everyday language, most people would understand *significant* to mean "important" in a general sense. However, in statistical research, the meaning of *significant* is more specific and relates to hypotheses and probability. The following examples illustrate this difference:

> Mandarin is a **significant** language in the world today. (important)

> The experiment found a **significant** increase in accurate language use among the study group compared to the control group. (statistically significant)

When using words with multiple meanings, consider the following questions that relate to context and audience:

- What does this word mean in the context of my writing?
- How might my reader interpret the meaning?
- Do I need to define the word, or will my reader understand what I mean?

Techniques for Defining and Classifying

When you define and classify key terms and concepts, your writing should be precise.

When to Define Key Terms

Write a definition if a key term or concept may be interpreted in more than one way and your reader may not be sure of your intended meaning without a definition. The following are three common ways to define terms.

1. Write a synonymous term or phrase in parentheses.

Technical term

Definition

As the younger generation became bilingual, the **heritage language** (the minority language spoken at home) became more endangered.

2. Write a sentence including the following: the term you are defining, the class it belongs to, and a distinguishing feature.

Defined term

Class

Distinguishing feature

Hungarian is one of several languages belonging to the Finno-Ugric language family and is characterized by sentence structure and vocabulary that differs from other European languages, with the exception of Estonian and Finnish.

3. Write a paragraph for a more detailed definition, especially when the meaning of a term has changed over time.

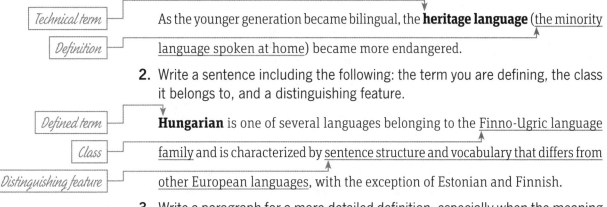

General understanding

Different meanings

Historical definitions

Bilingualism and Multilingualism

In simple terms, bilingualism refers to the ability to speak two languages, and multilingualism, to the ability to speak three or more languages. However, scholars have historically used the terms to emphasize different aspects of language use. In early definitions of bilingualism, Bloomfield (1933) emphasized speaking two languages to the ability of a native speaker as a key defining feature of bilingualism, Weinreich (1953) argued that bilingualism involved being able to alternate between two or more languages, and Haugen (1953) put forward the view that bilingualism requires complete and meaningful utterances in the second language. In recent years, however, there has been a shift of focus in how scholars understand bi- and multilingualism. Today, there is less emphasis on languages as separate, parallel, autonomous systems that learners should be able to speak with the same proficiency as a native speaker. Accordingly, our use of the terms *bilingual* and *multilingual* recognizes the hybrid nature of bi- and multilingualism and that people may have varying degrees of competence in different languages (Auer, 2007; Gajo, 2014; García, 2009; Grosjean, 1984, 2015; Heller, 2006; Lee & Marshall, 2012; Lüdi & Py, 1982, 2013; Marshall & Moore, 2013), and across different skills areas such as reading, writing, speaking, and listening.

ACTIVE AND CRITICAL READING

LANGUAGE LOSS: PROBLEMS AND SOLUTIONS

Language Endangerment

Read the text below on language endangerment and do the tasks that follow.

A feature of this article is the use of *which* as a relative pronoun in defining relative clauses, which is less common in North American varieties of English.

language planners: people working on policies to promote languages

(language) transmission: passing a language from one generation to another

cease: stop

dormant: not active

extinct: no longer existing

vigorous: strong and in good condition

on the verge of: near

vitality (of a language): extent of social use

What Is Language Endangerment?

Endangered Languages

Language endangerment is a serious concern to which linguists and **language planners** have turned their attention in the last several decades. For a variety of reasons, speakers of many smaller, less dominant languages stop

5 using their heritage language and begin using another. Parents may begin to use only that second language with their children and gradually the intergenerational **transmission** of the heritage language is reduced and may even **cease**. As a consequence there may be no speakers who use the language as their first or primary language and eventually the language may no longer

10 be used at all. A language may become **dormant** or **extinct**, existing perhaps only in recordings or written records and transcriptions. Languages which have not been adequately documented disappear altogether.

Defining Language Endangerment

Language endangerment is a matter of degree. At one end of the scale are

15 languages that are **vigorous**, and perhaps are even expanding in numbers of speakers or functional areas of use, but nevertheless exist under the shadow of a more dominant language. At the other end are languages that are **on the verge of** extinction (that is, loss of all individuals who continue to identify the language as being related to their identity). In between are

20 many degrees of greater or lesser **vitality**.

There are two dimensions to the characterization of endangerment: the number of *users* who identify with a particular language and the number and nature of the *uses* or functions for which the language is employed. A language may

be endangered because there are fewer and fewer people who claim that language as their own and therefore neither use it nor pass it on to their children. It may also, or alternatively, be endangered because it is being used for fewer and fewer daily activities and so loses the characteristically close association of the language with particular social or communicative functions. Form follows function and languages which are being used for fewer and fewer domains of life also tend to lose structural complexity, which in turn may affect the perceptions of users regarding the suitability of the language for use in a broader set of functions. This can lead to a **downward spiral** which eventually results in the complete loss of the language.

The concern about language endangerment is centered, first and foremost, around the factors which motivate speakers to abandon their language and the social and psychological consequences of language death for the community of (former) speakers of that language. Since language is closely linked to culture, loss of language almost always is accompanied by social and cultural disruptions. More broadly, the **intangible** heritage of all of human society is diminished when a language disappears. **Secondarily**, those concerned about language endangerment recognize the implications of the loss of linguistic diversity both for the linguistic and social environment generally and for the academic community which is devoted to the study of language as a human phenomenon.

Evaluating Language Endangerment

The best way to identify the level of vitality of a language has not always been clear. However, a scholarly consensus that can be applied worldwide is developing, and a global evaluation of the state of language vitality is becoming increasingly possible. **Sociolinguists** and **linguistic anthropologists** seek to identify trends in language use through the description of some direct measures of language vitality such as changes in the number of speakers or in the use of the language in certain **domains** or functions. Less directly, an increase in bilingualism, both in the number of bilinguals and in their **proficiency** levels, is often associated with these trends, though a high level of bilingualism is not, in itself, a sufficient condition for language shift or death. In addition there are numerous economic, political and social factors that affect a community's self perception and motivations.

Ethnologue reports data that are indicators of the two major dimensions of language use (users and functions). When data are available, we report the following factors which may contribute to the assessment of language endangerment:

downward spiral: process of becoming increasingly worse

intangible: that does not exist physically

secondarily: of secondary importance

sociolinguists: people studying language in relation to social factors

linguistic anthropologists: people studying the relationship between languages and cultures

domains: areas of activity and use (of languages)

proficiency: linguistic ability and knowledge

- The speaker population
70 - The ethnic population; the number of those who connect their ethnic identity with the language (whether or not they speak the language)
- The stability of and trends in that population size
- Residency and migration patterns of speakers
- The use of second languages
75 - The use of the language by others as a second language
- Language attitudes within the community
- The age range of the speakers
- The domains of use of the language
- Official recognition of languages within the nation or region
80 - **Means of transmission** (whether children are learning the language at home or being taught the language in schools)
- Non-linguistic factors such as economic opportunity or the lack thereof

Such factors interact within a society in dynamic ways that are not entirely predictable but which do follow recognizable patterns and trends. The general 85 scholarly consensus, however, is that the key factor in **gauging** the relative safety of an endangered language is the degree to which intergenerational transmission of the language remains intact.

Excerpt from Lewis, M. P., Simons, G. F., & Fennig, C. D. (Eds.). (2016). *Ethnologue: Languages of the world* (19th ed.). Dallas, Texas: SIL International. Retrieved from http://www.ethnologue.com/endangered-languages

means of transmission: ways languages are passed on

gauging: assessing or measuring

TASK 3 LOCATE STANCE

The article is written mainly in an objective style that does not explicitly present the authors' stance as being for or against measures to reduce or reverse language endangerment. Using your skills of inference, locate any information or statements that indicate the authors' stance on the topic.

_____

_____

_____

_____

_____

TASK 4 PARAPHRASE A KEY INTERRELATIONSHIP

In paragraph 3, the authors state that "form follows function." In your own words, explain how the article links the ideas of form, function, and language endangerment.

_____

_____

_____

Solutions to Language Loss

Read the following excerpts from an article on the topic of language nests and answer the questions that follow.

Back to the Future: Recreating Natural Indigenous Language Learning Environments through Language Nest Early Childhood Immersion Programs

by Onowa McIvor and Aliana Parker

What Are Language Nests?

[1] Language nests are places for young children that provide an immersion environment in their Indigenous language. **[2]** A language nest creates a space where young children can be "raised" in the language through meaningful interaction with proficient speakers, often Elders. **[3]** The immersion environment of the nest supports natural **language acquisition** instead of conscious language instruction, with the goal of facilitating first language acquisition of Indigenous languages. . . .

[4] While a language nest may operate similarly to a preschool or **Head Start**, unlike other programs, the driving purpose of the nest is language transmission. **[5]** The language immersion environment is the defining characteristic. **[6]** While other programs may involve a language component, such as having an Elder speaker attend the program or providing language during circle time,

it is *full immersion* that creates a language nest. **[7]** As Johnston and Johnson (2002) defined in their useful article on language nests, a nest "offers intensive exposure to only one language, focuses on learning the language through meaningful content, and is aimed at the youngest members of the community, who are best equipped to learn the language" (p. 108). **[8]** It is this full immersion that makes language nests a very challenging program to implement in **B.C.** due to the low numbers of fluent speakers. **[9]** As described in the *Report on the Status of B.C. First Nations Languages* (First Peoples' Cultural Council, 2014), almost 60% of all fluent speakers of First Nations languages are over the age of 65 and only one percent is under the age of 24. **[10]** Most communities in the province have few, if any, younger members who speak the language fluently, so they are dependent on Elders for the majority of their language programming. **[11]** As a result, all language nests in B.C. rely on Elders to come into the nest on a daily basis to speak the language with the children. **[12]** Anyone familiar with B.C.

immersion programs: programs where students are taught in a language that is not their main spoken language

language acquisition: learning and retaining knowledge of a language

Head Start: community-based education program for Indigenous children in Canada

B.C.: province of British Columbia, Canada

First Nations: Indigenous Canadians from over 630 groups

communities will attest to the astounding energy, commitment, and determination of First Nations Elders for sharing their languages. [13] Having Elders over 70 years of age contributing daily to early care and learning programs is a common occurrence throughout B.C.

References

First Peoples' Cultural Council (FPCC). (2014). *Report on the status of B.C. First Nations languages.* Retrieved from http://www.fpcc.ca/language/status-report/

Johnston, B., & Johnson, K. (2002). Preschool immersion education for Indigenous languages: A survey of resources. *Canadian Journal of Native Education*, *26*(2), 107–123.

Excerpts from McIvor, O., & Parker, A. (2016). Back to the future: Recreating natural Indigenous language learning environments through language nest early childhood immersion programs. *The International Journal of Holistic Early Learning and Development*, *3*, 21–35.

TASK 5 ANALYZE DEFINING SENTENCES

Check the statement that best describes the overall purpose of each group of sentences in defining language nests.

1. Sentences 1 to 4:

   ☐ describe the purpose of language nests.

   ☐ classify language nests.

   ☐ highlight a key distinguishing feature of language nests.

2. Sentences 5 to 7:

   ☐ describe the purpose of language nests.

   ☐ define immersion in language nests.

   ☐ highlight a key distinguishing feature of language nests.

3. Sentences 8 to 10:

   ☐ discuss linguistic fluency.

   ☐ evaluate by highlighting the problems language nests face.

   ☐ compare old and young speakers' abilities.

THE WRITING PROCESS

PROBLEMS, SOLUTIONS, AND EVALUATION

The Problem-Solution Essay Writing Process

Step 1: Describe the Situation or Context

In academic essays with a strong focus on problems and solutions, writers usually begin by describing the situation or context, including background or contextual information and statistics.

For example, in a problem-solution essay about language loss, a writer might begin by presenting facts on the number of languages in the world today, including endangered languages (statistics), followed by a description of how languages have been threatened more recently by globalization and the spread of languages such as English (contextual information).

Step 2: Describe the Problem

Next, the writer should describe the problem(s) in detail, mentioning contributing factors.

For example, the writer could explain how minority languages, including Indigenous languages, are disappearing in the world today at an alarming rate, highlighting the main reasons and describing how language loss has negative effects on communities' connections to their ancestors, land, and cultural heritage.

Step 3: Suggest Solutions

A discussion of possible solutions follows, in which the writer analyzes how the problem has been addressed in the past and how the problem(s) in question may be solved.

For example, the writer might review how communities have used the education system to protect and promote minority languages, highlighting cases where such actions have led to increases in the numbers of speakers.

Step 4: Evaluate the Solutions

In concluding the essay, the writer should remember to evaluate the suggested solutions. In other words, it is necessary to consider factors that may help or hinder the potential success of the solutions.

For example, the essay could end with recognition that the suggested solutions may be limited in their impact due to historical, cultural, social, or political factors.

ACTIVE AND CRITICAL READING

PROBLEMS, SOLUTIONS, AND EVALUATION RELATED TO INDIGENOUS LANGUAGES

Problems and Solutions in Abstracts

In previous chapters, you analyzed the abstracts of academic journal articles for questions and subquestions (Chapter 1); evidence of the research process (Chapter 2); and stance, opinion, and relevance (Chapter 11). When problems and solutions are central themes in academic articles, the problem(s) and solution(s) are usually highlighted in the abstract. The first abstract on the next page is another excerpt from the McIvor and Parker article (see p. 272 for the full source); the second is from an article about an Australian project in language preservation through digital literacy.

Abstract

[1] For a language to have a stable future, children need to be learning it. [2] Immersion for young children is the best method for rapid language regeneration as it can produce new proficient speakers within a few years. [3] Although early childhood language immersion programs, commonly known as language nests, have been recognized internationally as the most successful means available today for language revitalization, this method is not yet well subscribed to in Indigenous Canada. [4] This paper provides a picture of early childhood Indigenous immersion language programming and presents it as one viable solution to the challenge of Indigenous language loss in Canada. [5] In addition, it is hoped that this paper can be a starting point for Indigenous community members interested in immersion early childhood approaches to their children's health, identity development, and overall wellbeing.

TASK 6 IDENTIFY PROBLEMS AND SOLUTIONS IN THE ABSTRACT

Identify the problems and solutions that will be addressed in the McIvor and Parker article.

Problem(s): _____

_____

_____

_____

_____

Solution(s): _____

_____

_____

_____

_____

Getting in Touch: Language and Digital Inclusion in Australian Indigenous Communities

by Margaret Crew, Jennifer Green, Inge Kral, Rachel Nordlinger, and Ruth Singer

[1] Indigenous people in remote Australia face many dilemmas in relation to the status and vitality of their languages and communication ecologies. [2] Cultural leaders want to maintain endangered heritage languages, yet this concern is balanced against an awareness that English competency is a necessary life skill. [3] Remote Indigenous groups must also negotiate the effect of globalized media on language and cultural practices. [4] While public policy seeks to bridge the digital divide in remote Australia, little attention has been

paid to the dominance of English in the new digital environment and the potential impact that increased English language activities may have on endangered Indigenous languages. [5] In this paper we discuss the Getting in Touch project, a joint initiative between linguists, Australian Indigenous language speakers, and software developers. [6] Using a participatory, collaborative process, the project aims to develop ideas for digital resources that privilege Indigenous languages and knowledge systems. [7] We argue that taking Indigenous languages into account in app design may help enhance digital literacies in remote Indigenous communities and promote digital inclusion.

Excerpt from Carew, M., Green, J., Kral, I., Nordlinger, R., & Singer, R. (2015). Getting in touch: Language and digital inclusion in Australian Indigenous communities. *Language Documentation and Conservation*, 9, 307–323. doi:10.13140/RG.2.1.4940.5924

TASK 7 IDENTIFY PROBLEMS AND SOLUTIONS IN THE ABSTRACT

Identify the problems and solutions that will be addressed in the Carew et al. article.

Problem(s): _____

_____

_____

_____

_____

Solution(s): _____

_____

_____

_____

_____

Background Context and Problems

TASK 8 LOCATE THE BACKGROUND CONTEXT AND PROBLEM(S) IN AN ARTICLE

Read the following excerpt from the McIvor and Parker article (see p. 272 for the complete source). As you read, highlight what you consider to be important background and contextual information, and the problem(s) to be addressed.

Language Context

The context of language shift and loss has been well documented internationally (Crystal, 1997; Dixon, 1997; Krauss, 1992). This documentation attests to the current context of Indigenous languages, which represent 96% of the world's languages but are spoken by only four percent of its population
5 (Crystal, 1997). This leaves most of the world's language diversity in the stewardship of a very small number of people (UNESCO Ad Hoc Expert Group on Endangered Languages, 2003).

Prior to contact with Europeans, Indigenous languages flourished across North America
10 and were naturally continued from generation to generation. Following contact, warfare and the introduction of new diseases, both incidental and intentional, dramatically reduced Indigenous populations (Boseker, 2000).
15 Colonial legislation aimed to assimilate Indigenous people into the developing Euro-Canadian culture. The most damaging policies for Indigenous languages were the reserve system and the residential school system
20 along with the prohibition of traditional practices such as potlatches, and the loss of land through settlement, treaties, and destruction of natural habitat. These policies severely disrupted intergenerational language transfer (Stikeman, 2001; Warner, 2001).

The residential and day school system, which children were legally forced
25 to attend, largely forbade the use of Indigenous language (Milloy, 1999; Truth and Reconciliation Commission, 2015). Penalties for children caught speaking their languages included harsh punishment and public humiliation (Boseker, 2000). Indigenous people across Canada have shared their experiences of the tactics used to extinguish their languages. One Tlingit man
30 commented, "Whenever I speak Tlingit, I can still taste the soap" (Dauenhauer & Dauenhauer, 1998). It is no wonder that language recall and regeneration of use for some Indigenous people is so difficult.

All Indigenous languages in Canada face significant threats to their vitality, as there is very little political or economic support for these languages. Unlike
35 other minority language groups, Indigenous people cannot rely on new immigrants to maintain or increase the number of speakers (Norris, 1998), nor is there a "homeland" of speakers somewhere else in the world that they can visit if the language ceases to be used in Canada. There are now 60 Indigenous languages across 12 language families still spoken in Canada (Statistics
40 Canada, 2011). The province of British Columbia (B.C.) has the greatest diversity of Indigenous languages in Canada with 34 languages belonging to eight distinct language families (First Peoples' Cultural Council, 2014).

Many linguists agree that the average age of language speakers largely indicates a language's health and predicted longevity. UNESCO's "Atlas of the
45 World's Languages in Danger of Disappearing" (Wurm, 1996) noted that at

least one-third of the children should be learning the language to maintain its vitality. This is not the case in Canada, where:

> According to the 2006 Census, 18% of First Nations children across Canada had an Aboriginal language as their mother tongue (or first language learned), down from 21% in 1996. Older generations of First Nations people are generally more likely than younger generations to have an Aboriginal language as their mother tongue. (Bougie, 2010, p. 75)

However, more encouraging statistics report that those aged 34 and under "were more likely to report speaking an Aboriginal language at home that was different than their mother tongue. More specifically, it was more common among school-aged children" (Statistics Canada, 2011, p. 7), indicating a trend toward learning Indigenous languages as additional languages in childhood.

As B.C. is home to 60% of Canada's First Nations languages and most have the smallest number of speakers in Canada, the situation here is even more challenging. The *Report on the Status of B.C. First Nations Languages* (First Peoples' Cultural Council, 2014) explained only one percent of the proficient speakers of First Nations languages are under the age of 24, and proficient speakers make up only four percent of the total population. Therefore, it is crucial to concentrate Indigenous language learning efforts on the young children of every Indigenous Nation.

TASK 9 ANALYZE THE STRUCTURE

1. Reread the sections you highlighted in the text above. Indicate which of the following statements best describes how the authors present the background information and context, and the problems.

   ☐ The authors present all the background and contextual information together, and then they present all the problems together.

   ☐ The authors alternate between describing background and contextual information and related problems through the text.

2. Why might one of the structures described above be better than the other for this article?

   _____

   _____

   _____

   _____

   _____

Solutions and Evaluation

The following text is from a website for parents in New Zealand, which explains types of early childhood care. The article focuses on language nests designed to encourage the use of the endangered Maori language of the local Indigenous population.

Kohanga Reo

by Kylie Valentine

At Kohanga Reo all education and instruction is delivered in te reo Maori (Maori language). Learn more about Kohanga Reo and how it works in our article.

What Is Kohanga Reo?

Kohanga Reo is an early childhood education and care (ECE) centre where
5 all education and instruction is delivered in te reo Maori (Maori language). At Kohanga Reo *mokopuna* (children) are totally immersed in Maori language and *tikanga* (culture) from birth through to the age of six. This means that the only language spoken at Kohanga Reo is Maori.

Kohanga Reo is a *whanau* (family) dependent programme: parents and
10 whanau are closely involved with children's development and learning. They are also responsible for the management, operation and everyday decision making for the Kohanga Reo. Parents are also encouraged to take part in the daily programme provided by Kohanga Reo.

The translation of the words Kohanga Reo is 'language nest'. This translation
15 relates directly to one of the key objectives of the Kohanga Reo movement— the retention of the Maori language. Kohanga Reo totally immerses children in Maori language and culture in an effort to promote learning within a context/situation that is relevant to the children and which draws on Maori styles of learning and teaching. . . .

20 ## Whanau

Whanau and parents are ultimately responsible for the operation of Kohanga Reo. The whanau may consist of the parents of the children attending, elders and the community involved on the Kohanga.

The whanau is responsible for:
25 • the employment of the staff working in the Kohanga reo
   • the health and safety of the children attending the Kohanga reo
   • the early childhood education programme for the children attending
   • the management of Kohanga reo property and finances.

The reason for whanau involvement on such a large scale is
30 • to ensure children are supported
   • to share workload and responsibility
   • to ensure everyone is learning about te Kohanga Reo
   • to avoid domination of a few over the majority of the whanau. . . .

What Else Should I Know?

35 It is important to understand that although the primary aim of Kohanga Reo is to totally immerse children in order that they learn the Maori language and culture, including the spiritual dimension, the Education Review Office (ERO) makes us aware of some flaws in this ideal.

In ERO's report 'What Counts as Quality in Kohanga Reo', updated February 2005, an inability to find teachers fluent in, and therefore able to teach in, Maori was noted. This has implications where the total immersion of children in the Maori language is concerned.

Sixty-four percent of Kohanga reo were delivering their programmes entirely through te reo Maori. These Kohanga reo had good programmes in place to foster Maori language and cultural growth in children and to encourage children to communicate in Maori.

While they were committed to delivering programmes through te reo Maori, 27 percent of Kohanga reo were unable to do so consistently because of a lack of Maori language expertise within their Kohanga reo. Most of these whanau need to develop better strategies for promoting Maori language growth in children and in whanau members working with the children.

In nine percent of Kohanga reo, little or no Maori language was spoken by whanau and children. Where Maori was spoken by whanau it tended to be managerial rather than instructional. In almost all these Kohanga reo, children lacked stimulation and were often bored.

Excerpts from Valentine, K. (n.d.). Kohanga reo. *Kiwi Families*. Retrieved from http://www.kiwifamilies.co.nz/articles/kohanga-reo/

TASK 10 EVALUATE FACTORS THAT COULD LIMIT SUCCESS

As stated earlier, it is common to evaluate when writing about problems and solutions. List the points mentioned in the ERO report that are possible limiting factors in the success of Kohanga reo (Maori language nests).

_____

_____

_____

_____

_____

_____

_____

_____

_____

_____

TASK 11 DISCUSS

Find supplementary reading, writing, and critical-thinking activities online.

Look at the notes you took for Task 2, in which you discussed whether governments should take special measures to protect endangered minority languages rather than relying on survival of the fittest. Have your opinions developed or changed from reading the excerpts in the chapter? Discuss this question in small groups.

PROBLEMS, SOLUTIONS, AND EVALUATION

The following is a list of some of the most common ways to describe problems and solutions, and to evaluate the solutions.

Describing Problems

Language endangerment **poses several key problems** for linguistic minorities: . . .

There are three main problems to consider regarding language endangerment and linguistic minorities: . . .

One (major) problem to consider regarding . . . **is** . . .

When it comes to language loss, **one of the main problems is** . . .

Describing Solutions

A solution to the problem of language loss **is** . . .

An effective solution may be to . . .

Language planners **should** . . . **to solve the problem of** language loss among heritage language speakers.

An example of how language endangerment **has been solved / could be solved is** . . .

Instead of / Rather than . . ., policy-makers **should** . . .

The problem of language loss **should be addressed/tackled by** . . .

Evaluating Solutions

One factor that limited / may limit the chances for success is . . .

Increased funding **is unlikely to address the problem of** language loss **if/ unless** . . .

It is unlikely that increased funding alone **will/can solve the problem of** language loss . . .

Increased funding **was a successful/unsuccessful solution to the problem of** language loss **because** . . .

TASK 12 PRACTISE DESCRIBING PROBLEMS AND SOLUTIONS

Complete the following paragraph with appropriate expressions for describing problems and solutions.

Language loss _____ for linguistic minorities in the world today. _____ is the lack of intergenerational transmission, that is, an older generation being unable to pass on its language to a younger generation. Among Indigenous communities in Canada, historically, _____ the residential school system, through which young children were taken away from their families and communities and educated in residential schools, where they were punished if they spoke their Indigenous language. As a result, many Indigenous communities have very few speakers of their language today. _____

_____ by setting up language nests for very young children. Language nests allow elders to speak Indigenous languages with young children while they are at a young enough age to benefit from natural language acquisition. _____ is lack of time. In many communities, where only a small number of elders still speak the language, it is indeed a race against time. Moreover, language nests alone _____ language loss. They can work only if they are part of a broader, multifaceted approach.

EXTEND YOUR ACADEMIC VOCABULARY

Extend your knowledge of key vocabulary from this chapter.

broadly	fewer	lesser
characteristic	**implication**	means
consensus	intangible	refer to

*Words in bold type are AWL entries.

My eLab

Practise Chapter 13 vocabulary online.

EFFECTIVE SENTENCE STRUCTURE

MODALITY: LIKELIHOOD AND OBLIGATION

Modal auxiliary verbs express different aspects of modality such as likelihood, obligation, ability, permission, willingness, and necessity. There are also other words and phrases in the English language that express modality; for example, *have to* and *ought to* can be used to express obligation.

Modal Auxiliary Verbs to Express Likelihood

Modal auxiliary verbs are very important in academic writing; they can express three degrees of likelihood: possibility, probability, and certainty.

- Possibility: *may, might, could*
- Probability: *should*
- Certainty: *must, will*

TASK 13 IDENTIFY MODAL AUXILIARY VERBS THAT EXPRESS LIKELIHOOD

Reread the first paragraph of the Ethnologue text on page 268. Which modal auxiliary verb is used most, and does it express possibility, probability, or certainty?

_____

_____

TASK 14 IDENTIFY MODAL AUXILIARY VERBS THAT EXPRESS POSSIBILITY

Underline any modal auxiliary verbs that express possibility in the following excerpts from the chapter texts.

1. While a language nest may operate similarly to a preschool or Head Start, unlike other programs, the driving purpose of the nest is language transmission. The language immersion environment is the defining characteristic. While other programs may involve a language component, such as having an Elder speaker attend the program or providing language during circle time, it is *full immersion* that creates a language nest.

2. For example, the essay could end with recognition that the suggested solutions may be limited in their impact due to historical, cultural, social, or political factors.

TASK 15 ANALYZE THE USE OF *SHOULD*

Read the excerpt below, in which *should* is used to express a sense of future probability. Answer the questions that follow.

> One strategy that has been successful in reversing language loss in Indigenous communities, and which **should** continue to succeed in the future, is the setting up of "language nests." In language nests, young children spend time with community elders who speak to them in the community's Indigenous language while they are still young enough to learn it through immersion. (Introduction to language loss, p. 266)

1. Does the author's use of *should* give a sense of optimistic or pessimistic expectation?

_____

2. If the same author felt that certain languages were probably going to die out in the near future, which of the following sentences do you think would be more appropriate? Explain your answer.

1. Due to the lack of younger-generation speakers, at least 10% of endangered languages in the world **are probably going to** die out.

2. Due to the lack of younger-generation speakers, at least 10% of endangered languages in the world **should** die out.

_____
_____
_____
_____
_____
_____

TASK 16 ANALYZE THE USE OF *WILL*

Read the following sentence from one of the McIvor and Parker excerpts in this chapter and focus on the use of *will*. Does the use of *will* express certainty about the present or future, or a general prediction?

> Anyone familiar with B.C. communities **will** attest to the astounding energy, commitment, and determination of First Nations Elders for sharing their languages.

_____

_____

Modal Auxiliary Verbs to Express Obligation

Modal auxiliary verbs of obligation can express strong or mild obligation, coming from the speaker (internal) or as a result of pressure from society or other people (external).

TASK 17 ANALYZE EXPRESSIONS OF OBLIGATION

1. Read the following three sentences and compare the use of *must* and *have to* to express strong obligation. Indicate whether the sense of obligation is internal or external.

   a) I **must** study and improve my English if I want to be successful!

   ☐ internal (coming from the speaker) ☐ external (coming from society or other people) ☐ unclear

   b) Members of minority communities **have to** be bilingual to succeed in society.

   ☐ internal (coming from the speaker) ☐ external (coming from society or other people) ☐ unclear

   c) I **had to** study English to be successful.

   ☐ internal (coming from the speaker) ☐ external (coming from society or other people) ☐ unclear

2. Read the following excerpts and indicate whether the degree of obligation is strong or mild.

   a) Today, there is less emphasis on languages as separate, parallel, autonomous systems that speakers **should** be able to speak with the same proficiency as a native speaker.

   ☐ strong obligation ☐ mild obligation

b) Remote Indigenous groups **must** also negotiate the effect of globalized media on language and cultural practices.

☐ strong obligation　　　☐ mild obligation

Do Unit 13: Modal Auxiliary Verbs to Express Likelihood and Obligation in the Handbook, pp. 403–412.

c) UNESCO's "Atlas of the World's Languages in Danger of Disappearing" (Wurm, 1996) noted that at least one-third of the children **should** be learning the language to maintain its vitality.

☐ strong obligation　　　☐ mild obligation

WRITE, REVISE, AND EDIT

A PROBLEM-SOLUTION ESSAY

TASK 18 WRITE AN ESSAY

Write a two-page, double-spaced essay on one of the following topics:

1. What are the main problems that linguistic minorities face in preventing language loss? Describe problems, suggest solutions, and evaluate the proposed solutions. Incorporate vocabulary from the tasks in this chapter.

2. What are the main problems that international or first-year students face? Describe problems, suggest solutions, and evaluate the proposed solutions. Incorporate vocabulary from the tasks in this chapter.

Checklist for Revising and Editing

Use the checklist below to do a self-evaluation of your essay. Then, in groups of three, review each other's essays, using the same checklist. Make any necessary revisions.

☐ Clear explanation of problem(s), solution(s), and evaluation

☐ Clear and convincing opinions and final position

☐ Effective definition and classifying as required

☐ Effective use of modal auxiliary verbs for expressing likelihood and obligation

☐ Accuracy and range of grammar, vocabulary, and punctuation

CHAPTER 14

WRITING ABOUT CAUSES AND EFFECTS

> The fluttering of a butterfly's wing in Rio de Janeiro, amplified by atmospheric currents, could cause a tornado in Texas two weeks later.
>
> Edward Lorenz

In previous chapters, you studied two important aspects of causal relations. First, in Chapter 2, you studied correlation and causality in research and learned that many variable factors need to be eliminated before it can be stated that "*a* causes *b*" rather than "there is a link between *a* and *b*." Then, in Chapter 5, you studied logical fallacies based on cause and effect, including the need to avoid confusing chronological sequence and causality. The relationships between causes and effects can be complex, and writing about these relationships requires critical thinking and precise writing.

In this chapter, you will:

- read about the causes and effects of extreme weather events
- think critically about causality
- review definitions
- study language of cause and effect
- study inversion for emphasis
- review improving style
- write four paragraphs on causes, effects, solutions, and evaluation

TASK 1 EXPLORE THROUGH WRITING

The quotation from mathematician Edward Lorenz suggests that there could be a link between a butterfly flapping its wings in Rio de Janeiro and a tornado in Texas two weeks later. Do you agree? Why or why not?

Take five minutes to write about the question; then compare your writing in small groups.

EXTREME WEATHER

The term *extreme weather*, often used when describing hurricanes, tornadoes, flash floods, drought, and heat waves, refers to severe weather events that are unusual and significantly different from an expected weather pattern. Extreme weather events can be short-lived, lasting no more than a few hours, or can occur over an extended period of time, perhaps weeks or months. So severe are some extreme events that buildings can be badly damaged and people can lose their lives. Recently, scientists have linked extreme weather to global warming, with many suggesting that human-induced factors such as carbon emissions are the main cause. This view is challenged by climate change skeptics. Not only do they argue that the link between the two has yet to be scientifically proven, they also suggest that climate change is first and foremost a natural phenomenon.

Read the following introduction to an article on the topic of global climate change and its impacts on children's health. Then do the tasks that follow.

Global Climate Change and Children's Health

by Samantha Ahdoot and Susan E. Pacheco

[1] Global climate change is a leading public health threat to all current and future children. [2] Rising global temperature, known as "global warming," is causing major physical, chemical, and ecological changes in the planet. [3] The term "climate change" is used in this report to include these broader effects. [4] There is now broad consensus among the world's leading scientific organizations and approximately 97% of climate scientists that these changes are the result of human-generated greenhouse gas emissions.

[5] Rising greenhouse gas concentrations and climate change are part of a larger **constellation** of change resulting from contemporary human activity. [6] **Exponential** increases in human population, **habitat** transformation, energy production and consumption, and climate change are putting **unprecedented** pressure on the earth, resulting in physical, chemical, and ecological changes that are fundamentally altering the planet. [7] These accelerating changes threaten the biological systems on which the life, health, and prosperity of all children depend.

[8] There is wide recognition of climate change among scientific bodies, international agencies, and world religions, and it is important for **pediatricians** to be aware of the effects of climate change on the health and security of individuals, families, and communities. [9] Children are a uniquely vulnerable group that suffers **disproportionately** from these effects. [10] Children also have a fundamental right to justice in a matter as essential as the condition of the planet on which they will live and raise their own children. [11] Although uncertainties remain regarding risks and policy response, given the overwhelming scientific consensus on the cause and potentially **irreversible** harm associated with climate change, failure to take prompt, substantive action would be an act of injustice to all children.

constellation: group of related factors

exponential: increasingly fast

habitat: place where animals and plants live and grow

unprecedented: at a level never seen before

pediatricians: doctors specialized in children's health

disproportionately: too much when compared to others

irreversible: that cannot be undone

[12] Pediatric health care professionals should increase their understanding of the health consequences of climate change so they are able to recognize and anticipate climate-associated effects and serve as advocates for children in the development of mitigation and adaptation strategies to address this global challenge. [13] The purpose of this technical report is to educate pediatricians on the current knowledge of climate change and its effects on children's health. [14] Specific recommendations for pediatricians and governments are included in the accompanying policy statement from the American Academy of Pediatrics on global climate change and children's health.

Excerpt from Ahdoot, S., & Pacheco, S. E. (2015). Global climate change and children's health. *Pediatrics, 136*(5), e1468–e1484. doi:10.1542/peds.2015-3233

TASK 2 LOCATE KEY INFORMATION

In which sentence(s) did you locate the following information?

		Sentence(s)
1	Defining information for the term *climate change*	
2	A statement introducing the stance that human activity does cause climate change	
3	A thematic transition from climate change to children's health	
4	A suggested solution	
5	A statement of the reason for writing the article	

TASK 3 IDENTIFY THE SHIFT IN THE INTRODUCTION

In Chapter 7, you learned that many, but not all, introductions in academic writing shift from general to specific. Does the introduction above shift from general to specific or from specific to general?

TASK 4 IDENTIFY LANGUAGE OF CAUSE AND EFFECT

Reread the introduction and underline any words or phrases that are used to describe cause and effect.

CRITICAL THINKING

CORRELATION VERSUS CAUSALITY

According to the Ahdoot and Pacheco article, the vast majority of scientists believe that global warming is caused by human activity. Accordingly, a minority still challenge the view that there is a causal relation between the two.

TASK 5 DISCUSS

In Chapter 2, you studied how proving correlation and causality was a central goal in the process of doing quantitative research. Considering what you studied in Chapter 2, what you know about the climate change debate, and what you have just read, discuss the following question in small groups:

Do you believe that human activity is the cause of climate change?

ACTIVE AND CRITICAL READING

EL NIÑO AND GLOBAL CLIMATE

The following encyclopedia entry describes, in considerable detail, the El Niño phenomenon and its complex relation to extreme weather events. Read the article and answer the questions that follow.

El Niño

El Niño is a climate pattern that describes the unusual warming of surface waters in the eastern tropical Pacific Ocean. El Niño is the "warm **phase**" of a larger phenomenon called the El Niño-Southern **Oscillation** (ENSO). La Niña, the "cool phase" of ENSO, is a pattern that describes the unusual cooling
5 of the region's surface waters. El Niño and La Niña are considered the ocean part of ENSO, while the Southern Oscillation is its atmospheric changes.

El Niño has an impact on ocean temperatures, the speed and strength of ocean currents, the health of coastal fisheries, and local weather from Australia to South America and beyond. El Niño events occur irregularly at two- to seven-
10 year intervals. However, El Niño is not a regular cycle, or predictable in the sense that ocean tides are.

phase: period of time in a process

oscillation: moving from one position or state to another

simultaneously: at the same time

El Niño was recognized by fishers off the coast of Peru as the appearance of unusually warm water. We have no real record of what
15 indigenous Peruvians called the phenomenon, but Spanish immigrants called it El Niño, meaning "the little boy" in Spanish. When capitalized, El Niño means the Christ Child, and was used because the phenom-
20 enon often arrived around Christmas. El Niño soon came to describe irregular and intense climate changes rather than just the warming of coastal surface waters.

Led by the work of Sir Gilbert Walker in the
25 1930s, climatologists determined that El Niño occurs **simultaneously** with the Southern Oscillation. The Southern Oscillation is a change in air pressure over the tropical Pacific Ocean. When coastal waters become warmer in the eastern tropical Pacific (El Niño), the atmospheric pressure above the ocean decreases. Climatologists define these

30 linked phenomena as El Niño-Southern Oscillation (ENSO). Today, most scientists use the terms El Niño and ENSO interchangeably.

Scientists use the Oceanic Niño Index (ONI) to measure deviations from normal sea surface temperatures. El Niño events are indicated by sea surface temperature increases of more than 0.9° Fahrenheit for at least five succes-

35 sive three-month seasons. The intensity of El Niño events varies from weak temperature increases (about 4–5° F) with only moderate local effects on weather and climate to very strong increases (14–18° F) associated with worldwide climatic changes.

Upwelling

40 In order to understand the development of El Niño, it's important to be familiar with non-El Niño conditions in the Pacific Ocean. Normally, strong trade winds blow westward across the tropical Pacific, the region of the Pacific Ocean located between the Tropic of Cancer and the Tropic of Capricorn. These winds push warm surface water towards the western Pacific, where it

45 borders Asia and Australia.

Due to the warm trade winds, the sea surface is normally about .5 meter (1.5 feet) higher and 45° F warmer in Indonesia than Ecuador. The westward movement of warmer waters causes cooler waters to rise up towards the surface on the coasts of Ecuador, Peru, and Chile. This process is known as *upwelling*.

elevates: raises

nitrates: compounds containing nitrogen and oxygen

phosphates: compounds containing phosphorus

prey on: hunt and kill for food

50 Upwelling **elevates** cold, nutrient-rich water to the euphotic zone, the upper layer of the ocean. Nutrients in the cold water include **nitrates** and **phosphates**. Tiny organisms called phytoplankton use them for photosynthesis, the process that creates chemical energy from sunlight. Other organisms, such as clams, eat the plankton, while predators like fish or marine mammals

55 **prey on** clams.

Upwelling provides food for a wide variety of marine life, including most major fisheries. Fishing is one of the primary industries of Peru, Ecuador, and Chile. Some of the fisheries include anchovy, sardine, mackerel, shrimp, tuna, and hake.

60 The upwelling process also influences global climate. The warm ocean temperature in the western Pacific contributes to increased rainfall around the islands of Indonesia and New Guinea. The air influenced by the cool eastern Pacific, along the coast of South America, remains relatively dry.

El Niño Events

anomalies: exceptions to common rules

65 El Niño events are defined by their wide-ranging teleconnections. Teleconnections are large-scale, long-lasting climate **anomalies** or patterns that are related to each other and can affect much of the globe.

During an El Niño event, westward-blowing trade winds weaken along the Equator. These changes in air pressure and wind speed cause warm surface

70 water to move eastward along the Equator, from the western Pacific to the coast of northern South America.

These warm surface waters deepen the thermocline, the level of ocean depth that separates warm surface water from the colder water below. During an El Niño event, the thermocline can dip as far as 152 meters (500 feet).

75 This thick layer of warm water does not allow normal upwelling to occur. Without an upwelling of nutrient-rich cold water, the euphotic zone of the eastern Pacific can no longer support its normally productive coastal ecosystem. Fish populations die or migrate. El Niño has a devastating impact on Ecuadorian and Peruvian economies.

80 El Niño also produces widespread and sometimes severe changes in the climate. **Convection** above warmer surface waters brings increased precipitation. Rainfall increases drastically in Ecuador and northern Peru, contributing to coastal flooding and erosion. Rains and floods may destroy homes, schools, hospitals, and businesses. They also limit transportation and destroy
85 crops.

As El Niño brings rain to South America, it brings droughts to Indonesia and Australia. These droughts threaten the region's water supplies, as reservoirs dry and rivers carry less water. Agriculture, which depends on water for **irrigation**, is threatened.

90 Stronger El Niño events also disrupt global atmospheric circulation. Global atmospheric circulation is the large-scale movement of air that helps distribute thermal energy (heat) across the surface of the Earth. The eastward movement of oceanic and atmospheric heat sources causes unusually severe winter weather at the higher **latitudes** of North and South America. Regions
95 as far north as the U.S. states of California and Washington may experience longer, colder winters because of El Niño.

El Niño events of 1982–83 and 1997–98 were the most intense of the 20th century. During the 1982–83 event, sea surface temperatures in the eastern tropical Pacific were 9–18° F above normal. These strong temperature
100 increases caused severe climatic changes: Australia experienced harsh drought conditions; **typhoons** occurred in Tahiti; and record rainfall and flooding hit central Chile. The west coast of North America was unusually stormy during the winter season, and fish catches were dramatically reduced from Chile to Alaska.

105 The El Niño event of 1997–98 was the first El Niño event to be scientifically monitored from beginning to end. The 1997–98 event produced drought conditions in Indonesia, Malaysia, and the Philippines. Peru experienced very heavy rains and severe flooding. In the United States, increased winter rainfall hit California, while the Midwest experienced record-breaking warm
110 temperatures during a period known as "the year without a winter."

El Niño-related disruption of global atmospheric circulation extends beyond Pacific Rim nations. Strong El Niño events contribute to weaker **monsoons** in India and Southeast Asia. ENSO has even contributed to increased rainfall during the rainy season in sub-Saharan Africa.

convection: process in which heat moves through gas or liquid

irrigation: watering land via pipes and channels

latitudes: distances north or south of the equator

typhoons: powerful tropical storms

monsoons: periods of heavy rainfall in south Asia

thrive: grow successfully

cholera: water-borne disease causing vomiting and diarrhea

dengue, malaria: mosquito-borne diseases causing fever

respiratory: related to breathing

buoys: markers that float in water

humidity: water in the air

115 Diseases **thrive** in communities devastated by natural hazards such as flood or drought. El Niño-related flooding is associated with increases in **cholera**, **dengue**, and **malaria** in some parts of the world, while drought can lead to wildfires that produce **respiratory** problems. . . .

Monitoring El Niño

120 Scientists, governments, and non-governmental organizations (NGOs) collect data about El Niño using a number of technologies. The National Oceanic and Atmospheric Administration (NOAA), for instance, operates a network of scientific **buoys**. These buoys measure ocean and air temperatures, currents, winds, and **humidity**. The buoys are 125 located at about 70 locations in the southern Pacific Ocean, from the Galapagos Islands to Australia.

These buoys transmit data daily to researchers and forecasters around the world. Using data 130 from the buoys, along with visual imagery they receive from satellite imagery, scientists are able to more accurately predict El Niño and visualize its development and impact around the globe.

Excerpts from El Niño [Encyclopedic entry]. (n.d.). *National Geographic Society*. Retrieved from http://nationalgeographic.org/encyclopedia/el-nino/

TASK 6 SHOW YOUR UNDERSTANDING

Answer the following questions to show your understanding of the article on El Niño.

1. Describe the difference between El Niño, La Niña, and ENSO. [LINES 2–6]

_____

_____

_____

2. Which of the following sentences best describes the statement in lines 24 to 26?

☐ Sir Gilbert Walker led a group of climatologists and named El Niño and the Southern Oscillation.

☐ Sir Gilbert Walker and his team of climatologists figured out that El Niño takes place at the same time as the Southern Oscillation.

☐ Sir Gilbert Walker and his team of determined climatologists reached the conclusion that El Niño takes place at the same time as the Southern Oscillation.

3. Describe how upwelling has different impacts on the sea waters of Indonesia and the coastal waters of western South America. [LINES 46–49]

_____

_____

_____

4. In lines 120 to 133, the writer explains how the National Oceanic and Atmospheric Administration (NOAA) operates a network of scientific buoys. Describe the purpose of these buoys.

_____

_____

_____

TASK 7 CONSIDER THE STANCE ON HUMAN CAUSES

Does the article present a stance on the question of whether climate change is due to human activity or natural causes? Explain why or why not.

_____

_____

_____

EFFECTIVE WRITING STYLE

REVIEW: DEFINITIONS

In Chapter 13, you studied definitions in academic writing, focusing on the reasons definitions are required and on three ways to write definitions: write a synonymous term or phrase in parentheses; write a sentence including the term you are defining, the class it belongs to, and a distinguishing feature; and write a more extended definition in a paragraph.

TASK 8 ANALYZE DEFINITIONS

The encyclopedia entry about El Niño contains several definitions, with the information arranged in different ways. Read the definitions and answer the questions that follow.

1. El Niño is a climate pattern that describes the unusual warming of surface waters in the eastern tropical Pacific Ocean. El Niño is the "warm phase" of a larger phenomenon called the El Niño-Southern Oscillation (ENSO). La Niña, the "cool phase" of ENSO, is a pattern that describes the unusual cooling of the region's surface waters. El Niño and La Niña are considered the ocean part of ENSO, while the Southern Oscillation is its atmospheric changes.

Which of these definition strategies best describes excerpt 1?

☐ Each term is described in a defining sentence and in relation to different broader phenomena.

☐ Each term is described in a defining sentence and in relation to the same broader phenomenon.

☐ Each term is described in a defining sentence and in terms of its similarity to a broader phenomenon.

2. El Niño events are indicated by sea surface temperature increases of more than 0.9° Fahrenheit for at least five successive three-month seasons. The intensity of El Niño events varies from weak temperature increases (about 4–5° F) with only moderate local effects on weather and climate to very strong increases (14–18° F) associated with worldwide climatic changes.

   How would you describe the ordering of information in definition 2?

   _____

   _____

   _____

3. Due to the warm trade winds, the sea surface is normally about .5 meter (1.5 feet) higher and 45° F warmer in Indonesia than Ecuador. The westward movement of warmer waters causes cooler waters to rise up towards the surface on the coasts of Ecuador, Peru, and Chile. This process is known as *upwelling*.

   How does definition 3 differ from the definitions in excerpt 1?

   _____

   _____

   _____

4. El Niño events are defined by their wide-ranging teleconnections. Teleconnections are large-scale, long-lasting climate anomalies or patterns that are related to each other and can affect much of the globe.

   How would you describe the ordering of information in definition 4?

   _____

   _____

   _____

5. These warm surface waters deepen the thermocline, the level of ocean depth that separates warm surface water from the colder water below. During an El Niño event, the thermocline can dip as far as 152 meters (500 feet).

   How is the term *thermocline* defined in excerpt 5?

   _____

   _____

   _____

CAUSE AND EFFECT

Causal relations can be described in two ways: cause then effect, and effect then cause. The following two examples from the articles in this chapter illustrate the two ways.

1. The eastward movement of oceanic and atmospheric heat sources **causes** unusually severe winter weather at the higher latitudes of North and South America. (cause then effect)

2. These changes **are the result of** human-generated greenhouse gas emissions. (effect then cause)

In example 1, the writer presents the cause (movement of heat sources) and then the effect (severe winter weather). In example 2, the authors first present the effects ("these changes") and then the cause (human-generated greenhouse gas emissions). The second method is employed less in the two articles.

TASK 9 IDENTIFY CAUSE-THEN-EFFECT AND EFFECT-THEN-CAUSE PATTERNS

Read each of the following sentences from the two articles and identify the method used by the writers: cause then effect, or effect then cause.

1. The westward movement of warmer waters **causes** cooler waters to rise up towards the surface on the coasts of Ecuador, Peru, and Chile.

   ☐ cause then effect ☐ effect then cause

2. Rising greenhouse gas concentrations and climate change are part of a larger constellation of change **resulting from** contemporary human activity.

   ☐ cause then effect ☐ effect then cause

3. **Due to** the warm trade winds, the sea surface is normally about .5 meter (1.5 feet) higher and 45° F warmer in Indonesia than Ecuador.

   ☐ cause then effect ☐ effect then cause

4. The upwelling process also **influences** global climate.

   ☐ cause then effect ☐ effect then cause

5. Convection above warmer surface waters **brings** increased precipitation.

   ☐ cause then effect ☐ effect then cause

6. Regions as far north as the U.S. states of California and Washington may experience longer, colder winters **because of** El Niño.

   ☐ cause then effect ☐ effect then cause

Expressions of Cause and Effect

The following are some of the most common ways to describe cause and effect.

Describing Cause Then Effect

Structure	Expressions	Examples
Noun phrases	*a main/key/major cause of* *a contributing factor in* *a contributor to*	The El Niño phenomenon is **a main/key/ major cause of** extreme weather events. The El Niño phenomenon is **a contributing factor in / contributor to** extreme weather events.
Verbs	*cause* *contribute to* *lead to* *produce* *result in*	Rising sea temperatures **cause / contribute to / lead to / produce / result in** increases in extreme weather.
Linking words and phrases	*as a result* *consequently* *therefore* *so* *because* *as* *since* *as a result of* *because of* *due to*	1997–98 was an El Niño year. **As a result / Consequently / Therefore,** there were droughts in Indonesia and Malaysia. 1997–98 was an El Niño year, **so** there were droughts in Indonesia and Malaysia. **Because/As/Since** 1997–98 was an El Niño year, there were droughts in Indonesia and Malaysia. **As a result of / Because of / Due to** the droughts in Indonesia and Malaysia, local farmers suffered hardship.

As and *since* can also convey time relations, so avoid using them for cause and effect unless the meaning is clear.

Describing Effect Then Cause

Structure	Expressions	Examples
Noun phrases	*a main/key/major effect of* *a consequence of* *a result of*	Extreme weather events are **a main/key/major effect of** the El Niño phenomenon. Extreme weather events are **a consequence of / result of** the El Niño phenomenon.
Verbs	*caused by* *brought about by* *result from*	Typhoons in Tahiti were **caused by / brought about by** increases in sea temperatures. Typhoons in Tahiti **result from** increases in sea temperatures.
Linking words and phrases	*as a result of* *because of* *due to* *owing to* *because* *as* *since*	The sea is higher and warmer in Indonesia than in Ecuador **as a result of / because of / due to / owing to** warm trade winds. The sea is warmer in Indonesia than in Ecuador **because/as/since** warm trade winds blow westward.

TASK 10 PRACTISE USING VOCABULARY OF CAUSE AND EFFECT

Fill in the blanks in the following sentences describing causal relations, taken from the articles in this chapter.

1. Complete the sentences with verbs referring specifically to cause then effect.

   a) These changes in air pressure and wind speed _____ warm surface water to move eastward along the Equator, from the western Pacific to the coast of northern South America.

   b) The warm ocean temperature in the western Pacific _____ increased rainfall around the islands of Indonesia and New Guinea.

   c) Strong El Niño events _____ weaker monsoons in India and Southeast Asia.

   d) ENSO has even _____ increased rainfall during the rainy season in sub-Saharan Africa.

   e) El Niño also _____ widespread and sometimes severe changes in the climate.

   f) The 1997–98 event _____ drought conditions in Indonesia, Malaysia, and the Philippines.

2. Complete each sentence with one of the following verbs that explain *how* one thing affects another.
   - decreases
   - deepen
   - disrupt
   - thrive

   a) When coastal waters become warmer in the eastern tropical Pacific (El Niño), the atmospheric pressure above the ocean _____.

   b) These warm surface waters _____ the thermocline, the level of ocean depth that separates warm surface water from the colder water below.

   c) Stronger El Niño events also _____ global atmospheric circulation.

   d) Diseases _____ in communities devastated by natural hazards such as flood or drought.

3. Complete each sentence with one of the following expressions of effect then cause.

- because of / due to
- resulting from
- influenced by

a) Rising greenhouse gas concentrations and climate change are part of a larger constellation of change _____ contemporary human activity.

b) The air _____ the cool eastern Pacific, along the coast of South America, remains relatively dry.

c) Regions as far north as the U.S. states of California and Washington may experience longer, colder winters _____ El Niño.

4. Complete each sentence with one of the following phrases used to express cause and effect.

- can lead to
- due to / because of
- has an impact on
- is associated with
- is threatened
- the effects of X on . . .

a) Agriculture, which depends on water for irrigation, _____.

b) El Niño-related flooding _____ increases in cholera, dengue, and malaria in some parts of the world, while drought _____ wildfires that produce respiratory problems.

c) It is important for pediatricians to be aware of _____ climate change _____ the health and security of individuals, families, and communities.

d) El Niño _____ ocean temperatures, the speed and strength of ocean currents, the health of coastal fisheries, and local weather from Australia to South America and beyond.

e) _____ the warm trade winds, the sea surface is normally about .5 meter (1.5 feet) higher and 45° F warmer in Indonesia than Ecuador.

EXTEND YOUR ACADEMIC VOCABULARY

Extend your knowledge of key vocabulary from this chapter.

disproportionate	**irreversible**	susceptibility
exacerbation	receding	thrive
exponential	simultaneously	**unprecedented**

*Words in bold type are AWL entries.

Practise Chapter 14 vocabulary online.

EFFECTIVE SENTENCE STRUCTURE

INVERSION FOR EMPHASIS

It is possible to add emphasis to sentences by adding an emphatic adverbial word or phrase at the beginning of an independent clause. The following two examples are taken from the introductory paragraph on extreme weather on page 286.

1. **So severe are some extreme events** that buildings can be badly damaged and people can lose their lives.

2. **Not only do they argue** that the link between the two has yet to be scientifically proven, they also suggest that climate change is first and foremost a natural phenomenon.

Sentence 1 begins with the emphatic adverb *so* followed by the adjective *severe*. As a result, the subject-verb order has to be reversed: the verb *are* is positioned before the subject *some extreme events*. Sentence 2 begins with the adverbial phrase *not only* as a way to add emphasis. The following subject *they* and verb *argue* have to be changed to question form: *do they argue*.

A list of words and phrases that require inversion for emphasis can be found in Unit 14: Inversion for Emphasis in the Handbook (see p. 413).

The following are three ways that sentences are restructured when certain emphatic adverbs are used. The adverbs are in bold, and the inverted subjects and verbs, underlined.

1. With the verb *to be*

Climate change is a serious threat to coastal regions; it also plays a role in desertification inland.

Not only <u>is climate change</u> a serious threat to coastal regions, it also plays a role in desertification inland.

2. With auxiliary verbs

Greenhouse gas emissions are polluting the air and contributing to climate change.

Not only <u>are greenhouse gas emissions polluting</u> the air, they are also contributing to climate change.

Global temperatures have not risen so rapidly since the end of the last ice age.

Not since the end of the last ice age <u>have global temperatures risen</u> so rapidly.

Climate skeptics will accept that global warming is caused by human activity only after the presentation of conclusive scientific evidence.

Only after the presentation of conclusive scientific evidence <u>will climate skeptics accept</u> that global warming is caused by human activity.

3. With other verbs, use question structure.

I did not realize that monsoons and typhoons are different.

Little <u>did I realize</u> that monsoons and typhoons are different.

TASK 11 INVERT SUBJECTS AND VERBS FOR EMPHASIS

The following sentences are adapted from the two articles in this chapter. Add emphasis by beginning the independent clause with the word or phrase in parentheses and changing the order of the subject and verb as required.

1. Children should never lose their fundamental right to justice on the planet on which they will live and raise their own children. (Under no circumstances)

_____

_____

2. El Niño has an impact on ocean temperatures and on the speed and strength of ocean currents. (Not only)

_____

_____

3. El Niño is not a regular cycle. It is not predictable in the sense that ocean tides are. (Nor)

_____

_____

4. It was only in the 1930s that climatologists realized that El Niño occurs simultaneously with the Southern Oscillation. (Not until)

_____

_____

5. The air influenced by the cool eastern Pacific seldom becomes very humid. (Seldom)

_____

_____

6. The Ecuadorian and Peruvian economies have rarely come out unscathed during an El Niño year. (Rarely)

_____

_____

7. Scientists had data on an El Niño event from beginning to end after the event of 1997–98. (Only after)

_____

_____

8. El Niño-related disruption of global atmospheric circulation is not limited to Pacific Rim nations. (On no account)

_____

_____

9. El Niño-related flooding is so severe that it leads to increased rates of cholera, dengue, and malaria in some parts of the world. (So)

Do Unit 14: Inversion for Emphasis in the Handbook, pp. 413–420.

_____

_____

EFFECTIVE WRITING STYLE

REVIEW: IMPROVING STYLE

TASK 12 IDENTIFY ELEMENTS OF WEAK STYLE

The following paragraph contains several examples of weak style. Highlight each example and explain the weakness on the next page.

Extreme Weather

[1] *Extreme weather* is a term that you often hear when the weatherman is talking about things like hurricanes, tornadoes, flash floods, drought, and heat waves. [2] Some extreme weather events last for ages, and other extreme weather events don't last more than a few minutes. [3] A lot of scientists have linked extreme weather to global warming and suggested that man-made factors such as carbon emissions are the main cause, which has been challenged by climate change skeptics, who support the opinion that global warming is caused by natural things like solar flares, volcanoes, and natural temperature cycles. [4] How, then, should we reach an informed opinion when the two sides disagree about the origins and causes of global warming so vehemently? [5] Maybe the only way to do this is to have a go at analyzing reliable historical and current data that show how temperatures have changed during stages of industrialization carefully. [6] If we aren't able to do that, how will we be able to look into effective solutions?

Explanations of Weak Style

Sentence 1: _____

_____

_____

Sentence 2: _____

_____

_____

Sentence 3: _____

_____

_____

Sentence 4: _____

_____

_____

Sentence 5: _____

_____

_____

Sentence 6: _____

_____

_____

TASK 13 IMPROVE THE STYLE OF THE PARAGRAPH

Now rewrite the paragraph from Task 12, improving the style.

_____

_____

_____

_____

_____

_____

_____

_____

_____

_____

_____

_____

_____

_____

Find supplementary
reading, writing,
and critical-thinking
activities online.

PARAGRAPHS ABOUT CAUSES, EFFECTS, AND SOLUTIONS

Figure 1 opposite is a description of the potential effects of global climate change on the health of children, taken from the Ahdoot and Pacheco article. The figure presents a visual explanation of the following:

- how human-caused greenhouse gas emissions and natural causes contribute together to increase climate change
- four key environmental effects of accelerated climate change
- effects on children's health
- other effects indirectly related to children's health
- mitigating factors (i.e., factors that can lessen the impact of human-caused greenhouse gas emissions)
- adaptation factors (i.e., strategies that societies can employ to help people deal with the negative effects)

Think of the links between causes and effects, and problems and solutions. Figure 1 illustrates this interconnectedness between cause-and-effect analysis and problem-solution analysis, which is evident in the inclusion of the factors in the dotted rectangles for *mitigation* and *adaptation*.

Read the figure and do the writing task that follows.

Glossary for Figure 1

carbon capture: preventing carbon from entering the atmosphere, for example, from power stations

receding: moving backwards

susceptibility: state of being easily affected

post-traumatic stress: mental condition that emerges after stressful, shocking events

displaced: forced to move from one's home

exacerbations: making something bad worse

waterborne: spread or carried by water

foodborne: spread or carried by food

vectorborne: spread or carried by living organisms

novel: new

heat stroke: illness caused by exposure to excessive heat

nutrient: substance that helps growth and development

FIGURE 1 POTENTIAL EFFECTS OF GLOBAL CLIMATE CHANGE ON CHILD HEALTH

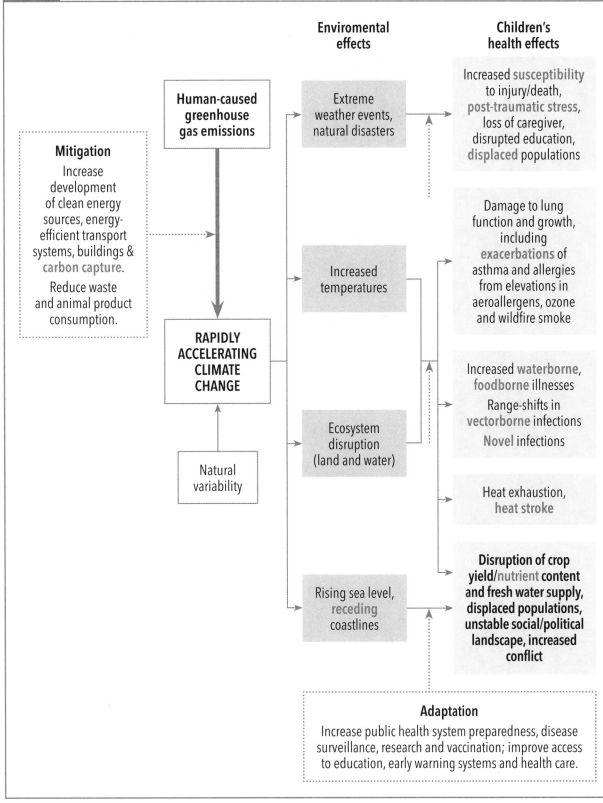

Ahdoot, S., & Pacheco, S. E. (2015). Global climate change and children's health. *Pediatrics*, *136*(5), e1468–e1484. doi:10.1542/peds.2015-3233

TASK 14 WRITE FOUR PARAGRAPHS

In four paragraphs, write about the causes, effects, and solutions described in Figure 1. In the fourth paragraph, evaluate the solutions suggested in terms of mitigation and adaptation by presenting your own personal opinion as to whether they would be likely to succeed, and why.

Checklist for Revising and Editing

Use the checklist below to do a self-evaluation of your paragraphs. Then, in groups of three, review each other's paragraphs, using the same checklist.

- [ ] Clear explanation of causes, effects, solutions, and evaluation
- [ ] Clear and convincing opinions and final position
- [ ] Effective use of language of cause, effect, solution, and evaluation
- [ ] Appropriate style
- [ ] At least two examples of inversion for emphasis
- [ ] Accuracy and range of grammar, vocabulary, and punctuation

CHAPTER 15

REVIEW AND CONSOLIDATION

If a job's worth doing, it's worth doing well.

Popular saying

This chapter presents summaries and review activities to help you consolidate your learning from Chapters 10 to 14.

In this chapter, you will first review the main content from Chapters 10 to 14:

- describing processes and statistical data
- writing arguments in essays
- making comparisons
- writing about problems and solutions
- writing about causes and effects

Then you will do consolidation tasks for the following features of successful academic writing that you studied in the chapters:

- critical thinking: assessing correlation and causality, cause and effect; engaging critically with statistical data; doing comparative analysis
- effective writing style: identifying and rewriting weak style, defining and classifying, incorporating information from a blog
- vocabulary: guessing the meaning from context; exemplification; describing statistics; making comparisons; describing problems and solutions, and evaluating the solutions; writing about causes and effects

TASK 1 EXPLORE THROUGH WRITING

When you read statistics in the media, how do you assess their reliability?

Take five minutes to answer the question. Read each other's writing in small groups.

CONTENT OVERVIEW

Describing Processes and Statistical Data

Chapter 10 focused on the ability to understand and critically engage with processes and data, and to write about them with precision. The chapter included the following related tasks:

- read and analyze texts on the topics of 3D printing and air pollution
- learn how to describe processes and statistical data
- study vocabulary to describe statistics
- critically engage with statistical data

At the end of the chapter, you wrote a process paragraph describing the pollution cycle, and a paragraph describing data from two bar charts about human and natural emissions.

Writing Arguments in Essays

The focus of Chapter 11 was on writing arguments, addressing controversy, and presenting a position in an ongoing debate. In the chapter, you studied and practised the following skills and stages involved in writing an argumentative essay:

- techniques for effective keyword searches
- identifying stance, opinion, and relevance in abstracts
- forming outlines for argumentative essays
- writing about statistical data
- including your life experience in essays

You ended the chapter by writing an argumentative essay on the pros and cons of using cellphones in higher education classrooms.

Making Comparisons

In Chapter 12, the focus was on making comparisons in academic writing and what effective comparative analysis entails, for example, looking for similarities and differences, and comparing like with like. You studied the following aspects of making comparisons in the context of comparing nuclear power with solar and wind power:

- reading texts for inference, stance, and bias
- key aspects of comparative analysis
- forming outlines for comparative essays
- analyzing effective comparative paragraphs
- language of comparison

Your writing task at the end of the chapter was either a research essay or two paragraphs comparing nuclear, solar, and wind power.

Writing about Problems and Solutions

Chapter 13 focused on analyzing problems and solutions, and evaluating suggested solutions, with reference to language loss in Indigenous communities. You studied the following aspects of writing about problems and solutions:

- identifying problems and solutions in abstracts
- analyzing articles for problems, solutions, and evaluation
- language of problems, solutions, and evaluation

To conclude the chapter, you wrote a two-page essay on either the problems faced by linguistic minorities or those of international or first-year students in higher education. You suggested solutions to the problems and evaluated your solutions.

Writing about Causes and Effects

In Chapter 14, you studied cause and effect, with specific reference to extreme weather events. You learned about the complex interrelationship between cause and effect and the need for critical thinking and precise writing skills when addressing causality. The chapter focused on the following skills:

- analyzing articles for cause and effect
- thinking critically about causality
- using language of cause and effect

At the end of the chapter, you wrote four paragraphs on causes, effects, solutions, and evaluation in response to an illustration of the causes of extreme weather events and their effects on children's health.

CRITICAL THINKING

CONSOLIDATION TASKS

Assessing Correlation and Causality, Cause and Effect

In Chapter 10, you reviewed the notions of correlation and causality, which you first studied in Chapter 2 (see p. 29). When researchers state that there is a correlation between *a* and *b*, it means they have established a link; for example, researchers may suggest that an experimental study showed a correlation between eating processed food and weight gain among the subjects. Accordingly, the authors of the study might write that "eating processed food was linked to weight gain," or "eating processed food may have caused weight gain." However, if they want to establish causality, they need to eliminate a range of variables, that is, other factors that may have had an effect on the weight of the study subjects, for example, age, socio-economic status, family history, and gender. Once they have eliminated the possible variable factors, the researchers can then state that eating processed food *caused* weight gain among the study subjects.

TASK 2 IDENTIFY STATEMENTS OF CORRELATION OR CAUSALITY

Read the following statements and indicate whether they describe a correlation or causality.

1. There is an indisputable link between carbon emissions and global warming.

   ☐ correlation   ☐ causality

2. There is no doubt whatsoever that global warming is the result of the burning of fossil fuels.

   ☐ correlation   ☐ causality

3. The closure of three coal-burning power stations may well have had an impact on improving air quality in the following months.

   ☐ correlation   ☐ causality

4. Increased air pollution brought about a rise in respiratory illnesses in the city.

   ☐ correlation   ☐ causality

TASK 3 ANALYZE CAUSE AND EFFECT

Read the following excerpt from the Eurostat article in Chapter 10 (see p. 210). Answer the questions that follow.

Air Pollution Statistics

[1] Air pollution caused by human activities, including industrial and energy production, the burning of fossil fuels and increased use of certain types of transport, causes serious health problems for hundreds of thousands of Europeans every year. [2] Environmental damage such as acidification, eutrophication, tropospheric (ground-level) ozone and reduced air quality, especially in urban areas, can be a local as well as a transboundary problem as air pollutants are transported in the atmosphere and harm human health and the environment elsewhere.

Excerpt from Eurostat. (2016, October 19). Air pollution statistics. *Statistics Explained*. Retrieved from http://ec.europa.eu/eurostat/statisticsexplained/index.php/Air_pollution_statistics

1. Does sentence 1 state that all air pollution is caused by human activities? Explain your answer.

   _____

   _____

   _____

2. Does sentence 1 state that there is a correlation between pollution caused by human activity and serious health problems or that the pollution *causes* the health problems? Explain your answer.

_____

_____

3. Does sentence 2 describe a correlation or causality regarding the health effects of air pollutants in the atmosphere? Explain your answer.

_____

_____

Engaging Critically with Statistical Data

In Chapters 10 and 11, you studied the importance of engaging critically with statistical data, first by reading critically and then by accurately representing what you find.

Read the text below and study the bar chart on the next page that shows the top sources of human-made fine particle emissions ($PM_{2.5}$) in New South Wales, Australia. Then do the task that follows.

evaporative emissions: emissions caused by liquids changing to vapour/gas

locomotives: trains

Air Emissions Data

Air quality in NSW is affected by human and natural sources, with the air quality in specific regions influenced by local sources and also by transport of pollutants and secondary pollutants. Emissions come from the following key sectors:

- industry sources, such as mining, power generation, manufacturing, waste management and agriculture

- motor vehicles, including heavy and light, commercial and private, diesel and petrol-powered vehicles; and including exhaust and **evaporative emissions** and particle emissions from brake and tyre wear

- non-road mobile sources, including shipping and **locomotives** and diesel equipment, used for example in mining, construction, waste management and port activities

- commercial activities, such as service stations, printing, dry cleaning and automotive repairs

- domestic sources, such as residential wood heating, lawn mowing and gardening equipment, aerosol and solvent use, and paints

- natural sources, such as vegetation emissions, bushfires and sea salt. . . .

The largest direct sources of human-made fine particle emissions in the Greater Metropolitan Region (GMR) are shown in Figure [1]. Coal mining, residential wood heaters, power generation and non-road diesel equipment are key sources of particle emissions.

Excerpt from State of NSW (2016, October). *Clean air for NSW* [consultation paper]. Retrieved from http://www.epa.nsw.gov.au/resources/air/clean-air-nsw-160415.pdf

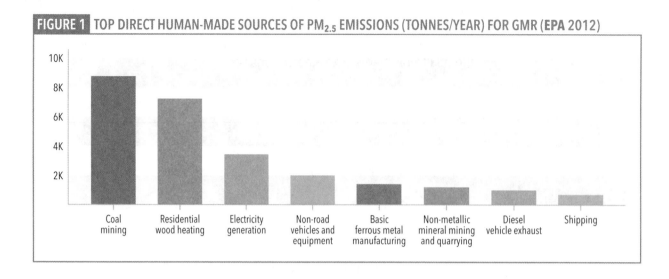

FIGURE 1 TOP DIRECT HUMAN-MADE SOURCES OF PM$_{2.5}$ EMISSIONS (TONNES/YEAR) FOR GMR (EPA 2012)

EPA: Environment
Protection Authority

TASK 4 ANALYZE ACCURACY

Read the sentences below, which refer to the text on air emissions data and the statistics shown in Figure 1. Indicate whether each sentence accurately and precisely represents the causes and effects stated in the text and the statistical data in the bar chart. If a sentence is incorrect or imprecise, rewrite it to make an accurate statement.

1. PM$_{2.5}$ emissions from coal mining exceeded eight tonnes in 2012.

   ☐ accurate   ☐ inaccurate

   _____

   _____

2. Human and natural sources may be having an effect on air quality in New South Wales.

   ☐ accurate   ☐ inaccurate

   _____

   _____

3. The figure for PM$_{2.5}$ emissions from non-road vehicles and equipment was one eighth of that for coal mining.

   ☐ accurate   ☐ inaccurate

   _____

   _____

4. The total figure for PM$_{2.5}$ emissions from coal mining was more than that of all the other sources combined.

   ☐ accurate   ☐ inaccurate

   _____

   _____

5. Air quality in the GMR is negatively affected in equal measure by four key sources: coal mining, residential wood heaters, power generation, and non-road diesel equipment.

☐ accurate   ☐ inaccurate

Doing Comparative Analysis

In Chapter 12, you learned the importance of comparing like with like versus comparing "apples and oranges."

Higher Education and League Tables

Numerous organizations rank universities and colleges nationally and internationally by establishing league tables. Many students consult these league tables when they make choices about the courses and institutions to which they are going to apply.

TASK 5 EXPLORE THROUGH WRITING

Take 15 minutes to write about the following question. Then compare your writing in groups of three.

If you were thinking of applying to a university ranked in the top 10 worldwide and to one ranked between 100 and 150, what factors would you consider when comparing them? Consider any of the following: criteria for rankings, reliability of statistics, socio-economic factors, educational factors, and personal life experience. Explain your choices.

EFFECTIVE WRITING STYLE

CONSOLIDATION TASKS

In Parts 1 and 2, you studied and reviewed various aspects of effective writing style. The focus of Chapters 10 to 14 was on identifying examples of weak style and rewriting them to improve the style, and on writing definitions and describing classifications. You also studied the style features of an academic blog.

Identifying and Rewriting Weak Style

TASK 6 IDENTIFY AND EXPLAIN WEAK STYLE

Identify the aspects of weak academic style in the following sentences.

1. *Multilingualism* is a technical term that is used in the fields of education and linguistics often.

2. You can use the term *multilingual* to refer to speakers of three or more languages.

_____

3. In contrast, the term *bilingual* has traditionally been used to describe speakers of two languages who can speak each language at the same level as a native speaker, or for speakers who can switch easily between the two languages, a definition that has been challenged by linguists in recent years, many of whom disagree with the idea that, to be called *bilingual*, a person should be able to speak each language like a native speaker.

_____

4. A multilingual person often speaks one of his languages more fluently than the others.

_____

5. First, in a city such as Montreal, Canada, the children of immigrants often speak three or more languages. For example, many children of immigrants speak a home language in addition to French and English. However, the children of immigrants do not always speak each language separately. Rather, they may mix the different languages when they speak. Linguists have called this form of multilingualism *codeswitching* and *translanguaging*.

_____

6. Lots of scientists have tried to find out how the brains of multilingual people differ from monolinguals' brains by doing experimental research.

_____

TASK 7 REWRITE THE SENTENCES FOR IMPROVED STYLE

Rewrite the sentences in Task 6 to improve the style.

1. _____

_____

2. _____

_____

3. _____

_____

_____

_____

_____

_____

4. _____

_____

5. _____

_____

_____

_____

_____

_____

6. _____

_____

Defining and Classifying

In Chapter 13, you studied three common strategies for defining: (1) write a synonymous word or phrase in parentheses; (2) write a sentence including the term you are defining, the class it belongs to, and a distinguishing feature; and (3) write a paragraph with a more detailed definition.

In Task 7 above, you rewrote classifying and defining information for the term *multilingual* to improve the academic style.

TASK 8 IDENTIFY FUNCTIONS OF CLASSIFICATION AND DEFINITION

Which of the sentences in Task 6 perform the following functions for the term *multilingual*?

	Function	Sentence(s)
1	Classify the term	
2	Define the term	
3	Distinguish the term from a similar term	
4	Expand the definition regarding usage	
5	Provide a real-world example	

Incorporating Information from a Blog

In Chapter 11, you described the style of an academic blog on the use of mobile devices in the college classroom. You analyzed the reliability of information from the blog and whether it could be cited in an academic essay. The blog was written in a style that was less formal, more personal, and more engaging than that of most academic journal articles. If you decided to paraphrase information from the blog in an essay, you would need to shift style to maintain a more formal tone.

TASK 9 SHIFT STYLE

The following sentences are from Maryellen Weimer's *Teaching Professor Blog* in Chapter 11 (see p. 236). Paraphrase the sentences to make the style more formal. The information in brackets provides additional explanations.

1. So apparently from the student perspective, we're not talking about a disruption they consider serious. [*Disruption* refers to using cellphones in class.]

_____

_____

2. I also wonder if it isn't getting under our skin because most of our policies really aren't working all that well. [*It* refers to students using their phones rather than paying attention to their instructors.]

_____

_____

3. Lots of points, but here's the bottom line: I think we can make the use of electronic devices more important than it merits.

_____

_____

VOCABULARY

CONSOLIDATION TASKS

In Chapters 10 to 14, you studied the following vocabulary strategies and topics:
- guessing the meaning from context
- exemplification
- describing statistics
- making comparisons
- describing problems and solutions, and evaluating the solutions
- writing about causes and effects

Guessing the Meaning from Context

You first studied different strategies for learning vocabulary in Chapter 1 (see p. 7). In Chapter 11, you practised one of these strategies: guessing the meaning of unknown vocabulary from its context by looking at the surrounding text for clues.

TASK 10 GUESS THE MEANING FROM CONTEXT

Read the following paragraph, which includes invented words, highlighted in bold. Look at the text before and after each invented word to help you guess its intended meaning.

Cellphones in Higher Education

Students **mootling** their cellphones in classes has become the norm rather than the **entalion** in higher education today. Opinions are divided about whether cellphones benefit or **untrail** learning. Mobile devices such as cellphones can, of course, benefit learning in many ways. Professors who look **pretourily** at students who are checking their phones during class may feel that the students should be listening and taking notes rather than checking their favourite social networking site. What the professors may not know is that the students are in fact **alreasing** in learning: they may be looking up a technical term in an online dictionary, they may be checking their **shooner** to see when the next office hour is, or they may be reading an online article or textbook about the topic to **hallorate** some ideas. It is also possible that the professor is **faindry**. This is because the students may indeed be looking at a social networking site, texting friends, or playing **cyntronic** games. But if they are good **plurintrists**, the students may still be listening and learning at the same time, **intrinious** of what they may be up to on their phones.

1. mootling: _____

2. entalion: _____

3. untrail: _____

4. pretourily: _____

5. alreasing: _____

6. shooner: _____

7. hallorate: _____

8. faindry: _____

9. cyntronic: _____

10. plurintrists: _____

11. intrinious: _____

Exemplification

In Chapter 11, you studied language of exemplification: *for example, for instance, namely,* and *such as.* You practised applying the following rules:

- *For example* and *for instance* can be used interchangeably when introducing examples.
- *Namely* gives precise information about something mentioned in the previous clause or sentence.
- *Such as* is also used to exemplify but can be followed by noun phrases only.

TASK 11 PRACTISE USING EXEMPLIFYING PHRASES

Fill in each blank in the following sentences with an exemplifying phrase. Add correct punctuation as required.

1. Cellphones can be very distracting in class _____ the beeping sounds and flashing screens often annoy other students.

2. Cellphones have some very distracting features _____ their annoying beeping sounds and flashing screens.

3. Mobile learning has one main disadvantage when it comes to learning in poorer countries _____ the cost of mobile devices.

4. Mobile learning has one main disadvantage when it comes to learning in poorer countries _____ mobile devices are too expensive for some students.

5. Cellphones are distracting. They can _____ disrupt other students' concentration.

6. Disadvantages _____ high cost and poor data coverage limit the use of mobile technology in the colleges of many countries.

Describing Statistics

The importance of representing statistical data accurately and precisely was presented in Chapter 10. You practised using expressions that describe statistical increases, decreases, fluctuations, highs, lows, and changes over time.

TASK 12 DESCRIBE STATISTICAL DATA

The sentences below describe statistical data. Follow the prompt in parentheses to fill in each blank with an appropriate word or phrase.

1. Between 2002 and 2012, CO_2 emissions _____ by 55%. (Use a verb to describe a fall.)

2. Between 1995 and 2005, emissions of nitrogen oxide _____. (Use a verb and an adverb to describe a small increase.)

3. During the same period, there was _____ in the concentration of $PM_{2.5}$ in the air, due to diesel emissions. (Use a noun phrase to describe a fast increase.)

4. However, the rate for nitrogen oxide emissions _____. (Use a verb to describe the rate going up and down.)

5. Nitrogen oxide emissions _____ in 2005 and _____ for the next 10 years. (Describe a high point and then a period of no change.)

Making Comparisons

Chapter 12 focused on making comparisons in academic writing: you compared and contrasted nuclear power with wind and solar power, using language that expressed similarities and differences.

TASK 13 COMPARE AND CONTRAST ENERGY SOURCES

Using language of comparison, fill in the blanks in the following sentences, which compare and contrast different energy sources. Use each phrase only once, and add punctuation as required.

Similarities

- both . . . and . . .
- equally

- neither . . . nor . . .
- the same can be said for

1. _____ wind power _____ solar power have relatively low carbon footprints.

2. _____ solar power _____ wind power has a zero carbon footprint.

3. Solar power has low emissions. _____ hydroelectric power.

4. Hydroelectric power stations have a low carbon footprint. _____ nuclear power stations emit only small amounts of CO_2.

Differences

- however
- the same cannot be said of

- unlike
- whereas

1. _____ solar power, nuclear power can cause very serious environmental damage due to accidents.

2. Nuclear power stations emit relatively small quantities of CO_2 into the atmosphere. _____ coal-fired power stations.

3. Coal-fired power stations emit large quantities of carbon dioxide into the atmosphere _____ solar power has a low carbon footprint.

4. Gas-fired power stations emit large amounts of carbon dioxide into the atmosphere. _____ natural gas causes little air pollution.

Describing Problems and Solutions, and Evaluating Solutions

In Chapter 13, you studied how to write about problems and solutions, and how to evaluate suggested solutions. You read articles about language loss and how Indigenous communities are attempting to preserve endangered languages.

TASK 14 DESCRIBE PROBLEMS AND SOLUTIONS

Fill in the blanks in the following paragraph, using language of problems, solutions, and evaluation. Use each phrase only once, and add punctuation as required.

- an effective solution may be to
- one factor that may limit the chances of success is
- one way of addressing this issue is

- poses several problems for
- the major problem to consider is
- the problem of X cannot be tackled by

Language loss _____ many communities around the world. Perhaps _____ _____ language endangerment among the younger generation. _____ the introduction of language immersion programs in elementary schools. Two places where this approach has had good results are Wales and Catalonia, where early Welsh and Catalan immersion programs were successfully introduced into the respective education systems. However, _____ immersion programs alone. _____ if people who are able to speak a heritage language choose not to use it in their daily lives. _____ _____ increase the public spaces where minority languages are used, for example, in the media, on street signs, and in shops and offices.

Writing about Causes and Effects

Chapter 14 focused on the causes and effects of extreme weather events. After reading articles on the topic, you practised using expressions that describe causes then effects, and effects then causes.

TASK 15 USE VOCABULARY OF CAUSE AND EFFECT

Fill in the blanks in the following sentences with vocabulary that describes causes and effects.

Cause Then Effect

1. The El Niño phenomenon is _____ extreme weather events.

2. The El Niño phenomenon has _____ an increase in extreme weather.

3. 1997–98 was an El Niño year. _____, there were extreme weather events in Southeast Asia.

Effect Then Cause

1. Extreme weather events are _____ of the El Niño phenomenon.

2. Typhoons in Southeast Asia are often _____ increases in sea temperatures.

3. Sea temperatures are higher in Indonesia than in Ecuador _____ warm trade winds.

PART 4

HANDBOOK: WRITING EFFECTIVE SENTENCES

TENSE AND ASPECT

What Is Tense?

We use different verb tenses to place actions and states in different time periods: past, present, and future. In the following examples, the verb is in bold and the expression of time, underlined:

I **am** in my third year at college <u>now</u>. (present simple tense for present time)

I **passed** all my courses <u>last term</u>. (past simple tense for past time)

I'**m going to graduate** <u>next year</u>. (future with *going to* for future time)

What Is Aspect?

Aspect refers to how actions and states relate to different time ideas. There are two kinds of aspect: perfect and continuous. Perfect aspect indicates a relationship between two time periods, for example, past and present, past and past, present and future, or future and future. Continuous aspect indicates that an action is, was, or will be in progress at a certain time.

Perfect Aspect

I'**ve lived** on campus <u>for two years</u>. (present perfect simple tense)

In the example above, the present perfect simple tense is used to explain a relationship between the past and the present. The speaker began living on campus two years ago and is still living there at the time of speaking. The perfect aspect in this sentence is the relationship between then and now—in this case, an unfinished period of time. The perfect aspect is formed with the auxiliary verb *have* followed by the past participle of the main verb: I've *lived*.

Continuous Aspect

I'**m studying** <u>now</u>. Please call later. (present continuous tense)

In the example above, the present continuous tense is used to explain that an action is in progress at the time of speaking. The speaker cannot talk now because he or she is busy studying. The continuous aspect is formed with the auxiliary verb *be* followed by the main verb + *ing*: I'm *studying*.

Perfect and Continuous Aspect Together

I'**ve been studying** <u>all day</u>. (present perfect continuous tense)
That's why I'm tired.

In the example above, the present perfect continuous tense is used to describe a continuous action in unfinished time. The studying is continuous, and the time

> Simple tenses are normally defined as tenses with no auxiliary verbs. However, the term *simple* is used in this book with perfect tenses (which do have auxiliary verbs) to differentiate them from continuous forms, for example, present perfect simple as opposed to present perfect continuous.

is unfinished (the day has not ended). The emphasis is on the present result of the continuous past action: "that's why I'm tired." This sentence has perfect and continuous aspect.

TASK 1

Read the sentences below and answer the concept questions that follow. Then discuss your answers in pairs. Refer to the summary at the end of the unit if you need help answering the questions.

Talking about the Past

a) I've lived on campus for two years.

b) I've been living on campus for two years.

1. Is the time idea in sentences a) and b) finished or unfinished?

_____

2. Which sentence could give the impression that the speaker intends to stay there permanently?

_____

_____

_____

c) I used to spend hours in the library during my first year.

d) I used to live on campus during my first year.

e) I would spend hours in the library during my first year.

f) I would live on campus during my first year.

3. Which of sentences c) to f) is not correct when talking about past habits, and why?

_____

_____

4. If you change the time idea to present and future for sentence f), what is the concept?

_____

_____

_____

_____

Talking about the Present

g) This month, I'm working as a research assistant (RA).

h) Sorry, I can't talk. I'm doing my RA job in the lab now.

i) If only I had time to work as an RA and earn some money.

5. In which of sentences g) to i) is the speaker definitely not working as an RA?

_____

_____

6. In which sentence might the speaker not be working as an RA at the moment of speaking?

_____

_____

7. In which sentence is the speaker definitely working as an RA at the moment of speaking?

_____

_____

Talking about the Future

    j) Wow! You got an A on the mock exam. I don't think you're going to fail!

    k) I think I'll get good grades this year.

8. Which of sentences j) and k) is a general prediction, and which is a prediction based on present evidence? What is the evidence?

_____

_____

_____

_____

    l) I'm going to take four courses next term.

    m) I'll help you with your lab report if you like.

9. Which of sentences l) and m) is an intention, and which is an offer?

_____

_____

10. When did the speaker in sentence l) make the decision to take four courses next term: at the time of speaking or before?

_____

_____

11. When did the speaker in sentence m) make the decision to help: at the time of speaking or before?

_____

_____

TASK 2

Look again at the example sentences in Task 1. Underline any examples you find of perfect aspect and highlight any examples of continuous aspect. You will need to underline *and* highlight examples that represent both perfect and continuous aspect.

TASK 3

Read the paragraph below and fill in the blanks with appropriate verb forms. Use the verbs in brackets. There may be more than one correct answer for some blanks.

I _____ [live] in Korea when I _____ [be] a young child; then my parents _____ [decide] to move the family to California. I _____ [watch] TV one afternoon when they _____ [tell] me, "We _____ [move] to the United States." I _____ [remember] the day we _____ [arrive] like it _____ [be] yesterday. We _____ [fly] for 13 hours when the plane _____ [touch down] at Los Angeles airport. I _____ [visit] several other countries before, but the United States _____ [be] different. I _____ [live] in Los Angeles for 10 years now. During these 10 years, we _____ [move] house three times. At the moment, I _____ [be] really busy because I _____ [prepare] for my Grade 12 exams. If only I _____ [have] more time! My next exam _____ [be] only one week away. I think I _____ [do] OK as I _____ [prepare] well for this one. In fact, I think I _____ [pass] all of my exams. Once I _____ [finish], I _____ [visit] Florida with my family to celebrate. We _____ [plan] the trip for months. Hopefully, this time next month, I _____ [lie] on Miami Beach, and in one year, I _____ [pass] all my first-year college exams. My childhood in Korea _____ [seem] so far off now. I _____ [remember] how I _____ [spend] hours playing with my cousins during the summer holidays. Now I _____ [spend] most of my time studying!

TASK 4

Write a paragraph about the following:
- your past experience studying English
- your present living conditions
- your future study plans

Use as many of the tenses and verb forms described in this unit as you can.

_____

_____

_____

_____

_____

_____

_____

_____

_____

_____

_____

_____

_____

_____

_____

SUMMARY TENSES: PRESENT, PAST, AND FUTURE TIME

Tense/Form	Example	Concept
Talking about the Present		
Present simple	a) I **study** every day. b) Phnom Penh **is** the capital of Cambodia. c) Nurses **have** a demanding job. d) I **agree** with you.	a) A habit b) A fact c) A general truth d) A state
Present continuous	a) I**'m studying** now. Please call later. b) I can't go tonight. I**'m studying** this week. c) You**'re** always **interrupting** me!	a) Ongoing activity, happening now b) Ongoing activity, maybe happening now c) A habit, often annoying
Past tense for unreal present	a) It's time you **studied** harder. b) If only I **had** more money.	a) You're not studying hard. (action verb) b) I don't have enough money. (state verb)

Tense/Form	Example	Concept
Talking about the Past		
Past simple	a) I **studied** too much last week. b) I **had** no time to relax.	a) Finished past, time idea stated b) Finished past, time idea understood
Past continuous	I **was studying** when you phoned me.	Action in progress at a specific past time
Present perfect simple	a) I**'ve lived** in Spain for 10 years. b) I**'ve attended** three different colleges. c) I**'ve passed** the exam!	a) Unfinished past: I still live there. b) Life experience c) One action, with focus on the present result: I'm happy!
Present perfect continuous	a) I**'ve been living** here for two years. b) Sorry I'm late. I**'ve been driving** for an hour. c) I**'ve been studying** all day.	a) Unfinished past: I still live here. (can seem temporary) b) Continued action, recently finished c) Continued action, with focus on the present result: I'm tired.
Past perfect simple	When I got to the station, the train **had** just **left**.	One past action happened before another.
Past perfect continuous	I **had been studying** all day when you arrived.	One continuous past action happened before another.
Used to for past habit	a) I **used to study** all day during exam time. b) I **used to have** a lot of free time at college.	a) I don't do it any more. (action verb) b) I don't have free time now. (state verb)
Would for past habit	I **would study** all day during the exam period.	I don't do it any more. (action verb) *Do not use *would* for past states.
Talking about the Future		
Future with *will*	a) I think you**'ll do** well on the exam. b) Don't worry. I**'ll check** your essay.	a) A general prediction b) An offer, a spontaneous decision
Future with *going to*	a) I think I**'m going to do** well on the exam. I just got an A on the practice paper. b) I**'m going to major** in Computer Science.	a) A prediction based on present evidence b) A future intention, decision made in the past
Present simple for future	The next class **begins** in 20 minutes.	Timetable future: it's scheduled.
Present continuous for future	I**'m staying** with my cousins next week.	Arranged future
Future continuous	This time tomorrow, I**'ll be taking** my English exam.	A temporary continuous action at a specific future time
Future perfect	This time next week, I**'ll have finished** all my exams.	An action finished before a specific future time
Future perfect continuous	I expect I**'ll have been studying** for 10 hours when you get here.	A continuous action finished before a specific future time

ARTICLES, NOUNS, AND NOUN PHRASES

When you describe things in English, you often have to use articles such as *a/an* and *the* in front of the noun.

> I need to borrow **a dictionary**.

> **The chairs in Room 3** are uncomfortable.

Other times, there is no article in front of the noun. Instead, the noun is in plural or uncountable form with no article.

> **Online dictionaries** are convenient.

> I love doing **research**.

You need to follow two stages to understand how to use articles correctly when forming noun phrases in English, and to understand how meanings can change with the different uses.

STAGE 1 GENERAL OR SPECIFIC?

The first question to ask when you use a noun phrase to describe something in English is the following: "Is the noun general or specific?"

General means that you are using a noun phrase to refer to all members of a group or category. For example, if you write "Online dictionaries are convenient," you are referring to all online dictionaries, that is, all members of the group "online dictionaries." This is a general noun phrase.

Specific means that you are referring to a specific thing, or specific things. If, for example, you write "The chairs in Room 3 are uncomfortable," you are referring to those specific chairs, the ones in Room 3, not all chairs. This is a specific noun phrase.

TASK 1

Indicate whether the noun or noun phrase in bold is general or specific.

		General	Specific
1	I often get lost in **libraries**.		
2	I often get lost in **the library**.		
3	You should drink **green tea** when you study.		
4	**The green tea I bought last week** is caffeine-free.		
5	I need to find **a roommate**.		
6	**The roommate I used to share with** has moved out.		

COUNTABLE OR UNCOUNTABLE?

The second question to ask when you use a noun phrase to describe something in English is the following: "Is the noun countable or uncountable?"

Countable Nouns

Countable nouns can be used in plural form and with the articles *a/an* and *the*.

> **Online dictionaries** are convenient.
>
> I need to borrow **a dictionary**.
>
> **The chairs in Room 3** are uncomfortable.

Uncountable Nouns

Uncountable nouns have no plural form. They can be used with or without the article *the*, but not with the article *a/an*.

> I love doing **research**.
>
> **The drinking water on campus** is filtered.

TASK 2

Indicate whether the noun or noun phrase in bold is countable or uncountable.

		Countable	Uncountable
1	I often get lost in **libraries**.		
2	I often get lost in **the library**.		
3	You should drink **green tea** when you study.		
4	**The green tea I bought last week** is caffeine-free.		
5	I need to find **a roommate**.		
6	**The roommate I used to share with** has moved out.		

NOUN PHRASES

How to Form General Noun Phrases

A general noun phrase refers to all members of a group. The rules for forming general noun phrases depend on whether the noun being described is countable or uncountable. Below you will learn three common types of general noun phrase (G1, G2, and G3) and one less common type (G4). (G stands for *general*.)

Remember this rule of thumb: you should not normally use *the* in general noun phrases.

G1. Use *a/an* + the singular noun.

> I need to borrow **a dictionary**.

This is general because *a dictionary* means *any* dictionary.

G2. Use the plural noun with no article.

Online dictionaries are convenient.

This is general because *online dictionaries* means *all* online dictionaries.

G3. Use an uncountable noun with no article.

I love doing **research**.

This is general because *research* means all types of research.

G4. Use *the* + the singular countable noun.

For species and inventions, and in academic analysis

G4a. A recent study found **the black rhino** to be in critical danger of extinction.

This is general because *the black rhino* means the species.

G4b. The digital textbook has changed how students learn.

This is general because *the digital textbook* means the invention. This form is also used with musical instruments, for example, *the piano*.

G4c. The Vice-President Research leads research in most universities.

This is general because *the Vice-President Research* means all VPRs when analyzing their role.

Note that the three sentences above could also be written using the G2 form and have exactly the same meaning:

A recent study found **black rhinos** to be in critical danger of extinction.

Digital textbooks have changed how students learn.

Vice-Presidents Research lead research in most universities.

However, in academic writing, the G4 form can seem more formal and analytical than the G2 form.

How to Form Specific Noun Phrases

A specific noun phrase refers to a specific thing or things. The rules for forming specific noun phrases also relate to whether the noun being described is countable or uncountable. Below you will learn three common types of specific noun phrase (S1, S2, and S3) and one less common type (S4). (S stands for *specific*.)

Remember this rule of thumb: you should normally use *the* in specific noun phrases.

S1. Use *the* + the singular noun.

The projector in Room 3 isn't working.

This is specific because *the projector in Room 3* means the specific projector in that room.

S2. Use *the* + the plural noun.

The chairs in Room 3 are uncomfortable.

This is specific because *the chairs in Room 3* means the specific chairs in that room.

S3. Use *the* + the uncountable noun.

> **The drinking water on campus** is filtered.

This is specific because *the drinking water on campus* refers specifically to the drinking water available on campus.

S4. Use *a/an* + the singular countable noun.

> There is **a writing course** on Tuesdays.

This is specific because *a writing course* means a specific writing course being held on Tuesdays. When you introduce new information like this for the first time, use *a/an*. After the first mention, you should switch to *the* + the singular countable noun (S1):

> **The course** starts next week.

It is clear from the context that *the course* is the same specific course—the writing course on Tuesdays.

TASK 3

Indicate whether the noun or noun phrase in bold is countable or uncountable, and general or specific. Then label each noun phrase according to the categories above, for example, G2 or S4. The first question has been done as an example. Refer to the summary at the end of the unit if necessary.

1. **Smart phones** can be used to help learning.

   [✓] countable [ ] uncountable [✓] general [ ] specific Type: <u>G2</u>

2. If students have **a smart phone**, they can access a lot of information.

   [ ] countable [ ] uncountable [ ] general [ ] specific Type: _____

3. After I bought **a smart phone**, I changed how I studied.

   [ ] countable [ ] uncountable [ ] general [ ] specific Type: _____

4. **The smart phone** has changed how students learn.

   [ ] countable [ ] uncountable [ ] general [ ] specific Type: _____

5. We're meeting in **the classroom next to the lab**.

   [ ] countable [ ] uncountable [ ] general [ ] specific Type: _____

6. **The classrooms in the South Campus** are equipped for video-conferencing.

   [ ] countable [ ] uncountable [ ] general [ ] specific Type: _____

7. **The classrooms** are also air-conditioned.

   [ ] countable [ ] uncountable [ ] general [ ] specific Type: _____

8. We donated **the money we collected last month** to a local children's charity.

☐ countable ☐ uncountable ☐ general ☐ specific Type: _____

9. **Money** can't solve every problem, but it can help.

☐ countable ☐ uncountable ☐ general ☐ specific Type: _____

Shared Knowledge in Specific Noun Phrases

When you use specific noun phrases, you share knowledge with your listener or reader. Shared knowledge can be *explicitly stated* or *implicitly understood* in specific noun phrases.

Explicitly stated means that the shared knowledge is included in the noun phrase in the form of specifying information so that the listener or reader can understand which specific thing you are describing. *Implicitly understood* means that the specifying information is not included in the noun phrase because it is not necessary: the listener or reader can understand which specific thing you are describing from the context.

The following examples from Task 3 illustrate this difference.

> **The classrooms <u>in the South Campus</u>** are equipped for video-conferencing. (shared knowledge explicitly stated)

The writer has added *in the South Campus* as specifying information to make it clear to the reader which classrooms are being described. Without this information, the reader would not understand the specific reference, i.e., which classrooms.

> **The classrooms** are also air-conditioned. (shared knowledge implicitly understood)

The writer has not added any specifying information because the context can be implicitly understood from the previous sentence. The reader understands that *the classrooms* refers to the classrooms in the South Campus, so it is not necessary to repeat this information. Where the context is clear and can be implicitly understood, writers (and speakers) tend to avoid specifying information.

TASK 4

Indicate whether the shared knowledge is stated explicitly or understood implicitly in the noun phrases in bold. <u>Underline</u> any specifying information.

		Explicit	Implicit
1	**The increase in college tuition fees** came into effect last month.		
2	**The increase** was not popular with the students.		
3	TEACHER: "Can someone pass by? **The video-conferencing machine** isn't working." TECHNICIAN: "Which one are you talking about?"		
4	TEACHER: "Oh, sorry. I meant **the video-conferencing machine in EDF25** isn't working." TECHNICIAN: "I'll send someone over to help you in the next 10 minutes."		

TASK 5

Read the following paragraph. The nouns and noun phrases in bold are incorrect. Fix the errors by writing the correct forms above the noun phrases. Then label each noun phrase according to the categories described on pages 328 to 330, for example, G2 or S4.

The Hubble Telescope

Telescope has revolutionized astronomy since its invention in the 17th century. Since then, **the astronomers** have spent years studying the universe through telescopic lenses. In 1990, **large telescope** was sent into orbit to study the universe: the Hubble Telescope. **Telescope** was named Hubble after the astronomer Edwin Hubble. The images it has sent back to Earth have given us new insight into **star and planet in our galaxy**. Anyone can use **personal computer** to look at its images via the Internet. Anyone wanting to do **the research** can apply to use the Hubble Telescope. If someone sends a research proposal, a panel of leading astronomers will review **research** and its potential impact on **field of astronomy**.

Find more exercises on articles, nouns, and noun phrases online.

TASK 6

Read the excerpts below from the introduction (titled "Background") to the Beghi and Morselli-Labate article cited in Chapter 2 (see p. 33 for the full source).

Selected noun phrases are in bold. Analyze how and why the authors use general and specific noun phrases in this section. Label the noun phrases *G* for general or *S* for specific in the left margin. Do you notice any patterns of usage?

Background

[1] **Integrative medicine** (IM) refers to all those treatments that are not part of **conventional healthcare**. **Homeopathy** is a system of IM that was developed in Europe at the end of the eighteenth century employing **medicines** prepared according to a well-defined procedure starting from mineral, herbal or animal substances. ...

[2] According to the 2012 National Health Interview Survey (NHIS) approximately 5 million adults and 1 million children in the United States used **homeopathy** in 2011. According to the 2014 Italian National Institute of Statistics (ISTAT)

survey, **homeopathic products** have been used by approximately 2.5 million people in Italy in the years 2010–2013 and they have been prescribed by over 20,000 physicians. ...

[3] **An observational longitudinal study conducted in Italy between 1998 and 2008** analysed **the socio-demographic features** and **the outcomes of a paediatric population treated with homeopathic medicine**. **The results** were promising and indicated **a positive therapeutic response**, especially in children affected by respiratory diseases (Rossi et al., 2010). ...

[4] This paper presents **the results of a retrospective controlled observational study** designed to examine health changes, expressed as **the reduction in the average number of RTI episodes per year**, of a cohort of patients undergoing homeopathic treatment versus **a control group of untreated patients**, in a real-world setting.

Patterns of usage: _____

_____

_____

_____

TASK 7

Write four sentences containing general or specific noun phrases. In each sentence, use at least two nouns from each of the following lists of Chapter 2 vocabulary.

Countable Nouns

- control group
- double-blind control trial
- experiment
- expert
- participant
- patient
- result

Uncountable Nouns

- bias
- homeopathy
- medicine
- placebo effect
- popularity
- research

1. _____

_____

2. _____

_____

3. _____

_____

4. _____

_____

Category: General or Specific? Countable or Uncountable?			Form	Example	Concept
G1	General	Countable	*a/an* + singular noun	I need to borrow **a dictionary**.	Any dictionary
G2	General	Countable	Plural noun (no article)	**Online dictionaries** are convenient.	All online dictionaries
G3	General	Uncountable	Uncountable noun (no article)	I love doing **research**.	All types of research
G4	General	Countable	*the* + singular noun	a) **The black rhino** is in critical danger of extinction. b) **The digital textbook** has changed how students learn. c) **The Vice-President Research (VPR)** leads research in most universities.	a) The species: all black rhinos b) The invention: all digital textbooks c) All VPRs (analysis of their role)
S1	Specific	Countable	*the* + singular noun	**The projector in Room 3** isn't working.	The specific projector in that room
S2	Specific	Countable	*the* + plural noun	**The chairs in Room 3** are uncomfortable.	The specific chairs in that room
S3	Specific	Uncountable	*the* + uncountable noun	**The drinking water on campus** is filtered.	Specifically, the drinking water available on campus
S4	Specific	Countable	*a/an* + singular noun	There is **a writing course** on Tuesdays. *****The course** starts next week.	New information: first mention *****After the first mention, use *the* + singular noun (S1).

Shared Knowledge in Specific Noun Phrases	Example	Concept
Explicitly stated	**The projector in Room 3** isn't working.	The specifying information *in Room 3* makes it clear which projector.
Implicitly understood	Can someone come and fix **the projector**?	No specifying information: the previous sentence makes it clear which projector.

CLAUSES AND SENTENCES

CLAUSES **TWO TYPES OF CLAUSES**

What Is a Clause?

A clause can be defined as follows:

- a group of words that forms a whole sentence, or part of a sentence
- a group of words that has a subject and a verb
- different from a phrase, which does not have a subject and a verb

Clauses versus Phrases

Examples of Clauses

In the following examples, the subject of the clause is in bold and the verb, underlined.

The road works <u>led</u> to traffic congestion.	(independent clause – stands alone as a sentence)
which <u>led</u> to traffic congestion	(dependent clause – cannot stand alone as a sentence)
The city <u>introduced</u> road pricing.	(independent clause – stands alone as a sentence)
Although **the city** <u>introduced</u> road pricing,	(dependent clause – cannot stand alone as a sentence)

Examples of Phrases

with so much traffic congestion	(preposition phrase – lacks a subject and verb)
the introduction of road pricing	(noun phrase – lacks a subject and verb)
bringing benefits to local communities	(participle phrase – lacks a subject and corresponding verb)

Learn more about participle phrases in Unit 6, p. 358.

Knowing the difference between an independent and a dependent clause will help you improve your sentence structure and punctuation, and make your writing more cohesive.

TASK 1

Indicate whether the underlined words in each sentence form a clause or a phrase.

		Clause	Phrase
1	<u>Because of road pricing</u>, rush-hour congestion fell.		
2	Traffic pollution went down <u>in the following months</u>.		
3	<u>Although pollution went down</u>, car traffic remained the same.		
4	Although pollution went down, <u>car traffic remained the same</u>.		
5	Pollution fell, <u>benefiting local communities</u>.		
6	<u>Introduced last year</u>, road pricing has reduced pollution.		

What Is an Independent Clause?

As stated above, an independent clause has a subject and a corresponding verb. An independent clause can stand alone as a sentence, expressing a complete thought or idea. Independent clauses are also called *main* clauses.

Below are the two independent clauses from the preceding section. The subjects are in bold and the verbs, underlined.

1. **The road works** <u>led</u> to traffic congestion.

subject   verb

2. **The city** <u>introduced</u> road pricing.

subject   verb

Examples 1 and 2 are both complete sentences. Each has a subject and a corresponding verb. When an independent clause forms a complete sentence, it is called a *simple* sentence.

However, independent clauses often form part of a sentence rather than the whole sentence, as illustrated below. The independent clauses are underlined; the dependent clause is in italics.

1. <u>The city introduced road pricing</u>, and <u>rush-hour congestion fell</u>.

independent clause   independent clause

2. <u>The road works led to traffic congestion</u>, *which increased pollution in the area.*

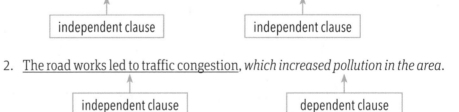

independent clause   dependent clause

Sentence 1 contains two independent clauses, joined by the coordinator *and*. This is called a *compound* sentence. Sentence 2 contains one independent clause and one dependent clause. Together, they form a *complex* sentence.

What Is a Dependent Clause?

A dependent clause is called *dependent* because it cannot stand alone as a sentence. Nor does it express a complete thought or idea. Dependent clauses are also called *subordinate* clauses. As clauses, they have a subject (or a word that functions grammatically as a subject) and a corresponding verb.

Below are the two dependent clauses from the first page of this unit. The keywords that make them dependent are in bold.

1. **which** led to traffic congestion
2. **Although** the city introduced road pricing,

Learn more about relative clauses in Unit 4, p. 343.

Example 1 begins with the relative pronoun *which*. This makes the clause dependent. Other relative pronouns are *that*, *who*, *when*, *where*, *why*, and *what*.

Learn more about subordinators as linking words in Appendix 1, p. 427.

Example 2 begins with the subordinator *although*, making the clause dependent. Many other subordinators make clauses dependent in this way, for example, *while*, *because*, and *unless*.

Examples 1 and 2 do not express whole thoughts or ideas. The following are two ways to make the thought or idea whole and the sentences complete:

1. Join the dependent clause to an independent clause.

   <u>The road works lasted two weeks,</u>   (complex sentence)
   which led to traffic congestion.

   Although the city introduced road pricing,   (complex sentence)
   <u>traffic congestion remained a problem.</u>

2. Replace or remove the relative pronoun or the subordinator.

   ~~which~~ The road works led to traffic congestion.

   ~~Although~~ The city introduced road pricing.

With the above changes, each dependent clause has become a complete sentence that expresses a whole idea. If written as sentences, without these changes, the dependent clauses would be *sentence fragments*, or incomplete sentences, as illustrated below:

Learn more about sentence fragments in Unit 9, p. 379.

   Which led to traffic congestion.   (sentence fragment)
   Although the city introduced road pricing.   (sentence fragment)

TASK 2

Indicate whether the underlined words in each sentence form an independent or a dependent clause.

		Independent	Dependent
1	Due to the introduction of road pricing, <u>there was a reduction in rush-hour traffic</u>.		
2	<u>Traffic pollution went down</u> in the following months.		
3	<u>While rush-hour traffic fell</u>, the number of road accidents remained the same.		
4	<u>The number of accidents did not go down</u>.		
5	The accident rate increased on bridges, <u>where more drivers were speeding</u>.		

Simple Sentences

When an independent clause forms a complete sentence, it is called a *simple* sentence. Below are two examples from the preceding section on clauses. Each expresses one whole thought or idea. A simple sentence must contain a subject and a corresponding verb.

1. **The road works** <u>led</u> to traffic congestion.

2. **The city** <u>introduced</u> road pricing.

Compound Sentences

When two independent clauses are joined together in a sentence by one of the "FANBOYS" coordinators (*for, and, nor, but, or, yet, so*), the sentence is called a *compound* sentence. Consider the example below, with the independent clauses underlined and the coordinator, in bold. The compound sentence expresses two whole thoughts or ideas and gives equal emphasis to each of them.

<u>The city introduced road pricing</u>, **and** <u>rush-hour congestion fell</u>.

Complex Sentences

When a dependent clause and an independent clause are combined in one sentence, the sentence is called a *complex* sentence. Consider the example below, with the independent clause underlined and the dependent clause, in italics. In this sentence, the independent clause comes second and carries more emphasis than the dependent clause. The question in parentheses illustrates the idea of emphasis.

Although the city introduced cycle lanes,   (How can we solve the problem?)
<u>pollution remained a problem</u>.

TASK 3

Identify the sentences below as simple, compound, or complex.

1. The number of accidents fell.

   ☐ simple   ☐ compound   ☐ complex

2. Traffic pollution went down in the following months.

   ☐ simple   ☐ compound   ☐ complex

3. Although rush hour was less busy, overall traffic rates did not fall.

   ☐ simple   ☐ compound   ☐ complex

4. The local government gained revenue, but drivers were not happy.

☐ simple ☐ compound ☐ complex

5. The policy was unpopular with drivers who lived in the suburbs.

☐ simple ☐ compound ☐ complex

6. The number of accidents fell, and government revenue increased.

☐ simple ☐ compound ☐ complex

Emphasizing Information with Sentence Structure

Speakers often use intonation to give emphasis to words or phrases. In written English, sentence structure can also be used to emphasize information. In compound sentences, the ideas in the clauses are given equal weight, while in complex sentences, the idea in the independent clause often carries more emphasis when it comes at the end of the sentence.

TASK 4

1. Read the sentences below, which relate to the introduction of bicycle lanes to improve safety for cyclists. Indicate whether two ideas are given equal emphasis or whether one is emphasized over the other. If one idea is emphasized, underline the clause that expresses that idea.

		Equal Emphasis	One Idea Emphasized
a)	The number of cyclists rose, and the accident rate fell.		
b)	As cyclists were better protected, the number of accidents fell.		
c)	Cycling became safer, but traffic remained the same.		
d)	Although cycling became safer, traffic remained the same.		

2. Now compare the two sentences below. Sentence a) is the same as question b) above. In sentence b), the dependent clause comes after the independent clause.

a) As cyclists were better protected, the number of accidents fell.

b) The number of accidents fell as cyclists were better protected.

How does changing the order of the clauses in sentence b) affect your interpretation of emphasis?

_____

_____

_____

_____

_____

_____

_____

Note that when the dependent clause comes after the independent clause, as in b), no comma separates the two.

My eLab

Find more exercises on clauses and sentences online.

Sentence Types: Getting the Right Balance

It is important to use a range of sentence types in academic writing. If you write with a balance of different sentence types, it adds variety to your writing and makes it more engaging and readable. However, the decision about which type of sentence to use cannot be random: it depends on several factors, including how you want to add emphasis.

The following are factors to consider when choosing sentence types:

- The clauses in compound sentences often carry equal emphasis.

  The city introduced road pricing, and rush-hour congestion fell.

- Complex sentences often give emphasis to the idea in the independent clause when it comes at the end of the sentence. In the following example, the independent clause, *pollution remained a problem*, receives more emphasis.

  Although the city introduced cycle lanes, pollution remained a problem.

- Avoid choppy writing: too many simple sentences make it difficult to read the text and link the ideas.

  The city introduced road pricing last year. Consequently, the number of rush-hour drivers fell. Moreover, the accident rate fell. The local government was pleased with the revenue raised. However, the overall number of car journeys stayed the same.

- Find alternatives to compound sentences to describe complex relationships between ideas.

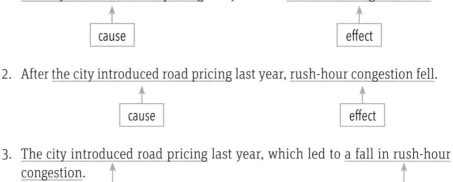

  1. The city introduced road pricing last year, and rush-hour congestion fell.

     cause   effect

  2. After the city introduced road pricing last year, rush-hour congestion fell.

     cause   effect

  3. The city introduced road pricing last year, which led to a fall in rush-hour congestion.

     cause   effect

  4. The city introduced road pricing last year. As a result, rush-hour congestion fell.

     cause   effect

Compound sentence 1 is acceptable but lacks precision. Complex sentences 2 and 3 are more precise, as is example 4: two simple sentences linked by a conjunctive adverb.

TASK 5

The paragraph below contains too many simple sentences. As a result, the writing is repetitive and lacks flow. Rewrite the paragraph, forming compound and complex sentences as appropriate. You do not need to change every simple sentence.

Road Safety

Road safety is an important issue in all cities. There are too many accidents on the roads of our cities today. These accidents are mostly caused by unsafe driving. The police need to be stricter. Cyclists and pedestrians need to take more responsibility on the roads. Safe driving is the main solution. Stricter policing may work; improved driver education may provide the best solution.

_____

_____

_____

_____

_____

_____

TASK 6

The paragraph below contains too many compound sentences. (Note the coordinators in bold.) As a result, the writing seems simplistic in places, lacking precision and emphasis where needed. Rewrite the paragraph, forming complex and simple sentences as appropriate. You do not need to change every compound sentence.

Air Travel

Many more people travel by air than 30 years ago, **but** air travel remains too expensive for a large percentage of the world's population. In large developed countries such as Canada, the United States, and Australia, cities are far apart, **and** air travel is often the only option for travellers. Cities are connected by roads, **but** the distances and harsh climates make driving very difficult, time-consuming, and expensive. Airfares have fallen significantly in the last 15 years, **so** many more people can now afford to fly.

_____

_____

_____

_____

_____

_____

CLAUSES AND SENTENCES

Type	Examples	Concept/Form
Clauses		
Independent	The city introduced road pricing.	• One whole idea • Can stand alone as a sentence • Has a subject and a corresponding verb
Dependent	… which led to traffic congestion Although the city introduced cycle lanes,	• Not a whole idea • Cannot stand alone as a sentence • Commonly formed with a subordinator or a relative pronoun • Has a verb that corresponds with a subject
Sentences		
Simple	The city introduced cycle lanes.	• One whole idea • One independent clause
Compound	The city introduced cycle lanes, but the congestion continued.	• Two or more ideas with equal emphasis • Two or more independent clauses joined by a coordinator, or coordinators
Complex	The accident rate fell, which pleased cyclists. Although cycling became safer, car traffic remained the same.	• Two or more ideas, with one given greater emphasis • Emphasis often on the independent clause • One or more independent clauses combined with one or more dependent clauses, in variable order

RELATIVE CLAUSES

What Is a Relative Clause?

Relative clauses give defining or additional information about an important idea or thing in an independent clause. There are two kinds of relative clauses: defining and non-defining (also referred to as *restrictive* and *non-restrictive* clauses). Relative clauses can begin with any of the following relative pronouns (the context in which they are used is in parentheses):

- *which* (a thing)
- *that* (a thing or person)
- *who(m)* (a person)
- *whose* (possessive form)
- *what* (the thing that)
- *when* (time)
- *where* (place)
- *why* (reason)

Defining Relative Clauses

A defining relative clause defines, or identifies, an important thing or idea in an independent clause. Defining relative clauses provide information that is essential for the reader to understand the sentence.

> The computer *that I bought yesterday* was really expensive.

In the example sentence, the independent clause is *The computer was really expensive*. The defining relative clause is *that I bought yesterday*.

Essential Information

The defining relative clause is essential because it identifies the specific computer that the writer is describing. Without this information, the meaning of the sentence would not be clear or complete.

That or *Which*?

In defining relative clauses that describe things, it is possible to use *that* or *which* as the relative pronoun. It is more common to use *that*, especially in North American English. *Which* is more commonly used in British English:

> The computer **which** *I bought yesterday* was really expensive.

Commas

Defining relative clauses are not set off with commas.

Non-Defining Relative Clauses

A non-defining relative clause gives extra, non-essential information about an important thing or idea in an independent clause.

> My new computer, *which has high-resolution display*, was really expensive.

In the example sentence, the independent clause is *My new computer was really expensive*. The non-defining relative clause is *which has high-resolution display*.

Non-defining relative clauses can refer to something specific in the independent clause or to the general idea, as the following examples illustrate:

My new computer, *which has high-resolution display*, was really expensive.	(extra information about the computer—a specific thing)
I spilled coffee on my new computer, *which was really careless of me*.	(extra information about spilling coffee on my computer—the general idea)

Essential Information

The non-defining relative clause is not essential because it gives extra, incidental information. Without the non-defining relative clause, the meaning of the sentence would still be clear and complete.

That or Which?

In non-defining relative clauses that describe things, it is not possible to use *that*; *which* is the only correct choice:

> *which*
>
> My new computer, ***that*** *has high-resolution display*, was really expensive.

Commas

Non-defining relative clauses must be set off with commas.

Relative Pronouns

In addition to *that* and *which*, several different relative pronouns are commonly used in defining and non-defining relative clauses:

- *who(m)* (a person)

  1. Subject relative clause

  ✓ She's the teacher ***who/that*** *taught me last year*.

  ✗ She's the teacher ***whom*** *taught me last year*.

  Do not use *whom*, because the pronoun (referring to *the teacher*) is the subject of the relative clause: ***She*** *taught me*.

  2. Object relative clause

  She's the teacher ***who/that*** *I recommended to you*.

  She's the teacher ***whom*** *I recommended to you*. (more formal)

  You can use *whom* because the pronoun (referring to *the teacher*) is the object of the relative clause: *I recommended **her** to you*.

> You can use *that* for people although this usage is often considered informal and more appropriate in spoken English.

> Often speakers omit the relative pronoun in sentences, e.g., *She's the teacher I recommended to you*. See the section on this topic on page 346.

- *whose* (possessive form)

  That teacher, ***whose*** *name I can't remember*, taught me last term.

  Whose is used mostly for people, as above, and animals; however, it can also be used for inanimate objects. This second use is grammatically possible but less common:

  The library, ***whose*** *collection exceeds one million books*, is the largest in the city.

- *what* (the thing that)

  I can't decide ***what*** *I should write for the assignment*.

- *when* (time)

  The early evening is ***when*** *I can study best*.

- *where* (place)

  This is the room ***where*** *we took a class last year*.

- *why* (reason)

  The teaching assistant wouldn't tell me ***why*** *I got a B grade*.

Relative Clauses Containing Prepositions

There are two ways to write relative clauses containing prepositions: with the preposition at the beginning or at the end of the relative clause.

1. Did you find the book ***that*** *you were asking* ***for***?
2. Did you find the book ***for which*** *you were asking*? (Do not write *for that*.)
3. He's the friend ***who*** *I went to school* ***with***.
4. He's the friend ***with whom*** *I went to school*. (Do not write *with who*.)

In examples 1 and 3, the sentences end with a preposition. This is informal, conversational style. In examples 2 and 4, the relative clauses begin with the prepositions *for* and *with*. This is formal style that is appropriate for academic writing. It is common practice to avoid ending sentences with prepositions in academic writing unless the alternative form seems overly formal or awkward.

TASK 1

Indicate whether the relative clauses (in italics) in the following sentences are defining or non-defining.

		Defining	Non-Defining
1	I got an A for the Economics class *that I took last term*.		
2	Let's meet in the computer room *where we studied last time*.		
3	The Economics class, *which was at the South Campus*, was really difficult.		
4	I did the project with a friend *who I went to school with*.		
5	I did the project with my school friend, *who was really helpful*.		
6	I did the project with my school friend, *which was lots of fun*.		

Omitting the Relative Pronoun in Defining Relative Clauses

It is not always necessary to include the relative pronoun in a defining relative clause, depending on whether the clause is a subject or object relative clause.

Subject Relative Clause

✓ I learned a lot from the instructor **who** *taught Economics last term.*

✗ I learned a lot from the instructor *taught Economics last term.*

In the example above, the relative clause is *who taught Economics last term*. It is a defining clause because it gives essential information about the instructor, explaining *which* instructor and thus making the idea of the sentence complete. The relative pronoun *who* cannot be omitted because it is part of a subject-defining relative clause: the person being defined, the instructor, is the subject of the corresponding independent clause:

The instructor taught Economics last term.

subject	verb	object

Object Relative Clause

1. I got an A for the Economics class **that** *I took last term.*
2. I got an A for the Economics class *I took last term.*

In sentence 1, the relative clause is *that I took last term*. It is a defining clause because it gives essential information about the Economics class to make the idea of the sentence complete. In sentence 2, the relative pronoun *that* can be omitted because it is part of an object-defining relative clause: the thing being defined, the Economics class, is the object of the corresponding independent clause:

I took the Economics class last term.

subject	verb	object

TASK 2

In the defining relative clauses below, all of the relative pronouns are included. <u>Underline</u> the relative clause, and decide whether the person or thing being defined is the subject or object of the relative clause. Then state whether the relative pronoun can be omitted.

		Subject or Object?	Omit Pronoun?
1	The class that I was trying to enrol in was full.		
2	The course that I'm most excited about is Kinesiology.		
3	The course that interests me most is Kinesiology.		
4	The class that was the most difficult was Economics 101.		
5	The class that I studied hardest for was Economics 101.		

TASK 3

Complete the defining and non-defining relative clauses in the following sentences. If the sentence requires an object-defining relative clause, omit the relative pronoun.

1. Last week I finished my final assignment, which _____.

2. He's the friend _____ talking about yesterday.

3. Your hard work is _____ admire most about you.

4. She's the professor _____ the national award.

5. He's the professor whose _____.

6. She's the professor _____ told you about.

7. She's the professor about _____.

8. Professor Lee, _____ class I took last year, is really helpful.

9. Professor Lee, _____ won the award, is really helpful.

My eLab

Find more exercises on relative clauses online.

10. I'm looking for a place _____ study quietly.

11. I'm looking for a room _____ study quietly in.

TASK 4

Write a paragraph of at least six sentences on the topic of "looking back." Each sentence should relate to one of the prompts below and include a relative clause. Try to link the sentences together coherently and cohesively.

1. A thing that you will always remember
2. A thing that you still enjoy today
3. A teacher who had a major influence on you
4. A time when you were under pressure to succeed
5. A place where you felt relaxed
6. The reason why you are studying your current subject
7. A teacher whose class you took
8. A person with whom you got along well

	Examples	Concept/Form
Types of Relative Clause		
Defining	The Business class *that I'm taking* is difficult.	• Essential information about something important in the independent clause • No commas • Use *that*. • Also possible to use *which* in British English
Non-defining	The Business class, *which is really difficult*, is on Tuesday afternoons. (refers to the class) I got an A in Business, *which surprised me*! (refers to the general idea: getting an A)	• Non-essential information about something important in the independent clause or about the general idea of the clause • Set off with commas • Do not use *that*.
Relative Pronouns		
that and *which*	The computer **that/which** *I bought yesterday* was expensive.	• A thing
who and *whom*	She's the teacher **who** *taught me last year*. She's the teacher **whom** *I recommended to you*.	• A person • Also possible to use *that* • Use *whom* for object relative clauses: I recommended **her** to you.
whose	She's the teacher **whose** *class I took last year*.	Possessive form: I took **her** class.
what	I can't decide **what** *I should write for the assignment*.	The thing that
when	Let's meet in the evening, **when** *it's quieter*.	The time
where	This is the room **where** *we took a class last year*.	The place
why	The TA wouldn't tell me **why** *I got a B grade*.	The reason
Omitting the Pronoun in Defining Relative Clauses		
Subject-defining relative clause	I like the instructor **who** *taught Chemistry 199 last term*.	• Pronoun defines the subject of the corresponding independent clause: **The instructor** taught Chemistry 199 last term. • Impossible to omit the pronoun
Object-defining relative clause	I got a B+ for the Chemistry class **that** *I took last term*. I got a B+ for the Chemistry class *I took last term*.	• Pronoun defines the object of the corresponding independent clause: I took **the Chemistry class** last term. • Possible to omit the pronoun
Relative Clauses Containing Prepositions		
Preposition at the end of the clause	Did you find the book **that** *you were asking* **for**? He's the friend **who** *I went to school* **with**.	• Rule: Place preposition at the end of the clause. • Style: Informal and conversational
Preposition at the beginning of the clause	Did you find the book **for which** *you were asking*? He's the friend **with whom** *I went to school*.	• Rule: *For that* or *with who* is incorrect. • Style: Formal, appropriate for academic writing (unless awkward)

PUNCTUATION: COMMAS AND SEMICOLONS

COMMAS ## THREE USES OF COMMAS

Commas are mostly used in two ways: to set off non-defining information in an independent clause, and before coordinating linking words such as *and*, *but*, and *so*. Another, less common use is to separate two or more adjectives before a noun. These rules for using commas are not always applied consistently by writers.

Adding Extra, Non-Defining Information to an Independent Clause

Note that some writers do not consistently use commas before independent clauses, especially in journalistic writing.

Before the Independent Clause

- Preposition phrases:

  Since the 1970s, there has been a mandatory life sentence for murder in Canada.

  After the change of law, many judges complained about government interference.

  Across the country, the crime rate has fallen.

  With the fall in crime, many people felt safer.

  In universities and colleges, criminology students are studying why crime has fallen.

- Conjunctive adverbs:

  However, not all types of crime have fallen continuously. Online fraud is one example.

  Moreover, financially motivated crimes such as theft and burglary tend to rise during economic slowdowns.

  Therefore, social and economic factors should be considered when reading crime statistics.

- Dependent clauses:

  While violent crime fell, financially motivated crime rates fluctuated.

  If unemployment rates drop, violent crime rates also fall.

  Although there is a link between crime and poverty, other factors need to be considered.

- Participle phrases:

  Sensing a change in public opinion, the government unsuccessfully attempted to reinstate capital punishment in 1987.

  Influenced by recent opinion polls, the government unsuccessfully attempted to reinstate capital punishment in 1987.

Within the Independent Clause

- Conjunctive adverbs:

  Not all types of crimes, **however,** have fallen continuously.

  Social and economic factors should be considered, **therefore,** when reading crime statistics.

- Non-defining relative clauses:

  The death penalty, **which is also known as *capital punishment*,** was abolished in Canada in 1976.

  After 1976, convicted murderers, **who might previously have received the death penalty,** would receive mandatory life sentences instead.

- Non-defining participle phrases:

  The death penalty, **also known as *capital punishment*,** was abolished in Canada in 1976.

  In 1987, the government, **sensing a change in public opinion,** unsuccessfully attempted to reinstate capital punishment.

- Non-defining noun phrases:

  Youth unemployment, **a root cause of financially motivated crimes,** has gone up in the current economic slowdown.

  Rates for burglary and car theft, **two of the most common financially motivated crimes,** have increased significantly.

After the Independent Clause

- Conjunctive adverbs:

  Financially motivated crimes such as theft and burglary tend to rise during economic slowdowns, **moreover**.

  Not all types of crimes have fallen continuously, **however**.

- Non-defining relative clauses:

  Criminologists have studied the deterrent effect of the death penalty, **which is its ability to prevent other crimes**.

  After 1976, mandatory life sentences applied for all convicted murderers, **who might previously have received the death penalty**.

- Non-defining participle phrases:

  Criminologists often study the pros and cons of the death penalty, **also known as *capital punishment***.

  In 1987, the government tried to change the law, **sensing a change in public opinion**.

- Non-defining noun phrases:

  The economic slowdown has led to increased youth unemployment, **a root cause of financially motivated crimes**.

  The police are targeting burglary and car theft, **two of the most common financially motivated crimes**.

Note that some writers avoid placing conjunctive adverbs within independent clauses because they feel such usage breaks the flow of the sentence.

Remember that defining information is not set off with commas: Criminals *who commit murder in Canada* face mandatory life sentences.

Adding a conjunctive adverb after an independent clause is grammatically possible but less common because such sentences may read awkwardly.

Coordination

To review compound sentences, see Unit 3, p. 338.

Before the "FANBOYS" Coordinators in Compound Sentences

Compound sentences are made up of two independent clauses joined by a coordinator (*for*, *and*, *nor*, *but*, *or*, *yet*, *so*).

- *and*

  Violent crime rates fell**, and** society became a lot safer.

- *but*

  Violent crime rates fell**, but** those for online fraud rose.

- *so*

  Mandatory life sentencing was introduced for murder**, so** the judiciary lost some of its independence.

Between the Items in Lists of Three or More Things

Stricter environments in some UK young offender institutions have resulted in inmates' [1] <u>having to wear uniforms</u>**,** [2] <u>being denied reading materials</u>**, and** [3] <u>ending their days at 10:30 p.m.</u>

No comma is required when only two things are joined by a coordinator:

Stricter environments in some UK young offender institutions have resulted in inmates' [1] <u>having to wear uniforms</u> **and** [2] <u>being denied reading materials</u>.

Separating Adjectives

Use commas to separate two or more adjectives belonging to the same category (e.g., opinion, shape, colour, material) when they come before the noun they describe:

Prisoners are now expected to live in a **harsher, more punitive** environment.

BUT

The local prison is a **big grey stone** building.

Variations on How to Use Commas

There are some variations on how to use commas that depend on the following factors.

British English

In British English, it is common to omit commas before coordinators such as *and*, *but*, and *so*, both in compound sentences and in lists of three or more things.

Violent crime rates fell with the increased police presence **and** the city became considerably safer in the months that followed.

Stricter environments in some UK young offender institutions have resulted in inmates' <u>having to wear uniforms</u>, <u>being denied reading materials</u> **and** <u>ending their days at 10:30 p.m.</u>

Journalistic Style

In journalistic style, commas are often omitted after introductory preposition phrases.

> **Since the 1970s** there has been a mandatory life sentence for murder in Canada.

> **With the fall in crime** many people felt safer.

To Avoid Confusion

Writers who usually omit commas (in British English and journalism, for example) sometimes have no choice but to include them to avoid confusing their readers. Consider the following examples:

1. With the fall in crime prevention became more of a focus than punishment.
2. With the fall in crime**,** prevention became more of a focus than punishment.

Sentence 1 would likely confuse the reader. This is because *crime prevention* is a common compound noun used in the discussion of crime. Without the comma, the reader might at first understand the sentence to be about "the fall in crime prevention." Readers often have to go back over such sentences two or three times to understand them. Sentence 2 is not confusing because there is a comma after the introductory phrase.

Sometimes writers add commas for clarity, to make it easier for the reader to process ideas or items in a list when confusion might arise. For example, although a comma is not needed before a coordinator joining two items, writers may include one to make the sentence more comprehensible.

1. Harsher environments in some prisons mean inmates receive fewer comforts that would make their stay in prison more tolerable and comfortable and stricter punishments if they break any of the rules of prison life.
2. Harsher environments in some prisons mean inmates receive <u>fewer comforts that would make their stay in prison more tolerable and comfortable</u>, and <u>stricter punishments if they break any of the rules of prison life</u>.

Sentence 1 could confuse the reader because the first item is *fewer comforts that would make their stay in prison more tolerable and comfortable*. Without the comma, the reader may think that the word *comfortable* is the beginning of the second item because it comes after the coordinator *and*. By placing the comma after the word *comfortable* in sentence 2, the writer avoids any confusion.

Personal Preference

Comma usage can also depend on the writer's personal style preferences. Writers may prefer not to use commas in some sentences if they feel it breaks the flow of the writing.

Remember: it is important to be consistent. Avoid using commas with some non-defining phrases and clauses but not with others.

TASK 1

In the following sentences, the commas have been removed. Add commas where required. Some sentences may require more than one comma; others may require none. Then identify each comma according to its function: addition of non-defining information (ND), coordination (C), or separation of adjectives (S).

Type of Comma

1. Although there is a link between alcohol consumption and crime other factors need to be considered. _____

2. During the last 30 years there has been a steady fall in crime rates in Canada. _____

3. There has nonetheless been an increase in certain crimes most notably cybercrimes. _____

4. Mandatory sentencing for the most violent crimes which takes some power away from judges has been popular with some members of the public but many judges disapprove. _____

5. Criminals who commit serious crimes in Sweden serve their sentences in a prison system that focuses on rehabilitation. _____

6. Aristotle said that poverty is the parent of crime which suggests a clear link between socio-economic factors and crime rates. _____

7. Violent crime rates have fallen across the country yet people still feel unsafe in some areas. _____

8. Crime policies aim for a safer more productive society. _____

9. The increased police presence aims to reassure people living in poor areas of the city. _____

TASK 2

The two sentences below could confuse readers. Explain why the sentences are confusing, and add commas to make them clearer.

1. After the mayor's promise to get tough on crime policies were implemented at the local level.

   _____

   _____

2. Due to the municipal government's measures to improve leisure facilities for at-risk youth clubs for sport and learning were set up in three areas of the city.

   _____

   _____

TWO USES OF SEMICOLONS

Semicolons are used like periods to separate two independent clauses. Periods separate sentences; semicolons separate independent clauses in a sentence. Semicolons are also used to separate items in lists.

Separating Independent Clauses in a Sentence

Use semicolons to separate independent clauses in a sentence when the clauses contain closely related ideas. In this way, semicolons give readers a clue that the next idea is related. In contrast, use a period to introduce a new idea in the following sentence. This difference between semicolons and periods is illustrated below:

The slow food movement supports local production and consumption; it also emphasizes ethical eating.	(closely related information)
The slow food movement emerged in Italy during the 1980s. The movement was originally seen as a reaction to the spread of fast food.	(new information)

Semicolons and Conjunctive Adverbs

You can also use semicolons in combination with conjunctive adverbs to separate closely related independent clauses:

The fair trade movement aims to improve the lives of small-scale farmers in developing countries; **however,** some farmers receive only minimal benefits.	(closely related information)
The fair trade movement aims to improve the lives of small-scale farmers in developing countries. **However,** some studies have shown that most consumers are more concerned about the price of products in their local supermarkets than about farmers' quality of life.	(new information)

Separating Items in a List

You have studied the use of commas to separate three or more items in a list. If one or more of the items contain a comma, you must use semicolons to separate them. Compare the examples below:

The fair trade movement needs to find strategies to address <u>expensive registration costs</u>, <u>excessive profits for intermediaries</u>, **and** <u>unstable product prices in world markets</u>.

The fair trade movement needs to find strategies to address <u>expensive registration costs, which disadvantage poor farmers</u>; <u>excessive profits for intermediaries</u>; **and** <u>unstable product prices in world markets, which fluctuate regularly</u>.

TASK 3

The following sentences are written without semicolons. Identify any places where commas or periods should be replaced with semicolons, and rewrite these parts of the sentences.

1. The fair trade movement has commendable aims. However, it has been argued that some intermediary buyers and sellers exploit the movement solely to make money for themselves.

_____

_____

2. Two of the most successful fair trade products are coffee and bananas. These two alone make up a large percentage of sales in richer countries.

_____

_____

3. Most shoppers can find fair trade coffee, bananas, and chocolate in local stores.

_____

_____

4. Most shoppers can find the following fair trade products in local stores: coffee, often imported from farms in Nicaragua, Kenya, and Colombia, bananas, primarily from Caribbean islands and Central America, and chocolate, made from cacao grown in countries such as Ivory Coast and Ghana.

_____

_____

TASK 4

Read the paragraph below. Replace periods with semicolons when you think ideas are closely related, and replace commas in lists with semicolons as needed.

Fair Trade

The fair trade movement dates back to the 1980s. Since its origin, thousands of small-scale farmers in developing countries have benefited from membership in fair trade programs. Today, the fair trade movement faces a number of challenges: fluctuating prices for products like coffee and bananas, which affect farmers' profits, mass-produced organic food, which competes in the ethical food market in developed countries, private and government intermediaries, who receive a percentage of every sale, and certification costs, which many small-scale farmers cannot afford. Certification costs should be the first problem to address. A reduction in these costs would allow more farmers to join and more profits to stay in local communities. Overall, fair trade has been a great success. However, the movement needs to become less *unfair* wherever possible.

TASK 5

Read the following paragraph, which is punctuated only with periods; it contains no commas or semicolons. Add commas and semicolons where necessary, and replace periods with semicolons when you think ideas are closely related.

Slow Food

The slow food movement is not just about eating slowly. It also relates to good and clean food. Agrillo Milano Roveglia and Scaffidi (2015) highlight two subjective factors in their definition of good food. The first is taste which relates to the subjective senses of the individual. The second is good knowledge of local culture environment and history of communities and their culinary practices. The role of promoting these values falls to local organizations called *convivia* established to educate people of all ages about "how food is produced and its production origins" (Page 2012 p. 3). Clearly the mission of slow food is to encourage lifestyles that promote good and clean food. However another important aspect is to eat in an ethically aware way.

Consumers have choices to make in their everyday interactions with food and the food industry. An example is the shopper who faces the decision to buy either a cheap mass-produced ready-made meal for microwaving or fresh local ingredients to cook the same meal from scratch. The slow food choice must be without doubt the latter.

My eLab

Find more exercises on commas and semicolons online.

SUMMARY   COMMAS AND SEMICOLONS

Function	Position	Examples
	Commas	
To set off extra, non-defining information in an independent clause	Before the independent clause, following: a) a preposition phrase b) a conjunctive adverb c) a dependent clause d) a participle phrase	a) **Since the 1970s,** there has been a mandatory life sentence for murder in Canada. **Across the country,** the crime rate has fallen. b) **Moreover,** financially motivated crimes such as theft and burglary tend to rise during economic slowdowns. **However,** not all types of crimes have fallen continuously. c) **If unemployment rates fall,** violent crime rates also fall. **Although there is a link between crime and poverty,** other factors need to be considered. d) **Sensing a change in public opinion,** the government attempted to reinstate capital punishment in 1987. **Influenced by recent opinion polls,** the government attempted to reinstate capital punishment in 1987.
	Within the independent clause, to set off: a) a conjunctive adverb b) a non-defining relative clause c) a non-defining participle phrase d) a non-defining noun phrase	a) Financially motivated crimes such as theft and burglary, **moreover,** tend to rise during economic slowdowns. Not all types of crimes, **however,** have fallen continuously. b) The death penalty, **which is also known as *capital punishment*,** was abolished in Canada in 1976. After 1976, convicted murderers, **who previously might have received the death penalty,** would receive mandatory life sentences instead. c) In 1987, the government, **sensing a change in public opinion,** attempted to reinstate capital punishment. The death penalty, **also known as *capital punishment*,** was abolished in Canada in 1976. d) Youth unemployment, **a root cause of financially motivated crimes,** has gone up in the current economic slowdown.

Function	Position	Examples
To set off extra, non-defining information in an independent clause	After the independent clause, preceding: a) a conjunctive adverb b) a non-defining relative clause c) a non-defining participle phrase d) a non-defining noun phrase	a) Not all types of crimes have fallen continuously, **however**. b) Criminologists have studied the deterrent effect of the death penalty, **which is its ability to prevent other crimes**. c) Criminologists often study the pros and cons of the death penalty, **also known as** *capital punishment*. d) The police are targeting burglary and car theft, **two of the most common financially motivated crimes**.
Coordination	Before the FANBOYS coordinators in compound sentences	Violent crime rates fell, **and** society became a lot safer. Violent crime rates fell, **but** those for online fraud rose. Mandatory life sentencing was introduced for murder, **so** the judiciary lost some of its independence.
	Between the items in lists of three or more things	Stricter environments mean inmates wear uniforms, books are limited, **and** lights are turned off at 10:30 p.m.
To separate adjectives before a noun	Between two or more adjectives of the same category	Prisoners are now expected to live in a **harsher, more punitive** environment.
Variations		
British English (omission of commas)	Before coordinators in compound sentences	Violent crime rates fell with the increased police presence **and** the city became safer in the months that followed.
	Before coordinators in lists of three or more things	Stricter environments mean inmates wear uniforms, books are limited **and** lights are turned off at 10:30 p.m.
Journalistic style (omission of commas)	After introductory preposition phrases	**Since the 1970s** there has been a mandatory life sentence for murder in Canada. **With the fall in crime** many people felt safer.
To avoid confusion (writers who usually omit commas)	After introductory phrases	**With the fall in crime,** prevention became more of a focus than punishment. (less confusing than "With the fall in crime prevention became …")
	Before coordinators that join two items	Inmates receive fewer comforts to make their stay in prison more tolerable and comfortable, **and** stricter punishments if they break any of the rules of prison life.
Personal preference	Writers may prefer not to use commas in some sentences if they feel it breaks the flow of the writing.	
Semicolons		
To separate independent clauses containing closely related information in a sentence	Between the independent clauses	The slow food movement supports local production and consumption; it also emphasizes ethical eating.
	After the first independent clause and before a conjunctive adverb	The fair trade movement aims to improve the lives of small-scale farmers in developing countries; **however,** some farmers receive only minimal benefits.
To separate three or more items in a list if one or more of the items contain a comma	Between the items in the list	The fair trade movement needs to find strategies to address expensive registration costs, which disadvantage poor farmers; excessive profits for intermediaries; **and** unstable product prices in world markets, which fluctuate regularly.

PARTICIPLE PHRASES

What Is a Participle Phrase?

Participle phrases (often called *participle clauses*) are similar to relative clauses. Both add information (defining or non-defining) about a thing or things in a related independent clause. Participle phrases follow the same rules of punctuation as those for relative clauses: commas are used to set off non-defining phrases, but not defining ones.

Participle phrases can be understood as reduced relative clauses. They express the same ideas as relative clauses, but in fewer words. In this way, participle phrases can give a sense of economy and add variety to your sentence structure.

The following examples illustrate how the relative clause (in italics) in sentence 1 can be reduced to a participle phrase (in bold) in sentence 2:

1. Fair trade products will become fairer when commodity producers receive a higher price, *which will bring benefits to local communities.*

2. Fair trade products will become fairer when commodity producers receive a higher price, **bringing benefits to local communities**.

In sentence 2, the present participle phrase *bringing benefits to local communities* expresses the idea conveyed by the relative clause in sentence 1, *which will bring benefits to local communities.*

Sentence 2 also illustrates an important feature of participle phrases, that is, the relationship between present and past participles does not correlate with present and past time. As can be seen in sentence 2, the present participle *bringing* refers to future time: "which will bring."

Present and Past Participle Phrases

As stated, the difference between present and past participle phrases does not relate to time. Present participle phrases are used as an alternative for clauses in the active voice, and past participle phrases, as an alternative for clauses in the passive voice.

The following sentences illustrate this difference.

Present Participle Phrases

1. Many registered fair trade coffee producers **living in Nicaragua** have invested in high registration costs in the hope of future benefits. (defining)

2. **Aiming for increased benefits for local communities**, Nicaraguan fair trade coffee producers campaigned for lower registration fees. (non-defining)

3. Fair trade producers will increase their market share in developed countries during the next 10 years, **leading to an increase in local development**. (non-defining)

Form: In the three phrases, the present participles are formed by adding *ing* to the verbs: *living*, *aiming*, and *leading*.

Concept: In the three example sentences, the participle phrases are used to convey the following meanings:

- Sentence 1: The participle phrase means "who live in."
- Sentence 2: The participle phrase means "because they were aiming for."
- Sentence 3: The participle phrase means "which will lead to" or "and it will lead to."

Time idea: Present participle phrases can be used with reference to past, present, or future time.

- Sentence 1 refers to present time: "who live in."
- Sentence 2 refers to past time: "because they were aiming for."
- Sentence 3 refers to future time: "which will lead to" or "and it will lead to."

Active voice: Present participle phrases are used in sentences in which the idea of the sentence would otherwise be expressed in an active-voice clause, as illustrated below.

Participle Phrase	Active-Voice Clause
Many registered fair trade coffee producers **living in Nicaragua** have invested in high registration costs in the hope of future benefits.	Many registered fair trade coffee producers who live in Nicaragua . . .
Aiming for increased benefits for local communities, Nicaraguan fair trade coffee producers campaigned for lower registration fees.	Because they were aiming for increased benefits for local communities, . . .
Fair trade producers will increase their market share in developed countries during the next 10 years, **leading to an increase in local development**.	. . . which will lead to an increase in local development.

Past Participle Phrases

1. The Fairtrade Labelling Organizations International (FLO), **set up in 1997**, coordinates registration and standards across the fair trade movement. (non-defining)
2. The FLO believes that money **received by local farmers** helps local communities to develop. (defining)
3. In the future, conscientious consumers will find an increasing variety of products **marked with fair trade logos**. (defining)

Form: In the three phrases, the first past participle is irregular (*set up*) while the second and third are regular, formed by adding *d* or *ed* to the verbs: *received*, *marked*.

Concept: In the three example sentences, the past participle phrases convey meaning in the same way as passive-voice sentences with regard to stated and unstated agents (the people or things doing the action).

- Sentence 1: The participle phrase *set up in 1997* has no stated agent as the agent is unknown or unimportant for the sentence.
- Sentence 2: The participle phrase *received by local farmers* emphasizes the stated agents (local farmers).
- Sentence 3: The participle phrase *marked with fair trade logos* has no stated agent as the agent is unimportant for the sentence.

Time idea: Past participle phrases can be used with reference to past, present, or future time.

- Sentence 1 refers to past time: "which was set up in."
- Sentence 2 refers to present time: "that is received by."
- Sentence 3 refers to future time: "that will be marked with."

Passive voice: Past participle phrases are used in sentences in which the idea of the sentence would otherwise be expressed in a passive-voice clause, as illustrated below.

Participle Phrase	Passive-Voice Clause
The Fairtrade Labelling Organizations International (FLO), **set up in 1997**, coordinates registration and standards across the fair trade movement.	The Fairtrade Labelling Organizations International (FLO), which was set up in 1997, . . .
The FLO believes that money **received by local farmers** helps local communities to develop.	The FLO believes that money that is received by local farmers . . .
In the future, conscientious consumers will find an increasing variety of products **marked with fair trade logos**.	. . . products that will be marked with fair trade logos.

TASK 1

<u>Underline</u> the participle phrase in each of the following sentences. Decide whether the participle phrase is replacing a clause in the active or passive voice and whether the participle phrase is present or past. Then state the time idea.

1. The slow food movement, originating in the 1980s, was a response to the spread of fast food restaurants in Italy.

   ☐ active voice ☐ passive voice ☐ present participle ☐ past participle

   Time idea: _____

2. Slow Food International, launched in 2001, brought greater worldwide attention to the movement.

   ☐ active voice ☐ passive voice ☐ present participle ☐ past participle

   Time idea: _____

3. Slow food promotes good, clean, and fair food for all, bringing together appreciation for the taste, culture, and local origins of food.

   ☐ active voice ☐ passive voice ☐ present participle ☐ past participle

   Time idea: _____

4. At slow food events, food produced by local farmers is showcased.

☐ active voice ☐ passive voice ☐ present participle ☐ past participle

Time idea: _____

5. In the future, it is hoped that slow food will spread globally, gaining a greater presence in large countries such as India and China.

☐ active voice ☐ passive voice ☐ present participle ☐ past participle

Time idea: _____

6. The benefits of ethical eating will be the focus of slow food events organized by future members of the movement.

☐ active voice ☐ passive voice ☐ present participle ☐ past participle

Time idea: _____

TASK 2

The following sentences contain relative clauses (in italics). First, rewrite each sentence, reducing the relative clause to a participle phrase. Then decide whether the participle phrase is replacing a clause in the active or passive voice and whether the participle phrase is present or past. Finally, state the time idea.

1. The fair trade movement, *which supports small-scale farmers and sustainability*, has a worldwide presence.

_____

_____

☐ active voice ☐ passive voice ☐ present participle ☐ past participle

Time idea: _____

2. Fair trade coffee and bananas, *which are grown primarily in Latin America and Africa*, are two of the best-selling products.

_____

_____

☐ active voice ☐ passive voice ☐ present participle ☐ past participle

Time idea: _____

3. A future goal of fair trade will be to tackle poverty more aggressively, *which will raise awareness of the need for a living wage for all farmers and their employees*.

_____

_____

☐ active voice ☐ passive voice ☐ present participle ☐ past participle

Time idea: _____

4. The move toward a living wage in fair trade will involve governments and international organizations as well as thousands of new farmers *who will be registered and certified as fair trade producers.*

_____

_____

_____

☐ active voice ☐ passive voice ☐ present participle ☐ past participle

Time idea: _____

5. In world markets *that are dominated by free trade*, the growth of fair trade alternatives may be slow.

_____

_____

☐ active voice ☐ passive voice ☐ present participle ☐ past participle

Time idea: _____

6. Regulators need to address the problem of price reduction due to overproduction, *which occurs when farmers receive a premium for their product, overproduce, and thus create surpluses.*

_____

_____

_____

☐ active voice ☐ passive voice ☐ present participle ☐ past participle

Time idea: _____

My eLab

Find more exercises on participle phrases online.

TASK 3

Read the following excerpt from the Suranovic article cited in Chapter 6 (see p. 128 for the full source), and decide whether the words in bold form a participle phrase. Explain why or why not.

> In the coffee industry, for example, from the early 1990s, four transnational companies—Nestlé, Phillip Morris, Sara Lee and Procter & Gamble—**accounted for more than 60 per cent of coffee sales in the major consuming markets**.

Participle phrase? ☐ Yes ☐ No

Why or why not?

_____

_____

Type	Example	Concept/Form
Defining	Many registered fair trade coffee producers **living in Nicaragua** have invested in high registration costs in the hope of future benefits.	• Essential information defining which coffee producers • No commas
Non-defining	The Fairtrade Labelling Organizations International (FLO), **set up in 1997**, coordinates registration and standards across the fair trade movement.	• Non-essential information about the FLO • Set off with commas
Present Participle Phrases		
Present participle phrases	Many registered fair trade coffee producers **living in Nicaragua** have invested in high registration costs in the hope of future benefits.	• Defining • Active-voice clause: "who live in Nicaragua" • Present time
	Aiming for increased benefits for local communities, Nicaraguan fair trade coffee producers campaigned for lower registration fees.	• Non-defining • Active-voice clause: "because they were aiming for . . ." • Past time
	Fair trade producers will increase their market share in developed countries during the next 10 years, **leading to an increase in local development.**	• Non-defining • Active-voice clause: "which will lead to / and it will lead to . . ." • Future time
Past Participle Phrases		
Past participle phrases	The Fairtrade Labelling Organizations International (FLO), **set up in 1997**, coordinates registration and standards across the fair trade movement.	• Non-defining • Passive-voice clause: "which was set up" • Past time
	The FLO believes that money **received by local farmers** helps local communities to develop.	• Defining • Passive-voice clause: "that is received by local farmers" • Present time
	In the future, conscientious consumers will find an increasing variety of products **marked with fair trade logos**.	• Defining • Passive-voice clause: "that will be marked with fair trade logos" • Future time

THE PASSIVE VOICE

The passive voice is commonly used in many forms of academic writing, particularly in forms that require an objective, scientific tone. Writing a sentence in the active or passive voice does not change the meaning. However, your choice to use one or the other can affect the tone that readers detect; it can also change the emphasis of information in the sentence in different ways.

Active and Passive Voice

The following examples show how to transform sentences in the active voice to the passive voice.

Active Voice

Active-voice sentences are formed with a subject followed by a corresponding verb, and sometimes an object:

1. Business leaders **require** sophisticated strategies when they work internationally.

2. Kamoche et al. (2015) **analyze** leadership strategies in Africa.

Passive Voice

To form a passive-voice sentence, place the object of an active-voice sentence in the subject position, use a form of the verb *to be* in the appropriate tense, and add a past participle:

1. Business leaders **require** sophisticated strategies when they work internationally. (active voice)

   Sophisticated strategies **are required** in international work. (passive voice – no stated agent)

2. Kamoche et al. (2015) **analyze** leadership strategies in Africa. (active voice)

   Leadership strategies in Africa **are analyzed** by Kamoche et al. (2015). (passive voice – stated agent: *by Kamoche et al. [2015]*)

The Passive Voice and Transitive Verbs

Passive-voice sentences are formed with transitive verbs, which are verbs that require an object. Intransitive verbs do not require an object. Some verbs can be used transitively or intransitively, depending on the context. In the active-voice examples below, the verbs are in bold and the objects, underlined.

Business leaders **face** <u>challenges</u> when they work internationally.	(transitive verb)
Leaders from Europe and Africa **talked** for three hours at the meeting.	(intransitive verb)
The European delegation **visited** <u>the site</u> three times.	(transitive or intransitive verb, used transitively)
The European delegation **visited** last year.	(transitive or intransitive verb, used intransitively)

TASK 1

Read the sentences below, and indicate whether the verbs are in the active or passive voice. If a verb is transitive and is in the active voice, rewrite the sentence in the passive voice. If a verb is in the passive voice, rewrite the sentence in the active voice. Key words to analyze and change are in bold.

1. **A recent study highlighted the need** to promote indigenous African knowledge in African transnational corporations.

   ☐ active voice   ☐ passive voice

   _____

   _____

2. In Section 3, **I will argue that** transcultural awareness is necessary in international business.

   ☐ active voice   ☐ passive voice

   _____

   _____

3. The role of women leaders in China, India, and Singapore **is discussed by** Peus, Braun, and Knipfer (2015).

   ☐ active voice   ☐ passive voice

   _____

   _____

4. **It has been documented that** Confucianism has greatly impacted leaders in the Chinese diaspora (Chai & Rhee, 2010).

   ☐ active voice   ☐ passive voice

   _____

   _____

5. It has been documented that **Confucianism has greatly impacted leaders** in the Chinese diaspora (Chai & Rhee, 2010).

   ☐ active voice   ☐ passive voice

   _____

   _____

6. **Scholars such as Kim and Moon (2015) and Peus, Braun, and Knipfer (2015) have addressed the relationship** between business leadership and local cultural knowledge.

   ☐ active voice   ☐ passive voice

   _____

   _____

The Passive Voice: Tone, Emphasis, and Agent

Use of the passive voice as opposed to the active voice does not change meaning. However, it can affect the tone of the sentence and the emphasis of information, as illustrated below.

Active Voice

1. Business leaders require sophisticated strategies when they work internationally.
2. Kim and Moon (2015) analyze leadership strategies in Asia.

Tone: Sentences 1 and 2 have an academic tone due to the vocabulary (*require*, *analyze*). The fact that they are in the active voice rather than the passive voice has little effect on their tone.

Emphasis: In sentence 1, the use of the active voice has little effect on which part of the sentence is emphasized. In sentence 2, *Kim and Moon (2015) analyze* is a citation phrase: *Kim and Moon* is the subject of the reporting verb *analyze*. In citation phrases, use of the active voice can emphasize the author more than the information cited.

Passive Voice

1. Sophisticated strategies are required in international work.

   (passive voice with no stated agent)

2. Leadership strategies in Asia are analyzed by Kim and Moon (2015).

   (passive voice – stated agent: *by Kim and Moon [2015]*)

Tone: Sentences 1 and 2 have an academic tone due to the vocabulary (*require*, *analyze*) and the use of the passive voice. The passive voice adds an extra tone of scientific objectivity.

Emphasis: In sentence 1, there is no stated agent: the writer does not indicate who requires the sophisticated strategies. This type of agentless passive-voice sentence is used here because the agent is unknown or unimportant and because the information in the sentence is a generally accepted fact. In this case, the stated strategies are more important than knowing who requires them. In sentence 2, the agent is stated: *Kim and Moon (2015)*. In this type of passive-voice sentence, the agent is emphasized.

TASK 2

Rewrite the following active-voice sentences as passive-voice sentences, following the prompts in parentheses. Explain your decisions about whether or not to state the agents.

1. In Section 2, I argue that traditional forms of knowledge in Africa and Asia should be seen as resources for business leaders.

   (Write a passive-voice sentence beginning with *it will* to create a less personal tone. Decide whether to add emphasis by stating the agent.)

   _____

   _____

   _____

   _____

   _____

2. Scholars such as Kim and Moon (2015) and Peus, Braun, and Knipfer (2015) have suggested that business leadership should be more closely tied to local cultural knowledge.

   (Write a passive-voice sentence beginning with *it has*. Decide whether to state the agent.)

   _____

   _____

   _____

   _____

   _____

Agentless Passives

Passive-voice sentences with no stated agent are also called *agentless passives*. As stated, agentless passives are used when the agent is unknown or considered to be unimportant. In cases of factual statements based on common knowledge, agentless passives pose few problems. However, in academic writing, agentless passives are problematic when the writer claims to represent the ideas of experts without stating explicitly who these experts are.

1. Local cultural knowledge was passed on orally before writing systems emerged.
2. It has been argued that intercultural awareness is as important as traditional leadership skills in business.
3. It has been argued that business leaders should pay more attention to local knowledge and culture.

In sentence 1, the agent is unknown and unimportant for the focus of the sentence. The sentence is not problematic because it states a generally recognized fact.

Sentence 2 has no stated agent. This example is problematic because the writer should state clearly who has put forward this argument. Similarly, sentence 3 is problematic because the writer should state who has argued this point about business leaders.

Passive-Voice Sentences with *to Get*

It is also possible to write passive-voice sentences using *to get* as the auxiliary verb in place of *to be*. Using *get* with the passive voice is more common in informal English than in formal academic style. It can also cause a change in meaning, suggesting the information conveyed is surprising or unpleasant.

1. My thesis proposal **was** rejected.
2. My thesis proposal **got** rejected.

In sentence 2, the writer has used *got* instead of *was* as the auxiliary verb in the passive-voice sentence, adding a sense of unexpectedness or unpleasantness to it. As such, the reader may interpret the sentence to mean that the writer was expecting the proposal to be accepted and is surprised or annoyed.

TASK 3

Read the following active- and passive-voice sentences, and answer the questions that follow.

1. My laptop was stolen yesterday afternoon. I left it in the room during the lunch break.

   Does the speaker seem surprised or annoyed?

   _____

2. I just found out that I got accepted for the scholarship!

   Does it seem like the speaker was expecting to be accepted?

   _____

3. The view that the MMR vaccine causes autism has been discredited.

   Why might an instructor add a margin note that asks, "By whom?"

   _____

4. The view that the MMR vaccine causes autism has been discredited by leading scientists.

   Why might an instructor add a margin note that asks, "Which ones?"

   _____

   _____

5. Leadership strategies in Asia are analyzed by Kim and Moon (2015).

   Does this sentence emphasize the agent?

   _____

Find more exercises on the passive voice online.

Voice	Examples	Form/Concept
Active voice	<u>Business leaders</u> **require** <u>sophisticated strategies</u> when they work internationally. <u>Kamoche et al. (2015)</u> **analyze** <u>leadership strategies in Africa</u>.	Form: <u>subject</u> + **verb** + <u>optional object</u>
Passive voice	a) <u>Sophisticated strategies</u> **are required** in international work. (no stated agent) b) <u>Leadership strategies in Africa</u> **are analyzed** by Kamoche et al. (2015). (stated agent)	• Active-voice object moves to subject position in the passive voice. • Form: *to be* + past participle • Verb must be transitive. • a) No stated agent 　b) Stated agent: *by Kamoche et al. (2015)*
Stating the Agent		
Passive voice, no stated agent	a) Sophisticated strategies are required in international work. b) Local cultural knowledge was passed on orally before writing systems emerged. c) It has been argued that business leaders should pay more attention to local knowledge and culture.	a) Agent is unimportant. b) Agent is unknown and unimportant for the sentence. c) Unstated agent is problematic: writer needs to state who the idea or argument belongs to.
Passive voice, stated agent	Leadership strategies in Asia are analyzed **by Kim and Moon (2015)**.	The agent is important for the sentence and is given emphasis.
Tone		
Active voice	In Section 3, I will argue that transcultural awareness is necessary in international business.	Personal, subjective style
Passive voice	In Section 3, it will be argued that transcultural awareness is necessary in international business.	Less personal, more objective style
Passive Voice with *to Get*		
Passive voice with *to be*	My thesis proposal **was** rejected.	Neutral
Passive voice with *to get*	My thesis proposal **got** rejected.	Sense of unexpectedness or unpleasantness

PUNCTUATION: COLONS AND APOSTROPHES

The rules for colons and apostrophes are not always agreed on in academic writing, nor are they always followed consistently. You will likely notice that writers use colons and apostrophes differently. This may be because they have followed a publisher's style guidelines, which are usually based on slightly different rules set out by organizations such as the APA and MLA. It may also be because they do not know how to use these punctuation marks correctly!

The following are the most common rules for colons and apostrophes.

COLONS

THREE USES OF COLONS

Colons are used to introduce examples and lists at the end of an independent clause, and to introduce direct quotations, also at the end of an independent clause. In addition, they are commonly used to separate main titles from subtitles when referring to written works.

Introducing Examples and Lists

Use a colon to introduce a list or examples after an independent clause:

> Two key factors affect business in Africa**:** globalization and dominant Western business practices.

Do not use a colon to introduce a list or examples that are incorporated grammatically into the sentence:

> Two key factors affecting business in Africa **are** globalization and dominant Western business practices.

Use a colon to create an economical style in a list containing long items. Compare the following paragraphs:

> In the above sections, I analyzed several factors related to business between Asia, Africa, and the West. First, I looked at strategies that promote intercultural understanding between regions. Second, I focused on the effects of globalization and dominant Western business practices in African and Asian countries. Finally, I considered the potential of crossvergence as opposed to convergence and divergence in international leadership.

> In the above sections, I analyzed the following factors related to business between Asia, Africa, and the West**:** strategies that promote intercultural understanding between regions, the effects of globalization and dominant Western business practices in African and Asian countries, and the potential of crossvergence as opposed to convergence and divergence in international leadership.

The items in the examples are separated by commas. If one of the items contained a comma, semicolons would be used to separate the items (see Unit 5, p. 354).

In the second paragraph, the insertion of a colon has taken away the need to use introductory linking words such as *first* and *second* as well as verb phrases such as *I looked at* and *I focused on*. Instead, with the colon, the list of noun phrases is sufficient.

Introducing Direct Quotations

Use a colon to introduce direct quotations at the end of an independent clause:

> Leadership assessments must be conducted as follows: "in a structured manner, primarily based on behavioral criteria" (Peus et al., 2012, p. 106).

Do not use a colon to introduce a direct quotation that is incorporated grammatically into the sentence:

> Leadership assessments should "be conducted in a structured manner, primarily based on behavioral criteria" (Peus et al., 2012, p. 106).

Separating a Main Title and a Subtitle

In titles of books, articles, and essays, it is common to use a colon to separate the main title (which indicates the general topic) and the subtitle (which shows the specific focus).

> Business Leadership in Africa: Rising to the Challenge
>
> Leadership Strategies in Chinese Corporations: Looking West or East?

TASK 1

Indicate whether the following sentences are correct or incorrect. If the sentence is incorrect, rewrite it.

1. Three trends in international business leadership have been analyzed: convergence, divergence, and crossvergence.

   ☐ correct   ☐ incorrect

   _____

   _____

2. The three trends studied for international business leadership are: convergence, divergence, and crossvergence.

   ☐ correct   ☐ incorrect

   _____

   _____

3. According to a famous entrepreneur, "business is 10% theory and 90% common sense."

   ☐ correct   ☐ incorrect

   _____

   _____

4. A famous entrepreneur once stated that: "business is 10% theory and 90% common sense."

☐ correct   ☐ incorrect

_____

_____

TASK 2

Insert a colon in the paragraph below and rewrite it in a more economical style.

Entrepreneurial Assets

Establishing a successful new business is not a simple task. Anyone trying to succeed needs several assets. First, it is essential to find a niche in the market and a product to sell in that space. Second, the entrepreneur needs to develop a sound marketing plan, with a clear focus on product, price, and placement. Third, he or she needs to guarantee quality and consistency in the production process. Finally, any entrepreneur starting a new project needs to be able to learn from mistakes.

_____

_____

_____

_____

_____

APOSTROPHES   TWO USES OF APOSTROPHES

Apostrophes are used mainly for possessives (showing that something belongs to something or someone) and contractions (short forms such as _doesn't_ instead of _does not_). For possessives, the position of the apostrophe depends on whether the noun it is added to is singular or plural.

Possessives

To form the possessive of a singular noun, add an apostrophe and an _s_:

Intercultural awareness can help **a business leader's decision-making** in international contexts.

For a singular noun ending in _s_, add an apostrophe and an _s_. Note, however, that some writers add only an apostrophe in such cases.

A clear marketing plan can promote **a business's growth** in its initial years.

A clear marketing plan can promote **a business' growth** in its initial years.

For a plural noun ending in _s_, add an apostrophe:

Intercultural awareness has an inevitable effect on **business leaders' beliefs**, values, and actions.

For a plural noun not ending in *s*, add an apostrophe and an *s*:

Many factors affect **women's chances** for advancement to leadership positions in international corporations.

For two or more individual possessives, add an apostrophe to each:

Guo's (2015) and **Li's** (2016) **analyses** of crossvergence in Asian contexts provide useful recommendations for international business leaders.

Note that the example above refers to two separate studies, so they qualify as individual possessives.

For joint possessives, add only one apostrophe to the final person or thing:

Kim and Moon's (2015) **analysis** of Corporate Social Responsibility (CSR) focuses on practices in several Asian countries.

Note that the example above refers to one co-authored study, so it qualifies as a joint possessive.

For a place name that ends with a plural noun ending in *s*, add an apostrophe:

The Unites States' historical position in support of free trade agreements may change in the next 20 years.

For an indefinite pronoun (e.g., *anyone*, *someone*), add an apostrophe and an *s*:

Someone's bag was left at the meeting.

For a name not ending in *s*, add an apostrophe and an *s*:

Lee's CSR plan was accepted by the board.

For a name ending in *s*, add an apostrophe and an *s*. Note, however, that some writers add only an apostrophe in such cases.

Carlos's CSR plan was accepted by the board.

Carlos' CSR plan was accepted by the board.

Awkward Possessive Apostrophes

Avoid using apostrophes that make words or phrases awkward to read or say.

For example, avoid sentences with too many possessives grouped together:

Ms. Lee's company's representative's proposal was accepted.

Rephrase such sentences to make them more readable:

The proposal put forward by the representative of **Ms. Lee's company** was accepted.

With names ending in an *s* pronounced *eez*, the pronunciation may become awkward by adding an extra *s*, so many writers use only the apostrophe.

Mr. Davies' CSR plan was accepted by the board.

Note that it is easier to pronounce *Mr. Davies'* than *Mr. Davies's*.

Contractions

Contractions are shortened words with a letter or letters omitted. They are often avoided in academic writing due to the perception that they can make the tone informal. Nonetheless, some writers use them; the choice to do so depends on the genre of writing, the reader(s), or the writer's personal preference.

Examples of Common Contractions

Negative Verbs	Subjects + Auxiliary Verbs
isn't (is not)	**I'm** (I am)
aren't (are not)	**I've** (I have)
hasn't (has not)	**you're** (you are)
haven't (have not)	**you've** (you have)
don't (do not)	**she's** (she is)
won't (will not)	**he'll** (he will)
wouldn't (would not)	**they're** (they are)
shouldn't (should not)	**they'd** (they would)

Numbers may also be contracted, specifically, in abbreviated forms of years, used in less formal English:

> During the **'90s** (During the 1990s)

Contraction Errors

The following are common errors to avoid when you use apostrophes in contractions.

***Its* and *it's*:** When *its* is used as a possessive, do not add an apostrophe. When *it's* is used as a contraction of *it is* or *it has*, add an apostrophe.

> ✓ The company is rebranding **its** logo.
>
> ✗ The company is rebranding **it's** logo.
>
> ✓ **It's** time we left.
>
> ✗ **Its** time we left.

***Whose* and *who's*:** Avoid confusing *whose* (a possessive relative pronoun) and *who's* (a contraction of *who is*).

> ✓ **Whose** idea are you using?
>
> ✗ **Who's** idea are you using?
>
> ✓ **Who's** been helping you with the proposal?
>
> ✗ **Whose** been helping you with the proposal?

Other possessive pronouns that never contain an apostrophe are *ours*, *yours*, *his*, *hers*, and *theirs*.

> ✓ The idea was **ours**.
>
> ✗ The idea was **our's**.

***Should've* and *should of*:** The contracted form of *should have* is *should've*. Some writers make the mistake of writing *should of* due to the similar pronunciation.

> ✓ We **should've** considered their proposal.
>
> ✗ We **should of** considered their proposal.

***Your* and *you're*:** *Your* is a possessive adjective. *You're* is the contraction of *you are*.

> ✓ It was **your** idea.
>
> ✗ It was **you're** idea.

✓ **You're** meeting us this afternoon.

✗ **Your** meeting us this afternoon.

Years in reference to periods, such as *the 1980s*: Many writers incorrectly add an apostrophe after years when referring to the decade.

✓ During the **1980s**, there was a global economic recession.

✗ During the **1980's**, there was a global economic recession.

TASK 3

Indicate whether the following sentences are correct or incorrect. If the sentence is incorrect, rewrite it.

1. Dealing with a glass ceiling can be a woman business leaders main hindrance to progress.

   ☐ correct   ☐ incorrect

   _____

   _____

2. The class's requests were dealt with by the course director.

   ☐ correct   ☐ incorrect

   _____

3. The classes' requests were dealt with by the course director.

   ☐ correct   ☐ incorrect

   _____

4. The marketing class analyzed the advertising of childrens products.

   ☐ correct   ☐ incorrect

   _____

   _____

5. The CEOs and managers roles in the company were very different.

   ☐ correct   ☐ incorrect

   _____

   _____

6. The United Arab Emirates oil reserves total almost 100 billion barrels.

   ☐ correct   ☐ incorrect

   _____

   _____

7. Is this anyones phone?

☐ correct ☐ incorrect

_____

8. Linda's office is the second on the left.

☐ correct ☐ incorrect

_____

9. Charles office is next to Lindas'.

☐ correct ☐ incorrect

_____

10. Dont be late for the meeting; your going to get an answer to your request for more staff.

☐ correct ☐ incorrect

_____

_____

11. Its time for the management to review it's procedures.

☐ correct ☐ incorrect

_____

TASK 4

The following paragraph contains no colons or apostrophes. Add them as required.

Richard Branson: Entrepreneur and Adventurer

Richard Branson, one of the worlds most famous entrepreneurs, set up Virgin Records in the early 70s in London, England. In the next 20 years, a radio station, an airline, and a phone company were added to the Virgin brand Virgin Radio, Virgin Atlantic Airways, and Virgin Mobile. By the middle of the 2000s, Bransons new company for space tourism, Virgin Galactic, was up and running. Branson has also caught peoples attention with his attempts at breaking world records, including an attempt to cross the Atlantic in a hot-air balloon. In 1987, Branson and a Swede, Per Lindstrand, set off to make the first transatlantic balloon flight. Branson and Lindstrands attempt went famously wrong when they had to jump into the ocean and be rescued. Branson was undeterred. His attitude to success and failure can be best summed up by the following quotation "Dont be embarrassed by your failures. Learn from them and start again."

My eLab

Find more exercises on colons and apostrophes online.

Function	Context	Examples
Colons		
To introduce a list or examples	After an independent clause *Do not use a colon when the list or examples are incorporated grammatically in the sentence.	Two key factors affect business in Africa: globalization and dominant Western business practices. *Two key factors affecting business in Africa are globalization and dominant Western business practices.
	After an independent clause, to create an economical style	**Less economical style:** In the above sections, I analyzed several factors related to business between Asia, Africa, and the West. First, I looked at strategies that . . . . Second, I focused on the effects of . . . . Finally, I considered the potential of crossvergence as opposed to . . . **More economical style:** In the above sections, I analyzed several factors related to business between Asia, Africa, and the West: strategies that . . ., the effects of . . ., and the potential of crossvergence as opposed to . . .
To introduce direct quotations	After an independent clause *Do not use a colon when the direct quotation is incorporated grammatically in the sentence.	Leadership assessments must be conducted as follows: "in a structured manner, primarily based on behavioral criteria" (Peus et al., 2012, p. 106). *Leadership assessments should "be conducted in a structured manner, primarily based on behavioral criteria" (Peus et al., 2012, p. 106).
To separate a main title and a subtitle	In titles of books, articles, and essays	Business Leadership in Africa: Rising to the Challenge Leadership Strategies in Chinese Corporations: Looking West or East?
Apostrophes		
To indicate possession	Singular nouns not ending in s **Rule:** Add 's.	Intercultural awareness can help **a business leader's decision-making** in international contexts.
	Singular nouns ending in s **Rule:** Add 's or only the apostrophe.	A clear marketing plan can promote **a business's/business' growth** in its initial years.
	Plural nouns ending in s **Rule:** Add only the apostrophe.	Intercultural awareness has an inevitable effect on **business leaders' beliefs**, values, and actions.
	Plural nouns not ending in s **Rule:** Add 's.	Many factors affect **women's chances** for advancement to leadership positions in international corporations.
	Two or more individual possessives **Rule:** Add 's to each possessive noun.	**Guo's** (2015) and **Li's** (2016) **analyses** of crossvergence in Asian contexts provide useful recommendations for international business leaders.
	Joint possessives **Rule:** Add 's only to the last possessive noun.	**Kim and Moon's** (2015) **analysis** of Corporate Social Responsibility (CSR) focuses on practices in several Asian countries.
	Place names ending with a plural noun that ends in s **Rule:** Add only the apostrophe.	**The Unites States' historical position** in support of free trade agreements may change in the next 20 years.
	Indefinite pronouns **Rule:** Add 's.	**Someone's bag** was left at the meeting.

Function	Context	Examples	
To indicate possession	Names not ending in *s* **Rule:** Add *'s.*	**Lee's CSR plan** was accepted by the board.	
	Names ending in *s* **Rule:** Add *'s* or only the apostrophe.	**Carlos's/Carlos' CSR plan** was accepted by the board.	
Contractions	Negative verbs	**isn't** (is not) **aren't** (are not) **hasn't** (has not) **haven't** (have not)	**don't** (do not) **won't** (will not) **wouldn't** (would not) **shouldn't** (should not)
	Subject + auxiliary verbs	**I'm** (I am) **I've** (I have) **you're** (you are) **you've** (you have)	**she's** (she is) **he'll** (he will) **they're** (they are) **they'd** (they would)
	Abbreviated forms of years (less formal)	During the **'90s** (During the 1990s)	
Avoiding contraction errors	*its* versus *it's*	The company is rebranding **its** logo. **It's** time we left.	
	whose versus *who's*	**Whose** idea are you using? **Who's** been helping you with the proposal?	
	Other possessive pronouns: *ours, yours, his, hers, theirs* **Rule:** No apostrophe.	The idea was **ours**.	
	should've versus *should of*	We **should've** considered their proposal.	
	your versus *you're*	It was **your** idea. **You're** meeting us this afternoon.	
	Years referring to a decade **Rule:** No apostrophe.	During the **1980s**, there was a global economic recession.	

SENTENCE FRAGMENTS, COMMA SPLICES, AND RUN-ON SENTENCES

Sentence Fragments

A sentence fragment is an incomplete sentence because it lacks at least one required component of an independent clause. The following sections describe the three most common types of sentence fragment.

Dependent Clause Written as a Complete Sentence

> Even though the aims of the fair trade movement are laudable.

The sentence begins with the subordinator *even though*, which makes the clause dependent. In informal conversation or digital communication, this type of sentence fragment is commonly used as a sentence. However, in academic writing, it needs to be corrected in one of the following two ways.

Remove the subordinator:

> ~~Even though~~ The aims of the fair trade movement are laudable.

OR

Connect the dependent clause to an independent clause, forming a complex sentence:

> Even though the aims of the fair trade movement are laudable, **it still needs to reform**.

Sentence without a Verb

> The slow food movement a challenge to fast-food culture.

This sentence fragment would work well as a headline of a news article if a colon was added:

> The slow food movement: a challenge to fast-food culture

However, to become a complete sentence, the fragment needs a verb:

> The slow food movement **represents** a challenge to fast-food culture.

Sentence without a Subject

> Gave the presentation on rehabilitation last night!

This type of sentence fragment is common in informal digital communication, for example, on social networking sites. However, in academic writing, a sentence needs a subject:

> **She** gave the presentation on rehabilitation last night.

Note also the removal of the exclamation mark in formal academic writing.

TASK 1

Correct the five sentence fragments below so that they become complete sentences.

1. Despite local farmers receiving a higher price for fair trade products.

   _____

   _____

2. Fast-food culture spreading worldwide.

   _____

   _____

3. Excessive fast-food consumption health problems in later life.

   _____

   _____

4. Discussed trading issues between southern Africa and the EU yesterday!

   _____

   _____

5. Because intermediaries make considerable profits in the fair trade chain.

   _____

   _____

Comma Splices

Comma splices are the result of the incorrect separation of two independent clauses with a comma instead of a semicolon or period.

Two Independent Clauses Separated by a Comma

> Excessive fast-food consumption can lead to weight gain, it can also cause health problems in later life.

To correct the comma splice, replace the comma with a period or semicolon. In this case, the semicolon is preferable because the two clauses are closely related.

> Excessive fast-food consumption can lead to weight gain**;** it can also cause health problems in later life.

> Excessive fast-food consumption can lead to weight gain**. It** can also cause health problems in later life.

Another way to correct the comma splice is to form a compound sentence, using *and* or *not only*:

> Excessive fast-food consumption can lead to weight gain, **and** it can cause health problems in later life.

> **Not only** can excessive fast-food consumption lead to weight gain, it can also cause health problems in later life.

Two Independent Clauses Separated by a Conjunctive Adverb with a Comma

> Local farmers receive a higher price for fair trade products, however, many still live in poverty.

To correct the comma splice, replace the comma at the end of the first independent clause with a semicolon or period. Again, the semicolon is preferable in this case because the two clauses are closely related.

> Local farmers receive a higher price for fair trade products**;** however, many still live in poverty.

> Local farmers receive a higher price for fair trade products**.** **However**, many still live in poverty.

You can also correct the comma splice by rewriting the sentence with a coordinator such as *but* or *yet* to form a compound sentence:

> Local farmers receive a higher price for fair trade products, **but/yet** many still live in poverty.

A third way to correct the comma splice is to rewrite the sentence with a subordinator such as *although* or *while* to form a complex sentence:

> **Although/While** local farmers receive a higher price for fair trade products, many still live in poverty.

Comma Splices and Genre

In some non-academic genres of writing, for example, literary writing and journalism, comma splices are used and deemed acceptable. Comma splices are also common in informal communication.

TASK 2

Correct the four comma splices below, using at least two of the methods described above. Use a semicolon rather than a period to join independent clauses with closely related ideas.

1. The Mediterranean diet has been shown to reduce the incidence of cardio-vascular disease, it may also prevent certain types of cancer.

   _____

   _____

   _____

   _____

2. Local farmers receive a higher price for fair trade products, therefore, consumers have to pay a premium at the supermarket.

   _____

   _____

   _____

   _____

3. Fast-food culture has grown worldwide due to lifestyle changes and marketing, nonetheless, traditional food is still preferred in many countries around the globe.

_____

_____

_____

_____

4. Today's international business leaders need to understand many different cultures, this is easier if they speak several languages.

_____

_____

_____

_____

Run-On Sentences

A run-on sentence is a sentence in which two or more independent clauses are joined without punctuation. Run-on sentences should be corrected in the same ways as the comma splices above.

> Excessive fast-food consumption can lead to weight gain it can also cause health problems in later life.

In the example above, there is no punctuation between the first independent clause, ending with *weight gain*, and the second one, beginning with *it*.

> The Mediterranean diet has been shown to reduce the incidence of cardiovascular disease it may also prevent certain types of cancer.

Here there is no punctuation between the first independent clause, ending with *cardiovascular disease*, and the second one, beginning with *it*.

Correct run-on sentences by adding a semicolon or period, or by modifying the sentence structure, as shown above in the section on comma splices.

TASK 3

Correct the following run-on sentences by applying at least two of the methods you have studied in this unit.

1. Fast-food consumption is on the rise worldwide young people in many countries are now eating more fast food and less local food.

_____

_____

_____

_____

2. The slow food movement promotes healthy and ethical eating it emerged as a reaction to the spread of fast-food culture.

_____

_____

_____

_____

TASK 4

The paragraph below contains sentence fragments, comma splices, and run-on sentences. Rewrite the paragraph, correcting the errors by applying the methods you have studied in this unit.

The Mediterranean Diet

The Mediterranean diet gets its name, unsurprisingly, from the food eaten in countries surrounding the Mediterranean Sea. Even though many of these foods are also eaten elsewhere in the world. The diet is characterized by high consumption of extra virgin olive oil, whole grains, green vegetables, and fresh fruit, dairy products and fish tend to be consumed moderately. Red meat and saturated fat are consumed much less. As are processed foods. Another important feature of the Mediterranean diet is a social dimension, meals are often eaten together as a family unit. Not in front of the TV or during a 10-minute lunch break. A number of studies have found that the Mediterranean diet can prevent heart disease, cancer, and diabetes in later life it has also been found to increase longevity.

_____

_____

_____

_____

_____

_____

_____

_____

_____

My eLab

Find more exercises on sentence fragments, comma splices, and run-on sentences online.

SENTENCE FRAGMENTS, COMMA SPLICES, AND RUN-ON SENTENCES

Problem	Examples	Correction Methods
Sentence Fragments		
Dependent clause written as a complete sentence	Even though the aims of the fair trade movement are laudable.	a) Remove the subordinator: The aims of the fair trade movement are laudable. b) Form a complex sentence: Even though the aims of the fair trade movement are laudable, **it still needs to reform**.
Sentence without a verb	The slow food movement a challenge to fast-food culture.	Add a verb: The slow food movement **represents** a challenge to fast-food culture.
Sentence without a subject	Gave the presentation on rehabilitation last night!	Add a subject: **She** gave the presentation on rehabilitation last night.
Comma Splices		
Two independent clauses separated by a comma	Excessive fast-food consumption can lead to weight gain, it can also cause health problems in later life.	a) Replace the comma with a semicolon or period: Excessive fast-food consumption can lead to weight gain; it can also cause health problems in later life. (preferable because the ideas are closely related) Excessive fast-food consumption can lead to weight gain. **It** can also cause health problems in later life. b) Form a compound sentence with *and* or *not only*: Excessive fast-food consumption can lead to weight gain, **and** it can cause health problems in later life. **Not only** can excessive fast-food consumption lead to weight gain, it can also cause health problems in later life.
Two independent clauses separated by a conjunctive adverb with a comma	Local farmers receive a higher price for fair trade products, however, many still live in poverty.	a) Replace the first comma with a semicolon or period: Local farmers receive a higher price for fair trade products; however, many still live in poverty. Local farmers receive a higher price for fair trade products. **However**, many still live in poverty. b) Form a compound sentence, adding a coordinator: Local farmers receive a higher price for fair trade products, **but/yet** many still live in poverty. c) Form a complex sentence, adding a subordinator: **Although/While** local farmers receive a higher price for fair trade products, many still live in poverty.
Run-On Sentences		
No punctuation joining independent clauses	a) Excessive fast-food consumption can lead to weight gain it can also cause health problems in later life. b) The Mediterranean diet has been shown to reduce the incidence of cardiovascular disease it may also prevent certain types of cancer.	Replace the comma with a semicolon or period, or modify the sentence structure (as for comma splices): a) Excessive fast-food consumption can lead to weight gain; it can also cause health problems in later life. b) **Not only** has the Mediterranean diet been shown to reduce the incidence of cardiovascular disease, it may also prevent certain types of cancer.

SUBJECT-VERB AGREEMENT

Subject-verb agreement means that subjects and their corresponding verbs should agree. In other words, if the subject is singular, the verb should be in a singular form; if the subject is plural, the verb should be in a plural form. While this may seem simple, there are some rules to learn to ensure that subjects and verbs agree consistently and accurately in your writing. The examples below illustrate some common rules for subject-verb agreement. The subjects are underlined and the corresponding verbs, in bold.

Basic Rules

For main verbs in the present tense, except irregular verbs such as *to be*, the third-person singular form requires an *s*. The other forms do not.

> <u>3D printing</u> **involves** using plastic or metal powders to create copies of objects.
>
> <u>3D printers</u> **form** thousands of horizontal layers to create objects.

For tenses with auxiliary verbs—for example, perfect, continuous, and future tenses—only the auxiliary verb agrees with the subject. Modal auxiliary verbs, however, do not change form in the third-person singular.

> In the last 10 years, <u>air pollution</u> **has damaged** more local environments.
>
> <u>Air pollutants</u> **are having** a particularly negative effect on urban environments.
>
> <u>Pollutant levels in the EU</u> **will** most likely **fall** further in the next decade.
>
> <u>Air pollution</u> **may rise** further if no action is taken.

Compound Subjects

A compound subject is made up of two or more nouns or pronouns, for example, A and B, X or Y.

Compound Subjects with *And*

If the subject of the sentence comprises two or more nouns or pronouns plus *and*, use the plural form of the verb:

> <u>Ammonia and nitrogen dioxide</u> **are** two major air pollutants.
>
> <u>Pollution, pesticides, and fast food</u> **have been linked** to ill health in children.

In some cases, however, two nouns joined by *and* represent a single idea and require a singular verb:

> <u>Research and development</u> into reducing air pollution **is** ongoing.

Compound Subjects with *Or* and *Nor*

If the subject of the sentence comprises two or more singular nouns or pronouns joined by *or* or *nor*, use the singular form of the verb:

> Fast food or lack of a balanced diet often **leads** to ill health in children.

> Neither fast food nor unhealthy eating fully **explains** why children become ill.

If the compound subject is made up of a combination of singular and plural nouns joined by *or* or *nor*, the verb should agree with the nearest noun or pronoun in the subject:

> Fast food or unhealthy eating habits often **lead** to ill health in children.

Compound Subjects with *As Well As* and *Along With*

If the compound subject is formed by two or more nouns or pronouns joined by *as well as* or *along with*, the corresponding verb should agree with the first noun in the subject. Compare the following sentences:

> Fast food, unhealthy eating, and lack of exercise **are** bad for children's health.

> Fast food, along with unhealthy eating and lack of exercise, **is** bad for children's health.

Indefinite Pronouns

Indefinite pronouns are pronouns that do not refer to a specific person, thing, or place, for example, *everyone*, *somebody*, *each*, and *neither*. Sentences with indefinite pronouns acting as subjects follow specific rules of subject-verb agreement.

Use a Singular Verb

When they form the subject of a sentence, the following indefinite pronouns require a singular verb: *another, anybody, anyone, anything, each (one), either, everybody, everyone, everything, neither, nobody, no one, nothing, one, other, somebody, someone,* and *something*.

> In my opinion, nothing **is** impossible with 3D printing.

> Something **isn't working** properly in the machine.

Use a Plural Verb

Use the plural form of the verb in sentences with the following indefinite pronouns as subjects: *both, few, many, others,* and *several*.

> A variety of objects today are made by 3D printing; many **are** prototypes.

> The workshop is now equipped with a 3D printer as well as a multifunction printer; both **require** regular maintenance.

Use a Singular or a Plural Verb

Some indefinite pronouns, for example, *all, none,* and *some*, may be followed by a singular or plural verb, depending on the context (whether they refer to a singular or plural noun).

> All of the objects on display **were made** with a 3D printer.

> All of the machinery **is** less than a year old.

Collective Nouns

Collective nouns are used to refer to groups of things or people. In most cases, they require singular verbs (although plural verbs may be used in less formal contexts). Some examples of collective nouns are *class, crowd, family, government, group, organization, population,* and *team.*

> The Environmental Sciences class **is going** on a field trip next week.
>
> The Environmental Sciences class **are collecting** samples. (informal)
>
> The government **has increased** funding for non-polluting fuel systems.

Plural verbs can also be used with collective nouns, when the members of the group are acting as individuals rather than together.

> The Environmental Sciences class **are doing** their individual projects.

TASK 1

Some of the following sentences have incorrect, or informal, subject-verb agreement. Identify the incorrect sentences and rewrite them.

1. In the last 10 years, air pollution phenomena has increased.

   ☐ correct   ☐ incorrect

   _____

2. The anti-pollution criteria for air filters has become much stricter.

   ☐ correct   ☐ incorrect

   _____

3. Neither stricter regulation nor technological development have halted damaging emissions.

   ☐ correct   ☐ incorrect

   _____

4. Stricter regulation, along with heavier fines, has only had a minimal effect.

   ☐ correct   ☐ incorrect

   _____

5. Both of the factories were absolved of any responsibility.

   ☐ correct   ☐ incorrect

   _____

6. The government are increasing funding for non-polluting fuel systems.

   ☐ correct   ☐ incorrect

   _____

Placing the Verb before the Subject

In some sentences, the verb is placed before the subject, for example, with the phrases *there is*, *there are*, *here is*, and *here are*. In such sentences, the verb agrees with the following noun or noun phrase:

> Here **is** <u>the exam schedule</u> for the Environmental Sciences class.

> Here **are** <u>the exam guidelines</u> for the Environmental Sciences class.

Nouns That Look Plural but Require Singular Verbs

Some nouns look plural but require singular verbs, for example, *news*, fields of study (*mathematics, economics*), expressions of time and distance (*three weeks, five hundred metres*), and amounts of currency (*20 dollars*).

> <u>The latest news about improvements in bioprinting</u> **is** promising.

> <u>Three weeks</u> **is** a long time to wait for exam results.

> <u>Five million dollars</u> **was invested** in bioprinting for regenerative science last year.

Note, however, that plural forms of currency require plural verbs when referring to the *type* of currency:

> <u>Euros</u> **are required** in many countries in Europe.

Avoid Common Errors

Be careful to make the verb agree with the subject when you write sentences containing the following structures.

One of the

> <u>One of the worst causes of air pollution</u> ~~are~~ **is** nitrogen dioxide.

> <u>One of the worst causes of air pollution</u> ~~are~~ **is** nitrogen oxides.

Nouns That Always Require a Plural Verb

> <u>The police</u> sometimes ~~arrests~~ **arrest** serious polluters.

> <u>People</u> ~~is~~ **are** responsible for recycling their own waste.

A Plural Noun Adjacent to the Verb

> <u>My friend who works for two environmental consultants</u> ~~are~~ **is** overworked.

> <u>Pollution from coal-fired power plants</u> ~~damage~~ **damages** air quality.

TASK 2

Some of the following sentences have incorrect subject-verb agreement. Identify the incorrect sentences and rewrite them.

1. There's air pollution in most urban centres.

   ☐ correct ☐ incorrect

   _____

2. There's many reasons for governments to invest in recycling.

   ☐ correct   ☐ incorrect

   _____

3. The news about the 3D printing for hip transplants were incredible.

   ☐ correct   ☐ incorrect

   _____

4. Five million euros have been raised so far for local hospitals.

   ☐ correct   ☐ incorrect

   _____

TASK 3

Correct the subject-verb agreement errors in the following paragraph.

3D Printing

One of the most useful technological innovations of recent years have been 3D printing. Everyday household objects, machine parts, and even surgical implants has been constructed by 3D printing. Some experts have gone as far as stating that nothing is impossible with these machines. One of the most beneficial uses of 3D printing are surgical implants. Here is some examples of the types of implants that can be printed three-dimensionally. Recently, in Australia, surgeons successfully implanted a 3D-printed neck vertebra into a patient suffering from cancer. Another common use are dental implants. In fact, several million dollars have been spent on developing these technological advances. International collaboration, as well as local fundraising initiatives, has helped the development of the technology.

_____
_____
_____
_____
_____
_____
_____
_____
_____
_____
_____

My eLab ✎

Find more exercises on subject-verb agreement online.

Context	Rule/Explanation	Examples
Basic rules	a) Present-tense verbs, except irregular verbs (e.g., *to be*): the third-person singular form requires an *s*. b) Tenses with auxiliary verbs: only the auxiliary verb agrees with the subject. (Modal auxiliary verbs: No change of form in the third-person singular.)	a) <u>3D printing</u> **involves** using plastic or metal powders to create copies. <u>3D printers</u> **form** thousands of horizontal layers to create objects. b) Recently, <u>air pollution</u> **has damaged** more local environments. <u>Air pollutants</u> **are having** a negative effect on urban life. <u>Pollutant levels in the EU</u> **will fall** further in the future. <u>Air pollution</u> **may rise** further if no action is taken.
Compound subjects made up of two or more nouns or pronouns	a) With *and*: use plural verbs. b) With *or/nor* and singular nouns/pronouns: use singular verbs. c) With *or/nor* and a combination of singular/plural nouns: the verb agrees with the nearest noun/pronoun. d) With *as well as* and *along with*: the verb agrees with the first noun in the subject.	a) <u>Ammonia and nitrogen dioxide</u> **are** two major air pollutants. <u>Pollution, pesticides, and fast food</u> **have been linked** to ill health. b) <u>Fast food or lack of a balanced diet</u> often **leads** to ill health. <u>Neither fast food nor unhealthy eating</u> **explains** why children become ill. c) <u>Fast food or unhealthy eating habits</u> often **lead** to ill health. d) <u>Fast food, along with unhealthy eating,</u> **is** bad for children's health.
Indefinite pronouns	a) Use a singular verb with *another, any-body/one/thing, each, either, every-body/one/thing, neither, nobody, no one, nothing, one, other, some-body/one/thing*. b) Use a plural verb with *both, few, many, others, several*. c) Use either a singular or a plural verb with *all, none,* and *some*.	a) In my opinion, <u>nothing</u> **is** impossible with 3D printing. <u>Something</u> **isn't working** properly in the machine. b) A variety of objects today are made by 3D printing; <u>many</u> **are** prototypes. c) <u>All of the objects on display</u> **were made** with a 3D printer. <u>All of the machinery</u> **is** less than a year old.
Collective nouns	a) Use a singular verb with *class, family, government, team*, etc. b) Use a plural verb when referring to individual members of the group.	a) <u>The Environmental Sciences class</u> **is going** on a field trip next week. b) <u>The Environmental Sciences class</u> **are doing** their individual projects.
Verb before the subject	The verb agrees with the following noun.	Here **is** <u>the exam schedule</u>. Here **are** <u>the exam guidelines</u>.
Nouns that look plural but require singular verbs	a) *news* b) Fields of study (*mathematics*), expressions of time/distance (*three weeks, five hundred metres*), and amounts of money *BUT* c) Types of currency, in the plural, require a plural verb.	a) <u>The latest news about improvements in bioprinting</u> **is** promising. b) <u>Three weeks</u> **is** a long time to wait for exam results. <u>Five million dollars</u> **was invested** in regenerative science last year. c) <u>Euros</u> **are required** in many countries in Europe.
Errors to avoid	a) *One of the . . .* + **singular verb** + singular/plural noun b) *The police/people* + **plural verb** c) Avoid conjugating the verb with the nearest noun.	a) <u>One of the worst causes of air pollution</u> ~~are~~ **is** nitrogen dioxide. <u>One of the worst causes of air pollution</u> ~~are~~ **is** nitrogen oxides. b) <u>The police</u> sometimes ~~arrests~~ **arrest** serious polluters. c) <u>My friend who works for two environmental consultants</u> ~~are~~ **is** overworked.

CONDITIONAL SENTENCES

Conditional sentences have two clauses: the main clause and the conditional clause (also known as the *if clause*). In a conditional sentence, the action or state in the main clause will occur only if a condition in the *if* clause is met. To understand and use conditional sentences correctly, answer the following three questions:

- **Concept:** Is the action or state real or imaginary, possible or impossible?
- **Time idea:** Is the time idea past, present, future, or any time?
- **Form:** How are verb tenses used in the two clauses?

There are three main types of conditional sentence: first, second, and third conditional. In addition, there is a form called the *zero conditional*, and there are combinations of mixed conditionals.

Zero Conditional

In zero-conditional sentences, the action in the main clause always happens. This conditional form is used for factual statements:

> If international students **take** courses at Central University, they **pay** higher tuition fees.

Concept: Factual reality

Time idea: Any time

Verb forms: Present tense (*if* clause) and present tense (main clause)

In the example above, the writer believes that all international students always pay higher tuition fees if they take courses at the university.

First Conditional

The first conditional is used for real possibilities:

> If the college **implements** its mobile learning strategy, most students **will be** pleased.

Concept: Real possibility

Time idea: Present to future

Verb forms: Present tense (*if* clause) and future tense (main clause)

In the example of the first conditional, the writer believes that the actions or states in the two clauses have a real chance of occurring. This statement would be appropriate in the context of a college that has consulted students about introducing mobile learning, leading students to believe it is a real possibility.

Second Conditional

The second conditional is used for imaginary, hypothetical actions and states:

> If the college **implemented** a mobile learning plan, most students **would be** pleased.

Concept: Imaginary, hypothetical reality

Time idea: Present to future

Verb forms: Past tense (*if* clause) and *would* + base form of the verb (main clause)

> Note that the standard second-conditional form of the verb *to be* is *were* for all persons, including *if I were* and *if he/she/it were*.

The second-conditional sentence has the same time idea as the first-conditional example on the preceding page. However, the writer is thinking hypothetically, imagining what would happen if the college were to introduce a mobile learning plan. This statement matches the context of a college that students feel has no stated intention of introducing mobile learning.

Third Conditional

The third conditional is used for ideas about changing the past, which is impossible:

> If my college **had provided** more courses, I **would have graduated** in four instead of six years.

Concept: Impossible reality

Time idea: Past

Verb forms: Past perfect (*if* clause) and *would have* + past participle (main clause)

The writer is looking back at her college years and wondering why it took six years to graduate. She comes to the conclusion that the college did not provide enough courses, hence the statement. The third conditional is often used when people look back on the past and imagine how things might have been different.

TASK 1

Read the following conditional sentences and answer the questions that follow.

1. If you don't study, you fail.

   a) Is the speaker presenting failure as a possible result of not studying or as a factual consequence?

   _____

   b) Is the sentence a zero or first conditional? _____

   c) Does the statement read as encouragement or as a warning?

   _____

2. If you don't study hard, you'll fail.

   a) Does the speaker believe not studying and failure are possible or imaginary?

   _____

b) Is the sentence a first or second conditional? _____

c) Would the speaker be more likely to say this to a good or bad student?

_____

3. If you studied harder, you'd pass.

a) Does the speaker believe studying harder and passing are possible or imaginary?

_____

b) Is the sentence a first or second conditional? _____

c) Would the speaker be more likely to say this to a good or bad student?

_____

4. If I had studied harder, I would have passed with an A.

a) Is the speaker describing a situation that is possible or impossible to change?

_____

b) Is the sentence a second or third conditional? _____

c) Do you think the speaker is looking back with regret or imagining future possibilities?

_____

Mixed Conditionals

It is also possible, and quite common, to mix the *unreal* second and third conditional forms by combining an idea of impossible past with an imaginary present or future.

Combining Impossible Past with Imaginary Present

In the sentences below, the speaker is imagining how, if things had been different in the past (third conditional in the *if* clause), he or she would have more job opportunities in the present (second conditional in the main clause).

> If I **had studied** foreign languages at university, I**'d be** more employable now.
>
> I**'d be** more employable now if I **had studied** foreign languages at university.

> If the *if* clause comes second in a conditional sentence, there is no comma before *if*.

Combining Impossible Past with Imaginary Future

In the sentences below, the speaker is imagining how, if things had been different in the past (third conditional in the *if* clause), he or she would be able to start a new job in the future (second conditional in the main clause).

> If I **had studied** foreign languages at university, I think I**'d be starting** a job in Paris next month.
>
> I think I**'d be starting** a job in Paris next month if I **had studied** foreign languages at university.

Alternative Conditional Forms

Modal Auxiliary Verbs

It is possible to replace the auxiliary verbs in the main clause of first, second, and third conditionals with one of the four modal auxiliary verbs *may*, *might*, *could* or *should* to add a more nuanced sense of possibility or probability.

In first-conditional sentences, the use of *should* (sentence 1) adds a sense of future probability and positive expectation. The use of *may*, *might*, and *could* (sentences 2 and 3) adds a sense of present or future possibility.

1. If the college adopts mobile learning, most students **should** be pleased.
2. If the college adopts mobile learning, some students **may/might** be pleased.
3. If the college adopts mobile learning, it **could** have positive results.

In second-conditional sentences, the use of *might* and *could* adds a sense of present or future possibility:

If the college gave more tutorial support, more students **might/could** pass their exams.

In third-conditional sentences, the use of *might* and *could* adds a sense of past possibility. Note that it is not possible to use *should* in the main clause of a third-conditional sentence to express past probability.

If my college had provided more courses, I **might/could** have graduated in four instead of six years.

When, As Soon As, and Unless

Another variation of conditional sentences involves replacing *if* with *when*, *as soon as*, or *unless* in first-conditional sentences.

1. **When** the college adopts mobile learning, most students will be pleased.
2. **As soon as** m-learning is adopted, students will need to have smart phones.
3. **Unless** the college adopts mobile learning, exam results will continue to fall.

In sentence 1, the use of *when* suggests that mobile learning is *definitely* going to be adopted. In sentence 2, *as soon as* adds the idea that students will need to have smart phones *immediately after* the policy is implemented. In sentence 3, the use of *unless* means "if not": "if the college does not adopt mobile learning."

Should Instead of If

In first-conditional sentences, *should* can replace *if* to add a sense of formality:

1. **If** you require any assistance, please feel free to ask.
2. **Should** you require any assistance, please feel free to ask.

Sentence 2 is more formal than sentence 1. This form is often used in formal documents and letters.

Were and Was

In second-conditional sentences, *were* and *was* can be used in the *if* clause. *Were* is the standard form; *was* is informal.

If I **were** you, I would make use of the Student Learning Office.

If I **was** you, I would make use of the Student Learning Office.

Were To and *Was To*

In second-conditional sentences, *were to* and *was to* can also be used in the *if* clause:

1. If I graduated in three years, I would be amazed.
2. If I **were to** graduate in three years, I would be amazed.
3. If I **was to** graduate in three years, I would be amazed.

Sentence 1 is the most common form of second conditional, using the past-tense verb. Sentences 2 and 3 have the same meaning as sentence 1; the use of *were* in sentence 2 is standard while *was* in sentence 3 is informal.

Had I and *If I Had*

It is possible to use *had I/you/we/*etc., instead of *if I/you/we/*etc. *had*, in third-conditional sentences:

1. **If I had** studied foreign languages at university, I'd be more employable now.
2. **Had I** studied foreign languages at university, I'd be more employable now.

Sentences 1 and 2 have the same meaning. The use of *had I* in sentence 2 adds formality.

TASK 2

Follow the prompts and write a corresponding conditional sentence.

1. **Third conditional:** You are looking back and wondering how your life would have been different if you hadn't learned English as a child.

   _____

   _____

2. **Mixed conditional:** You are looking back and wondering what you would be doing now if you hadn't learned English as a child.

   _____

   _____

3. **Second conditional:** You are imagining how your life would be if you had to give up access to mobile devices for one month.

   _____

   _____

4. **Second conditional:** You are recommending to your boss, who is rather formal, to focus more on enjoying life and less on work.

   _____

   _____

5. **Second conditional:** You are recommending to your best friend to focus more on work and less on enjoying life.

_____

_____

6. **Zero conditional:** Explain what happens if you drop a smart phone in water.

_____

_____

7. **Second conditional:** Ask a group of colleagues how they would be affected if they gave up using their cellphones for one month; use *were to*.

_____

_____

8. **First conditional:** Explain to your friend that his or her smart phone will work better immediately after upgrading the operating system; use *as soon as*.

_____

_____

9. **First conditional:** Tell your classmates that they need to share ideas for the group project to get a good grade; use *unless*.

_____

_____

10. Explain to your friend that his or her smart phone will probably work better if he or she upgrades the operating system; you are optimistic.

_____

_____

11. Explain to your friend that his or her smart phone will possibly work better if he or she upgrades the operating system; you are not sure.

_____

_____

12. Advise your friend to change service provider to get better coverage on his or her phone; use *if I were you*.

_____

_____

My eLab 🖉

Find more exercises on conditional sentences online.

TASK 3

Practise using the different conditional forms you have learned in this unit by answering at least five of the questions below in a short paragraph.

1. When you look back at your previous studies, do you have any regrets?
2. When you graduate from your planned studies, what do you think you are likely to do next?
3. What would you love to do after graduating, but you think it is an unrealistic hope?
4. What do you plan to do immediately after class today?
5. What reassurance did your family give you recently for your future studies?
6. What warnings did they give you about your studies?
7. What will possibly happen if you pass your academic writing course with a top grade?
8. What do you think will probably happen during your first year at university?

_____

_____

_____

_____

_____

_____

_____

_____

_____

_____

_____

SUMMARY CONDITIONAL SENTENCES

Type of Conditional	Concept/Form	Examples
Zero conditional	**Concept:** Factual reality **Time idea:** Any time **Verb forms:** Present tense and present tense	If international students **take** courses at Central University, they **pay** higher tuition fees.
First conditional	**Concept:** Real possibility **Time idea:** Present to future **Verb forms:** Present tense and future tense	If the college **implements** its mobile learning strategy, most students **will be** pleased.
Second conditional	**Concept:** Imaginary, hypothetical reality **Time idea:** Present to future **Verb forms:** Past tense and *would* + base form of the verb	If the college **implemented** a mobile learning plan, most students **would be** pleased. If mobile learning **were** of use to me, I **would get** a smart phone.

Type of Conditional	Concept/Form	Examples
Third conditional	**Concept:** Impossible reality **Time idea:** Past **Verb forms:** Past perfect and *would have* + past participle	If my college **had provided** more courses, I **would have graduated** in four instead of six years.
Mixed conditionals	a) Impossible past (third conditional) + imaginary present (second conditional) b) Impossible past (third conditional) + imaginary future (second conditional)	a) If I **had studied** foreign languages at university, I**'d be** more employable now. b) If I **had studied** foreign languages at university, I think I**'d be starting** a job in Paris next month.
Alternative Conditional Forms ♦		
First conditional + modal auxiliary verbs	a) *Should*: sense of future probability and positive expectation b) & c) *May*, *might*, and *could*: sense of present or future possibility	a) If the college adopts mobile learning, most students **should** be pleased. b) If the college adopts mobile learning, some students **may**/**might** be pleased. c) If the college adopts mobile learning, it **could** have positive results.
Second conditional + modal auxiliary verbs	*Might* and *could*: sense of present or future possibility	If the college gave more tutorial support, more students **might**/**could** pass their exams.
Third conditional + modal auxiliary verbs	*Might* and *could*: sense of past possibility Note: It is not possible to use *should* in the main clause of a third-conditional sentence.	If my college had provided more courses, I **might**/**could** have graduated in four instead of six years.
First conditional with *when*, *as soon as*, and *unless*	a) *When*: suggestion that event is **definitely** going to happen b) *As soon as*: idea that event will happen **immediately** c) *Unless*: same meaning as "if not"	a) **When** the college adopts mobile learning, most students will be pleased. b) **As soon as** m-learning is adopted, students will need to have smart phones. c) **Unless** the college adopts mobile learning, exam results will continue to fall.
First conditional with *should*	• More formal than with *if* • Often used in formal documents and letters	**Should** you require any assistance, please feel free to ask. (**If** you require any assistance, . . .)
Second conditional with *was*	• Less formal than *were* • Non-standard form	If I **was** you, I would make use of the Student Learning Office. (If I **were** you, . . .)
Second conditional with *were/was to*	• Same meaning as the more usual form with past-tense verb: "If I graduated in three years, . . ." • The use of *were to* adds formality.	a) If I **were to** graduate in three years, I would be amazed. b) If I **was to** graduate in three years, I would be amazed.
Third conditional with *had I*	More formal than *if I had*	**Had I** studied foreign languages at university, I'd be more employable now. (**If I had** studied foreign languages at university, . . .)

PARALLEL STRUCTURE

The term parallel structure (also known as *parallelism*) refers to the use of the same types of words and phrases by writers when they provide a series of items or examples in a sentence. In academic writing, the use of parallel structure adds cohesion to sentences and accords equal importance to ideas. Consider the examples below:

1. Solar energy is cheap, clean, renewable, and effective. (parallel)
2. Solar energy is cheap, clean, renewable, and delivers power efficiently. (not parallel)

Sentence 1 has parallel structure because each of the four items in the series is an adjective: *cheap*, *clean*, *renewable*, and *effective*. Sentence 2 does not have parallel structure because three of the four items are adjectives (*cheap*, *clean*, *renewable*), but the fourth is a verb phrase (*delivers power efficiently*).

1. Solar power costs less than other energy forms, uses natural energy sources, and delivers power efficiently. (parallel)
2. Solar power has three main benefits: it costs less than other energy forms, uses natural energy sources, and efficient power delivery. (not parallel)

Sentence 1 has parallel structure because each of the three benefits includes a verb: ***costs*** *less than other energy forms*, ***uses*** *natural energy sources*, and ***delivers*** *power efficiently*. Sentence 2 does not have parallel structure because the first two benefits include verbs while the third is a noun phrase: *efficient power delivery*.

Different Forms of Parallel Structure

The following are the most common parts of a sentence that may, or may not, form parallel structures.

Adjectives and Adverbs

1. Solar energy is **cheap**, **clean**, **renewable**, and **effective**. (parallel)
2. The new wind power policy was implemented **quickly**, **fairly**, and **efficiently**. (parallel)
3. The new wind power policy was implemented **fairly**, **efficiently**, and **in two years**. (not parallel)

Sentence 1 has parallel structure because each item is an adjective. Sentence 2 also has parallel structure because each item is a single-word adverb. Sentence 3 does not have parallel structure because two single-word adverbs are followed by a preposition phrase: *in two years*.

A gerund is a verb + *ing* that functions as a noun in a sentence, and an infinitive is the form of a verb that follows *to*.

Gerunds and Infinitives

1. Nuclear energy is often applauded for **reducing** carbon emissions, **providing** a reliable energy supply, and **cutting** fuel bills. (parallel)

2. All energy providers aim to **reduce** carbon emissions, **provide** a reliable energy supply, and **cut** fuel bills. (parallel)

3. Nuclear energy is often applauded for **reducing** carbon emissions, **the provision** of reliable energy, and **because it cuts fuel bills**. (not parallel)

The structure is parallel in sentences 1 and 2 because the actions are expressed as gerunds and infinitives, respectively. The structure of sentence 3 is not parallel because the actions are expressed as a gerund, a noun phrase, and a clause.

Verbs Followed by a Gerund or an Infinitive

When a verb can be followed by either a gerund or an infinitive, keep the structure parallel.

1. Due to public pressure, energy suppliers began **consulting** with local communities, **implementing** environmental audits, and **promoting** the benefits of cheap energy. (parallel)

2. Due to public pressure, energy suppliers began to **consult** with local communities, **implement** environmental audits, and **promote** the benefits of cheap energy. (parallel)

3. Due to public pressure, energy suppliers began **consulting** with local communities, **implementing** environmental audits, and **to promote** the benefits of cheap energy. (not parallel)

Sentences 1 and 2 have parallel structure because they contain series of gerunds and infinitives, respectively. The structure of sentence 3 is not parallel because the series contains two gerunds, followed by an infinitive: *to promote*.

Verb Phrases

1. Solar power **costs less than other energy forms**, **uses natural energy sources**, and **delivers power efficiently**. (parallel)

2. Solar power is popular because it **uses natural energy sources**, **delivers power efficiently**, and **for its low long-term costs**. (not parallel)

Sentence 1 has parallel structure because each item is a verb phrase. Sentence 2 does not have parallel structure because the first two items are verb phrases while the third is a preposition phrase: *for its low long-term costs*.

TASK 1

Indicate whether the structure of the following sentences is parallel or not. Underline any words, phrases, or clauses that break the parallel structure.

1. Solar energy requires large areas of land, produces power intermittently, and takes time to yield financial returns.

   ☐ parallel   ☐ not parallel

2. Solar energy is environmentally friendly, renewable, and does not pollute the air.

   ☐ parallel   ☐ not parallel

3. The new wind power station was set up within three years, built on budget, and welcomed by the local community.

    ☐ parallel   ☐ not parallel

4. This proves that wind power can be set up quickly, cost-effective, and welcomed by communities.

    ☐ parallel   ☐ not parallel

TASK 2

Rewrite any sentences that do not have parallel structure. Not all of the sentences require changes.

1. Solar energy requires large areas of land, cannot produce power continuously, and is slow to yield financial returns.

    _____

    _____

2. The new wind power station was set up within three years, popular with the local community, and built on budget.

    _____

    _____

3. Solar power has three main benefits: it is more carbon-friendly than other energy forms, it does not pollute the air, and its popularity with the public.

    _____

    _____

4. The new-generation nuclear power station was built quickly, fairly, and efficiently.

    _____

    _____

5. The energy produced from the nuclear power plant will reduce carbon emissions, provide a reliable energy supply, and cut fuel bills.

    _____

    _____

6. The owners of the plant have three key aims: to provide power to hundreds of thousands of homes, to meet government production targets, and low carbon emissions.

    _____

    _____

7. Solar panels are cheap, efficient, and do not harm the environment.

_____

_____

8. Many environmentalist groups are known for opposing nuclear energy, promoting solar power, and their support for other renewable sources.

_____

_____

Find more exercises on parallel structure online.

TASK 3

When you have finished the first draft of the writing task for Chapter 12 (see p. 264), reread your draft to look for parallel structure, or lack of it. You can do this by looking specifically for series of items and for keywords such as *and* and *or*. Correct any sentences that lack parallel structure.

SUMMARY PARALLEL STRUCTURE

Parts of the Sentence	Parallel Examples	Non-Parallel Example with Explanation
Adjectives and adverbs	Solar energy is **cheap, clean, renewable,** and **effective**. The new wind power policy was implemented **quickly, fairly,** and **efficiently**.	The new wind power policy was implemented **fairly, efficiently,** and **in two years**. The structure is not parallel because two single-word adverbs are followed by a preposition phrase: *in two years*.
Gerunds and infinitives	Nuclear energy is often applauded for **reducing carbon emissions, providing a reliable energy supply,** and **cutting fuel bills**. All energy providers aim to **reduce carbon emissions, provide a reliable energy supply,** and **cut fuel bills**.	Nuclear energy is often applauded for **reducing carbon emissions, the provision of reliable energy,** and **because it cuts fuel bills**. The structure is not parallel because the items in the series are a gerund, a noun phrase, and a clause.
Verbs followed by a gerund or an infinitive	Due to public pressure, energy suppliers began **consulting** with local communities, **implementing** environmental audits, and **promoting** the benefits of cheap energy. Due to public pressure, energy suppliers began to **consult** with local communities, **implement** environmental audits, and **promote** the benefits of cheap energy.	Due to public pressure, energy suppliers began **consulting** with local communities, **implementing** environmental audits, and **to promote** the benefits of cheap energy. The structure is not parallel because two gerunds are followed by an infinitive: *to promote*. When a verb can be followed by either a gerund or an infinitive, keep the structure parallel.
Verb phrases	Solar power **costs less than other energy forms, uses natural energy sources,** and **delivers power efficiently**.	Solar power is popular because it **uses natural energy sources, delivers power efficiently,** and **for its low long-term costs**. The structure is not parallel because two verb phrases are followed by a preposition phrase: *for its low long-term costs*.

MODAL AUXILIARY VERBS TO EXPRESS LIKELIHOOD AND OBLIGATION

Modality

Modal auxiliary verbs express different aspects of modality. The term *modality* refers to the attitude of writers or speakers when they are describing things. Common aspects of modality that are expressed with modal auxiliary verbs are likelihood, obligation, ability, permission, willingness, and necessity.

Other words and phrases in the English language also express modality; for example, *have to* and *ought to* can be used to express obligation. Although some linguists claim that such phrases are not modal auxiliary verbs, they are included in this unit in cases where they express degrees of modality.

When you write essays involving the analysis of problems and solutions, and evaluation, you need to be able to present attitudes clearly. For example, you need to express your view of actions as possible, probable, or certain; equally, if you are arguing that certain actions are required to solve a problem, you should make it clear whether you think there is a strong or mild obligation to apply these solutions.

In this unit, the focus is on modal auxiliary verbs that express likelihood and obligation. Remember that when writers or speakers express likelihood and obligation, they are expressing their attitude: whether they think something is, was, or will be possible, probable, or certain; and whether they believe that there is a strong or mild sense of obligation for something to happen.

Two Ways to Express Attitude

There are always two or more ways to write a sentence expressing modality. In the following examples, sentence 1 expresses likelihood or obligation using a modal auxiliary verb, and sentence 2 expresses the same idea in other terms.

Likelihood: Possibility

1. The government's new policies **may/might/could** protect linguistic minorities.
2. **I think** the government's new policies **will possibly** protect linguistic minorities.

Likelihood: Probability (with Positive or Optimistic Expectation)

1. The government's new policies **should** be successful.
2. **I think** the government's new policies **will probably** be successful.

Mild Obligation

1. Schools **should** do more to help students from all minority backgrounds.
2. **I believe** schools **have an obligation to** do more to help students from all minority backgrounds.

Strong Obligation

1. Schools **must** do more to help students from all minority backgrounds.
2. **I strongly believe** schools **have an obligation to** do more to help students from all minority backgrounds.

The examples above illustrate three important points to remember about modal auxiliary verbs:

1. There are always alternative ways of expressing modality.
2. Modal auxiliary verbs represent the subjective attitude of the speaker.
3. The same modal auxiliary verb can express different aspects of modality. For example, in the sentences above, *should* is used to express probability as well as mild obligation.

MODALITY # LIKELIHOOD

Use the following modal auxiliary verbs to express degrees of likelihood. Affirmative sentences are indicated by a + and negative sentences, by a −.

I'm Certain . . .

Will

Time Idea	Examples
Present	Who's texting you? + That **will be** my boss asking where I am. − It **won't be** my boss. She's on holiday this week.
Future	+ If someone calls later, it**'ll be** my boss. Tell her I'm on my way. − If someone calls later, it **won't be** my boss. She's on holiday this week.
Past	Someone called last night. + That **will have been** my boss. I was running late. − It **won't have been** my boss. She never calls at night.

Will is used in the examples above to express certainty. The certainty is based on the speaker's knowledge of the habits, routines, and characteristics of her boss.

Must

Time Idea	Examples
Present	Someone's at the door. + That **must be** my roommate. − That **can't be** my roommate.
Future	There is no future form of *must* for certainty.

Time Idea	Examples
Past	Someone called last night. + It **must have been** my roommate. − It **can't/couldn't have been** my roommate.

Must is used in the examples above to express certainty. Unlike *will*, *must* gives no indication of knowledge of others' habits, routines, and characteristics.

I Think It's Probable . . .

Should

Time Idea	Examples
Present	+ The projector **should be working**. Let's check. − There ***shouldn't be** any problems. The projector is brand new.
Future	+ You **should pass** the exam tomorrow. I'm confident you're ready. − You ***shouldn't have** any problems tomorrow. Be confident!
Past	+ You ***should have passed** the exam. What went wrong? − You ***shouldn't have failed** the exam. What went wrong?

Should is used in the examples above to express probability. The use of *should* for probability expresses an idea of positive or optimistic expectation. Avoid using it in other contexts; for example, if you thought that a friend is probably going to fail his exam, and you said "You should fail," it would sound like you wanted him to fail! Also note the examples marked by an asterisk (*). These examples could be misinterpreted because *should* is also used to express obligation.

I Think It's Possible . . .

May, Might, and Could

Time Idea	Examples
Present	+ You **may/might/could be** in the wrong classroom. Have you checked your planner? − The exam **may/might not be** in this building. Can you check your planner for me?
Future	+ You **may/might/could pass** the exam tomorrow. I think you have a chance. − You **may/might not pass** the exam tomorrow. Prepare yourself.
Past	+ You **may/might/could have passed** the exam, but you won't know your grade until the end of term. − You **may/might not have passed** the exam, so you should work hard on your term paper.

May, *might*, and *could* are used in the examples above to express possibility in the affirmative for all time ideas. However, only *may* and *might* can be used in the negative forms, not *could*. The three forms have similar degrees of certainty. *May* is the most common form used in academic writing as it carries a sense of formality.

TASK 1

Fill in the blanks in the sentences below with modal auxiliary verbs that express likelihood. Decide whether the form should be affirmative or negative and whether the time idea is present, future, or past. Use the verbs (and adverbs) in brackets, and follow the prompts in parentheses.

1. It _____ [be] easy moving to another country as an international student. (I'm sure it wasn't.)

2. You _____ [miss] your friends and family. (I'm certain you are.)

3. Working for a few years _____ [also be] an option. (I think it would have been possible.)

4. You _____ [experience] any problems getting used to life as a student here and succeeding in your studies. (I'm optimistic: I think it's probable that you won't.)

5. You _____ [even decide] to live and work here for a few years after you graduate. (I think it will be possible.)

MODALITY OBLIGATION

Use the modal auxiliary verbs below, and the following phrases, to express degrees of obligation. Affirmative sentences are indicated by a + and negative sentences, by a −.

Strong Sense of Obligation

Must

Time Idea	Examples
Present	+ You **must focus** more. I'm trying to explain! − You **don't have to study** much because you're so clever! − Students ***mustn't bring / aren't allowed to bring** phones into the exam room.
Future	+ You **must study** harder next year. − You **don't/won't have to study** harder next year. − Students ***mustn't bring / won't be allowed to bring** phones into the exam room tomorrow.
Past	+ I **had to study** hard, but I passed! − I **didn't have to study** much. It was easy. − Students ***weren't allowed to bring** phones into the exam room.

Must is used in the affirmative examples above to express strong obligation for present and future time. The affirmative form of *must* in the past tense is *had to*.

Use *have to* for most negative sentences; *mustn't* is used in the negative form only when something is forbidden, as illustrated in the examples marked with an asterisk. Use *mustn't* or *not allowed to* for prohibition in the present and future, but only *wasn't/weren't allowed to* in the past.

Have To

Time Idea	Examples
Present	+ You **have to pay attention** to this. You need to know it to pass the quiz. − You **don't have to study** much to get good grades. You're so lucky!
Future	+ You **(will) have to study** hard next year if you want to get a scholarship. − You **don't/won't have to improve** your grades next year to keep the scholarship.
Past	+ I **had to study** hard, but I passed! − I **didn't have to study** much. It was easy.

The use of *have to* in the examples above expresses strong obligation, as does *must* in the previous examples. However, there is a difference between the sense of obligation in *must* and *have to* in some cases, as the following sentences illustrate:

1. You **must focus** more. I'm trying to explain! (internal obligation)
2. You **have to pay attention** to this for the scholarship. (external obligation)

In sentence 1, the speaker uses *must* to emphasize that the obligation is internal; in other words, it is up to the person being addressed to make the effort to focus more. In sentence 2, the speaker uses *have to* because the obligation is external to the person; it comes from an external source: the scholarship requirements.

Mild Sense of Obligation

Should

Time Idea	Examples
Present	+ Schools **should do** more to support minority languages. + You ***should consider** getting a private tutor for help. − Schools **shouldn't spend** so much time on formal assessment. − You ***shouldn't waste** money on a private tutor.
Future	+ Schools **should increase** their budgets for teaching assistants next year. + You ***should live** near the campus when you start college in September. − Schools **shouldn't reduce** their budgets for teaching assistants next year. − You ***shouldn't live** far from the campus when you start college in September.
Past	+ The school **should have done** more to support its international students. + You ***should have considered** getting a private tutor for help. − The school **shouldn't have focused** so much on formal assessment. − You ***shouldn't have wasted** your money on a private tutor.

Should is used in the sentences above to express mild obligation. The negative *shouldn't* and the past form *should have* are used consistently, without changes in meaning. The sentences marked with an asterisk express recommendation.

TASK 2

Fill in the blanks in the sentences below with modal auxiliary verbs that express obligation. Decide whether the form should be affirmative or negative and whether the time idea is present, future, or past. Use the verbs in brackets, and follow the prompts in parentheses.

1. I _____ [study] harder! (It's up to me to achieve this.)

2. I _____ [maintain] a B average to keep my scholarship. (It's a requirement of the scholarship.)

3. Next term, I _____ [take] four courses. I have no choice. (It's a condition of the program.)

4. Students _____ [smoke] within 15 metres of any building. It's the law. (The law forbids smoking near buildings.)

5. Now that I'm living on campus, I _____ [take] the bus to class every day. (I can walk.)

6. Last week, I _____ [prepare] for two mid-term exams. (The mid-terms were compulsory.)

7. You _____ [take] too many courses during your first term. (I'm making a recommendation.)

Other Ways to Express Obligation

Need To

Need to is used to express necessity. It is often used as an alternative to *have to* when there is little difference in meaning between necessity and obligation. The examples below show the different forms of *need to*.

Time Idea	Examples
Present	+ You **need to ask** someone to lend you their lecture notes. − You **don't need to ask** anyone for extra help. You're doing fine. − You ***needn't ask** anyone for extra help. You're doing fine.
Future	+ You **(will) need to take** the bus to the downtown campus tomorrow. − I **won't/don't need to ask** for a ride to the downtown campus tomorrow. − I ***needn't ask** for a ride to the downtown campus tomorrow.
Past	+ I **needed to ask** for a ride to the campus this morning. There were no buses. − You **needn't have given** me a ride to campus. I could have walked. Thanks, though. − He **didn't need to give** me a ride to campus. I walked.

Need to is used in the present and future forms and means "it is / will be necessary" and "it isn't / won't be necessary." The negative form *needn't* is marked with an asterisk because it is less common and rather old-fashioned. In the past negative form, there is an important distinction to note between *needn't have* and *didn't need to*: use *needn't have* when something took place but was unnecessary; use *didn't need to* when something did not take place and was unnecessary.

She gave me a ride ⟶ You **needn't have given** me a ride to campus.

He didn't give me a ride ⟶ He **didn't need to give** me a ride to campus.

Ought To

Ought to can be used as an alternative to *should* for likelihood and obligation. The negative form of *ought to* is *ought not (to)* or *oughtn't (to)*. The past forms are *ought to have* and *ought not (to) have*. *Ought to* is more common in British English and often seems rather old-fashioned and formal. The negative and past forms are not commonly used in modern English.

+ You **ought to pass** the exam. (I think it's probable, and I'm hopeful.)

+ Schools **ought to do** more to support minority languages. (I think it is their duty.)

Have Got To

Have got to is commonly used, especially in British English, as a less formal alternative to *have to*. The negative forms are *hasn't/haven't got to*. The past forms are *had to* and *didn't have to*.

+ You **have got to pay attention** to this. You need to know it to pass the quiz.

– You **haven't got to study** much to get good grades. You're so lucky!

+ I **had to** study so hard!

– You **didn't have to** study much. Lucky you!

TASK 3

Rewrite the paragraph below about a student's life during the first term of a new degree program. Use modal auxiliary verbs and phrases of likelihood and obligation that you have studied in this unit. Focus on the underlined words, which express modality.

When I got a call at 8:00 last night, I said to myself, "I'm certain that is my parents calling as they always call at this time on a Sunday." They wanted to know how I was and reminded me that I am required to maintain a B average as a condition of my student visa. They also said it was up to me to be focused and organized and that no one else can help me with that. I am certain that my parents are missing me a lot and want to come to visit. It is probable (and I hope) that they will be able to visit me during spring break next year. If so, I'm certain they won't have as bad a time as they did when they visited my brother at college last year. When they bought their tickets to Los Angeles, the travel agent forgot to tell them that it was necessary for them to have a biometric passport to get into the country. <u>I think it would have been a good idea for them to have checked</u> because when they tried to check in at the airport, they were told that <u>they were prohibited from boarding</u> the plane with their old-style passports. They missed the flight!

_____

_____

_____

_____

_____

_____

_____

_____

_____

My eLab ✎
Find more exercises on modal auxiliary verbs online.

_____

_____

_____

SUMMARY MODAL AUXILIARY VERBS TO EXPRESS LIKELIHOOD

Time Idea	Examples	Explanation
Certainty		
Present	Who's texting you? + That **will be** my boss asking where I am. − That **won't be** my boss. She's on holiday this week.	**Will** is used to express certainty based on the speaker's knowledge of the habits, routines, and characteristics of her boss.
Future	+ If someone calls later, it**'ll be** my boss. Tell her I'm on my way. − If someone calls later, it **won't be** my boss. She's on holiday this week.	
Past	Someone called last night. + That **will have been** my boss. I was running late. − It **won't have been** my boss. She never calls at night.	
Present	Someone's at the door. + That **must be** my roommate. − That **can't be** my roommate.	**Must** is used to express certainty. Unlike *will*, the use of *must* gives no indication of the speaker's knowledge of the habits, routines, and characteristics of her roommate.
Future	There is no future form of *must* for certainty.	
Past	Someone called last night. + It **must have been** my roommate. − It **can't/couldn't have been** my roommate.	

Time Idea	Examples	Explanation
Probability		
Present	+ The projector **should be working**. Let's check. − There ***shouldn't be** any problems. The projector is brand new.	***Should*** is used to express probability. The use of *should* for probability carries an idea of positive, optimistic expectation. The examples marked by an asterisk could be misinterpreted as mild obligation.
Future	+ You **should pass** the exam tomorrow. I'm confident you're ready. − You ***shouldn't have** any problems tomorrow. Be confident!	
Past	+ You ***should have passed** the exam. What went wrong? − You ***shouldn't have failed** the exam. What went wrong?	
Possibility		
Present	+ You **may/might/could be** in the wrong classroom. Have you checked your planner? − The exam **may/might not be** in this building. Can you check, please?	***May***, ***might***, and ***could*** express possibility in the affirmative for all time ideas. For possibility, only *may* and *might* can be used in the negative forms, not *could*. The three forms have similar degrees of certainty. *May* is the most common form used in academic writing as it carries a sense of formality.
Future	+ You **may/might/could pass** the exam tomorrow. You have a chance. − You **may/might not pass** the exam tomorrow. Prepare yourself.	
Past	+ You **may/might/could have passed** the exam, but you won't know your grade until the end of term. − You **may/might not have passed** the exam, so you should work hard on your term paper.	

SUMMARY MODAL AUXILIARY VERBS TO EXPRESS OBLIGATION

Time Idea	Examples	Explanation
Strong Obligation		
Present	+ You **must focus** more. I'm trying to explain! − You **don't have to study** much because you're so clever! − Students ***mustn't bring / aren't allowed to bring** phones into the exam room.	***Must*** expresses strong obligation in the present and future; the affirmative form of *must* in the past is *had to*. Use *have to* for negative sentences. *Mustn't* is used only when something is forbidden: see the examples marked with an asterisk. Use only *wasn't/weren't allowed to* for prohibition in the past.
Future	+ You **must study** harder next year. − You **don't/won't have to study** harder next year. − Students ***mustn't bring / won't be allowed to bring** phones into the exam room tomorrow.	
Past	+ I **had to study** hard, but I passed! − I **didn't have to study** much. It was easy. − Students ***weren't allowed to bring** phones into the exam room.	
Present	+ You **have to pay attention**. You need to know this for the quiz. − You **don't have to study** much to get good grades. You're lucky!	***Have to*** expresses strong obligation, as does *must*.
Future	+ You **(will) have to study** hard next year to get a scholarship. − You **don't/won't have to improve** your grades next year to keep the scholarship.	
Past	+ I **had to study** hard, but I passed! − I **didn't have to study** much. It was easy.	

Time Idea	Examples	Explanation
	Internal versus External Obligation	
	a) You **must focus** more. I'm trying to explain! b) You **have to pay attention** to this for the scholarship.	a) The obligation is internal: it is up to the person being addressed to become more focused. b) The obligation is external: it comes from the scholarship requirements.
	Mild Obligation	
Present	+ Schools **should do** more to support minority languages. + You *****should consider** getting a private tutor for help. − Schools **shouldn't spend** so much time on formal assessment. − You *****shouldn't waste** money on a private tutor.	*Should* expresses mild obligation, without changes in meaning in the negative and past forms *shouldn't* and *should have*.
Future	+ Schools **should increase** their budgets for TAs next year. + You *****should live** near the campus in September. − Schools **shouldn't reduce** their budgets for TAs next year. − You *****shouldn't live** far from the campus in September.	The sentences marked with an asterisk express recommendation.
Past	+ The school **should have done** more for international students. + You *****should have considered** getting a private tutor for help. − The school **shouldn't have focused** so much on assessment. − You *****shouldn't have wasted** your money on a private tutor.	
	Other Forms	
Present	+ You **need to ask** someone to lend you their lecture notes. − You **don't need to ask** anyone for extra help. You're doing fine. − You *****needn't ask** anyone for extra help. You're doing fine.	*Need to* expresses necessity and can be used instead of *have to* for obligation.
Future	+ You **(will) need to take** the bus to the campus tomorrow. − I **won't/don't need to ask** for a ride to the campus tomorrow. − I *****needn't ask** for a ride to the campus tomorrow.	*Needn't* is marked with an asterisk because it is less common and sounds old-fashioned.
Past	+ I **needed to get** a ride from a friend. There were no buses. − You **needn't have given** me a ride. I could have walked. − He **didn't need to give** me a ride to campus. I walked.	Use *needn't have* when something took place but was unnecessary. Use *didn't need to* when something did not take place and was unnecessary.
Present	+ a) You **ought to pass** the exam. + b) Schools **ought to do** more to support minority languages. − a) You **ought not to fail** the exam. − b) Schools **ought not (to) reduce** their budgets for minority language programs.	*Ought to* means the same as *should* for likelihood (a) and obligation (b). It is more common in British English, and more formal than *should*.
Past	+ a) You **ought to have passed** the exam. What happened? − b) You **ought not (to) have said** that. He was offended.	The negative and past forms are uncommon in modern English.
Present	+ You **have got to pay attention** to pass the quiz. − You **haven't got to study** much to get good grades. You're lucky!	*Have got to* is common, especially in British English, as a less formal alternative to *have to*.
Past	+ You **had to pay attention** to the questions because the sound quality was poor. − I **didn't have to study** hard for the test. It was easy.	The past forms are the same as for *have to*: *had to*, *didn't have to*.

INVERSION FOR EMPHASIS

It is possible to add emphasis to sentences by adding emphatic adverbs or adverbial phrases at the beginning of the independent clause. These are generally words or phrases that have a negative connotation, and they are usually placed at the beginning of the sentence.

EXPRESSIONS ## EMPHATIC ADVERBS

When the following emphatic adverbs (in bold) are placed at the beginning of an independent clause, the usual subject-verb order (underlined) is reversed.

1. **At no time** <u>should residents leave</u> their homes during a tornado.
2. **Hardly** <u>had the rain ended</u> when our home became flooded.
3. **Little** <u>did we know</u> that the storm would last for three days.
4. **Never** <u>have I been</u> so frightened as during that storm.
5. **No sooner** <u>had the rain ended</u> than the heavy winds began.
6. **Not once** <u>did I panic</u> while I was inside my house.
7. **Not only** <u>were trees felled</u> by the winds, (but) local rivers also flooded.
8. **Not since** my childhood <u>have I lived through</u> such extreme weather.
9. **Not until** the weather settled <u>did life return</u> to normal.
10. **Only after** the weather settled <u>did life return</u> to normal.
11. **On no account** <u>should people leave</u> their homes during a tornado.
12. **Rarely** <u>have I witnessed</u> such rain damage.
13. **Seldom** <u>does so much rain fall</u> in one day.
14. **So** heavy <u>was the rain</u> that local rivers broke their banks.
15. **Under no circumstances** <u>should you approach</u> a fallen power line.
16. People living away from the coast were not affected. **Neither** <u>were the people</u> living on higher land.
17. People living away from the coast were not affected. **Nor** <u>were the people</u> living on higher land.

FORM ## INVERSION

Three Forms of Inversion

When beginning independent clauses with certain emphatic adverbs, change the subject-verb order in one of the following three ways:

1. When the main verb is *to be*, change the subject-verb order.

   <u>Climate change is</u> the result of both human activity and natural phenomena.

   Not only <u>is climate change</u> the result of human activity, it is also caused by natural phenomena.

2. For verbs with auxiliaries, change the subject-auxiliary order.

   <u>Pacific storms have become</u> so severe that evacuation of communities is now a regular occurrence.

   So severe <u>have Pacific storms become</u> that evacuation of communities is now a regular occurrence.

3. For other verbs, use question structure, with a form of the auxiliary verb *to do*.

   <u>El Niño rarely leaves</u> coastal Pacific communities unscathed.

   Rarely <u>does El Niño leave</u> coastal Pacific communities unscathed.

Forms without Inversion

If the emphatic adverbs listed on page 413 are used within an independent clause that begins with *it is/was*, the subject-verb order in the following dependent clause (*that …*) is not reversed.

Not until the end of the storm <u>did people venture</u> out of their shelters.	(subject-verb order changed)
It was not until the end of the storm that <u>people ventured</u> out of their shelters.	(subject-verb order unchanged)
Only after coastal erosion affected communities <u>was action taken</u>.	(subject-verb order changed)
It was only after coastal erosion affected communities that <u>action was taken</u>.	(subject-verb order unchanged)

Not Only

If the independent clause begins with *not only*, it requires inversion when the writer wishes to emphasize the action of the verb, as in the following example:

Not only <u>does El Niño damage</u> coastal communities, it also affects people living further inland.

However, in other cases, an independent clause can contain the phrase *not only*, or even begin with it, and yet not require inversion, as illustrated in the following examples:

<u>El Niño affects</u> **not only** coastal communities **but also** people living further inland.

Not only coastal communities **but also** <u>people living further inland suffer</u> during El Niño years.

Learn more about correlative conjunctions as linking words in Appendix 1, p. 430.

In these examples, there is no inversion because *not only* is not an emphatic adverb, modifying the verb *affects* or *suffer*, but the first part of a correlative conjunction (*not only … but also*) joining two noun phrases: *coastal communities* and *people living further inland*.

TASK 1

Rewrite each of the following sentences to add emphasis, beginning with the emphatic adverb in parentheses.

© ERPI Reproduction prohibited

1. People living in the town are not allowed to return until the storm clears. (Under no circumstances)

   _____

   _____

2. The storm damaged many small homes in the area as well as local crops. (Not only)

   _____

   _____

3. Local residents were able to return home two months later. (Only after)

   _____

4. A storm of such intensity had not struck the town since 2005. (Not since)

   _____

5. People living in the town were not allowed to return until the storm had cleared. (Not until)

   _____

6. People with homes in the area should not return without authorization. (At no time)

   _____

7. People with homes in the area should not return until the flooding subsides. (On no account)

   _____

   _____

8. Areas of Argentina and southern Brazil are seldom affected by El Niño-related extreme weather events. (Seldom)

   _____

   _____

9. In all its history, the coastal town has rarely been so badly affected by storms. (Rarely)

   _____

10. The town was so badly affected by the storm that many residents were forced to live in temporary shelters. (So badly)

    _____

    _____

11. People fleeing the flooding had no shelter. They didn't have food either. (Nor)

_____

12. As soon as the storm cleared, people left their homes to assess the damage. (No sooner)

_____

13. As soon as the storm cleared, people left their homes to assess the damage. (Hardly)

_____

14. They were completely unaware that an even stronger storm was on its way. (Little)

_____

15. Local people were not aware that a new storm was on its way. The meteorologists weren't either. (Neither)

_____

_____

16. During my 20 years in the country, I have never experienced such extreme weather. (Not once)

_____

_____

17. Extreme weather has never been so severe as during the last seven years. (Never)

_____

TASK 2

The following sentences are from the results on a search engine when the keywords *extreme weather* were combined with the emphatic adverbs listed on page 413. In the sentences, the adverbs have been replaced with blanks. Fill in each blank with an emphatic adverb that fits conceptually and grammatically. Try to use each adverb only once. In some cases, more than one answer is possible.

1. The signs of climate change are right in front of us, says the assessment's chapter on agriculture, one of the few comprehensive reports to explicitly point to certain events—like the 2012 drought—as an example of the consequences of climate change. _____ will weather affect crop growth, but it will encourage invasive species and pests, lower the quality of forage for livestock and lead to changing land uses across the country, the report says.

(https://www.scientificamerican.com/article/deadly-heat-waves-flooding-rains-crop-failures-among-climate-change-plagues-already-afflicting-americans/)

2. A near-record year for wind events. _____ 2007 have so many storms exceeded gusts of 90 kilometres per hour and Alberta broke the previous record with 41 wind storms—up from the high of 37 in 2007. (http://www.huffingtonpost.ca/2012/12/20/calgary-hail-stor-environment-canadas-top-10-extreme-weather-events_n_2339941.html)

3. As the sea ice melts, sea surface temperatures will remain at around zero degree Celsius (32 °F) for as long as there is ice in the water, since the extra energy will first go into melting the ice. _____ the ice has melted will the extra energy start raising the temperature of the water. (http://arctic-news.blogspot.ca/2016/07/extreme-weather-events.html)

4. The Himalayan Mountains have long kept a dark secret. In 1942, hundreds of human skeletons dating back to the 9th century were discovered around an upland lake in northern India. They had all died at the same time. But _____ 2007 did scientists offer an explanation for their mysterious demise. All the bodies showed similar wounds: deep cracks in the skull. Scientists came up with a stunning explanation. They were killed by cricket-ball-sized hailstones.

(https://www.allianz.com/en/about_us/open-knowledge/topics/environment/articles/130903-hailstorms-threaten-rising-losses.html/)

5. There are many caves and potholes. Unless you are part of a properly equipped, experienced and supervised group, stay well away from them. The substantial quarry on the Southernmost section of the reserve on Moughton Fell is a fully operational site, and _____ should you cross its perimeter. If you hear a siren, it may indicate imminent blasting at the quarry—you should move well away from the boundary.

(http://www.inclusivelondon.com/information/Ingleborough%20National%20Nature%20Reserve/103010/info/information.aspx)

6. To reduce your chance of encountering a bear: travel in large groups; avoid areas of obvious recent bear activity; avoid carrion (dead meat); camp well inland of the coast or in areas with good visibility in all directions; and cook less odorous food. _____ should you approach a polar bear. If a bear is encountered, noise-makers such as bear bangers and air horns may scare the bear away. Pepper spray, used at close range, may deter polar bears, but it has not been thoroughly tested.

(http://www.pc.gc.ca/eng/pn-np/nt/aulavik/visit/visit4/a.aspx)

7. I have lived in Australia for 16 years (minus the two I spent wandering the globe), and in all that time _____ did a cyclone even come close to where we live in south-east Queensland. Now we had two bearing down on us, with one showing the possibility of changing that fact very quickly!

(https://onewanderlustlife.wordpress.com/2015/02/23/australian-summer-extreme-weather-edition/)

8. _____ does one hear any working scientist say that science is "settled." Science is never settled. It is, by definition, an ever-evolving body of human knowledge, and climate science is exactly like all the other sciences in that way.

(http://www.nytimes.com/interactive/projects/cp/climate/2015-paris-climate-talks/how-can-science-be-settled)

9. Pagliuca, Stephenson and McKenzie, along with their guests, awoke to a brilliant sunrise early on April 11. The coal stove in the Auto Road's Stage Office (the Observatory's early home) took the chill off the room. "_____ did we realize as we were enjoying a fine view of the Atlantic Ocean that we were to experience during the next 48 hours one of the worst storms ever recorded in the history of any observatory."
—Log Book entry, Sal Pagliuca

(https://www.mountwashington.org/about-us/history/world-record-wind.aspx)

10. Air France said it had cancelled 210 flights and booked more than 2,000 hotel rooms for its stranded passengers. At sea, the ferry services connecting the northwestern department of Brittany with nearby islands were all suspended— and the inaugural voyage of the Roscoff-Plymouth ferry service was post-poned. _____ bad was the weather that northeastern France was put on "orange alert" and the French navy deployed three rescue vessels to be on stand by in case of maritime accidents.

(http://www.telegraph.co.uk/news/worldnews/europe/france/4580079/French-storms-leave-half-a-million-without-electricity.html)

11. Ladies and gentlemen, _____ has the global community been under such stress. The ties that bind us, as humankind, are fraying. We must work especially hard to preserve them, at this critical juncture, in the interests of our common future. Thank you very much and I will be happy to answer your questions. —Ban Ki Moon

(http://unic.org.in/display.php?E=1068&K=Press_Conference)

12. The potato has also given traders like Amina Nakate a business edge. At her stall in Nylon market, Mbale, time passes quickly for Nakate. _____ _____ has she served a customer than another falls in line. In her 10 years of trading there, none of her products—like plantain and cassava—have sold as fast as the sweet potato, she said. In a day, she can sell about five 200kg bags of the product, yielding an income of 700,000 shillings ($208) per day—compared to $50 previously.

(http://www.braced.org/news/i/?id=d7a1eaab-3dcf-4488-b1f2-4a8030777228)

13. If you are happy to be contacted by a BBC journalist please leave a telephone number that we can contact you on. In some cases a selection of your comments will be published, displaying your name as you provide it and location, unless you state otherwise. Your contact details will never be published. When sending us pictures, video or eyewitness accounts _____ _____ should you endanger yourself or others, take any unnecessary risks or infringe any laws. Please ensure you have read the terms and conditions.

(http://www.bbc.com/news/world-europe-36483045)

14. In the beginning, there were no searing head winds, but after the Hawi turnaround, all that changed. The relentless cross winds hit at 35 mph. The tall grass bent over backward and told me this was going to take a while. I needed to be patient, not become agitated or frustrated. I signed up for this, right? After a few more hours battling the winds and extreme heat, _____ was I so happy to see an airport. Landmark! It was 10 miles to the end of this oven-like ride, 125 degrees from lava rocks and road, with vicious winds.

(http://www.cnn.com/2015/10/30/health/ironman-championship-final-hawaii/)

15. _____ did I know that exactly two months later, the largest scientific organization in the world and publisher of the leading academic journal *Science* would launch an initiative aimed at doing just that—move the conversation forward by telling Americans "What We Know." It boils down to three main points—97 percent of climate scientists agree that climate change is here and now, that this means we risk abrupt and irreversible changes to the climate, and the sooner we act, the lower the costs and risks we face.

(http://www.ecowatch.com/how-scientists-are-moving-climate-change-conversation-forward-1881880099.html)

My eLab

Find more exercises on inversion for emphasis online.

INVERSION FOR EMPHASIS

Expression/Form	Examples
Emphatic Adverbs	
At no time	**At no time** <u>should residents leave</u> their homes during a tornado.
Hardly	**Hardly** <u>had the rain ended</u> when our home became flooded.
Little	**Little** <u>did we know</u> that the storm would last for three days.
Never	**Never** <u>have I been</u> so frightened as during that storm.
No sooner	**No sooner** <u>had the rain ended</u> than the heavy winds began.
Not once	**Not once** <u>did I panic</u> while I was inside my house.
Not only	**Not only** <u>were trees felled</u> by the winds, (but) local rivers also flooded.
Not since	**Not since** my childhood <u>have I lived through</u> such extreme weather.
Not until	**Not until** the weather settled <u>did life return</u> to normal.
Only after	**Only after** the weather settled <u>did life return</u> to normal.
On no account	**On no account** <u>should people leave</u> their homes during a tornado.
Rarely	**Rarely** <u>have I witnessed</u> such rain damage.
Seldom	**Seldom** <u>does so much rain fall</u> in one day.
So + adjective	**So heavy** <u>was the rain</u> that local rivers broke their banks.
Under no circumstances	**Under no circumstances** <u>should you approach</u> a fallen power line.
. . . Neither	People living away from the coast were not affected. **Neither** <u>were the people</u> living on higher land.
. . . Nor	People living away from the coast were not affected. **Nor** <u>were the people</u> living on higher land.
Inversion	
To be as main verb	a) <u>Climate change is</u> the result of both human activity and natural phenomena. b) **Not only** <u>is climate change</u> the result of human activity, it is also caused by natural phenomena.
Verbs with auxiliaries	a) <u>Pacific storms have become</u> so severe that evacuation of communities is now a regular occurrence. b) **So severe** <u>have Pacific storms become</u> that evacuation of communities is now a regular occurrence.
Other verbs	a) <u>El Niño rarely leaves</u> coastal Pacific communities unscathed. b) **Rarely** <u>does El Niño leave</u> coastal Pacific communities unscathed.
Within an independent clause that begins with *it is/was*: no inversion	It was **not until** the end of the storm that <u>people ventured</u> out of their shelters. It was **only after** coastal erosion affected communities that <u>action was taken</u>.
Use of *not only* without inversion (correlative conjunction *not only . . . but also*)	**Not only** <u>does El Niño damage</u> coastal communities, it also affects people living further inland. (inversion) *BUT* <u>El Niño affects</u> **not only** coastal communities **but also** people living further inland. (no inversion) **Not only** <u>coastal communities</u> **but also** <u>people living further inland suffer</u> during El Niño years. (no inversion)

APPENDICES

APPENDIX 1

LINKING WORDS IN ACADEMIC WRITING

Linking words in academic writing connect ideas and add cohesion. In doing so, they make it easier for readers to understand the interrelationships between ideas, for example, emphasis, addition, cause and effect, and contrast.

In this appendix, you will study five groups of linking words:

- conjunctive adverbs
- coordinators
- subordinators
- correlative conjunctions
- other linking words and phrases

CONJUNCTIVE ADVERBS

Conjunctive adverbs are used to join ideas and arguments in different clauses and sentences. The conjunctive adverb you choose to use gives an indication to your reader of how you think your ideas are related. Conjunctive adverbs can be placed at the beginning of independent clauses, in the middle, or at the end.

Meaning

Conjunctive adverbs convey a range of meanings, most commonly:

- addition: *moreover, in addition*
- contrast: *however, nonetheless*
- result: *therefore, consequently*

> The Mediterranean diet has been linked to reduced rates of heart disease**; moreover,** it may also reduce cancer rates. (addition)
>
> Many doctors recommend olive oil**; however,** it is more expensive than other oils used for cooking. (contrast)
>
> The Mediterranean diet is low in unhealthy fats**; therefore,** it may reduce cholesterol. (result)

As you have learned in the preceding chapters, conjunctive adverbs and adverbial phrases are also used for other functions, including the following:

- introducing: *to begin with, first(ly)*
- summarizing: *in brief, in short, to summarize, to sum up*
- concluding: *in conclusion, to conclude*

Conjunctive Adverbs That Refer to a Previous Idea

Certain conjunctive adverbs are used specifically to connect the second part of a sentence, or a new sentence, to an idea stated previously. The conjunctive adverb may show contrast with the previous idea (*in contrast, on the other hand*), contradict or challenge it (*instead, on the contrary*), or restate it, with or without expanding on it (*in other words, specifically*).

Accuracy and Punctuation

Use conjunctive adverbs between, within, or after independent clauses. If the conjunctive adverb is placed between two independent clauses, set it off with a period or semicolon, and a comma. If it is placed within an independent clause, set it off with commas.

Between Independent Clauses

The Mediterranean diet has been linked to reduced rates of heart disease. **Moreover,** it may also reduce cancer rates. (with a period and comma)

The Mediterranean diet has been linked to reduced rates of heart disease; **moreover,** it may also reduce cancer rates. (with a semicolon and comma)

Within an Independent Clause

Some doctors**, however,** believe the health benefits are overstated. (with commas)

After an Independent Clause

Some doctors believe the health benefits are overstated**, however.** (with a comma and period)

Style

Conjunctive adverbs add a sense of formality to your writing. However, if you begin too many successive independent clauses with conjunctive adverbs, your writing may lack flow and appear formulaic. If this is the case, consider combining conjunctive adverbs with alternatives. Compare the following two paragraphs:

The Mediterranean diet has been linked to reduced rates of heart disease**; moreover,** it may also reduce cancer rates. **As a result,** many doctors recommend olive oil. **However,** olive oil is unaffordable for many people. **Therefore,** nutritionists should suggest cheaper alternatives. (formulaic and lacking in flow)

The Mediterranean diet, which has been linked to reduced rates of heart disease, may also reduce cancer rates. Many doctors are, therefore, recommending olive oil. Because olive oil is unaffordable for many people, nutritionists should also suggest cheaper alternatives. (rewritten for more variety and better flow)

Some writers would not set off *therefore* with commas in the second example because they feel the commas break the flow of the sentence.

Summary: Conjunctive Adverbs and Adverbial Phrases

Conjunctive Adverbs	Use	Examples
Addition		
additionally furthermore in addition moreover	To add ideas	Olive oil is high in monounsaturated fats**; additionally / furthermore / in addition / moreover,** it contains polyphenols, which may prevent heart disease.
equally likewise similarly	To express similarity	Olive oil is widely used in salads**. Equally/ Likewise/Similarly,** grapeseed oil is a healthy option for salads and mayonnaise.
in other words specifically	To restate, or expand on, a previously stated idea	Foods high in sugar and saturated fat are linked to poor health**; in other words,** people should avoid them. Foods high in sugar and saturated fat are linked to poor health**, specifically,** obesity and heart disease.
Contrast		
however nevertheless nonetheless still	To express contrast	Olive oil is a healthy option**. However/ Nevertheless/Nonetheless/Still,** it is too expensive for many families to use regularly.
as opposed to in contrast on the other hand	To express contrast with a previously stated idea	Processed food is often unhealthy **as opposed to** homemade meals, which tend to contain less sugar, salt, and fat. Processed food with high levels of sugar, salt, and fat should be avoided. **In contrast / On the other hand,** homemade alternatives can offer a balanced and healthy diet.
instead on the contrary rather	To contradict or challenge a previously stated idea	Many people believe low-fat food to be healthy**; instead / on the contrary / rather,** a balanced diet can be more beneficial.
Result		
as a result consequently therefore thus	To describe results or effects	The Mediterranean diet may help prevent heart disease. **As a result / Consequently / Therefore / Thus,** it has gained in popularity.

Note that *in other words* is set off by a semicolon and a comma because it precedes an independent clause, but *specifically* is set off by commas because it is placed within the independent clause.

Coordinators are used for two main purposes: to link two or more independent clauses and to join items in a series or list. There are seven coordinators, known as the "FANBOYS": *For*, *And*, *Nor*, *But*, *Or*, *Yet*, *So*.

Meaning

When you link two ideas with a coordinator, it is important to consider the relationship between the two ideas and to select the coordinator that best conveys your intended meaning. The FANBOYS coordinators convey the following meanings:

- addition (including alternatives): *and, nor, or*
- contrast: *but, yet*
- cause and effect: *for, so*

> The final exam was yesterday, **and** 80 students were present. (addition)
>
> The exam was difficult, **but** some students still got high grades. (contrast)
>
> I knew the exam would be difficult, **so** I prepared for two weeks. (result)

Emphasis

To review compound sentences, see Unit 3 in the Handbook, p. 338.

If a writer joins independent clauses with a coordinator, they form a compound sentence. Generally speaking, compound sentences give equal emphasis to the ideas in each independent clause, as in the following example:

> Students can take the exam in person, **or** they can choose to do it online.

Accuracy and Punctuation

Use coordinators to join independent clauses. In North American varieties of English, it is normal to place a comma before the coordinator; in British and other varieties of English, no comma is required.

> I had no time to prepare for the exam, **yet** I still got an A. (with comma)
>
> I had no time to prepare for the exam **yet** I still got an A. (no comma)

Style

If you use too may compound sentences, your writing style may seem rather simple and repetitive. If the relationship between two independent clauses is cause and effect or contrast, you may want to consider alternatives with different structures, for example:

I knew the final exam would be difficult, **so** I prepared for two weeks.	(compound sentence with the coordinator *so*)
I knew the final exam would be difficult; **therefore,** I prepared for two weeks.	(two independent clauses joined by the conjunctive adverb *therefore*)
Since I knew the final exam would be difficult, I prepared for two weeks.	(complex sentence formed with the subordinator *since*)

Summary: Coordinators

For has a literary, narrative tone; it is uncommon in most academic writing.

When *nor* is placed at the beginning of an independent clause, invert the subject-verb order (see Unit 14 in the Handbook, p. 413).

Coordinator	Use	Example
for	To express a reason	My school years were happy, **for** I had not a care in the world.
and	To add information and examples	The final exam took place yesterday, **and** 80 students were present in the exam hall.
nor	To add information and examples in negative sentences	Students could not check their notes, **nor** were they allowed to use calculators.
but	To join ideas when there is an idea of contrast	The final exam was difficult, **but** some students still got high grades.
or	To add alternative information and examples	Students can take the exam in person, **or** they can choose to do it online.
yet	To express an unexpected idea of contrast	I had no time to prepare for the exam, **yet** I still managed to get an A.
so	To express an effect or result	I knew the final exam would be difficult, **so** I prepared for two weeks.
In Series or Lists		
and	To add a similar item to a series or list	To prepare for the writing test, I revised articles, tenses, **and** punctuation.
or	To add an alternative item to a series or list	I had three choices: retake the course, retake the final exam, **or** accept the N (incomplete) grade.

SUBORDINATORS

To review dependent clauses and complex sentences, see Unit 3 in the Handbook, pp. 337 and 338.

Subordinators can be used to link the ideas in two clauses. When subordinators are used at the beginning of a clause, they make it dependent. The dependent clause (also called a *subordinate clause*) should be joined to an independent clause to make a complete, complex sentence.

Meaning

When you link two clauses with a subordinator, you can convey a range of meanings about how the two clauses interrelate:

- time: *before, while*
- contrast: *although, whereas*
- reason: *because, since*
- condition: *if, whether*

> **Before** nuclear power was developed, most power stations were coal-fired. (time)
>
> **Although** nuclear power is efficient, it does present serious risks. (contrast)
>
> Many people oppose nuclear power **because** they worry about accidents. (reason)
>
> Climate change activists are unsure **whether** the risks outweigh the benefits. (condition)

Emphasis

Complex sentences are often written with a dependent clause preceding the independent clause. In such cases, the information in the independent clause usually carries more emphasis. If the independent clause precedes the dependent clause, the emphasis is less clear.

1. **Although** nuclear power is efficient, it does present serious risks.
2. Many people oppose nuclear power **because** they worry about accidents.

In sentence 1, the idea of serious risk is emphasized as the independent clause comes second in the sentence. In sentence 2, the dependent clause comes second in the sentence; in this case, it is less clear whether the writer is emphasizing opposition or accidents.

Accuracy and Punctuation

Use a comma to separate dependent and independent clauses if the dependent clause comes first in the sentence. No comma is required if the dependent clause comes second in the sentence.

> **Although** nuclear power is efficient**,** it does present serious risks. (with comma)

> Many people oppose nuclear power **because** they worry about accidents. (no comma)

Style

The use of subordinators and complex sentences adds a degree of formality and sophistication to academic writing. This is especially the case when two clauses are related by an idea of time, contrast, or cause and effect.

> Most power stations used to be coal-fired; **then** nuclear energy was developed.

> **Before** nuclear power was developed, most power stations were coal-fired. (improved academic style)

> Nuclear power is efficient, **but** it does present serious risks.

> **Although** nuclear power is efficient, it does present serious risks. (added formality)

> Many people oppose nuclear power, **and** they worry about accidents. (imprecise expression of cause and effect)

> Many people oppose nuclear power **because** they worry about accidents. (improved academic style)

Summary: Subordinators

Subordinators	Use	Examples
Time		
after *as long as* *as soon as* *before* *until* *when* *while*	To convey time relations	**Before** nuclear power was developed, most power stations were coal-fired. **After** an earthquake caused a nuclear meltdown at a nearby power plant, public confidence in nuclear power declined. **When** the site for the power station was announced, local people expressed concern about health risks. **While** the site was being developed, the environment protection agency carried out a detailed assessment. Construction began **as soon as** the assessment was complete. **As long as** people need electricity, nuclear power will have a place in the energy market. The plant didn't open **until** all safety checks had been made.
Contrast		
although *even though* *whereas* *while* *whilst* (British English)	To express contrast	**Although** nuclear power is efficient, it does present serious risks. The project was completed **even though** it ran over budget by $20 million. (stronger contrast than *although*) The UK power plant took seven years to build **whereas/while/whilst** its Korean equivalent was finished in five.
Reason		
because *as* *since*	To describe reasons	Many people oppose nuclear power **because/as/since** they worry about accidents.
Condition		
if *unless* *whether*	To describe conditions	**If** nuclear power reduces global CO_2 emissions, should it be supported in the fight against climate change? **Unless** the risks are reduced, many people may remain suspicious of nuclear energy. Environmentalists are divided over **whether** they should support nuclear power. (two possibilities)

As and *since* can also convey time relations, so avoid using them to describe reasons unless the meaning is clear.

Correlative conjunctions are linking words that are used in pairs to join two or more related ideas in a sentence.

Meaning

Correlative conjunctions can be used to express the following meanings, often with a sense of emphasis:

- addition: *both . . . and, not only . . . (but) also*
- one or the other: *either . . . or, neither . . . nor, whether . . . or*

> **Both** English **and** Mandarin are major world languages. (addition)
>
> **Neither** English **nor** Spanish majors can take the course. (not one or the other)

Accuracy

If a sentence contains two subjects joined by a pair of correlative conjunctions, the verb agrees with the nearer subject.

> **Neither** Mandarin classes **nor** individual instruction **is offered** at the university.
>
> **Either** Advanced English **or** elective foreign language courses **are taken** in the second year.

Maintain parallel structure when using correlative conjunctions.

> English majors can study **not only** English literature **but also** linguistics.
>
> English majors can complete their programs by **either** studying linguistics **or** taking elective foreign language courses.

To review subject-verb agreement and parallel structure, see Units 10 and 12 in the Handbook, pp. 386 and 399.

Style

Correlative conjunctions add a formal, academic style to writing.

Summary: Correlative Conjunctions

Correlative Conjunctions	Use	Examples
Addition		
both . . . and *not only . . . (but) also*	To add ideas and examples	**Both** English **and** Mandarin are major world languages. Mandarin is **not only** difficult to pronounce, it is **also** hard to write.
One or the Other		
either . . . or *neither . . . nor* *whether . . . or*	To express the idea of one or the other	English majors can take **either** 19th century poetry **or** modern fiction. **Neither** French **nor** Spanish majors can take the course. **Whether** you take Spanish **or** choose another elective, the courses will be for four credits.

The following are additional linking words and phrases that are common in academic writing.

Linking Words for Exemplification

Learn more about linking words for exemplification in Chapter 11, pp. 241–242.

A specific group of conjunctive adverbs is used to introduce examples in sentences:

- *for example*
- *for instance*
- *namely*
- *such as*

1. College writing poses many challenges, **for example,** when students have to learn and use different citation styles.
2. College writing poses many challenges, **for instance,** academic vocabulary and correct citation style.
3. College writing is challenging**; for example,** students need to use formal English and correct citation style.

In sentence 1, *for example* is set off by commas because the following example is a dependent clause. In sentence 2, *for instance* is set off by commas because the following examples are noun phrases. In sentence 3, *for example* is set off by a semicolon and a comma because the following example is an independent clause.

4. Citation styles **such as** APA and MLA are challenging.
5. Most college essays**, such as** lab reports and response papers**,** require specific structures.

In sentence 4, *such as* introduces a defining phrase, so no commas are required. In sentence 5, *such as* introduces a non-defining phrase, so commas are required.

6. Good college writing is based on two key skills**, namely,** effective reading and critical thinking.
7. Good college writers use two key skills**; namely,** they read effectively and think critically.

In sentence 6, *namely* is set off by commas because the following examples are noun phrases. In sentence 7, *namely* is set off by a semicolon and a comma because the following example is an independent clause.

Linking Words for Enumeration

Another type of conjunctive adverb is commonly used to add cohesion in academic writing by expressing sequence:

- *first(ly)*
- *second(ly)*
- *third(ly)*
- *finally*

College writing poses several challenges to first-year students. **First,** it is often very different from the writing they did in secondary school. **Second,** students have to learn how to write many different types of essay. **Third,** they often get less support from their instructors. **Finally,** the stakes are much higher.

APA CITATION STYLE

APA (American Psychological Association) citation style is used in many publications, particularly in social and behavioural sciences. The following APA formats for writing in-text citations and references lists are some of the most common forms you will need for academic writing. You can find complete guidelines for APA citation style in the *Publication Manual of the American Psychological Association*, Sixth Edition.

IN-TEXT CITATIONS

Every time you use a statistic, idea, image, or creative work that is not your own, you are required to acknowledge your source with a citation in the text—an *in-text citation*. Each in-text citation should match a corresponding entry in the reference list at the end of the essay.

APA in-text citations should include the author's or authors' surname(s) and the year of publication, separated by a comma, in parentheses after the cited information. If a source has no date, use the letters *n.d.* in the parentheses instead.

> **Surname and year:** (Casanave, 2002)
>
> **Source with no date:** ("El Niño," n.d.)

For direct quotations, include page numbers, preceded by *p* or *pp*, a period, and a space. The APA manual also recommends, but does not require, that paraphrased information include page numbers.

> **Page numbers only:** (pp. 118–119)
>
> **Source and page numbers:** (Morton, Storch, & Thompson, 2015, p. 9)

Authors

Inclusion of the Author's Name in the Citation Phrase

If you include the name of the author in the citation phrase, it is not necessary to repeat it in the following parentheses.

> Casanave (2002) suggests that academic writing is like a game and writers need to learn the rules of the game to succeed.

If the name of the author is not part of the citation phrase, include it in the following parentheses.

> It has been suggested that academic writing is like a game and writers need to learn the rules of the game to succeed (Casanave, 2002).

Unless marked with an asterisk (*), the examples throughout the appendix refer to texts cited in this book.

More Than One Author

If two authors' names are included in a citation phrase, join them with *and*; if they appear in parentheses, join them with an ampersand (&).

> Richards and Stedmon (2016) discuss the issue of delegation and control in autonomous cars.

> Delegation and control in autonomous cars are key safety concepts to consider (Richards & Stedmon, 2016).

For sources with three to five authors, list them all the first time the source is cited. Further citations should include the first author only and *et al.* (not italicized).

> **First citation:** Marshall, Zhou, Gervan, and Wiebe (2012) analyze the factors that relate to first-year university students' sense of belonging in a Canadian university.

> **Next citation:** Sense of belonging is clearly an important aspect of student success to consider during the first year of higher education (Marshall et al., 2012).

For sources with six or more authors, write the name of the first author followed by *et al.* in all citations.

> *Aman et al. (2015) review the health and environmental safety of solar energy systems.

No Author

For sources that do not have an author, cite the title of the work. For short works, for example, journal articles and book chapters, place the title in quotation marks. For longer works, such as books, use italics. If a work has a long title, you may shorten it in parentheses.

> *In "Brexit and Parliament, Questions of Sovereignty" (2016), the complex interrelationships between the UK and European parliaments are discussed in terms of competing views of sovereignty.

> *The complex interrelationships between the UK and European parliaments have been discussed in terms of competing views of sovereignty ("Brexit and Parliament," 2016).

Multiple Sources in a Citation

When you include two or more sources in an in-text citation, order the authors (or titles of works with no author) alphabetically, and separate them with semicolons.

> A number of studies in recent years have analyzed paraphrasing, patch-writing, and plagiarism (Badge & Scott, 2009; Bailey & Challen, 2015; Ellery, 2008; Harwood & Petric, 2012).

Print Sources

Multiple Works by the Same Author

If you cite more than one work by the same author and published *in the same year*, differentiate the works by adding the letters *a, b, c*, etc., after the year. The letters refer to the alphabetical order in which the reference list entries appear.

> *Canagarajah (2013a) discusses individual choices, power relations, and agency in intercultural communication.

If you cite more than one work by the same author but published *in different years*, separate the years of the works with commas.

> The history of homeopathy in Germany and its central role in the development of the double-blind control trial is discussed by Stolberg (1999, 2006).

> The Nuremberg salt test of 1835 played a central role in the history of homeopathy in Germany and the development of the double-blind control trial (Stolberg, 1999, 2006).

Secondary Sources

If you are citing a source that you read about elsewhere, without having read the original work, begin the in-text citation with the phrase *as cited in*.

> Spady argues that post-secondary students' social integration is informed by a social system (the campus) and the sum of its parts (as cited in Marshall et al., 2012).

Citing Multiple Pages

Use the following formats to cite information from multiple pages of the same work.

> **Consecutive pages:** Marshall et al. (2012) address critiques that have been made of Spady's (1971) model of student integration (pp. 118–119).

> **Non-consecutive pages:** Marshall et al. (2012) consider the critiques that various authors have made of Tinto's (1975) model of student retention (pp. 119, 134).

Direct Quotations

Direct Quotations of Fewer Than 40 Words

Direct quotations of fewer than 40 words should be integrated grammatically into sentences and enclosed in quotation marks. Page numbers should be provided in parentheses immediately after the quotation. If the quotation appears at the end of a sentence, place the final punctuation mark outside the parentheses.

> In their conclusion, Morton, Storch, and Thompson (2015) highlight "the unpredictable and unexpected practices contributing to the students' progress as academic writers" (p. 9).

> Writing teachers need to become more aware of the "unpredictable and unexpected practices contributing to the students' progress as academic writers" (Morton, Storch, & Thompson, 2015, p. 9).

Punctuation from the original text, for example, question marks, should remain within the quotation marks; punctuation that you add should be placed outside the quotation marks.

> **Original punctuation:** Morton, Storch, and Thompson (2015) ask the following question: "Do the students' perceptions of themselves as academic writers change?" (p. 3).

> **Added punctuation:** Should we agree with Morton, Storch, and Thompson's conclusion (2015) that progress in academic writing is the product of "unpredictable and unexpected practices" (p. 9)?

Direct Quotations of 40 Words or More

Direct quotations of 40 words or more should be dropped one line, indented a half inch (1.25 cm) from the left margin, and not enclosed in quotation marks. The final period should be placed before the in-text citation rather than after.

> Many linguists agree that the average age of language speakers largely indicates a language's health and predicted longevity. UNESCO's "Atlas of the World's Languages in Danger of Disappearing" (Wurm, 1996) noted that at least one-third of the children should be learning the language to maintain its vitality. This is not the case in Canada, where:
>
> > According to the 2006 Census, 18% of First Nations children across Canada had an Aboriginal language as their mother tongue (or first language learned), down from 21% in 1996. Older generations of First Nations people are generally more likely than younger generations to have an Aboriginal language as their mother tongue. (Bougie, 2010, p. 75)

Omitting Words from Direct Quotations

If you omit words from a direct quotation, indicate the omission with an ellipsis (three spaced periods: . . .).

> With reference to students taking the ALC course, Marshall et al. (2012) stress the need to focus on "the academic literacy development of students . . . and to recognize and respect the varied social, cultural, and linguistic backgrounds of students" (p. 135).

Adding Words to Direct Quotations

If you add words to improve the clarity of a direct quotation, enclose the added word(s) in square brackets.

> With reference to students taking the ALC course, Marshall et al. (2012) stress the need to focus on "[writers'] social, cultural, and linguistic backgrounds" (p. 135).

Online Sources

With an Author

If an online source has an author, it should be cited by the author's name and year of publication, as for print sources.

> Diesendorf (2016) aims to dispel what he sees as myths in the renewable versus nuclear power debate.

No Author

If the online source has no author, you should include the title of the work being cited and the year of publication in the in-text citation. As for print sources, use quotation marks for short works (e.g., journal articles and book chapters), and italics for longer works (e.g., books). If a work has a long title, you may shorten it in parentheses. If it has no date, write *n.d.*

> The effects of extreme weather events on coastal communities in Ecuador have been well documented by National Geographic ("El Niño," n.d.).

No Author or Title

If the information you are citing is from a website that has no author or title, cite the website address only, in parentheses. In such cases, you are not required to include a matching reference list entry at the end of the essay.

> Today, over 70 so-called generation III reactors are under construction, including 29 in energy-hungry China (www.world-nuclear.org/info/Current-and-Future-Generation/Nuclear-Power-in-the-World-Today).

With Numbered Paragraphs

If you are directly quoting information from an online source with no page numbers but with numbered paragraphs, indicate the paragraph numbers in parentheses, using the abbreviation *para*, followed by a period, a space, and the paragraph number, for example, (para. 5).

Personal Communications: Conversations, Interviews, and E-Mail

Use the following format to cite personal communications such as a conversation, interview, or e-mail correspondence. Do not include a corresponding entry in the reference list.

> (D. Moore, personal communication, November 21, 2016)

REFERENCE LISTS

APA reference lists should include one entry for each source that has been cited with an in-text citation. APA format requires that the reference list appear at the end of the essay, on a separate page, with the title *References* centred at the top of the page.

Reference list entries should be double-spaced, arranged alphabetically by the author's surname or by the title of an unauthored source. All lines other than the first line of each entry should be indented by a half inch (1.25 cm) from the left margin. The examples below illustrate the most common types of reference list entries. However, they are not double-spaced, as would be required in an essay.

Number of Authors

An article, chapter, or book may have no author or different numbers of authors. Use the following formats, depending on the number of authors.

No Author

Begin the reference list entry with the title of the article, chapter, or book:

> *Brexit and parliament: Questions of sovereignty (2016, November 12). *The Economist*, 54–55.

One Author

Begin the reference list entry with the author's surname and initial(s):

> Casanave, C. P. (2002). *Writing games: Multicultural case studies of academic literacy practices in higher education.* Mahwah, NJ: Lawrence Erlbaum Associates.

Two Authors

Begin the reference list entry with the first author's surname and initial(s), followed by a comma, an ampersand (&), and the second author's surname and initial(s):

> McIvor, O., & Parker, A. (2016). Back to the future: Recreating natural Indigenous language learning environments through language nest early childhood immersion programs. *The International Journal of Holistic Early Learning and Development, 3,* 21–35.

Three to Seven Authors

Write the reference list entry as above, adding authors as in the following example:

> Marshall, S., Zhou, M., Gervan, T., & Wiebe, S. (2012). Sense of belonging and first-year academic literacy. *Canadian Journal of Higher Education, 42*(3), 116–142.

Eight or More Authors

List the first six authors' surnames and initials, add three spaced periods, and then list the final author's surname and initial(s):

> *Aman, M. M., Solangi, K. H., Hossain, M. S., Badarudin, A., Jasmon, G. B., Mokhlis, H., . . . & Kazi, S. N. (2015). A review of Safety, Health and Environmental (SHE) issues of solar energy system. *Renewable and Sustainable Energy Reviews, 41,* 1190–1204.

Formats for Print Sources

Use the following formats for different sources.

Journal Article

Include the DOI (digital object identifier) if available.

Surname(s), Initial(s). (year). Title of article. *Title of Journal, volume number*(issue number), page number(s). doi:xxxxx

> Bailey, C., & Challen, R. (2015). Student perceptions of the value of Turnitin text-matching software as a learning tool. *Practitioner Research in Higher Education, 9*(1), 38–51.

Chapter in an Edited Collection

Surname(s), Initial(s). (year). Title of chapter. In Initial(s). Surname(s) (Ed[s].), *Title of book* (pp. xxx–xxx). Place of publication: Publisher.

> Suranovic, S. (2015). The meaning of fair trade. In L. T. Raynolds, & E. A. Bennett (Eds.), *Handbook of research on fair trade* (pp. 45–60). Cheltenham, UK: Edward Elgar.

Magazine Article

Surname(s), Initial(s). (year, Month day). Title of article. *Title of Magazine, volume number*(issue number), page number(s).

> *Loder, N. (2016, December). Crumbs of comfort. *The Economist 1843,* 104–105.

Newspaper Article

Surname(s), Initial(s). (year, Month day). Title of article. *Title of Newspaper,* p(p). xxx.

*Brody, J. E. (2017, January 16). Why we need to emancipate ourselves from smartphones. *The Globe and Mail*, p. L3.

Book

Surname(s), Initial(s). (year). *Title of book.* Place of publication: Publisher.

Casanave, C. P. (2002). *Writing games: Multicultural case studies of academic literacy practices in higher education*. Mahwah, NJ: Lawrence Erlbaum Associates.

Multiple Publications by the Same Author

If you have cited two or more works by the same author and published in the same year, order the works alphabetically according to their titles, and add *a*, *b*, *c*, etc., to the year for each different work.

*Canagarajah, A. S. (2013a). Agency and power in intercultural communication: Negotiating English in translocal spaces. *Language and Intercultural Communication*, *13*(2), 202–224.

*Canagarajah, A. S. (2013b). The end of second language writing? *Journal of Second Language Writing*, *22*(4), 440–441.

If you have cited two or more works by the same author and published in different years, order the works by year, with the earliest work first.

Casanave, C. P. (2002). *Writing games: Multicultural case studies of academic literacy practices in higher education*. Mahwah, NJ: Lawrence Erlbaum Associates.

Casanave, C. P. (2010). Taking risks?: A case study of three doctoral students writing qualitative dissertations at an American university in Japan. *Journal of Second Language Writing*, *19*(1), 1–16.

Works Published by Organizations

If you have cited a work published by an organization (governmental or non-governmental), list the entry by the name of the organization, not the title of the work.

Name of Organization. (year). *Title of work*. Place of publication: Publisher.

European Environment Agency. (2016). *Explaining road transport emissions: A non-technical guide*. Copenhagen: EEA.

Formats for Online Sources

Reference list entries for electronic sources require the inclusion of the URL in most cases. It is only necessary to include a retrieval date if it is likely that the source will change, for example, a wiki. The following are common forms of reference list entries for electronic sources.

Web Page with an Author

Begin the reference list entry with the author's surname and initial:

Surname, Initial. (year, Month day). Title of document. Retrieved from URL

Weimer, M. (2015, October 14). How concerned should we be about cell phones in class? [Web log post]. Retrieved from http://www.facultyfocus. com/articles/teaching-professor-blog/how-concerned-should-we-be-about-cell-phones-in-class/

Web Page with No Author

Begin the reference list entry with the title of the web page or article, or the name of the organization:

Title of article/page. (year, Month day). *Title of Site*. Retrieved from URL

OR

Name of Organization. (year, Month day). Title of article/page. *Title of Site*. Retrieved from URL

El Niño [Encyclopedic entry]. (n.d.). *National Geographic Society*. Retrieved from http://nationalgeographic.org/encyclopedia/el-nino/

Eurostat. (2016, October 19). Air pollution statistics. *Statistics Explained*. Retrieved from http://ec.europa.eu/eurostat/statisticsexplained/index. php /Air_pollution_statistics

Article from an Online Academic Journal

Many online academic journal articles now have a digital object identifier (DOI). In such cases, the APA manual stipulates that the DOI should be used instead of the article's URL, with no retrieval date required.

Surname(s), Initial(s). (year). Title of article. *Title of Journal, volume number*(issue number), page numbers. doi:xxxxx

Ma, L., & Tsui, A. S. (2015). Traditional Chinese philosophies and contemporary leadership. *The Leadership Quarterly, 26*(1), 13–24. doi:10.1016/j. leaqua.2014.11.008

Online Newspaper Article

Surname(s), Initial(s). (year, Month day). Title of article. *Title of Newspaper*. Retrieved from URL

James, E. (2014, November 26). Prison is not for punishment in Sweden. We get people into better shape. *The Guardian*. Retrieved from http://www. theguardian.com/society/2014/nov/26/prison-sweden-not-punishment-nils-oberg

Online Magazine Article

Surname(s), Initial(s). (year, Month day). Title of article. *Title of Magazine*. Retrieved from URL

Harford, T. (2015, May 29). Mind the fair trade gap. *FT Magazine*. Retrieved from https://next.ft.com/content/fc9a2e14-03e1-11e5-a70f-00144feabdc0

Online Encylopedia Entry

Title of article. (year, Month day). In *Title of Encyclopedia*. Retrieved from URL

3D printing. (2016, January 26). In *Encyclopædia Britannica*. Retrieved from https://www.britannica.com/technology/3D-printing

MLA CITATION STYLE

MLA (Modern Language Association) citation style is used mainly in the humanities, such as English and modern languages, cultural and literary studies. The MLA formats presented in this appendix include the most common forms you will need for academic writing. You can find complete guidelines for MLA citation style in the *MLA Handbook*, Eighth Edition.

IN-TEXT CITATIONS

Every time you use a statistic, idea, image, or creative work that is not your own, you are required to acknowledge your source with an in-text citation. Each in-text citation should match a corresponding entry in the list of works cited at the end of the essay.

MLA in-text citations should usually include, in parentheses, the author's or authors' surname(s) and/or the page number(s) of the information cited, with no comma separating the two. MLA in-text citations do not include the year of publication.

> Unless marked with an asterisk (*), the examples throughout the appendix refer to texts cited in this book.

Surname: (Casanave)

Surname and page number: (Casanave 25)

Page number only: (25)

If you are citing an online source that does not have page numbers, cite the paragraph numbers, if available, by using the abbreviations *par.* or *pars.* You are not required to cite page numbers or paragraph numbers if none are available.

Authors

Inclusion of the Author's Name in the Citation Phrase

If you include the name of the author in the citation phrase, do not repeat it in the following parentheses.

> Stolberg describes how homeopathy was popular in the 19th century in the kingdom of Bavaria (642).

If the name of the author is not part of the citation phrase, include it in the following parentheses.

> Homeopathy had gained considerable popularity in the kingdom of Bavaria during the 19th century (Stolberg 642).

Two Authors

If two authors' names are included in a citation phrase, join them with *and*. In parentheses, also join them with *and*.

> Richards and Stedmon discuss the issue of automation and human performance with reference to autonomous cars (384).

> Another important issue to consider with regard to autonomous cars is the relationship between automation and human performance (Richards and Stedmon 384).

Three or More Authors

For sources with three or more authors, cite the surname of the first author, followed by *et al.* (not italicized).

> Marshall et al. concluded that the sense of belonging of the first-year university students in their study was affected by a wide range of social and linguistic factors (134).

> First-year university students' sense of belonging can be affected by a wide range of social and linguistic factors (Marshall et al. 134).

No Author

For sources that do not have an author, cite the title of the work, or an abbreviated title in parentheses. For short works, for example, journal articles and book chapters, use quotation marks. For longer works, such as books, use italics.

> *In "Brexit and Parliament, Questions of Sovereignty," the complex interrelationships between the UK and European parliaments are discussed in terms of competing views of sovereignty.

> *The complex interrelationships between the UK and European parliaments have been discussed in terms of competing views of sovereignty ("Brexit and Parliament").

> No page or paragraph numbers are available for this source.

Multiple Sources in a Citation

When you include two or more sources in an in-text citation, separate the sources in parentheses with semicolons.

> A number of studies in recent years have analyzed paraphrasing, patchwriting, and plagiarism (Bailey and Challen; Ellery).

Print Sources

Multiple Works by the Same Author

When you cite more than one work by the same author in the same sentence or paragraph, include the title of the work in parentheses to make it clear to the reader which work you are citing.

> Stolberg describes the history of homeopathy in Germany ("Homeopathy in the Kingdom of Bavaria") and later analyzes the invention of the double-blind control trial ("Inventing the Randomized Double-Blind Trial").

Secondary Sources

If you are citing a source that you read about elsewhere, without having read the original work, begin the in-text citation with *qtd. in*.

> Spady argues that post-secondary students' social integration is informed by a social system (the campus) and the sum of its parts (qtd. in Marshall et al. 119).

Citing Multiple Pages

Use the following formats to cite information from multiple pages of the same work.

> **Consecutive pages:** Marshall et al. address critiques that have been made of Spady's model of student integration (118–119).

> **Non-consecutive pages:** Marshall et al. consider the critiques that various authors have made of Tinto's model of student retention (119, 134).

Direct Quotations

Direct Quotations of Fewer Than Four Lines

Direct quotations of fewer than four lines should be integrated grammatically into sentences and enclosed in quotation marks. Page numbers should be provided in parentheses immediately after the quotation.

> In their conclusion, Morton et al. highlight "the unpredictable and unexpected practices contributing to the students' progress as academic writers" (9).

> Writing teachers need to become more aware of the "unpredictable and unexpected practices contributing to the students' progress as academic writers" (Morton et al. 9).

Punctuation from the original text, for example, question marks, should remain within the quotation marks; punctuation that you add should be placed outside the quotation marks.

> **Original punctuation:** Morton et al. ask the following question: "Do the students' perceptions of themselves as academic writers change?" (3).

> **Added punctuation:** Should we agree with Morton et al.'s conclusion that progress in academic writing is the product of "unpredictable and unexpected practices" (9)?

Direct Quotations of Four Lines or More

Direct quotations of four lines or more should be dropped one line, indented by half an inch (1.25 cm) from the left margin, and not enclosed in quotation marks. The final period should be placed before the in-text citation rather than after.

> UNESCO's "Atlas of the World's Languages in Danger of Disappearing" noted that at least one-third of the children should be learning a language to maintain its vitality. Bougie highlights the difference in Canada as follows:
>
>> According to the 2006 Census, 18% of First Nations children across Canada had an Aboriginal language as their mother tongue (or first language learned), down from 21% in 1996. Older generations of First Nations people are generally more likely than younger generations to have an Aboriginal language as their mother tongue. (qtd. in McIvor and Parker 23)

Omitting Words from Direct Quotations

If you omit words from a direct quotation, indicate the omission with an ellipsis (three spaced periods: . . .).

> With reference to students taking the ALC course, Marshall et al. stress the need to focus on "the academic literacy development of students . . . and to recognize and respect the varied social, cultural, and linguistic backgrounds of students" (135).

Adding Words to Direct Quotations

If you add words to improve the clarity of a direct quotation, enclose the added word(s) in square brackets.

> With reference to students taking the ALC course, Marshall et al. stress the need to focus on "[writers'] social, cultural, and linguistic backgrounds" (135).

Online Sources

With an Author

If an online source has an author, cite the author's name.

> There are a number of contested myths in the renewable versus nuclear power debate (Diesendorf).

No Author

If the online source has no identifiable author, cite the title of the work: for short works (e.g., journal articles and book chapters), use quotation marks, and for longer works (e.g., books), use italics. If a work has a long title, you may shorten it in parentheses.

> The effects of extreme weather events on coastal communities in Ecuador have been well documented by National Geographic in its online encyclopedia ("El Niño").

No Author or Title

If the information you are citing is from a website that has no author or title, cite the website name only, in parentheses. Do not include the URL in the parentheses; include it in the Works Cited entry, which should begin with the website name.

> Today, over 70 so-called generation III reactors are under construction, including 29 in energy-hungry China (*World Nuclear Association*).

With Numbered Paragraphs

If you are directly quoting information from an online source with no page numbers but with numbered paragraphs, indicate the paragraph numbers in parentheses, using the abbreviation *par.* or *pars.* Separate the author's name from the paragraph number(s) by a comma.

Personal Communications: Conversations, Interviews, and E-Mail

Use the following format to cite personal communications such as a conversation, interview, or e-mail correspondence. Include a corresponding entry in the Works Cited list.

> (Moore, Personal communication)

MLA reference lists should include one entry for each source that has been cited with an in-text citation. MLA format requires that the reference list appear at the end of the essay, on a separate page, with the title *Works Cited* centred at the top of the page.

Reference list entries should be double-spaced, arranged alphabetically by the author's surname or by the title of an unauthored source. All lines other than the first line of each entry should be indented half an inch from the left margin. The examples below illustrate the most common types of entries. However, they are not double-spaced, as would be required in an essay.

Number of Authors

An article, chapter, or book may have no author or different numbers of authors. Use the following formats, depending on the number of authors.

No Author

Begin the reference list entry with the title of the article, chapter, or book:

> *2010 Encyclopedia Britannica World Atlas*. Encyclopedia Britannica Editorial, 2010.

One Author

Begin the reference list entry with the author's surname and name, separated by a comma:

> Casanave, Christine. *Writing Games: Multicultural Case Studies of Academic Literacy Practices in Higher Education*. Lawrence Erlbaum Associates, 2002.

Two Authors

Begin the reference list entry with the first author's surname and name, followed by a comma and *and*, then the second author's name and surname:

> McIvor, Onowa, and Aliana Parker. "Back to the Future: Recreating Natural Indigenous Language Learning Environments through Language Nest Early Childhood Immersion Programs." *The International Journal of Holistic Early Learning and Development*, vol. 3, 2016, pp. 21–35.

Three or More Authors

Begin the reference list entry with the first author's surname and name, followed by a comma and *et al.*:

> Marshall, Steve, et al. "Sense of Belonging and First-Year Academic Literacy." *Canadian Journal of Higher Education*, vol. 42, no. 3, 2012, pp. 116–142.

Formats for Print Sources

Use the following formats for different sources.

Journal Article

Surname, Name (, and Name Surname). "Title of Article." *Title of Journal,* vol. xx, no. xx, year, pp. xxx–xxx.

> Bailey, Carol, and Rachel Challen. "Student Perceptions of the Value of Turnitin Text-Matching Software as a Learning Tool." *Practitioner Research in Higher Education*, vol. 9, no. 1, 2015, pp. 38–51.

Chapter in an Edited Collection

Surname, Name (, and Name Surname). "Title of Chapter." *Title of Book*, edited by Editor's Name(s), Publisher, year, pp. xxx–xxx.

> Suranovic, Steven. "The Meaning of Fair Trade." *Handbook of Research on Fair Trade*, edited by Laura Raynolds and Elizabeth Bennet, Edward Elgar, 2015, pp. 45–60.

Magazine Article

Surname, Name (, and Name Surname). "Title of Article." *Title of Magazine*, day Month year, pp. xxx–xxx.

> *Loder, Natasha. "Crumbs of Comfort." *The Economist 1843*, Dec. 2016, pp. 104–105.

Note that month names that are longer than four letters are abbreviated in a newspaper or magazine reference. Use the following abbreviations: Jan., Feb., Mar., Apr., Aug., Sept., Oct., Nov., and Dec.

Newspaper Article

Surname, Name (, and Name Surname). "Title of Article." *Title of Newspaper*, day Month year, p. xxx.

> *Brody, Jane E. "Why We Need to Emancipate Ourselves from Smartphones." *The Globe and Mail*, 16 Jan. 2017, p. L3.

Book

Surname, Name (, and Name Surname). *Title of Book.* Publisher, year.

> Casanave, Christine. *Writing Games: Multicultural Case Studies of Academic Literacy Practices in Higher Education.* Lawrence Erlbaum Associates, 2002.

Multiple Publications by the Same Author

If you have cited two or more works by the same author, list the works in alphabetical order (disregarding words such as *a*, *an*, and *the*). Use the above formats for the first entry. Thereafter, use three hyphens ---, followed by a period, to replace the author's name.

> *Canagarajah, Suresh. "Agency and Power in Intercultural Communication: Negotiating English in Translocal Spaces." *Language and Intercultural Communication*, vol. 13, no. 2, 2013, pp. 202–224.

> *---. "The End of Second Language Writing?" *Journal of Second Language Writing*, vol. 22, no. 4, 2013, pp. 440–441.

Works Published by Organizations

If you have cited a work published by an organization (governmental or non-governmental), list the entry by the name of the organization, not the title of the work.

Name of Organization. *Title of Work*. Publisher, year.

> European Environment Agency. *Explaining Road Transport Emissions: A Non-Technical Guide*. EEA, 2016.

Formats for Online Sources

MLA citation style encourages the inclusion of a URL for electronic sources. If you provide a URL, only the www. address is required; you should leave out the *https://*. Indicate page or paragraph numbers if available, and the date you accessed the source, preceded by the word *Accessed*, to indicate the version you consulted, especially if the source is undated.

The following are some common forms of MLA reference list entries for electronic sources.

Web Page with an Author

Begin the reference list entry with the author's surname and name:

Surname, Name. "Title of Article." *Title of Site/Page*, Sponsor or Publisher (if different from site), date of publication (if available), URL. Accessed date.

> Weimer, Maryellen. "How Concerned Should We Be about Cell Phones in Class?" *Faculty Focus*, 14 Oct. 2015, www.facultyfocus.com/articles/ teaching-professor-blog/how-concerned-should-we-be-about-cell-phones-in-class/. Accessed 25 Nov. 2016.

Web Page with No Author

Begin the reference list entry with the title of the web page or article:

"Title of Article." *Title of Site/Page*, Sponsor or Publisher (if different from site), date of publication (if available), URL. Accessed date.

> "El Niño." *National Geographic*, www.nationalgeographic.org/encyclopedia/ el-nino/. Accessed 12 Nov. 2016.

Article from an Online Academic Journal

Many online academic journal articles now have a digital object identifier (DOI). When citing such articles, include the DOI rather than the URL, and the online database where you found the article (if applicable).

Surname, Name. "Title of Article." *Title of Journal,* vol. xx, no. xx, year, pp. xxx–xxx. *Online Database* (if applicable), doi:xxxxx. Accessed date.

> Ma, Li, and Anne S. Tsui. "Traditional Chinese Philosophies and Contemporary Leadership." *The Leadership Quarterly*, vol. 26, no. 1, 2015, pp. 13–24. *ScienceDirect*, doi:10.1016/j.leaqua.2014.11.008. Accessed 7 Sept. 2016.

Online Newspaper Article

Surname, Name. "Title of Article." *Title of Newspaper*, date of publication. *Online Database* (if applicable), URL. Accessed date.

> James, Erwin. "Prison Is Not for Punishment in Sweden. We Get People into Better Shape." *The Guardian*, 26 Nov. 2014, www.theguardian.com/society/2014/nov/26/prison-sweden-not-punishment-nils-oberg. Accessed 15 June 2016.

Online Magazine Article

Surname, Name. "Title of Article." *Title of Magazine*, date of publication, URL. Accessed date.

> Harford, Tim. "Mind the Fair Trade Gap." *FT Magazine*, 29 May 2015, next.ft.com/content/fc9a2e14-03e1-11e5-a70f-00144feabdc0. Accessed 5 Aug. 2016.

Online Encylopedia Entry

"Title of article." *Title of Encyclopedia*, date of publication (if available), URL. Accessed date.

> "3D Printing." *Encyclopædia Britannica*, 26 Jan. 2016, www.britannica.com/technology/3D-printing. Accessed 2 Nov. 2016.

Personal Communications: E-Mail

Surname, Name. "Re: Subject Line." Received by Name Surname, date.

> Hynes, Patricia. "Re: Editing Questions." Received by Steve Marshall, 21 Nov. 2016.

35 MISTAKES TO AVOID IN ACADEMIC WRITING

A complete list of mistakes to avoid in academic writing would be endless. Here are 35 common mistakes that writers make.

PUNCTUATION

The following are common mistakes when using commas, semicolons, and colons.

1. Comma Splices

Avoid writing comma splices: sentences in which two independent clauses are joined by a comma.

✗ Crime prevention strategies have been successful during the last year**,** they also have the support of the central government.

✓ Crime prevention strategies have been successful during the last year**;** they also have the support of the central government.

✓ Crime prevention strategies have been successful during the last year**.** They also have the support of the central government.

2. Commas: Inconsistency

It is important to use commas consistently. For example, you should avoid including commas in some sentences and not in others (e.g., before coordinators and after introductory phrases—in bold in the following examples).

✗ **Between 2002 and 2012** crime fell gradually within the European Union. **During the same period,** violent crime fell in some EU countries **yet** figures rose in others. The inconsistency in violent crime rates is difficult to explain**, and** criminologists are looking for explanations.

✓ **Between 2002 and 2012,** crime fell gradually within the European Union. **During the same period,** violent crime fell in some EU countries**, yet** figures rose in others. The inconsistency in violent crime rates is difficult to explain**, and** criminologists are looking for explanations.

3. Commas: Confusing Sentences

In several writing genres, for example, journalistic and informal writing, commas are not used consistently after introductory phrases before an independent clause. If you are not including commas after introductory phrases, avoid confusing your reader due to the lack of commas.

✗ To reduce **crime prevention** is a more effective focus than punishment.

✓ To reduce **crime, prevention** is a more effective focus than punishment.

Because *crime prevention* is a common compound noun, if the writer omits the comma, the first part of the sentence could be read as "to reduce crime prevention" rather than "to reduce crime."

4. Semicolons: Incorrect Use in Complex Sentences

It is incorrect to use a semicolon to separate a dependent and independent clause in a complex sentence. Use a comma instead.

    ✗ Although the fair trade movement benefits many small-scale farmers world-wide**;** it benefits intermediaries even more.

    ✓ Although the fair trade movement benefits many small-scale farmers world-wide**,** it benefits intermediaries even more.

5. Semicolons: Incorrect Use in Lists of Items

Use semicolons to separate items in a list only if at least one of the items includes a comma.

    ✗ The fair trade movement needs to find strategies to address three important issues: expensive registration costs**;** excessive profits for intermediaries**;** and unstable product prices in world markets.

    ✓ The fair trade movement needs to find strategies to address three important issues: expensive registration costs**,** excessive profits for intermediaries**,** and unstable product prices in world markets.

    ✓ The fair trade movement needs to find strategies to address three important issues: expensive registration costs**,** which affect farmers**;** excessive profits for intermediaries**;** and unstable product prices in world markets.

6. Colons: Incorrect Use When Introducing Examples and Lists

Do not use a colon when you introduce a list or examples that are incorporated grammatically into the sentence.

    ✗ Two key challenges in international business relations in Africa are**:** responding to globalization and adapting to Western business practices.

    ✓ Two key challenges in international business relations in Africa are responding to globalization and adapting to Western business practices.

    ✓ Two key challenges in international business relations in Africa are **the following:** responding to globalization and adapting to Western business practices.

    ✓ Business leaders in Africa face two key **challenges:** responding to globalization and adapting to Western business practices.

7. Colons: Incorrect Use When Introducing Direct Quotations

It is correct usage to place a colon at the end of an independent clause to introduce direct quotations. However, do not use a colon to introduce a direct quotation that is incorporated grammatically into the sentence.

    ✗ It is important for leadership assessments to be performed**:** "in a structured manner, primarily based on behavioral criteria" (Peus et al., 2012, p. 106).

✓ It is important for leadership assessments to be performed "in a structured manner, primarily based on behavioral criteria" (Peus et al., 2012, p. 106).

✓ Leadership assessments should be performed to link organizational structure and work patterns **as follows:** "in a structured manner, primarily based on behavioral criteria" (Peus et al., 2012, p. 106).

LINKING WORDS

Avoid the following mistakes when you use linking words to join your ideas and arguments.

8. *Although* and *Even Though* Followed Directly by a Comma

Do not introduce a sentence with the subordinators *although* or *even though* followed by a comma.

✗ Certain nutritionists recommend olive oil. **Although,** it is too expensive for many families to use on a daily basis.

✓ Certain nutritionists recommend olive oil. **However,** it is too expensive for many families to use on a daily basis. (Use a conjunctive adverb such as *however*.)

✓ **Although** certain nutritionists recommend olive oil, it is too expensive for many families to use on a daily basis. (Move the subordinator to form a dependent clause.)

9. *Although* and *Even Though* with *But*

This is a common mistake when translating from certain languages into English.

If you begin a dependent clause with *although* or *even though*, do not begin the following independent clause with *but*. The idea of contrast has already been expressed by the subordinator.

✗ Although certain nutritionists recommend olive oil, **but** it is too expensive for many families to use on a daily basis.

✓ Although certain nutritionists recommend olive oil, it is too expensive for many families to use on a daily basis.

10. *In Contrast* versus *On the Contrary*

Use *in contrast* to introduce contrasting information. Use *on the contrary* to contradict or disagree with an argument stated previously.

✗ High school writing often involves formulas such as the five-paragraph essay. **On the contrary,** college writing varies greatly across the disciplines.

✓ High school writing often involves formulas such as the five-paragraph essay. **In contrast,** college writing varies greatly across the disciplines.

✓ It has been argued that high school writing is too easy. **On the contrary,** I found that many students wrote a range of challenging texts in Grades 11 and 12.

Avoid the following mistakes with nouns and verbs commonly used in academic writing.

11. *Criteria* and *Phenomena*: Singular versus Plural Forms

Nouns that have their origins in Greek, for example, *criteria* and *phenomena*, are often used incorrectly, even by experienced academics. Avoid confusing the singular and plural forms of these nouns.

✗ The criteria for the in-class essay **was** confusing.

✓ The criteria for the in-class essay **were** confusing.

✗ There are many important **criterion** for college success.

✓ There are many important **criteria** for college success.

✗ The essay was about a weather **phenomena** known as *urban heat islands*.

✓ The essay was about a weather **phenomenon** known as *urban heat islands*.

✗ Several **phenomenon** cause urban heat islands.

✓ Several **phenomena** cause urban heat islands.

12. *Effect* versus *Affect*

Avoid making mistakes with *effect* and *affect* when describing causal relations. Each word can be used as a noun or a verb with different meanings. In most contexts, *effect* is a noun and *affect*, the corresponding verb, as illustrated below.

✗ Higher temperatures and pollution had a negative **affect** on air quality in the city.

✓ Higher temperatures and pollution had a negative **effect** on air quality in the city. (noun)

✗ Higher temperatures and pollution **effected** air quality in the city.

✓ Higher temperatures and pollution **affected** air quality in the city. (verb)

Effect can also be used as a verb meaning "to bring something about or make happen." *Affect* as a noun refers to an emotion that is related to behaviour. The following examples illustrate these less common usages.

✓ The new anti-pollution policies **effected** little change in the city.

✓ **Affect** is an important psychological factor in individuals' responses to requests and instructions.

13. *Affect* versus *Effect on, Emphasize* versus *Emphasis on*

In several cases, when you have the choice of expressing relationships of cause and effect or emphasis with either a verb or a corresponding noun, use the preposition *on* with the noun.

✗ Higher temperatures and pollution **affected on** air quality in the city.

✓ Higher temperatures and pollution **affected** air quality in the city.

✓ Higher temperatures and pollution **had an effect on** air quality in the city.

✗ The new mayor **emphasized on** tackling air pollution when he came to office.

✓ The new mayor **emphasized** tackling air pollution when he came to office.

✓ The new mayor **placed an emphasis on** tackling air pollution when he came to office.

HOMOPHONES

Some words sound the same but have different meanings and spellings. The following examples are commonly confused.

14. *There, Their,* and *They're*

✗ **Their** are several benefits to using cellphones for learning.

✓ **There** are several benefits to using cellphones for learning.

✗ Many teachers don't allow students to use cellphones in **there** classes.

✓ Many teachers don't allow students to use cellphones in **their** classes.

✗ Students may distract others when **there** texting friends.

✓ Students may distract others when **they're** texting friends.

15. *Your* and *You're*

✗ Please check **you're** phone for updates to the schedule.

✓ Please check **your** phone for updates to the schedule.

✗ **Your** arriving at 16:45 tomorrow afternoon.

✓ **You're** arriving at 16:45 tomorrow afternoon.

SPELLING: DOUBLE CONSONANTS

16. Incorrect Double Consonants

Writers sometimes make mistakes when they are spelling multi-syllable words that may or may not require double consonants when adding a suffix. If the suffix begins with a vowel (*ed, ing*), you can apply the following rule: a) double the consonant after *a short stressed vowel sound*; b) do not double the consonant after *an unstressed vowel sound*.

✗ The artefacts were **intered** 2,000 years ago.

✓ The artefacts were **interred** 2,000 years ago.

✗ The archaeologists **enterred** the site after a year of preparation.

✓ The archaeologists **entered** the site after a year of preparation.

RELATIVE CLAUSES

The following are some of the most common mistakes that writers make when they form relative clauses.

17. Confusing Defining and Non-Defining Relative Clauses

Avoid writing non-defining relative clauses as defining relative clauses, and vice versa.

In each example below, the defining relative clause gives essential information about the subject of the independent clause. It explains that the writer is referring to a specific Business class—the one she is taking this term, not the other Business classes she may have taken. Do not set off defining clauses with commas, and use the relative pronouns *that* or *which* for things.

✗ The Business class**, that I'm taking this term,** is difficult.

✓ The Business class **that I'm taking this term** is difficult.

✓ The Business class **which I'm taking this term** is difficult. (British English)

In the next two examples, the non-defining clause gives non-essential information about the noun *exam* in the independent clause. It provides extra information— that the Business exam was more difficult than expected. Set off non-defining clauses with commas, and use the relative pronoun *which* for things, not *that*. Note that the incorrect non-defining clause suggests that there was more than one exam: one that was more difficult than expected and one that wasn't.

✗ I got an A in the Business exam **which was more difficult than expected**.

✓ I got an A in the Business exam**, which was more difficult than expected**.

18. *That* versus *Where*

Avoid incorrect use of *that* and *where* in defining relative clauses that require a verb and corresponding preposition. The following examples show incorrect and correct usage of *that* and *where* in phrases that refer to the following idea: I lived in that country when I was a child.

✗ That is the country **that I lived** when I was a child. (The preposition *in* is missing.)

✗ That is the country **where I lived in** when I was a child. (The preposition *in* is unnecessary.)

✓ That is the country **that I lived in** when I was a child.

✓ That is the country **where I lived** when I was a child.

✓ That is the country **in which I lived** when I was a child. (formal)

19. *Whom* versus *Who*: Direct Objects

Whom can be used when referring to a person who is the direct object of the relative clause.

✗ He's the teaching assistant **whom** taught the lab class last term.

✓ He's the teaching assistant **who** taught the lab class last term.

✓ Is he the teaching assistant **whom** you recommended?

The first sentence is incorrect because *whom* should be *who* (as in sentence 2); it is the subject of the relative clause, referring back to *he*: *He* taught the lab class last term. The third sentence is correct because *whom* is the object of the relative clause, replacing *him*: You recommended **him**.

20. *Whom* versus *Who*: After Prepositions

Whom should also be used after prepositions.

    ✗ She's the student with **who** you took the lab class last term.

    ✓ She's the student with **whom** you took the lab class last term.

DANGLING MODIFIERS

Dangling modifiers are phrases or clauses, usually at the beginning of sentences, that "dangle"—in other words, they do not correspond to the grammatical subject of the main clause.

21. Dangling Modifiers: Participle Phrases

Dangling modifiers are most common in sentences that begin with participle phrases.

    ✗ **Originating in the 1980s,** I became interested in the slow food movement.

    ✓ **Originating in the 1980s,** slow food emerged in response to the spread of fast food.

    ✗ **Launched in 2001,** they soon learned about Slow Food International.

    ✓ **Launched in 2001,** Slow Food International gained worldwide attention.

The first incorrect sentence can be read as meaning the writer originated in the 1980s, not the slow food movement. The second incorrect sentence reads as if "they" were launched in 2001.

22. Dangling Modifiers: Preposition Phrases

In addition, avoid dangling modifiers in sentences that begin with preposition phrases.

    ✗ **At the age of 25,** the slow food movement became an integral part of my life.

    ✓ **At the age of 25,** I became very involved in the slow food movement.

PRONOUNS

Pronouns are words that take the place of a noun or noun phrase. For example, in the following sentence, the pronoun *him* refers to the noun *Michael*.

    I bumped into Michael and asked **him** if I could borrow his lecture notes.

23. *I* versus *Me*

Use *and I* if a verb follows immediately. Use *and me* if no verb follows.

    ✗ **You and me** should attend the lecture next week.

    ✓ **You and I** should attend the lecture next week.

    ✗ She lent her lecture notes to **you and I**.

    ✓ She lent her lecture notes to **you and me**.

24. Ambiguous Pronouns

Avoid using pronouns that may confuse your reader by referring to more than one noun. In the following sentence, it is not clear whether the classmates or the lecture notes are not helpful.

    ✗ My classmates rarely share lecture notes because **they** aren't very helpful.

    ✓ My classmates rarely share lecture notes because they are too competitive.

    ✓ My classmates rarely share lecture notes because the notes they take aren't very helpful.

DESCRIBING QUANTITY

Be careful not to make mistakes with quantifiers such as *some*, and with phrases such as *a large number of* and a *large amount of*.

25. *Some* versus *Some of*

Use *some of* before determiners such as *the*, *those*, *my*, etc. The same rule applies for other quantifiers, for example, *many*, *a few*, etc.

    ✗ **Some of** questions in the quiz were very difficult.

    ✓ **Some** questions in the quiz were very difficult.

    ✓ **Some of the** questions in the quiz were very difficult.

26. *A Large Amount of* versus *A Large Number of*

Use *a large amount of* with uncountable nouns (nouns that have no plural form). Use *a large number of* with plural countable nouns.

    ✗ **A large amount of** students dislike final exams.

    ✓ **A large number of** students dislike final exams.

    ✓ There was **a large amount of** confusion about the final exam format.

27. *Less* versus *Fewer*

Use *less* with uncountable nouns and *fewer* with countable nouns. Avoid the common mistake of using *less* with plural countable nouns.

    ✗ The final exam had **less problem-solving questions** than the mid-term test.

    ✓ The final exam had **fewer problem-solving questions** than the mid-term test.

28. *Little, A Little, Few,* and *A Few*

Before uncountable nouns, *little* means "virtually none" while *a little* means "a small amount."

    I had **little difficulty** answering all the questions. (virtually no difficulty)

    I had **a little difficulty** answering all the questions. (a small amount of difficulty)

Before plural countable nouns, *few* means "virtually none" while *a few* means "a small number." *Little* means "small" when used with countable nouns.

> There were **few questions** that I couldn't answer. (virtually no questions)
>
> There were **a few questions** that I couldn't answer. (a small number of questions)
>
> I had **a little problem** with the final question. (small, not serious problem)

✗ There were **little questions** that I couldn't answer. (This means the questions were physically small.)

✓ There were **few questions** that I couldn't answer.

✗ I hope there are **few questions** that I will be able to answer. (This means the speaker does not want to be able to answer the questions!)

✓ I hope there are **a few questions** that I will be able to answer.

IN-TEXT CITATIONS AND REFERENCE LISTS

The following are seven common mistakes to avoid when citing sources and writing reference list entries.

29. Reference List Not in Alphabetical Order

It is a requirement for APA and MLA citation styles that reference list entries be ordered alphabetically by author's surname (or by publishing organization, or title for works with no identifiable author). Occasionally, titles of a work begin with a number; such works should be ordered numerically, coming before titles beginning with a letter. The following examples of an APA reference list illustrate this point.

✗ Casanave, C. P. (2002). *Writing games: Multicultural case studies of academic literacy practices in higher education.* Mahwah, NJ: Lawrence Erlbaum Associates.

Bailey, C., & Challen, R. (2015). Student perceptions of the value of Turnitin text-matching software as a learning tool. *Practitioner Research in Higher Education, 9*(1), 38–51.

European Environment Agency. (2016). *Explaining road transport emissions: A non-technical guide.* Copenhagen: EEA.

3D printing. (2016, January 26). In *Encyclopædia Britannica.* Retrieved from https://www.britannica.com/technology/3D-printing

✓ 3D printing. (2016, January 26). In *Encyclopædia Britannica.* Retrieved from https://www.britannica.com/technology/3D-printing

Bailey, C., & Challen, R. (2015). Student perceptions of the value of Turnitin text-matching software as a learning tool. *Practitioner Research in Higher Education, 9*(1), 38–51.

Casanave, C. P. (2002). *Writing games: Multicultural case studies of academic literacy practices in higher education.* Mahwah, NJ: Lawrence Erlbaum Associates.

European Environment Agency. (2016). *Explaining road transport emissions: A non-technical guide.* Copenhagen: EEA.

30. No Corresponding Reference List Entry for an In-Text Citation

Every in-text citation in the main body of the essay requires a corresponding entry in the reference list (except personal communications in APA style). Always cross-reference each in-text citation to avoid this mistake.

31. No Corresponding In-Text Citation for a Reference List Entry

Every reference list entry should correspond with an in-text citation in the main body of the essay. Always cross-reference each reference list entry to avoid this mistake.

32. Mismatch between the In-Text Citation and Reference List Entry

A reference list entry should begin with the same surname, organization, or work title as is indicated parenthetically in the corresponding in-text citation. Avoid a mismatch between the two as illustrated below.

In-text citation: ("3D printing," 2016)

References

✗ *Encyclopædia Britannica*. (2016, January 26). 3D printing. Retrieved from https://www.britannica.com/technology/3D-printing

✓ 3D printing. (2016, January 26). In *Encyclopædia Britannica*. Retrieved from https://www.britannica.com/technology/3D-printing

33. Formatting Inconsistencies

Avoid mixing up different citation styles as the following example illustrates. APA style is in bold, and MLA style is underlined.

✗ Recent research has focused on different aspects of the business leadership nexus between China and the West: for example, how three leading Chinese philosophies—Daoism, Confucianism, and Legalism—can complement Western-influenced leadership in China **(Ma & Tsui, 2015)**, and the need for Chinese approaches to stem the shift of Chinese leaders toward Western practices <u>(Li 1–2)</u>. **Kim and Moon (2015)** focus on leadership and Corporate Social Responsibility (CSR), comparing CSR in Asia (from Pakistan eastward to Japan) and Western CSR, while the determinants for success in business leadership and the role of women leaders in China, India, and Singapore are discussed in **Peus, Braun, and Knipfer (2015)**. A recent study has also highlighted the need to promote Indigenous African forms of knowledge to meet the needs of the African workforce, addressing the growth in Asia-Africa relations <u>(Kamoche et al. 331)</u>.

34. Ungrammatical Incorporation of Quotations

All short direct quotations (fewer than 40 words in APA style or four lines in MLA style) should be incorporated grammatically into sentences. Use a colon before direct quotations only if the quotation does not flow grammatically in the sentence.

Original information: Drawing on articles that reported interviews of fifteen business leaders, we code their leadership behaviors according to the school they exemplify. We use these fifteen cases to illustrate, rather than as a test of, the propositions. Finally, we discuss how traditional culture could be a rich source of understanding for future leadership research in China and beyond. (Ma & Tsui, 2015, p. 14)

> ✗ Ma and Tsui (2015) present interviews with 15 Chinese business leaders in their analysis of traditional Chinese culture and its **potential "a** rich source of understanding for future leadership research" (p. 14).

> ✗ Ma and Tsui (2015) present interviews with 15 Chinese business leaders in their analysis of traditional Chinese culture and its **potential as: "a** rich source of understanding for future leadership research" (p. 14).

> ✓ Ma and Tsui (2015) present interviews with 15 Chinese business leaders in their analysis of traditional Chinese culture and its **potential as "a** rich source of understanding for future leadership research" (p. 14).

35. Lack of Concision in Quotations

Direct quotations should be concise and include only key ideas. Other information should be paraphrased.

Original information: Although learning reflects knowledge acquired from teachers and others, thinking reflects digesting and internalizing what is learned. Ideal students of Confucius would use self-reflection to rigorously identify their own faults and develop actions for self improvement in the pursuit of self-perfection. (Ma & Tsui, p. 16)

> ✗ Ma and Tsui (2015) suggest that even though "learning reflects knowledge acquired from teachers and others, thinking reflects digesting and internalizing what is learned," and that ideally, "students of Confucius would use self-reflection to rigorously identify their own faults and develop actions for self improvement in the pursuit of self-perfection" (p. 16).

> ✓ Ma and Tsui (2015) suggest that learning is a reflection of what is learned from teachers and others, and that thinking is a reflection of how knowledge is internalized. According to the authors, from a Confucian perspective, self-reflection should be employed by learners as part of the process of "self improvement in the pursuit of self-perfection" (p. 16).

CREDITS

Text Credits

Chapter 1, pp. 4–7, 18, 22 Excerpts from "What Our Students Tell Us: Perceptions of Three Multilingual Students on Their Academic Writing in First Year" by Janne Morton, Neomy Storch, and Celia Thompson © 2015 Elsevier Inc. All rights reserved.

Chapter 2, pp. 36–38, 45–46 Excerpts from "Inventing the Randomized Double-Blind Trial: The Nuremberg Salt Test of 1835" by Michael Stolberg © Michael Stolberg, Institut für Geschichte der Medizin, Würzburg, Germany.

Chapter 3, pp. 52–55 Excerpts from "To Delegate or Not to Delegate: A Review of Control Frameworks for Autonomous Cars" by Dale Richards and Alex Stedmon © 2015 Elsevier Ltd. and The Ergonomics Society. All rights reserved. pp. 59–60 "Driverless Cars Work Great in Sunny California. But How About in a Blizzard?" by Brian Fung © 1996–2017 The Washington Post.

Chapter 4, pp. 78–81 Excerpts from "Student Perceptions of the Value of Turnitin Text-Matching Software as a Learning Tool" by Carol Bailey and Rachel Challen © 2015 University of Cumbria. pp. 87–89 Excerpts from "Here's What Makes a Song a Ripoff, according to the Law: How You Think about Music ≠ How the Courts Think about Music" by Reggie Ugwu © 2017 BuzzFeed Inc.

Chapter 5, pp. 105–106 "'Prison is not for punishment in Sweden. We get people into better shape'" by Erwin James © 2016 Guardian News & Media Ltd.

Chapter 6, pp. 130, 134 "Slow Food Revisited" by Jessica R. Page © Taylor & Francis Group, LLC. pp. 130, 131, 134 "Mind the Fair Trade Gap" by Tim Harford © 2017 Used under licence from the Financial Times. All rights reserved.

Chapter 7, pp. 155–156 Excerpt from "Traditional Chinese Philosophies and Contemporary Leadership" by Li Ma and Anne. S. Tsui © 2014 Elsevier Inc. All rights reserved. p. 158 Excerpt from "Understanding the Varieties of Chinese Management: The ABCD Framework" by Xin Li, reproduced with permission of the author. p. 159 Excerpt from "Dynamics of Corporate Social Responsibility in Asia: Knowledge and Norms" by Rebecca Chunghee Kim and Jeremy Moon © 2015 Palgrave Macmillan, a division of Macmillan Publishers Ltd. pp. 160–161 Excerpt from "On Becoming a Leader in Asia and America: Empirical Evidence from Women Managers" by Claudia Peus, Susanne Braun, and Kristin Knipfer © 2014 Elsevier Inc. All rights reserved. pp. 161–162 Excerpt from "The Dynamics of Managing People in the Diverse Cultural and Institutional Context of Africa" by Ken Kamoche, Lisa Qixun Siebers, Aminu Mamman, and Aloysius Newenham-Kahindi © 2015 Emerald Group Publishing Limited.

Chapter 8, p. 173 Excerpt from "Traditional Chinese Philosophies and Contemporary Leadership" by Li Ma and Anne. S. Tsui © 2014 Elsevier Inc. All rights reserved. p. 174 Excerpt from "Understanding the Varieties of Chinese Management: The ABCD Framework" by Xin Li, reproduced with permission of the author. pp. 175–176 Excerpt from "Dynamics of Corporate Social Responsibility in Asia: Knowledge and Norms" by Rebecca Chunghee Kim and Jeremy Moon © 2015 Palgrave Macmillan, a division of Macmillan Publishers Ltd. p. 178 Excerpt from "On Becoming a Leader in Asia and America: Empirical Evidence from Women Managers" by Claudia Peus, Susanne Braun, and Kristin Knipfer © 2014 Elsevier Inc. All rights reserved.

Chapter 10, pp. 206–208 "3D Printing" Reprinted with permission from Encyclopædia Britannica, © 2016 by Encyclopædia Britannica, Inc. pp. 210–211 Excerpt from "Air Pollution Statistics" © European Union, 1995–2016. p. 218 "Modern Life Is KILLING Children: Gadgets, Pollution and Pesticides Are Blamed as Cancer Rates Soar 40 per cent in Just 16 Years" by Simon Holmes © Associated Newspapers Ltd.

Chapter 11, pp. 237–238 "How Concerned Should We Be about Cell Phones in Class?" by Maryellen Weimer © 2017 Faculty Focus, Magna Publications.

Chapter 12, pp. 246–247 Excerpt from "Second Life or Half-Life? The Contested Future of Nuclear Power and Its Potential Role in a Sustainable Energy Transition" by M. V. Ramana © 2016 The Editors and the Author, published by Palgrave Macmillan. pp. 251–253 Excerpts from "Renewable Energy versus Nuclear: Dispelling the Myths" by Mark Diesendorf © The Resurgence Trust.

Chapter 13, pp. 268–270 Excerpt from "What Is Language Endangerment?" Used by permission, © 2016 SIL, Permission required for further distribution. pp. 271–272, 274, 276–277 Excerpts from "Back to the Future: Recreating Natural Indigenous Language Learning Environments through Language Nest Early Childhood Immersion Programs" by Onowa McIvor and Aliana Parker © The Authors, reproduced with permission of the authors. pp. 278–279 Excerpts from "Kohanga Reo" by Kylie Valentine © 2017 Kiwi Family Media Ltd.

Chapter 14, pp. 286–287, 303 Excerpts from "Global Climate Change and Children's Health" by Samantha Ahdoot and Susan E. Pacheco © 2015 American Academy of Pediatrics. pp. 288–291 Excerpts from "El Niño" © 1996–2017 National Geographic Society. All rights reserved.

Chapter 15, p. 308 Excerpt from "Air Pollution Statistics" © European Union, 1995–2016.

Photo Credits

Fotolia

p. 3 © Ivan Kruk; p. 6 © Rawpixel.com; p. 10 © javarman; p. 16 © YakobchukOlena; p. 23 © Rawpixel.com; p. 28 © Leigh Prather; p. 29 © Ints Vikmanis; p. 32 © cassis; p. 36 © miwa; p. 44 © mars58; p. 47 © Swapan; p. 51 © martialred; p. 59 © robsonphoto; p. 70 © WavebreakmediaMicro; p. 75 © fantom_rd; p. 79 © wong yu liang; p. 84 © Brian Weed; p. 88 © Vibe Images; p. 95 © stokkete; p. 105 © HappyAlex; p. 111 © Gernot Krautberger; p. 117 © pemaphoto; p. 128 © uniartpawlak; p. 131 © bonga1965; p. 135 © klublu; p. 136 © WavebreakmediaMicro; p. 145 © Fotofreundin; p. 153 © imtmphoto; p. 156 © TMAX; p. 159 © fpdress; p. 160 © Jenner; p. 162 © Minerva Studio; p. 171 © nakophotography; p. 174 © superjoseph; p. 178 © michaeljung; p. 181 © leungchopan; p. 190 © travnikovstudio; p. 193 © rolffimages; p. 195 © cristovao31; p. 199 © RioPatuca Images; p. 201 © Monkey Business; pp. xi, 203, 204 © StockRocket; p. 208 © palickam; p. 217 © Tyler Olson; p. 226 © beeboys; p. 228 © WavebreakMediaMicro; p. 230 © Photographee.eu; p. 237 © Syda Productions; p. 249 © nixki; p. 253 © Frank Fennema; p. 258 © MAXFX; p. 263 © jetrel2; p. 269 © davidyoung11111; p. 271 © De Visu; p. 275 © Bürgel & Gutekunst; p. 276 © Duke; p. 282 © Photokanok_1984; p. 287 © Arabella Carter-John; p. 288 © Kseniya Ragozina; p. 291 © mur162; p. 297 © D. Ott; p. 300 © Tom LiMa; p. 302 © Digitalpress; p. 307 © Netfalls; p. 308 © sborisov; p. 311 © Skowron; p. 315 © Monkey Business; p. 318 © richsouthwales.

Shutterstock

pp. x, 1, 2 © Dragon Images; p. 27 © SFIO CRACHO; p. 49 © A. and I. Kruk; pp. x, 101, 102 © GaudiLab; p. 103 © Gwoeii; p. 125 © guruXOX; p. 149 © GaudiLab; p. 205 © Art Konovalov; p. 225 © Syda Productions; p. 245 © Daniel Prudek; p. 265 © Mona Makela; p. 285 © AC Rider; p. 305 © Stock-Asso; pp. xii, 319, 320 © ESB Professional; pp. 421, 422 © Rawpixel.com.